The Twelve Month's Volunteer Volume 2 1847

The Twelve Month's Volunteer Volume 2 1847

The recollections of a member of the 1st Tennessee Cavalry during the Mexican War

George C. Furber

LEONAUR

The
Twelve Month's
Volunteer
Volume 2
1847
The recollections of a member
of the 1st Tennessee Cavalry
during the Mexican War
by George C. Furber

First published under the title
*The Twelve Month's Volunteer or
Journal of a Private in the
Tennessee Regiment of Cavalry
in the Campaign in Mexico, 1846-7*

Leonaur is an imprint
of Oakpast Ltd

Copyright in this form © 2009 Oakpast Ltd

ISBN: 978-1-84677-766-0 (hardcover)
ISBN: 978-1-84677-765-3 (softcover)

http://www.leonaur.com

Publisher's Notes

In the interests of authenticity, the spellings, grammar and place names used have been retained from the original editions.

The opinions of the authors represent a view of events in which he was a participant related from his own perspective, as such the text is relevant as an historical document.

The views expressed in this book are not necessarily those of the publisher.

Contents

March of the Generals	9
Camp Scenes	65
Operation of the Divisions	115
Amusements at Sea	181
Return March	265
Appendix	322

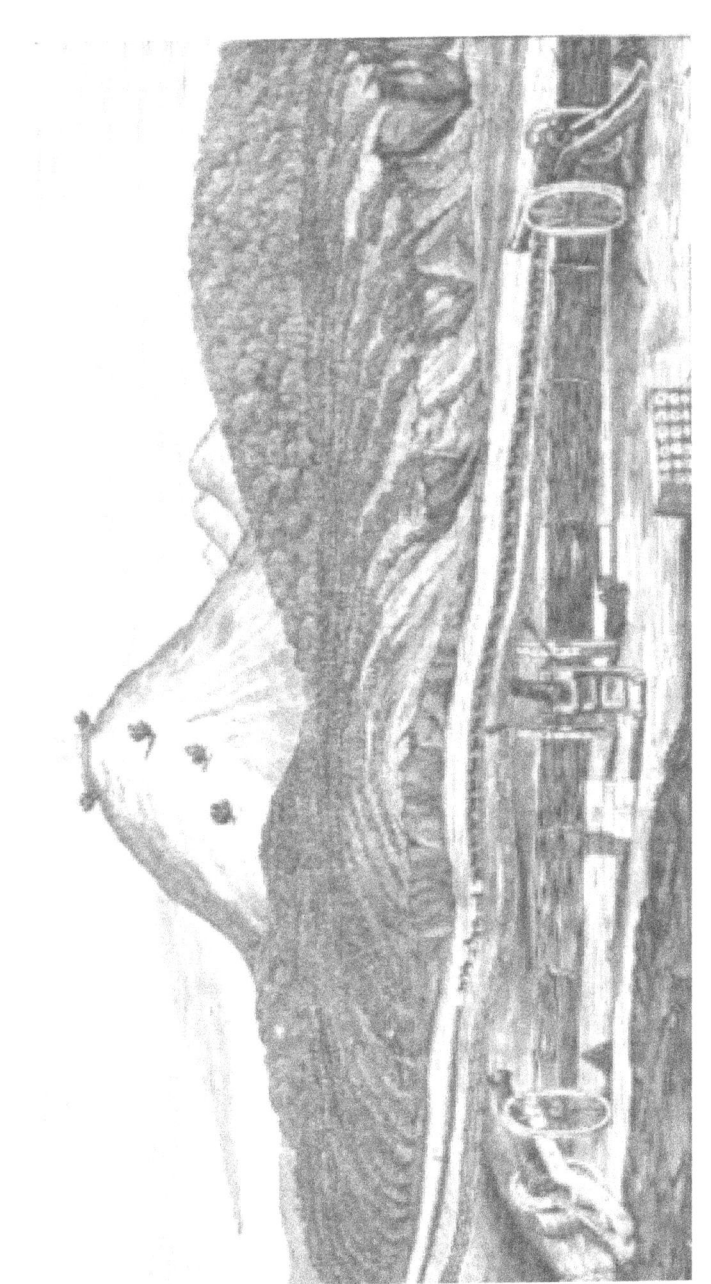

Hills of Cerro Gordo and Telegrafo

CHAPTER 1

March of the Generals

Friday, January 5th, 1847. A busy morning.—The bugles and numerous drums and fifes, on the clear, morning air, roused up the army early.—After a quick breakfast, General Patterson's division, now consisting of four regiments: our own, of cavalry, Colonel Thomas', the First and Second Tennessee Infantry, under colonels Campbell and Haskell, all of General Pillow's brigade, and the Third Illinois, under Colonel Foreman, which last was with us before, and a company of artillery—struck their tents, and the wagons, being loaded, with the heavy train, commenced the march; passing by the town, there turned to the left, took the road over the spur of the mountain, towards Tampico; General Twiggs' division of regulars, as before said, being one day in advance, and General Quitman to follow the next day, with his force, consisting of the Fourth Illinois and Georgia regiments, the Baltimore battalion, and Captain Haynes' company of cavalry, the second time detached from the regiment; we saw no more of him, or of our comrades of his company, until our arrival near Tampico.

General Patterson took a detail from our regiment of twenty men and a sergeant, to ride with him, as his guard; and General Pillow required a like detail of twelve men to attend him.—On General Patterson's guard, the author was placed, on the march now commenced.—Attended by his guard, the general before following the column of troops, that, under General Pillow, were already on the road, went down to General Taylor's camp, to bid him farewell.—The old general's quarters looked lonely; of the thousands that were round him, yesterday, the lines of tents of May's dragoons were all that were left.

After the parting between the generals, we came up through the space, so lately crowded, now so deserted; the camp fires were still smoking.—Many Mexicans, wrapped in their *horongos*, were stepping over the ground, collecting clothing, &c., but apparently fearful of taking it away, while any of us were yet near.—A little farther on, we came to a detail of our regiment, engaged in the melancholy duty of burying a comrade (James Brown, who died last night).—The general stopped at the grave, asked a few questions, and directed the men to put a few stones on its surface, to prevent it from being disturbed, and then we rode on towards the town.—Passing near, and leaving it to the right, we crossed the rocky stream, and took the road for Tampico. Now, this was, for miles, stretched out with troops, and the long train, of which, while the head was already over the first spur of the mountain, the rear had not yet left camp, where, also, the rear guard of cavalry, under Captain Sneed, were drawn up, waiting, in patience, for it to start.

When ascending the first spur of the mountain, the view caught of the plain behind, was indeed most beautiful.—It extended far down upon the town, and adjoining country) dotted with ranches, with bright groves of orange trees, and large fields of sugarcane, and interspersed by the hills of *chaparral*, which, from above, appeared level.—The scope of vision included a wide area of many miles along the foot of the rugged mountains, with their wild peaks above.—The town was immediately below, and one could see its whole length and breadth; while the rocky brook meandered along, visible in its every turn, for miles.—General Quitman's camp was in view, on the left; its many lines of tents looked small and white; far on the right, just visible, could be seen the few, of General Taylor; while the long lines of our division and train winding up the ascent, and coming over the plain, were stretched back to the camp, and their movements gave animation to the scene.—It was, altogether, one of the most beautiful and extensive mountain landscapes that any of us had ever gazed upon; and it attracted universal attention.

We passed up the spur, and on the top found it hilly for some miles.—The column of troops raised a heavy dust, to avoid which, the general put his horse into a brisk canter, we following him closely.—We soon met Captain Bragg, with his artillery, going back to General Taylor.

We saw our old general no more during the campaign; he had hot work to do in less than six weeks after this, at Buena Vista; for this movement and division of forces, became immediately known to Santa Anna, by the death of Lieutenant Ritchie, (who was lassoed at the town of Villa Grande, a few days before this), and the capture of his dispatches, which he was bringing from Monterey to Victoria. These were duplicates of those brought by Captain Haynes, and were, by the Mexicans, immediately sent to Santa Anna, and he thus saw, at once, the position of the American forces, and that General Taylor was left with a small army.

Here, then, was the opportunity, by a sudden march, to rout that little army, and retake the whole valley of the Rio Grande. Santa Anna had with him over twenty thousand men, and a large number of pieces of artillery, with abundance of material of war. His troops had the utmost confidence in him, for he, as yet, had not been in the field during this war, and his former reputation was great with them. He had excited them, by his endeavours and speeches, to a pitch of enthusiasm, so that all were eager to march against the *Americanos*; and many were the threats among his legions, that they would not leave an American alive.

At San Louis Potosi, he received these dispatches, in less than a week after this time; and, in two more weeks he bad his powerful army in motion, marching to the north, towards Saltillo, to annihilate General Taylor's little force.

On the next day to that of our departure from Victoria, General Taylor, with less than a thousand men, commenced his return march for Monterey. Of his departure, a friend, who was with Quitman's brigade, thus writes:

There was a general rush to see the old hero leave; all his old soldiers, except the Mississippians, who went back with him, had departed for Tampico. Everyone seemed to be melancholy at the separation. It was thought that all the fighting, all the honours, and all the laurels would be down on the coast, at Vera Cruz, and towards the Capital It looked, then, as if Old Zach had been sent back to the rear, where he would have only to guard the country of the Rio Grande.

Little thought those who saw the old hero, as he quietly rode through the *plaza* and streets of Victoria, in a plain citizen's dress, with some late papers in his hand, carelessly sitting on his Mexican pony, and politely bidding *adieu* to all those who remained behind him, slowly followed by May's dragoons, Bragg's battery, and Davis' Mississippians, that ere another six weeks should roll around, he would stand on the bloody field of Buena Vista, at the head of a gallant little army, to triumph over Mexican veterans. Even that recall, that countermand, which then seemed almost like disgrace, soon afforded him an opportunity of covering himself with greater glory, than in all his life before, he had won.

Now, we will again enter upon the smaller incidents of the march.—We skirted the foot of the mountain during the day, through beautiful scenery, and at three p.m., the advance reached a pretty mountain stream, called *Rio de Floris*, (or river of flowers).—A *rancho* was near it on an eminence. The water of the stream was clear, and ran with a continual murmur over the rocks; along its banks were trees of rose-wood, *lignum-vitae*, and musquit of large size, and to our surprise, we saw also, several of our old acquaintances, the sycamore; the growth of which, we had left a thousand miles or more, to the north-east.

Difference of elevation, however, has the same effect on climate and growth of timber, as difference of latitude; a thousand feet elevation, in these regions, having as much effect, in producing coolness of air. as five hundred miles or more distance on the low plains towards the north would have.—Those men, who climbed these mountains at Victoria, say that the little rough appearance they present against the sky, is made by oak trees, both post and red, of considerable size; but none of these grow down here, and we had not seen one for hundreds of miles back.

The column of infantry soon began to come into camp, followed by the wagon train. The men were covered with dust, and it was caked on their sweaty faces, giving them an odd appearance.—Multitudes of them soon lined the banks of the creek, up and down, standing on the rocks, in the water, and washing their hands and faces in the clear stream, that rapidly coursed along.—One or two had the luxury of a towel, that they had got from the Mexicans; a very few had handkerchiefs, some a piece of an old tent, with which to wipe their faces after washing; but the most had nothing of the kind, for their wardrobe was becoming scanty. These allowed the sun and fresh air to dry their faces and heads.—As their company wagons came in, their lines of tents went up, and before sunset all were in, and the little hills and hollows all around, were covered with busy life; and, after night, shone bright with many hundred fires.

We, of the guard, twenty men, under Sergeant McKamy, soon found that we were placed in a different situation than before, and in a much better one, for we had no roll-calls, no guard to stand, nor any of the ordinary camp duties to perform; we drew our provisions by ourselves, as a separate company, and our forage in the same way.—We were in three messes, and our tents and mess-bags were carried in one of the general's large wagons, all of which had good teams, and moved at the head of the train, behind the artillery, and consequently were always in camp the first at night; our tents, therefore, were up quickly, and we had time to rest at evening.

We had not, either, to march in the dusty column by day, for the general kept clear of that; often we would ride ahead, and rest in the shade, until the column came up.—Moreover, we always had the best possible position in camp at night, for water; for the general, when coming on the ground, always selected his position on the upper part of the creek or river, when at one; and beside this, we were not crowded for room; for the body of the army was always placed a short distance from his quarters, and our horses got a fine chance at the little grass that was to be found along.—Not only so, but he allowed us to have our forage carried in one of his wagons; thus taking much weight off our horses (and by a private bargain with one of his wagoners, who had a fine large wagon, six excellent mules, and a light load, we got our saddle-bags of clothing, &c., carried; and not only so, but our blankets we wrapped up each morning, and stowed away in there also; thus reducing the weight on our horses to ourselves and arms).—The effect of this was immediately perceptible in their movements and appearance.—Our duty was light, simply to keep our arms in first-rate order, and to assist at camping, in putting up the three marquees, &c., and in taking them down in the morning.—Our sergeant was an accommodating man, and we were as jovial as larks.

Saturday, January 16th. The *reveille* was beat at an early hour, and the camp was lit up before day.—Hearing quite a confusion at the general's quarter, we went up there, being near.—There were many curious, natural holes in the rock about here, which we had noticed the last night; they were round, like wells, and about ten or twelve feet deep.—General Patterson, while walking around in the dark, preparatory to starting, fell into one of these, and went down, against the bottom, with such a concussion as deprived him of the power of making any exertion to get out. He lay there, a few moments, before he could call for help; when his power of speech returned to him, however, he exercised it lustily, by calling for his Irish servant, Lawless.

Lawless heard the general's voice, rapidly calling him, but, from the nature of the sound, coming up out of the ground, he was for the moment, in the darkness, completely unable to tell from which direction it came. He kept answering, however, and run around completely confused; seizing a light, he at last struck the direction, and groped his way through a large bunch of cactus, that pierced him in an hundred places; he cursed this, and answered the general's call in the same breath; pushing through it, he saw the hole, and, extending the light over it, the general in the bottom.

Surprised, as he bent over, he called out, "And is it under the ground that ye are, gineral? and what in the divil brought you here?"—

"What brought me here? I fell here; get me out," replied the general, in a passionate voice.—With the help of the aids, he was out before we got up there. He was much bruised, and his ankle severely sprained; but after a little rest, was enabled to mount his horse, when the marquees were taken down, and the march was commenced.

About this time, Lieutenant Williams, one of the general's aids, was hunting in every direction for a bottle of brandy, which was taken out of the general's stores the night before, for his benefit and that of the aids; but on account of the lateness of the hour, had been laid by, still corked, for the morning.

"Have you seen anything of a bottle of brandy about here?" said he to the sergeant of the guard.

"Men, have you seen anything of a bottle of brandy about here?" shouted the sergeant, without answering directly the question of the aid.

The nearest man, still without answering, repeated the question to the others quickly, "I say, men, don't you hear the sergeant; have you seen anything of a bottle of brandy about here?"

"Bottle of what?" inquired one or two.

Lieutenant Williams replied aloud, and uneasily, for there was a strong probability that he would lose his morning dram, "A bottle of brandy that the general brought from Philadelphia with him."

"Have you seen anything of the general's bottle of brandy?" called out several; and in an instant after another man, a little farther off, was heard at the same, but with a cough at first, and a hem!

"Have you,"—another hem!—"seen anything of the general's brandy,—hem!—Charley?"

"I don't keep the general's brandy," replied he; "I wish I did."

The sergeant called out, "Look after it, men;" and all went to looking, but could not find it in the darkness; so they returned to saddling their horses, at which they were at first engaged.

But all the time that this calling had been made, another conversation had been carried on in whispers in the darkness:— "Drink quick, Jim; don't you hear the lieutenant inquiring after it?"

"I will; but it's so d—m—d strong," said Jim, as he bent behind his horse and drank, and then called out aloud, "Have you seen," &c.

"Hand the bottle over here," said Charley, in an earnest whisper;—"Ha! the best brandy I ever drank in my life.—Stop! let me have another swallow."

"Don't you hear McKamy calling to us to look after it?" said another—"put it there by that rock; we'll find it when we come back."

The aid stormed and swore about the infantry sentinels, that had stood there in the night; said he knew the company that they were detailed from, and he threatened all sorts of vengeance against them.

"D—m it," said he to Colonel Abercrombie, the other aid, "there is nothing left but whisky, now, and I hate that."—

The guard returned, and the bottle was passed around among a few whom they knew would not "blow;" and it might have been observed that morning, that these were in excellent spirits.

We struck out on the road, and marched several miles before the sun became warm; but when it did so, it was excessively hot. The road was very dusty. It lay for the whole march up and down the high mountainous spurs, and over bodies of good valley land, but with no habitations.—the general, being used up from the effects of his fall, and in much pain, was compelled to halt, and wait for the buggy of the surgeon of his staff, Dr.

Wright. This was the only buggy in the army, and was very convenient for the doctor. While halted, we of the guard got round under the musquit bushes, for shade. There was no other growth in this dry valley, save the many varieties of the cactus, some of which have already been described. The country here was covered with them.

Some of the scenery passed over today, of hill and valley, was indeed striking.—From the top of the hills we were watched all day, closely, by parties of the enemy; and some talk was among the boys of the prospect of a fight before long; for there were so many of these parties, and some so numerous, that it was thought that the enemy might be crossing from Tula, on the west, to give us a trial; but they molested us none. Captain Caswell made a chase after one party, on a high hill, but they saw him so far, coming through the valley, that they were off beyond the reach of pursuit, and that evening we saw no more of them. The spyglass showed more of these than we had an idea of without it, all lancers. It was provoking to the men, to see them far up on the heights, and know that it was useless to try to catch them.

At four, p. m., after marching near twenty-five miles, we encamped near a pretty brook of bluish water, which afforded an abundant supply for the whole army. As it had been so very dusty today, another washing scene took place, after which all betook themselves to their supper and rest.—this encampment was on some hills covered with a scattered growth of large musquit trees; with but little cactus. We of the guard found much grass for our horses. How the regiment made out we knew not, for we went not to it, not knowing on what part of the ground it was.[1]

---

1. When there are several regiments together, after encamping, there is not much running about. One might almost as easily find a particular person in a city in which he was not acquainted, as to find him in a camp; he will have as many inquiries to make to do it; and, besides,—men do not become so much acquainted as is, by many, supposed. A person will get acquainted with all his own company in two or three weeks, but not with all his regiment in as many months; if he does in six, he has a good faculty for making acquaintances; but with other regiments, he knows only a few. Soldiers get into the habit of staying in their own companies; not only so, but they have a peculiar attachment to their own tents.

Sunday, January 17th. There is no Sabbath in camp; one day is precisely like another, and it is with the greatest difficulty that one can tell what day it is;—in fact but few know;—not one man in twenty can tell whether it is Sunday or Thursday, Monday or Saturday; they know not, neither do they care.

We were on the march early, the general riding in a little hospital wagon, in which he lay upon his back, being unable to sit up. The road lay over high hills, beautiful plains, and extensive valleys. The elevated range of mountains we were leaving to the right, where their massive peaks rose up against the western sky; now, from distance, they appeared of a hazy blue.

These hills, over which we passed this day and the day before, are indeed singular,—long and straight, ending abruptly at either end; the tops level as a line for the whole extent. They are called by the Mexicans *mesas*, or tables, (see picture p.21). When on them, some of them are found not to be of more than a few yards in width;—to look up to them from the valley below, you would suppose a large plain on the top; but when the steep ascent has taken you up perhaps eight hundred or a thousand feet, immediately you see far down into the opposite valley, directly before you.

Neither do these long hills run in any particular way; they are thrown, as it were, in all directions, making all angles with each other, and enclosing fertile plains and valleys of every possible diversity of shape and appearance. The lover of beautiful landscape could here find enough, to give him full scope for admiration of changing scenes, for weeks. These scenes are not so rugged and imposing as those of the main chain of mountains, but they are beautiful, and there is an endless variety of them.

We had seen but few Mexican soldiers today, for the hills are more accessible, and if they had showed themselves, we would have had a better chance of catching them.—Some were on a high hill passed to the right, this morning. In some of the valleys, we passed over large bodies of lava, though no mountain is now volcanic in this immediate vicinity.

At nine o'clock, we came to a little brook, deep, and of good water. Here the general, after ascertaining from the Mexican guide, Valencia, that it was twenty-one miles to the next water, determined to encamp, and halted the advance. Colonel Abercrombie directed us of the guard to encamp in the same beautiful grove that the general was to occupy, on the bank of the creek.—the army soon came up and encamped.

We had now nearly the whole day before us, in which to do as we pleased.—the general's tents, and our own, were soon up, and some of the guard went hunting, as did many of the infantry.—They covered, in crowds, the high hills around, and wandered about nearly all the day; many of them endeavouring to shoot Mexicans, not content with deer and turkeys;— but they were unsuccessful; for, although they came in view of those in the distance, they could not come up with them.—We had passed no habitations during the day, and the country was entirely wild, and there were some deer and many turkeys;— monkeys and apes, the Mexicans told us, were in numbers in the hills.—In a few hours, the boys returned;—they had killed a few turkeys and deer.

There was much fun and sport going on among the troops during the day.—the infantry have become so accustomed to marching, that they do not mind it at all. The second Tennessee regiment appears to be the liveliest, although all are enough so; but their pranks are innumerable. If there are any cattle within miles of the camp, they are sure of having them; and not only so, but Mexicans stand a poor chance with them, for, having some of their men murdered and shockingly mutilated, near Camargo, when they first came to the country, they have since had a hatred against the class that perpetrated these murders, and have paid them in their own coin, sending many of them to their "long home."—The first Tennessee is much smaller in number than the second, having been much cut up at Monterey; but they are still an efficient body.

Sometimes, when, before day, the reveille beats, after it is done, a great number commence to crow for the dawn, and then, all over the camp, such an universal crowing takes place, that one would think that all the chicken cocks in the country were collected, and endeavouring to outdo each other.—There was a single little dog, that belonged to one of the infantry, and which accompanied the march. Whenever, in the morning, on the march, he made his appearance, he was received with a yell that frightened the poor little fellow almost out of his life;—tucking his tail between his legs, he fled as fast as his feet could carry him, but always took the road; and as he passed company after company, moving on, the yell was kept up, until he had cleared the infantry, and taken refuge with the horses of the cavalry.—Every morning he is thus greeted.

We came to a new species of palm tree, called, by the Mexicans, *palmetto del sol,* or sun palm, (see picture p.21):—It is a singular tree,—large at the bottom of the trunk, of a spongy texture of wood, rough bark, and but few branches; each one of them surmounted by a bunch of large, grass-like blades, which hang down.—These are preferred by the Mexicans to all other, for the purpose of making hats, or *sombreros.*

On the ground that we occupied this night, General Twiggs encamped the night before, and General Quitman on the next following. Both the camps of these divisions could plainly be seen with the glass this evening, from the top of the high rocky hill overlooking ours.

January 18th. As usual now, we were upon the march before day.—when the sun arose, it revealed to us a succession of beautiful scenery. Far on the right appeared the lofty chain of mountains, which, by our course, south-east, we were gradually leaving; this range here running about south. On the left, too, far in the distance, another range of lofty irregular peaks rose up. Between these, the extensive valley was filled by the high, flat-topped hills, or *mesas,* mentioned before, thrown promiscuously around, in its vast extent. Fleecy clouds, of dazzling whiteness in the sun, rolled around the mountains and enveloped the tops of these hills, clinging to them, as it were, by one part, and the other floating buoyantly off from them in the still air; but after the sun became hot, the clouds vanished, and the whole scene,

1 2 3 4 5
Cactus Gigantea, La Palma Bendita, Sword Palmetto, etc.

in vast extent, in the embrace of the mountains, was below. The road, as before, lay up and down these hills, and over beautiful plains. We now came to many palm trees, which, singly and in groves, were seen for the remainder of the route.—this, with the *cactus gigantea*, the sun palm, the sword palmetto, the prickly pear, rose-wood, ebony, *lignum vitae*, musquit, and an infinite variety of other cactus, were the growth now met with, for several days in succession. For the appearance of the first five, (see picture p. 21.)

In the middle of the day it became so dusty, that one could hardly see across the road, which appeared, in many places, like a long bed of dry ashes.—At noon we came to a *rancho*, the houses of which were built of stone, and whitewashed, and were much neater than others that we had seen . Here the contractors stopped to procure beef for the night; and many of the men obtained from the *peones peloncillas* of about a pound and a half weight of good sugar, for a *medio*, or *picayune* each.—beyond this *rancho*, we descended a rocky hill, and came to the Rio de Lemon. (So called on Arista's map, but by the inhabitants called *Rio Follon*. It flows to the southward, and runs into the river Panuco). This beautiful, rapid stream, we immediately forded, followed by the infantry, artillery, and train; all of which got a good washing off; the water taking the infantry nearly to their armpits.

After crossing, the general determined to continue on farther, and we followed the river down about seven miles, and encamped along the road. The musquit trees, on either hand, were so thick, that the division was much cramped for want of room.—The tents were soon up, and it being close to the river, everyone who could raise a line and hook, went a fishing in the deep stream; which here was quiet, of gentle current, and deep; though falling above in large cascades, over massive rocks. It was stocked with catfish, and the finest perch; and many of the men caught large strings of them.

Mexican lancers have been during the day, hanging round us, but have kept off' far; or else, when near, were so concealed, in the thickets, that we did not perceive them.—We passed to-day, three large crosses by the side of the road, each with a pile of small stones around it; two of them were old and decaying; the other was firm, and had been erected at a later date; it had, upon the cross-bar these words, in red paint: *"Un Ave-Maria, un Padre nuestro por la alma de Juan Gonzales, que estaba matado el 25 de Abril, de 1842."* (One prayer to the Virgin Mary, one Lord's prayer, for the soul of Juan Gonzales, who was murdered on the 25th of April, 1842.) We had often seen these crosses and piles of stones before, and we met them often, by the highways, afterwards; but few of the men, however, made any inquiry into the reason of their erection; many passed along, thinking them to be sign-posts!

Whenever a Mexican is murdered, one of these is put up, by the people of the neighbourhood, on the ground where the blood is spilled, and the soul departs; and the reason is this: as such a person died without confession to the priest, or absolution given of his sins, or partaking of the sacrament; and without the extreme unction, or anointing with the holy oil;—all of which are administered to a dying man,—he consequently goes directly into purgatory, with his sins upon his head, unabsolved, unanointed, unsanctified; and, consequently, in a most terrible situation; and, therefore, these crosses are erected, calling on all passers-by to say these prayers for that soul, in order that the intense suffering, consequent upon entering purgatory in such a condition, may be alleviated; for they quote from the Bible, that the "prayers of the righteous availeth much," and a large number of these prayers, they believe, will induce the Virgin Mary to use her intercession with our Saviour, to have such a soul placed in a better situation.

Each pious *"cristiano,"* as they call themselves, that passes, turns to the cross, says over the prayers, and in token thereof, places a small stone on the heap there accumulating. These heaps are never disturbed; not even a boy can be found that will take off from the pile one of the little stones that has been blessed with a prayer; but rather, he, also, in turn, stops, says his prayer, and adds another stone.—The women never neglect it, and the author was informed, by a gentleman who had long resided in Mexico, that the largest pile he had ever seen there, was placed almost entirely by women; and this appeared the more singular, as the object of their solicitude was killed by an injured husband in public!—Distance marched this day, about twenty-five miles.

January 19th. At an early hour we were on the route, and marched five miles by the time it was well light. That distance brought us to the Lemon or Follon River again, which we immediately forded, and the infantry got another wetting, which was not very agreeable to them, for it was too early in the day. It was amusing to look back from the bank opposite, and see them crossing, and hear their noise and yells. We thought the Illinoisans made noise and fun enough about such fordings, but the Tennesseans made the more. The water run off from all when they got over; but they did not mind the wetting, save some who did not succeed in keeping their crackers dry.—There was a *rancho* on the top of the hill, with many houses.

While on this bank, one of the beef contractors, named Bigelow, found occasion to go back to the *rancho* mentioned yesterday, twelve miles, to see about the supply of beef to be furnished to Quitman's brigade, for the night. He was warned not to do it; but mounting his splendid horse, he determined to try it, and away he went.[2] After crossing the Follon, the hills became lower, and the mountains were but just discernible on the distant horizon in the rear. We now passed over a beautiful country of hills and rolling plains, with more grass than we had before seen in

---

2. He passed the wagontrain, not yet all crossed, then the rear guard. Before he got to the encampment just left, a party of Mexican cavalry filed into the road before him. He was about to turn back, when he saw a large number behind him; then putting spurs to his noble horse, he broke through the front line, and, amid the volley fired at him, received but one ball, which shattered his right leg below the knee; but he kept his seat, while they pursued him back over the Follon, and by the rancho spoken of, until he came in view of part of Captain Haynes' company, under Lieutenant Chamblis, the advance guard of Quitman's division. He was immediately placed in the hospital wagon, and made the rest of the march in that way, being unable to walk for many weeks afterward.

several weeks; groves of the palm tree were here and there, scattered over the face of the country.

About three, p. m., after a pleasant march of twenty-two miles, we encamped on the banks of a pretty brook, and the general selecting his quarters under the foliage of a large rose-wood tree, surrounded by others of thick shade, Colonel Abercrombie appointed to us our place about fifty yards from him, under a shade equally pleasant, and so thick that we concluded not to put up our tents, but to fix our sleeping-places in this, a sort of natural arbour.

The general's marquees were soon up, and we sat down to conversation, having nothing else to do, save to watch the long lines of cavalry and infantry, followed by the wagon train, that were coming down over the beautiful hills, towards the camp, as they continually arrived.—Colonel Abercrombie came down to us, and asked if anyone would cut down a large palm tree that stood near, a most majestic object; to oblige him, as he wished to examine the "cabbage," or tender wrapping of the buts of the leaves, at the top of the trunk, which cabbage the Mexicans here eat, and pronounce it fine.

A dozen men instantly offered to serve the colonel, (who, having the power to command, chose, rather in such a case to request), and procuring axes, the noble tree was soon stretched on the ground. Its leaves were taken off from the body, and the top of this cut off. After stripping the tough outside covering off, the inside was found white and tender, and somewhat like a cabbage; this, however, was small, not weighing more than seven or eight pounds. (We afterwards found these "cabbages;" to sell in the markets of Tampico, and other places).—For the appearance of this tree, and those of others which have been mentioned as growing about here, see the picture p.21, where it is numbered 2.

> Note to the reader this picture, showing most accurately the appearance of the plants and trees, was drawn upon the ground by the author. A single cavalry soldier was placed in the foreground, to show, by comparison, the height of

the trees; and the engraver was directed to copy these in every line, and moreover, to place a small scouting party in the back ground. To the author's surprise, when the picture was completed, he found that the engraver had put in the scouting party, but had set them all to cooking; and the volumes of smoke inserted, would convey the idea that the scouts were more anxious for their dinner, than to catch the enemy, that, at this place, were hanging so thickly around us.

This is wrong; and the reader will therefore, in imagination, put out the engraver's fire, and place the party in a position of vigilance. The soldier in front, also, though dressed correctly, and having all right about him, has, by the engraver's command, taken off his sword and cartridge box, and set them up against that sun palm, together with his gun, which, too, the engraver has cut, not a carbine, but rather a fowling piece.

This is incorrect: for no scout was caught in this fix. His holsters are right, but his sword should be upon his side, and his carbine slung to his shoulder, or in his hand, ready to act in an instant. Owing to these mistakes, the author would not have inserted this picture, but for the remarkable correctness of the trees and plants which it represents, and the excellent workmanship of the whole cut

The others, 1, 3, 4, 5, have been mentioned before, in this work. This palm is connected with one of the religious ceremonies of this people, which we will mention. The tree is called, by the Mexicans, in distinction from all others of the palm kind, *la palma bendita*, or the blessed palm.—(Valencia, our Mexican guide, said that this was the tree whose branches were broken off and strewed in the way of our Saviour, in his entry into Jerusalem, mentioned by the evangelists, and that, on this account, it was since prized by Christians. This may be the opinion (*St. John, chap. 12, verse 13,*) taught them by the priests, and probably is.

It was the only reason that the author received, for the custom of blessing the leaves, on Palm Sunday).—Palm Sunday is a festival kept by all the population of Mexico. It comes on, or near the 27th of March, of each year.—On that day, the people, in their holiday dresses, take bunches of the large leaves of this tree, and carry them to the priests, who, in a formal and solemn manner, bless them, thus making them sacred. They are then taken home, torn up into strips, and plaited in numberless beautiful forms; everyone has a cross worked in it, trimmed with ornaments of ribbon, &c., and sent as presents. They are from friend to friend, from young to old, and the contrary, and especially passed between the young of both sexes, as sacred tokens of love. Crosses are plaited, of the same material, and put up over the windows and doors of each house, and these so guarded, cannot be entered by Satan or any of his evil spirits.—on this day is general rejoicing and all are made holy. The priests, in the morning, consecrate, in every church, a large quantity of holy water, called *agua bendita*, which is sent for by all persons, drank, and used for sickness—with great success, they say. No wonder, then, that the Mexicans regard *La Palma Bendita* with attachment, and call it "blessed."

The whole of this tree is not shown in the picture, but enough is visible to show its form and beauty. A diamond shaped network, composed of the buts of the older leaves, which have fallen off, sometimes descends half way down the trunk; in this one, however, but little of it can be seen, directly under the leaves, at the top of the visible part of the trunk.

The column-like cactus, growing up under the tree, marked (No. 1) beneath, is called by the Mexicans, *la cactus gigantea*, or more commonly, *brazos de Alexandr*a (arms of Alexander); it bears a fruit, something in shape, like a pear.

The trunk of the sword *palmetto*, (No. 3) is only used for posts for fences; gardens and yards being enclosed with them, when split, and set to one another, like pickets. The root of this is called article; is soft and juicy, and rubbed upon clothing, is used for soap; and is effectual in removing dirt and stains; in many sections, this tree is known by the name of the soap-plant; and was so called by some of our soldiers.

The *palmetto del sol* or palm of the sun (No. 4,) is used only as said before, for making *sombreros* (hats) and little baskets.

The prickly pear is part of their national emblem, and can be seen on every Mexican dollar, under the eagle.—The use made of it in this section, is to feed their mules and cattle on, when there is no grass. To do this, they cut it down, and making a fire of brush, throw the thick leaves into it, which half roasts them, and burns the needles off;—in this state it is eaten greedily by their animals. It is also used when thus roasted, to cure wounds and bruises upon their mules and horses, and for that purpose, is very effectual. Farther south, it feeds the cochineal insect, which is so valuable for dyeing.—Two flat-topped hills, such as we had been passing over for some days before this, are in the back ground.

In the camp, this evening, we had quite a scene, occasioned by the dry grass taking fire; and this spread with great rapidity, scorching and snapping, among the prickly pear; it gave quick employment to hundreds, to extinguish it; which, in the camp, was done without much labour, but, outside of that, it ran for miles, and could be seen by its light, after dark.—On the trees round the camp, and in the thickets, were numbers of the *guano*, a new species of animal to us. They are of the lizard family;—one kind were jet black in colour; the body of one of these was about a foot long, and the tail as much longer; legs like a lizard, but large in proportion to the body; sharp teeth, bright eyes, and very long, keen claws; from the head a row of black bristles ran along the back; the remainder of the surface was naked, and of a shining black; the stout tail was covered with knotty projections; taking them altogether, this kind were ugly looking "varmints."

Another kind was more pleasing to the eye, but still as singular in shape; their colour was green; the body of one about four inches long; had a high, flat crest on the head; with the tail slender, and nearly two feet in length: giving the animal the appearance of a green snake, with a large head, and four legs near to it. They were all extremely agile, and run over the ground and up the trees, with surprising quickness. Colonel Campbell, of the first Tennessee, had caught one near his tent, of this latter kind; and we examined it closely.—Our Mexican guide, Valencia, informed us, that there were many kinds of them in this part of the country; that all were harmless, save the large black ones, which bite severely.

General Patterson sent on a detachment of our regiment of cavalry, to an *hacienda* ahead, to procure corn for the supply in the train was about giving out. These were to remain at the *hacienda* until we came up.—We had gained, this day, five miles on General Twiggs; he encamping last night that distance in our rear, and passing over this ground today.

January 20th. The *reveille* was beat, fires lit up, breakfasts finished, wagons loaded, and all were on the march by daylight. The infantry, as we passed them, were, from one end of the line to the other, enjoying their usual amount of fun and sport, as they marched on.—The road lay over extensive, open valleys; grassy, and with, here and there among them, thick groves of timber; and then, again, nothing for miles, save dry grass, and, occasionally, a musquit bush.—There were many rocky hills on the first part of the day's march.

Nine miles distance brought us to the *hacienda* of Alomita, (or little cottonwood). Some few small trees of cottonwood grew on the bank of the stream, that flowed along the base of the hill upon which the *hacienda* is situated.—We crossed the stream, toiled up the hill, and entered the town, (for the collection of houses of the *peones* of the estate, made quite a town). Here we found the company of cavalry that had been sent on by the general last night. They and their horses had fared sumptuously, by command of the owner of the *hacienda*, Don Juan Cardonas—the fairest complexioned Mexican we had seen; affable, polite; a gentleman in appearance, and a prince in estate.

When he heard that General Patterson had come in,—which was earlier in the morning than he expected—for the general, taking only the guard with him, had left the advance of the army three miles back,—he came out in a hurry to meet him; was very anxious to have him alight, and take a cup of coffee, &c.; but Patterson could not do it. He only wanted corn; and the demand was made for it, and a reasonable price offered.—(General Patterson had improved in this respect, of attending to the wants of horses as of men, since he had been with old Zach. again; and, on this march to Tampico, we had no reason to complain, for want of forage.)—We remained halted, at the edge of the square or *plaza* of the *hacienda*, while the general and the *"don"* made their arrangements, by means of an interpreter, Selby, an American who accompanied us. Don Juan was a man who had travelled much, and knew a little English.

We were struck with the population of his *hacienda*, which could not have been less than twelve or fifteen hundred —The large buildings for himself, his *administrador,* or overseer, officers, &c., called *la casa grande*; were built of stone, and occupied two sides of the large square:—part of one side was occupied by the church, which was not a *capilla*, like the other *haciendas,* but a *parochia*, in which a curate officiated, having ecclesiastical jurisdiction over all the *capillas* in the surrounding country, comprehended in the limits of his curacy.

The *parochia* was finely built of stone, and a great profusion of carved work, of large proportions, covered its front towards the square. Three heavy bells were in its tower, and in religious convenience, the people of this *hacienda* seemed to be as well accommodated as though they were in a city. The curate, with his long black robe, and three-cornered cap, walked out to the corner, and politely touched his hat to the guard, with the expression "*Buenos dias Señores*." He had a good-humoured, intelligent countenance, pleasant appearance, and seemed in no ways alarmed or disconcerted at our presence; but on the contrary, all the time he was there, he seemed to be interested in us; and especially his attention was taken by the size of the horses. One of his *tenientes*, or under priests, was with him, and for a few moments they carried on a brisk conversation, and passed back toward *la casa grande*.

Their conduct was quite a contrast to that of the *capillan*, mentioned on January 4th, who, as we appeared in sight, opened the ceremony of *"nuestro Señor esta patente"* and by the dismal tolling of the bell, set the whole populace of the *hacienda*, wherever they were scattered within the sound, to crossing themselves, and praying earnestly to the saints for deliverance.

This valley adjoining the town, (for so we might call the *hacienda*), spread out, below the crossing of the road, into a spacious area, which was watered by ditches that diverted the water from the brook;—this valley was very fertile, and productive,[4] and cultivated with care. Don Juan promised the general immediately to send a large number of his *peones* into this valley and gather one piece of corn, (which contained about fifty acres), and have it shelled out in season for the wagons to take this evening. He was to receive one dollar and twenty-five cents per *fanega*, nearly two bushels. (This seemed a heavy job, but with the force he had, he easily accomplished it).

Although this town was so large, yet it was but part of the domain of Don Juan.—On a high hill, far to the north, was another town to be seen;—this, too, was part of the same *hacienda*.[5]

The head of the cavalry had come up to the town during the time in which this arrangement was going on, and the general,

---

4. Immense tracts of land, fertile in quality of soil, are left entirely uncultivated in Mexico, in every part, for the want of water upon them. As a general rule, no land is fit to cultivate, save that which can be watered by ditches; for the long dry season parches every other. Many tracts of these uncultivated regions, however, afford, during the rainy season, and for some time afterward, excellent grass for pasturage; other immense bodies, about in the mountains, are perfectly bare; and where so, no animal lives. Where water is plenty, as was the case from Victoria to Tampico, at every few miles distance, some deer and other wild animals are found. The *haciendas* and *ranchos* are only on or near the streams.

5. These *haciendas* are on tracts of land granted, in former times, to particular individuals, by the king of Spain. No actual surveys were made, but the boundaries were designated by the points in view, and the principal intention being, fully to cover the water courses. They are described in the grant, somewhat in this way: "Beginning at the crest of such a mountain named, at the commencement of its descent; running about such a course, towards another mountain named, so many hours' or days' ride; thence towards another mountain, about such a course, to the mountain, or so many hours' ride;" and so on through the whole. Notwithstanding the vagueness of the boundaries, few disputes arise, because they are almost always bounded by dry tracts, of no value.

followed by us, moved ahead.

He gave permission for one out of each of the three messes in the guard to leave the lines to hunt; with the caution, however, to look out for the lancers, a body of whom, we had learned, were in the vicinity, and had remained at this *hacienda* two nights before.—Three men went; but two of them soon returned; the other one we saw no more of until night.—We found the hills now spreading out in an undulating surface, beautiful to the eye, with, here and there, groves of *la palma bendita,* musquit, sword palmetto, &c. At other places, there was nothing on them but grass.

The range of mountains were now at a great distance in the rear; the mesas, or flat-topped hills had disappeared; —but we were nearing the lofty isolated peak of Mont Bernal, which was to our front and right, to the southward of our route, as we passed down toward the coast.—Eighteen miles march from Alomita brought us to a pretty creek, with high banks, at which General Twiggs had encamped the night before: the general crossed the creek, and selected the place for his marquees; and our situation was appointed near. The regiment of cavalry followed, and encamped

These *haciendas* are often very large, some of them taking in a thousand or more of square miles. When one is sold, the original grant from the king of Spain is assigned over to the purchaser, accompanied by another instrument containing the indebtedness of each *peon* on it, and these are also passed over, and the *peones* labour for the new master as they did for the old. on the opposite side of the creek; while the three regiments of infantry crossed it. The wagontrain was on both sides.

In the evening our mess-mate, R. S. Courteney, came in, his horse dripping with sweat.—He had been chased over hill and valley, for some distance, by several lancers, who only desisted when coming on a hill in view of the army. The speed of his horse saved him.—Courteney thought he had made a narrow escape, and at night he patted his horse, rubbed him, and talked to him, as though he thought that the animal could understand his words. (The lancers this day attacked the rear of General Quitman's brigade. They only killed one man, however, and took another prisoner, when they were dispersed by some of Captain Haynes' company, of our regiment, now with that brigade).

Much anxiety was felt in company G, of the cavalry, for the safety of two men, Corporal Rhoton and Private N. W. Ragland, who left the lines to scout and hunt, and had not come up at night.[6]—Distance marched this day, twenty-seven miles.

Thursday, January 21st. We resumed the march at an early hour.—We had now come down into an extensive rolling prairie, covered with grass, but mostly dead;—the mountains still faintly visible in the distance, in the rear; but on the right, over a great distance of rolling prairie, the mountain of Bernal raised its lofty peak above the clouds, and stood out alone, a massive, noble object, overlooking the whole country. It rose gradually, for a long distance, and then, as it were, suddenly shot its vast bulk upwards, nearly perpendicularly; appearing, from its very loneliness, the more imposing.—Its summit was rent and seamed, and it presented every appearance of an extinct volcano (See picture p.37).—We passed over the rolling lands of fine soil, but dry, with much grass upon them, on which large droves of horses, mules, and cattle were feeding; and at ten a. m., after a march of twenty-one miles, we arrived at the *hacienda* of Chocoi; after passing on the route, several *ranchos*, and much cultivated land, enclosed with brush fences.

We halted a little while in front of *la casa grande* (the owner's house), on a sort of square, and then proceeded on near the *tanque*, or artificial pond of water, for the use of the *hacienda*; here, turning to the right, we passed down a gentle slope along a fence of musquit sticks and brush, and the general selected his

---

6. The next day, Captain Sneed, of company G, sent back four men, to look for the lost two; but the day passed away, the march was made, and none had come up at the succeeding morning. The company was halted, and half remained at camp, while the other half went back for the six, and were fortunate enough to find them; the four had found the lost two, and were bringing them up. The Mexicans had not seen them, being deterred from coming near the road by Quitman's brigade advancing. The company was reunited, and all joined the regiment the succeeding day.

quarters under the shade of some *lignum-vitae* and rose-wood trees, in the little valley, while our position, by the aid, was appointed to us, up a little higher, near the musquit fence.

The cavalry soon came in, in long columns, and filed to the left of the *hacienda*, encamping in and about the extended lots.—The infantry regiments followed; and their position was assigned in the middle space, on the bare knolls, and around the *tanque*; while most of the wagon train drew up in long lines between the general and the infantry.—As usual, two hours, or more, elapsed, before the rear guard made its appearance; and shortly after that, the tents were all up, in every direction, and all were busy in the camp, which immediately appeared as though it had been occupied a month or more.

Wood was scarce; plenty of green *lignum-vitae*, on the little hills on the right—this, in its outside appearance of bark, resembles hickory; but did not burn like it,—for one might as well attempt to burn a brick, as a piece of it green.—The men of the guard being obliged to have fuel, pulled up some of the stakes, and burned a little of the brush of the old fence. It was amusing to see them watch the general's quarters, while they collected enough of this for fires; which they knew would expose them to severe punishment, if found out; but hunger, and the want of fuel to get their meals, made them run all risks.—(It has not been mentioned, that dry musquit makes as good a fire as our best hickory, and that it burns freely, and with intense heat, and yet lasts well, being close grained and heavy; so much so, that when a dry and sound piece is lifted, and struck with a quick blow, it has a peculiar, short, ringing sound, somewhat like that of metal).

This *hacienda* of Chocoi was not as large as that of Alomita; not having, according to appearances, more than a hundred or two *peones*; though the number of these is not easily estimated, they being stowed so thickly in the rude buildings, and many living about in *la casa grande*.—The owner, Don Ramon Prieto, was a man of the old Spanish blood, light in complexion, and gentlemanly in appearance; he had travelled much in the United

States, and in England, and spoke the English language pretty well, as also did his son, who had spent some time at school in Philadelphia.—Whenever we came across these higher order of Mexicans, who have resided or visited in the United States, we found them quite friendly, and apparently attached to our country, and also to our customs; though not so much so, as to make them alter their own very materially.—As an instance of this the don of this *hacienda* still had his old fashioned Spanish carriage, in preference to one of our style.

This old carriage, of the kind used altogether in the interior, is worth a description, from its singular shape and appearance, and as it excited much curiosity in those who walked up to the *casa grande,* where it stood under the large *piazza.* The hind wheels were large and strong, about five and a half feet in diameter; the fore ones stout, but low, not being more than two and a half feet; the axles were both very heavy, as also was the high bolster on the fore one; two large pieces, looking like small timbers for a house, ran from the hind axle-trees to the bolster, and connected the two; two heavy uprights stood from the hind axle, and corresponding two from the bolster; these had cross pieces equally large, and carved; all this made the frame; stouter and heavier than that of any six horse wagon, larger also; for the width between the wheels or track, was about eight feet and a half, and from the fore-axle to the hind one, between eleven and twelve feet.

The reader can judge what a cumbrous frame this was; but the body supported by it, was not larger than that of one of our common carriages, seating only six persons on the two seats; this body was hung on huge leather braces, that passed, from the cross piece on the fore-axle, to that over the hind one; of course the fore-wheels were before the carriage, and the hind ones as much behind it. The harness was cumbrous, heavy, loaded with brass, and had heavy coverings or bags for the tails of the mules. Seven were harnessed to the heavy carriage: two at the wheels, then three abreast, then two more, with three riders along, there being no driver.

January 22nd. We, of the guard, were roused about midnight, by one of our men, who dreamed that it was day, made up a large fire, and waking us, soon set us all to cooking, when we found that it was not near daylight; and, on coming out of the bushes, we saw that each of the regiments around, were all asleep but the sentinels.—However, we finished our breakfast, fed our horses, wrapped ourselves in our blankets, and again lay down to sleep, with some muttered exclamations against the wakefulness of our old mess-mate.—We slept but little, however.—We were again awakened by the reveille.—In a few moments all were in motion; the roll calls of every company were called; the fires were kindled, breakfast dispatched, tents down, and in the wagons; and all were on the march by daylight, save company G, of the cavalry, which halted, as before mentioned, to hunt up its missing members.

General Patterson had now determined to go to Tampico in two days, though it was three days' march for the troops; and, this morning, he detached two companies of the cavalry,—Captain Caswell's and Lieutenant Lacy's,[7] —to go with him; and, taking the guard, with these he set out, leaving the division under the command of General Pillow.—General Patterson was still unable to ride on horseback, and continued in the wagon, which could not be driven very rapidly.—The detachment, therefore, did not gain much on the division coming behind, for some hours.—The mountain of Bernal was still upon our right; a view of which, as well as of an *atajo*[8] (drove of pack mules), with their accompanying *arrieros*, or drivers, that we met near this place, see sketch.

As we met these continually on the marches, and as little has been said about them, and as the whole internal commerce of Mexico is carried on by means of these *arrieros*, or muleteers,

---

7. This is the company mentioned before as Captain Lenow's. That officer returned from Matamoras home, on furlough, and while there, declining to return to the war, sent back his resignation. The command then fell on the first lieutenant for the remainder of the campaign, and he discharged its duties with honour to himself and satisfaction to his company.
8. *Atajos, Arrieros*, Merchants, and Custom House Officers in Mexico:

Mount Bernal, Mexican Atajo, American Army - Lechugas

supplying the place of railroads, canals, and wagons in our country, and as, throughout the country, as well as in old Spain, the same system is pursued, an account of this class of people will be found interesting. One who pursues the business of an *arriero* has his *atajos* of mules, which are his own property, and, together with their halters, pack-saddles, or *aparejos*, are his whole stock in trade. A full *atajo* consists of sixty mules, though a smaller number is called the same name. A good mule, with its *aparejo*, is worth about thirty dollars.

He also has a trained, docile horse for himself, and five or six others for his attendants; beside these, he has a gentle horse, commonly a white, gray, or clay-bank, with a bell on his neck. This horse always goes before, and the mules will follow after him, though they will not follow one of their own kind, even if belled. A horse of a light colour is selected on account of the ease by which the mules can recognize him at a little distance. The sight of him, and the sound of the bell, starts them all towards him. (The author's horse, a handsome clay-bank, with long and full white mane and tail, at Camp Ringgold, near Matamoras, was always, when turned loose, followed by two or three Mexican mules, belonging to the train, and it was with great difficulty that they could be driven away from him. For this, then, the author was at a loss to account, but did so easily afterwards; for, as pack mules in the service of an *arriero* they had followed a horse of the same colour).

The *arriero* has in his service six *peones* for every *atajo* he owns; these are bound by debt to him, in the same manner that the general class are bound to the owners of the *haciendas* or *ranchos*. These are each provided with a lasso for catching the refractory mules, and each has a long straight sword and sometimes a gun, for their defence against the *ladrones*, or robbers, which infest all the highways. The *arriero* ready with his *atajo* and attendants, for a journey to any part of the republic. A merchant in Saltillo, for instance, proceeds to the coast to buy his goods, or perhaps he may go to New Orleans, or have them shipped from England. They arrive at Matamoras; they are passed through the custom house, where they are strictly examined, to see that they contain nothing but what is allowed to come into the country, for there are many articles that are not admitted. This examination, however, is slight, or entirely omitted, if the merchant gives to the collector, or administrador, a bribe.

When the goods are landed, the merchant must pay upon them a port duty, of from fifty to four hundred *per cent* His goods are now at the custom house; his next inquiry is for an *arriero* to take them to the interior. He finds one, and a bargain is concluded at so much a cargo, that is, a mule load, (three hundred pounds in our weight). The mules are driven up to the custom house and packed with the goods. Another duty is now laid upon these, called an extraction duty; this is eighteen per cent. The merchant, before the goods are taken, must give security that he will pay this amount within one, two, three, four, or five months, or longer, according to the distance they are to be taken. On this account, the merchant commonly states his destination to be much farther than he really means to carry them. He therefore states his destination to be Monterey, Saltillo, and Durango. On a stamped paper is made out a list of the goods, the boxes, marks and contents, and the certificate of the collector, that the merchant has paid the port duties on the goods, and given security for the extraction duty, and he is therefore allowed to take the goods to Monterey, Saltillo, and Durango, or elsewhere, according as he has stated his destination. This paper is called a *guia*,

The *arriero* and his men load on the mules, over their pack-saddles, which are simply immense pairs of leather saddlebags, stuffed with straw. He gives the merchant a receipt for the number of boxes, and then, commonly accompanied by the latter, the *atajo* sets off on its journey. The mules travel about twenty miles a day; at night are unloaded and turned out to graze; and poor picking they have, too. However, they are so hardy, that dry grass and weeds go very well with them; and, if not too hardly driven, they are commonly in good order. In the morning they are driven up to the piles of merchandise and row of pack-saddles; and so well do they know their own, that one will go to no other. They stand in a row, and the muleteers load them again, and all, as before, start off after the bell horse.

During the day, the time of the *arriero* and his men is continually employed in seeing that the loads are right. If a box slips, two of them ride up to the mule bearing it, and put a leathern blind-fold over his eyes; the string of this is dropped over his long ears, and the blind coming down, prevents him from seeing; he instantly stops, and nothing can induce him to move while this is on. They then fix his load and lash it firmly, take off the blind, which they carry on their arm, (see picture); the mule resumes his march; and thus, day by day, do the patient animals plod along. They come near a town.

Here, too, is a custom house; for Mexico is not like our country, in having custom houses only on the ports and borders, and goods once in pay no more; but here, they are in every town; and duties are to be paid in the interior, as well as on the coast Mounted guards are on the hills and approaches to the town. These see the *atajo* coming; they take command, and accompany it to the custom house. The long line of mules is stopped; the questions asked, and the *guia* examined. If the merchant does not wish to sell there, the custom house has nothing to do with him, and the drove passes on, until after a few days' patient labour, the next town is reached; the same thing takes place; at the next the same; the next also; and the same at every town passed.

After many days, the *atajo* approaches its destination. The guards, in the same way as before, come forward and take it to the custom house; the *guia* is exhibited; the goods are examined, slightly, if a bribe is given, and unloaded there. The merchant pays the *arriero*; who now seeks for a load to carry to some other place. If successful, he starts off loaded; if not, he goes empty to another town, on his way back to the coast. The custom house officers do not interrupt or hinder him, when he has no burdens.

These *arrieros* are, as said before, the common carriers of Mexico. They have more to do with foreigners, (i. e. Americans,

English, French, and Italians; for the majority of the merchants of the interior are of these nations), than any other class, and, from them, they learn honour and fidelity to their employers. They are the more honest and trusty class in Mexico, from the *Don* of the extensive *hacienda*, down to the Indian *peon*. They can be trusted alone, with goods to carry from one end of the republic to the other, against all incidents but robbery; but they will not, although armed, defend with vigour their *cargas* against the *ladrones*, or robbers, that swarm upon the public roads, without the owner is with them. If he is along, especially if he is an American, Englishman, or Frenchman, whom they know will expose his life to save his property, they will then second his defence with vigour and bravery; consequently, when such owner is along, the *atajos* are seldom attacked. Such are the *arrieros*, a good-humoured, honest set; the same today as a class, that they were fifty years since, and will be as long as the present population remains.

But as we were obliged to bring in the merchant, as well as the custom house, in order to give a correct account of the *arriero*, let us follow them through; for, although two duties have been exacted from him, on the goods brought, still the custom house has not done with him yet. He has paid the port duty, and given bond for the exaction duty of eighteen per cent; and has paid the *arriero* for the transportation, and the goods now lie in the custom house stores in the place of his final destination.

He wishes to take them to his store to sell. Before he can do this, he must pay the third duty of eighteen per cent, called the internal duty; and not only so, but a fourth one, municipal duty, to the corporation of the town, for the privilege of selling them there. After this, he is allowed to open them for sale.

But suppose that he finds that he has too much for the market, or that, while he was engaged in this long transportation, another had brought a supply, and he wishes to send his to the next large town. In that case, the custom house again gets hold of him, if that town is out of his state; for, before he can start with them, he must take out a *guia*, as before; and upon that must pay another internal duty of eighteen *per cent*, and another municipal duty at the town to which he is sending them. The four original duties on the same goods are yet not all the exactions; for still another comes, in an indirect manner. He has given bond and security to pay the extraction duty of eighteen per cent in the first port; this he must take in specie; but, as it enters the town, it is taken to the custom house, and although it came to pay to them, yet it is regarded as coming to be exported, and another duty of ten per cent is taken from it The whole system is calculated to exact every *quartilla* possible, from the merchants and people.

No wonder that the merchant should endeavour to avoid this enormous taxation; which, however, at last, comes not out of him, but from the people; as, for every tax he pays, he increases the price of his goods so much; and thus the government grind down the people, not only into poverty, but even into slavery, or the system of *peonage*, the same; and, although we are digressing, yet let us follow the subject far enough to see its effects upon the bondage of the *peon*.

The law obliges him to take two-thirds of his scanty wages, of his master, in goods for himself and his family. Now the merchant who brings these, adds to their original cost, the amount of the five taxes, then his profit, and at the gross amount sells them to the owner of the *hacienda*. He, too, has his profit on the whole, which, by universal custom, is one hundred per cent, on the merchant's prices; and at this, the articles are sold to the peon. Can he ever be out of debt to his master?

But to the merchant again. He sometimes succeeds in getting more goods in, than are marked in his *guia*; or else, he brings in a contraband article that pays him a high profit. He does this by continual bribery of the custom house officers. When the *atajo* is approaching the town of its final destination, all the goods that are contraband, or that are not marked in the *guia*, which he has brought along by bribery of the officers, the *arriero* places on separate mules, and some of his men drive these to a by-place in the mountains near, or to some place of concealment.

The remainder of the goods, that are regularly marked, and have paid the duties so far, are driven in towards the guards boldly, and taken by them to the custom house. The merchant finds the guard who stands at such a point; a few dollars given him, and the mules secreted can be driven in by him at night, and he will never see them, even should they brush him with their burdens; or he suddenly finds that an *atajo* is trying to slip in on another side of town, and he leaves his post to go there, &c. The mules are silently driven to an appointed place, and the gates of the high court yard receive them within. They are unloaded, and the goods stowed away. A little extra present to the *arriero*, for his part of the game, and all is right If, by accident, the custom house officers suspect the matter, a bribe to them makes them forget to search.

And now the author asks pardon of the reader, for the insertion of so long a note; but, as it describes the whole manner of transportation in Mexico, by the *arrieros* shown in the picture, and also the system of her internal and external duties; the corruption of her public officers, and the bearing of the whole system upon the people, he hopes that it will repay the perusal. The reader, of course, will understand, that in the ports taken by the United States' forces, all these duties are, for the time held by them, abolished.

After proceeding about fourteen miles, over a beautiful, undulating country, of rich soil, but with no inhabitants, with high hills in the distance, on either hand, and splendid views continually opening anew, we came to a swamp of large timber, thick; and under it was a close growth of *lechugas*, or the thorny flag mentioned.—The soil of this swamp, now hard as a rock, and having the impress, plainly, of tracks made months since, is very boggy when, wet.—Four miles through this, brought us out to the bank of the upper bay of the large lake of Carpentero, at which was a *rancho* of several buildings.

While watering the horses of the detachment here, the advance of the division came in sight, and filed out to encamp.— (Here the author left the guard of General Patterson, on account of his horse being taken violently sick, and unable to proceed; but, by the kindness of Dr. Wright, the surgeon of General Patterson's staff, the author was furnished with powerful medicines, which saved his horse).—General Patterson ordered him to remain with the division, to come up with it; and, when arrived at Tampico, to report himself to Colonel Abercrombie, his aid.—(The comparative dignity of generals, and some of the inferior officers, has been mentioned. This was exemplified at this moment.

The sick horse, on the ground near the general's wagon, required immediate bleeding, but not a fleam, nor even a penknife, could be procured, with which to do it. A lieutenant, who had been speaking to the general, was standing near the wagon. The author, being pretty well acquainted with him, asked him to lend his penknife, to bleed the horse.—It was amusing to see the haughty air with which he drew himself up, and, without making any reply, (struck speechless, with the arrant impudence of such a request, made by a long bearded private, to his smoothly shaven, nicely dressed lordship, and that, too, in the immediate presence of the major general), looked our author in the face, to rebuke his insolence, with as much severity as it was possible for a man to put on.

He, however, was thinking of little else save the sickness of his favourite horse and was not struck with much terror at the lieutenant's frowning countenance.—General Patterson saw it all,—for it was within a few feet of him; and, waiting a moment, seeing that the officer did not intend to comply with the request, immediately, with a smile, he handed his own splendid knife to the author, telling him to use every exertion to save so good a horse, &c.

The lieutenant immediately looked astonished, then deeply mortified; mortified, though, not at his action, but at being so quietly rebuked for it, by the general).—The detachment shortly afterward moved on. The author now found himself in an unpleasant situation; his mess gone, and forage all missing;—his company were behind.—Shortly however, he was kindly invited by Colonel Thomas, to come to his tent and table, until the division again came up with the general; of which kind invitation he availed himself so far as to procure his meals, and shared the tent of the assistant surgeon, Dr. Stout.—The colonel also divided with him the forage of his own horses.

This place, at which we were now encamped, was on a wide plain, bare of vegetation; for some distance back it was of alluvial soil, deposited by the lake, which, at times, overflowed the most of it.—On the bank of the lake was, as said before, a *rancho* of fifteen or twenty houses. This was here situated, for the raising of stock.—The lake, winding around, was spread out in the distance, in a smooth sheet; far across it, rose a range of high hills.—Distance marched this day eighteen miles.

Saturday, January 23rd. The whole division was on the march, before sunrise. The author's horse, not being yet entirely recovered, but sufficiently so to go leisurely, he got on, according to the general's directions, as easily as he could. Sometimes he was near the cavalry; then the artillery and the infantry would pass him; and, as he stopped to rest his horse, half, or more, of the train would go by; but when rested, he could again pass these, the infantry, and artillery, and come up to the cavalry again: and thus he spent the day very agreeably; for he had an opportunity to notice the passage of the whole division, from the advance to the rear, and to observe the continual sport and hilarity of the infantry.

The most of this, however, was found in the "mustang cavalry"—a description of force unknown to the army regulations, but which accompanied us from Victoria.—It was composed of numbers, from the three regiments of infantry. Any one that could raise the means to buy a long-eared *burro* (jackass), or a mule, or old Mexican horse, or any such conveyance, immediately entered the mustang cavalry. Such animals could be bought for from three to five dollars.—Some of the riders had procured Mexican saddles, with their horse-hair housings, and bridles also; while some had bridles, but no saddles;—others had saddles, without bridles; while others, again, had neither.

Here was a soldier large as life, with his musket in his hand, on a little jackass, without saddle or bridle, and so small, that the rider had to lift his feet from the ground;—the little *burro* jogged along with him, occasionally stopping to gather a bite of grass.—Here was another, on an old Mexican horse, whose bones showed plainly against his tight hide, having sunken eyes, and not able to go out of a walk.—Here was another little jack that refused to proceed, while a stout man had his shoulder to his rump, heaving him on; he had half a dozen muskets and cartridge-boxes for his load.

There was a soldier endeavouring to pull a mule along, by the *lariat*, while another was beating him.—Another was boasting how finely his little burro carried him without saddle or bridle, when the animal purposely turned under a long, thorny musquit limb, and brushed him off quickly, tearing him with the thorns.—Here went one loaded with mess-bags, camp-kettles, &c., followed by a larger *burro*, with two riders and no saddle. This mustang cavalry, too, had an officer; as much of a jackass as any with the long ears. He was a small man and rode a miserable, poor, little horse, with an old, torn saddle, but no bridle, but with a rope round the horse's nose; he paid no attention to the fun going on about him, but, filled with dignity, rode on, the most ridiculous object to be seen.—His appearance of importance was so amusing, that the author made some inquiries of the men, as to who he was, and found him to be a commissary, or else a quarter-master of one of the regiments.

MUSTANG CAVALRY

We passed, on the march, another *atajo*, or drove of mules, bound from Tampico, into the interior; these were heavily laden, but moved along with steadiness.—On the way along, we noticed, that the musquit was generally in bloom, having upon it thousands of small balls, each the size of a marble, of white and yellow colours, and pleasant fragrance.—After twenty-one miles march, over a beautiful, undulating country, of rich soil, mostly free from timber, having passed several *ranchos* on the way, we arrived at the old town of Altamira, on the same lake—Carpentero. Here we encamped, on the border of this lake, near the town, into which many went up, and soon came back, telling all that there was chewing tobacco to sell there.—Many of the men had, for a long time, been without this article, which, in the interior, was not to be procured; and now, everyone who could raise *"dos reales"* (twenty-five cents), went up to buy;—it was not very good, but still appeared, to those who had been so long without, a great luxury. (See note at end of chapter)

We found the town of Altamira to be a dilapidated place, having nothing of interest in its streets and squares, save a massive old church, that had been standing for two or three centuries; and it appeared as though it might stand as much longer. It was a curious structure, high, extensive, and heavy. On taking a side view of it, one would hardly know, whether to pronounce it an old feudal castle, a heavy fort, or a gloomy prison, similar to the Bastille; certainly a church would be the last thing he would think of. It had heavy stone abutments, running up against the walls, appearing like the piers of our bridges, when built out, as defences against ice.

There was a heavy, eight-sided dome on the top, which was a little different from the common style of their churches. We were informed that much wealth belonged to this old church; and that its interior had been most superbly finished in former times, and still so continued;—we had no opportunity to examine it. The name Altamira signifies a high view, and was probably applied to this place on account of the lovely prospect out on the lake, which is studded with green islands; in no other direction is the view extensive.—Lake Carpentero communicates with the Panuco river; and the inhabitants informed us, that vessels, drawing less than five feet of water, might come up the river by Tampico, into the lake, and wind their way along in the channels between the numerous islands, and come up to the town. They might do so, but there is nothing at Altamira for them to come for.—With the lovely country around it well settled and cultivated, it would be the garden spot of the nation.

The men found here plenty of brandy, *muscal*, and other liquors to sell, of which many of them partook rather too freely.—One liquor that is much in use in every part of Mexico, but more especially towards the centre and southern, was also for sale here, as well as in every town that we have passed. This is *pulque*, the fermented juice of the *agaue Americana*, or maguey; plenty of which we had already seen growing. The wild maguey, of which the strong liquor muscal, is made, has already been mentioned. A description of this enormous plant, which lives and thrives to the age of from fifty to eighty years, will not give to the reader as correct an idea of its appearance, as a representation in a view. The author, therefore, sketched the appearance of two of these plants, which were growing near a *rancho*, two days before reaching Altamira.

This view, in the picture, shows the two plants, of not more than twenty or twenty-five years old, and not fit yet to tap, to obtain the juice, or *pulque*. The size of the leaves can be seen by comparison with the height of the Mexican, smoking his *cigarro*, near.—Of the manner of obtaining the *pulque*, we will speak, when giving the account of all Mexican liquors, and methods of

---

9. This maguey is very useful to the Mexicans. It not only furnishes them with *pulque* and *muscal*, but of the strong fibres in its leaves they manufacture rope, and sacking of all kinds (called *guangoche*); beside, shoe thread (*peta floxa*), and strong sewing thread (called *peta torrida*). The upright shoot of the wild plants, when roasted, is sold in small pieces, by the name of *quiote*. This is prized for chewing, on account of its sweetness, as they would chew sugar-cane; and men, women and children, when not smoking, frequently have this *quiote* in mastication. The ancient Mexicans made as much use of this plant as those of the present race; and beside, formed from its leaves a coarse kind of paper.

Maguey Plant, Rancho, Dress of the Mexican

distillation, &c. (see ch. 2). The leaves of this plant are covered, on either edge, with thorns, and are pointed with the same.[9]—In this view, also, is shown a small *rancho*, on the little brook, in the back ground; a field enclosed by a stick fence, near the *rancho*; a corner of another fence, on the right of the foreground, and an irrigating ditch, by which the water was diverted from the brook above, and carried to a field below. (This ditch in front, the engraver has hid too much, by the grass on its bank).

January 24th. Another, and the fourth change of appearance of country since we had left Victoria, here met our view.—Near Victoria, we had travelled over mountainous scenery, with a few rapid streams;—then we struck the *mesas*, or table-topped hills, with extensive valleys between;—next, we left those, and came out into a vast undulating prairie, with some water, rich soil, and but little timber;—now, we passed over low, sandy lands, with heavy timber, thickly growing; the whole appearing entirely different from the former sections.—In the first section, it had been dry, lonely, but grand;—in the second, still bare and lonely, but pleasing, from its endless change of views and landscapes;—in the third, still more pleasing, being enlivened by extensive views of rounded swells, succeeding each other, until lost on the horizon—high, distant mountains, overlooking the whole: the view of the landscape improved by the grass, the palms, and scattered groves; the large herds of horses, mules, and cattle.

The fourth, upon which we had now entered, was refreshing and delightful to gaze upon, on account of its lofty oaks, of unknown species to us, it's beautiful palms, its lofty, graceful cocoas, of different kinds its sabre trees, with large trunks and limbs, appearing, in colour and smoothness, as if bronzed; its spreading banyans, each with several trunks; its trees of orange, lemon, and lime; its tall bananas, and sugarcane; its pineapples, and other fruits; its flocks of noisy parrots, of brilliant plumage; and of many kinds of birds which, before, we had never seen.—Our old acquaintance, the musquit, left us entirely; but very little cactus could we find; the trees, now seen, were without thorns: nothing was thorny, save the *lechugas*, or thorny flag, and the maguey.

After commencing the march in the morning, the road wound along the lovely shores of the lake, which, in hundreds of pretty indentations, formed little bays and inlets, upon the green shore. Never before had we seen a lake so crowded and studded with the most verdant and beautiful small islands.—Over the road the tall trees bent their limbs, covered with foliage of as lively green as though the season had been May.

We now, for the first time in Mexico, saw little patches of land,—enclosures upon which was the residence of one family only,—cultivated by one man, who appeared to be the owner. These little fields now began to succeed each other rapidly; and in each one we saw a smoking coalpit, put up in our manner.—About each house were three or four patient *burros*, who were waiting for their loads of coal, to take into the city; while others were going in, and others yet returning.—We noticed that many of these little enclosures had beds of vegetables: cabbages, beans, onions, garlic, tomatoes, red pepper, &c., growing for market. The air was different from before. Again we felt the sea breeze, that in an instant can be told, as it falls upon the cheek, by its peculiar freshness and invigorating power.—The whole scene was so new, that the morning's march seemed but a few moments[10] pleasant ride—and was short; for eight miles brought us to the little *rancho* of *La Encarnacion*, where, being plenty of water, and only ten miles from Tampico, the division encamped, around and under the thick, shady trees.

The author continued on to Tampico,—for he yet belonged to the general's guard, which had gone in,—arrived there, and reported himself to Colonel Abercrombie, as directed by the general. He was released from any farther duty of the guard, which had now been discharged from that duty; and had been ordered, with the two companies—Caswell's and Lacy's —who had come in with the general, to return to the duty of camp. These two companies, with the guard, started out, towards camp; but the author remained in town until the following morning, when he returned to the camp at La Encarnacion, where all the regiment (save company G) and the division then were.—That company, on the night of their arrival, were ordered to Tampico, and immediately sent over the river Panuco, into the state of Vera Cruz, as a guard to the topographical engineers; who were directed, by General Patterson, to reconnoitre the country. They were gone upon this service three days.

Tuesday, January 26th. We have been two days in this camp, and they had been devoted entirely, by all the regiments, to rest and sleep. Plenty of corn and hay had been sent out from Tampico for our use, and our wearied horses at once began to fare well.—As for ourselves, we spent the most part of the day, after the sun got. up, in sleep or in conversation under the thick shade of the trees around; and everyone seemed determined to make up for all that he had lost, on the march from Victoria.—No drill or parade was required of us here, and a glorious time of "napping it," we had.—General Quitman's brigade, which had come one day in the rear of us, passed through our camp, and continued on to a position within about three miles of the city. Captain Haynes' company of our regiment, had marched with this brigade from Victoria. That officer, at the request of the author, furnished to him some incidents of his march, which will be found in the note below—We wished much to go in near town, also; but we had no orders so to do. We were satisfied to remain where we were, for we had a fine, shady camp, plenty of forage, plenty of provisions, and nothing in the world to do; and beside that, were, at that time, most remarkably fond of repose.

General Hayne's Company with General Quitman's Brigade:

"At Victoria, my company having been detached from the regiment, to march with General Quitman's brigade, and being ordered by General Quitman to remain behind the troops, till all the wagons, &c., had left the city, we took our post near the plaza. Here we saw the Mississippi regiment of volunteers, Captain Bragg's and Lieutenant Thomas' companies of light artillery, and Colonel May's squadron of dragoons, headed by Old Rough and Ready, pass from their encampment, through the city, on their counter-march towards Monterey. The general was dressed very plainly, and accompanied by his staff. His appearance is that of a plain, blunt, and honest farmer, rather than that of an old regular officer; who are generally great sticklers for military dress. Not so with General Taylor. In plain citizen's dress, with forage cap, mounted upon a small Mexican horse, which was, perhaps, captured in some of the battles, he did not look like the great general, and the great military chieftain. At least, so said those who had not seen him before.

"'Why,' said one, to whom he was pointed out, 'is that General Taylor? I never should have taken that man for General Taylor!'

"'He is not as tall as I supposed he was,' said one.

"'He is a younger man than he is represented to be,' said another.

Bowing politely to all, and occasionally stopping to bid *adieu* to some old soldier or volunteer, who had lingered on the streets to catch a parting glimpse of their beloved general, Old Rough and Ready passed out of Victoria, followed by the kind wishes of the whole army. His little army, that went back with him, numbered only between seven hundred and fifty, and eight hundred.

"About noon, we left the city of Victoria. The Mexican population flowed out to see the army march off, apparently much disconcerted, to see columns march off towards the south, and the north; and many were their inquiries, as to which route General Taylor would march.

"Being obliged to remain until all the troops of both armies had left, my company patrolled the city, in different directions. Availing myself of the promising appearance of the interior of a Mexican *fonda* (eating-house), kept by a *señora*, who had made herself very obliging to those who liked Mexican dishes, with a friend or two, I entered her house, called for '*cafe, pan, gallinas, huevos*" which means coffee, bread, chickens, and eggs. Everything was soon ready, and our hostess assured us, that it was all done up in American style.

"Having seen a commotion amongst the soldiery, she inquired if we were all going away. We told her yes. She wished to know if General Taylor was gone. We told her, all, but us; and we would be off immediately. Assuming a thoughtful air, she exclaimed, '*Yo soy triste! Mui triste!*' (I am sad I am grieved); and then, as if soliloquising, she continued: '*entonces, no puedo vender mas cafe, ni pan, ni huevos, ni mas gallinas*' (Then, I shall sell no more coffee, nor bread, nor eggs; no more chickens.) '*Americanos, mui amigos! Mexicanos, mal!*' (Americans, good friends; Mexicans, bad.)

"Much amused at the sadness of this money-loving dame, we mounted our horses, and marching round the *plaza*, we left the city at one side, as a Mexican body of cavalry (as we afterwards learned), entered it at the other.

"Everything went on quietly, till the evening of the second day; when a small party of my company, who had gone out to drive in beeves, saw a party of Mexican cavalry, about six miles ahead of our camp. Next morning, a beef-contractor, named Bigelow, who started from the centre brigade, in the morning, to come back to ours, was fired upon, and pursued for some distance, by a party of Mexican cavalry, who shot him through the leg. The fleetness of his horse enabled him to reach an advanced party of my company. That evening, Lieutenant Chambliss, with twenty of the Giles' troopers, went forward some miles, to ascertain the position of the Mexicans, but they had disappeared in the *chaparral*.

"Two days afterwards, a party of Mexican cavalry, armed with lances and rifles, attacked a few men of the Georgia Regiment and Baltimore Battalion., who had dropped behind the rear guard, and killed one, took another prisoner, and were in pursuit of others, who were relieved by the gallantry of Henry Pitts, David Myres and P. C. Morton, privates of my company. Being in the rear of the column near two miles, and hearing the guns in their rear, they charged back in a gallop. The lancers, seeing them approaching, supposed a body of cavalry was near, and fled to the thick *chaparral*. One man with difficulty saved himself from their lances, by climbing a small thorn-tree, the leaves of which hid him from their view.

"Before day the next morning, my company marched back, by order of General Quitman, and lay in ambush, on the roadside, hoping that the lancers would follow on, but they had taken the alarm. There was a body of Mexican cavalry, who had been, until then, following in our rear.

"The only remaining incident is to be told. At Altamira, which is a town of between one and two thousand inhabitants, a horse was stolen from my company, as we left the encampment. In the evening I returned from our next camp with ten men, and calling on the *alcalde* of Altamira, inquired of him whether any Mexican had brought an American horse into the town. He said, at first, that he did not know; then that he would inquire, and soon after said 'yes; there was a horse, which he had sent into the country.' His evasive answers led to a suspicion of his honesty, and I immediately took him prisoner, and placed a man on each side of him, with a loaded carbine.

"This produced quite an excitement in the town. The crowd gathered round us quite boldly, and the second *alcalde* came forward, to remonstrate against the arrest of his brother. His remonstrance soon exhibited the fact, that he had secreted another horse, which had been stolen from the Tennessee Cavalry; so he was ordered to take his seat between the sentinels as a prisoner. They were then told, that unless the horses were forthcoming in half an hour, they would be carried off. They immediately ordered out some men on horseback, to bring in the stolen animals. In ten minutes, one was brought in; in half an hour another, and shortly after, a third, with the two men who had received the horse from the thief; but the thief was allowed to escape.

"Taking possession of the recovered horses, the *alcaldes* were ordered to mount, and we started with them to the camp, with the assurance that we would keep them prisoners, until the thief should be brought to us; but the junior *alcalde* offered, if we would allow him to remain, to have the thief captured. We left him, therefore, with a promise, that if he did not send us the thief the next day, we would return and take him to camp also.

"About this time, some Mexicans, six or seven in number, armed with swords and pistols, rode up near us; these we quickly disarmed and made prisoners, also. Our party was ten in all Our prisoners, one *alcalde*, three horse-thieves, six pack mules, bearing forty or fifty gallons of *muscal*, six or seven disarmed men, and another, who could speak a little English, and begged us to take him a prisoner also, as he was determined to die with his particular friend, the *Señor Alcalde*.

"His request was promptly granted, and he was ordered into line. With this cavalcade of prisoners, mules, and recaptured horses, we entered our camp, sometime after midnight. Early in the morning the thief was captured, and placed at our command, and we released the *alcalde*, whose rejoicings, at his deliverance, were only equalled by the fright during his captivity. This was the last horse stolen by the citizens of Altamira."

Some complaint was soon after made by the Mexicans, to General Quitman, of this capture, who reported the affair to General Patterson, who very wisely passed the matter over. It was said, at the time, that these gentlemen attached some blame to Captain Haynes, for having thus summarily dealt with the rascals, who aided and abetted in the stealing of his horses. Rather than of censure, for capturing them, that officer was deserving of praise. If officers higher in command than him, had acted in the same prompt way that he did, when in command of his separate detachment, it would have been better than the milder, temporizing course that was pursued.

January 27th. Company G returned from its scout in the state of Vera Cruz, where they had been in the neighbourhood of a large Mexican force, under General Cos, which has been there collected for some time; with that general's head quarters at Tuspan, about seventy-five or eighty miles to the southward.

The engineers sent out, under protection of the company, finished their observation satisfactorily.—They reported that section of country as being fertile, producing in abundance pineapples, cocoa nuts, and every kind of the richest fruits, and most fragrant and beautiful flowers;—of tall trees, of growth and luxuriance previously unknown to them;—of most lovely lakes spread out, winding in a thousand shapes;—of fields of maguey, larger even than any before seen; of lofty hills;—of most luxuriant valleys of green;—of the air refreshed by the sea breeze, which is loaded with the fragrance of the orange blossoms;—of the valleys having fields of sugar-cane, of great size; and, in one word, as a perfect earthly paradise. It was amusing to observe the enthusiasm with which all of the company spoke of it, officers and men.

We heard before their return, from the Mexicans, that the country south of the Panuco, and up along its bank, was extremely beautiful and fertile, and therefore we did not discredit the accounts of the men, though, as said before, it was amusing to hear how flowing were their descriptions of its attractions.

This little place of *La Encarnacion* had only a few houses, one of which was of stone, with a store. Here, too, was the largest garden of bananas that we had seen. The growth of this tall plant, with its fruit, is well known in the southern part of the United States.—Here it was about ten feet high, with its long waving leaves of green, and hanging bunches of cucumber-shaped fruit, making a fine appearance, especially as it was planted so thickly. It seemed to be the main "staff of life" with the inhabitants of this section of Mexico.

We found here a stone idol, of the ancient Mexican, or Aztec race, which idol, we were informed by the intelligent owner of the house, was dug up not far from this place, with many other things, instruments and utensils, which he said were now all lost. This idol is about three feet high, and with its pointed pedestal, is one piece; of a rude style of sculpture, but cut with great care. A sketch of it was taken by the author, both side and front view, which will be seen below.

It is one of the numerous idols that were worshipped by the ancient Mexicans, before the conquest of Mexico by Cortes, in the year 1521.—It has much resemblance to the old Egyptian style of sculpture; and from this, as well as the similar customs, in some respects, the present pyramids in both countries, the similar ancient calendars, &c., some reasons might be obtained to establish the similarity, or identity, of the two races.—The carved apron in front of this image was curiously wrought, and the two figures in the centre, now worn by time, appear to be the disfigured remains of two large hieroglyphics.—The ears of the image are large, and nearly square, and stand directly out from the head;—the pointed pedestal appears as if made to fit into a socket. Of its general appearance, the reader can get a good idea from the sketch below, which is a correct likeness.

There was considerable sickness in the regiment now, and one man, James Allen, of Captain Gillaspie's company, died to-day. His comrades made a coffin from a gun box, which they were so fortunate as to procure.—Most of those who have died have been buried without coffins, for no material of which to make them could be procured.

January 28th. Our regiment of cavalry, the first and second Tennessee infantry, comprising, in all, the Tennessee brigade, under General Pillow, were this morning ordered by him to strike their tents, and march to an encampment selected near Tampico.

The morning was very pleasant, and the work of striking tents, loading wagons, saddling up, &c., was quickly performed,

and we were soon in lines and on the march. The second battalion of our regiment, under Major Waterhouse, were in advance; then we of the first battalion, under Lieutenant-Colonel Allison, followed; then came the first Tennessee regiment of infantry, under Colonel Campbell; then the second regiment, Colonel Haskell; then a small train of company wagons; then the rear guard.

Our battalion being a little behind hand, had some trouble to pass the infantry, to get into our position.—The sun was hot, but we were shaded from it by the lofty oaks, the extended branches of which, in some places, nearly met over the wide road.—Five miles took us through this sandy level forest, to the cultivated hills. Here we halted for a little while, to allow the infantry to come up; for on the good road we had got nearly a mile in advance of them.—In this halt we had leisure to observe the surpassing beauty of the scenery around us.

On our right, far down at the base of the hills, was the wide lake, spread out more beautiful still than we had before seen it, on account of our height above it, which enabled us to look down on its extent, and over the numberless beautiful green islands, with which its calm surface was relieved. Here and there, among the islands, could be seen the long slender lines of the boats of the inhabitants, moving almost imperceptibly on the brilliant surface of the water, which was unruffled even by a ripple. The natural beauty of this lake, as seen from these hills, with the tall blue eminences far beyond it, rising in the horizon, is seldom excelled.—But, on the other hand, the prospect, to the left, was delightful:—The hills were clothed in perpetual green, of a heavy growth of tropical trees, of the richest appearance;— here in forests, there singly or in groves; while ranchos were thickly scattered around far down in the vales, or perched, as it were, high up on the hill-sides.—The bloom of nature, the fresh green of all vegetation, was delightful.—Orange trees, lemon, and many other kinds, and vines, with soft leaves and luxuriant foliage, were thickly growing.—We saw no musquit, so thorny; no prickly pear, as much so, no sword palmetto to pierce, and but little cactus, of any species. This seemed to be a garden spot, from which most of the thorns had been expelled.

After a little time spent in gazing on this scene, in itself so beautiful as to be worth a journey of a hundred miles to see, the infantry came near, and we were ordered on over the hills, up and down their long, cultivated sides.—Among these, three miles from town, in a beautiful place, was Quitman's brigade encamped. Passing this, we were again halted at the last hill, before reaching town, for the infantry.

Here was another view as beautiful as before, but somewhat different.—On the right was still the level lake, here merging into the river;—it's pretty islands, which we had passed behind, were succeeded by others equally picturesque. More boats were seen, far below, upon its surface.—On the left, as we stood, were still the fertile hills and valleys, with extensive fields of sugar-cane, banana, corn, pineapples, and other products.—But, to the front, was the main picture:—The city of Tampico lay before and below us, with its white buildings and large extent. The American flag, from a lofty staff, was seen flying out above it;—the forests of masts of vessels, with their colours, were in the river beyond, giving animation to the scene.

This river flowed around in front, and passed far off to the left, where a little patch of the blue sea, at its mouth, could be perceived, with the tall black dots, as it were, of the heavy ships that there lay at anchor.—Over the river, in front, and bounding the view, were a long range of hills, not bare in a single spot, but covered with a forest of the freshest green. In the foreground, on looking down the road, were the line of cavalry, seen halted all the way down the hill;—beyond them, the road was thickly studded with men, and small droves of jacks and mules, going to, and returning from market; and wagons with their white covers, bringing out provisions, &c., to the camp of General Twiggs, which was near this place, and General Quitman's, still farther back.—Beyond these objects, as the road again rose the hill to enter the town, was in view, first, the stone cemetery, on the right; the new fortification in front; and down still farther than these, to the left, near the margin of another lake, was a new fort, yet unfinished, and upon which scores of men were then at work.—That lake spread out on that side of the city, between the hill upon which the fort was built, and a long, wide, level plain, that again, beyond, stretched away to the river.

Upon the river, in the distance, towing up vessels, were several steamers, throwing long lines of black smoke behind them. The other view, first mentioned, was lovely, but this extensive scene exceeded it in beauty; for it united sea and land, lakes, river, islands, forests, city, vessels, army, camp, roads, fields, and crowds of men at different labours.—Where could a scene more comprehensive, more beautiful, be found?

After the infantry again came up, we were ordered to proceed. We passed down the long hill, and rose upon the other, of more gentle slope. Proceeding by the cemetery, we struck the town at the fortification, near a large two story stone building—the military hospital; and, winding through the long streets, descended to the main *plaza*. From there, we passed on through the business portion of the city, though continually descending, until we reached the river's edge;—here we turned to the left, and, following the road that led out of the city towards the mouth of the river, a short distance brought us to a stone bridge, thrown over the canal, which connects the smaller lake spoken of, to the left, with the river.

When this was crossed, we came out upon a spacious plain, level as a floor, bounded by the river on the right, the lake on the left, and high hills in front. As we proceeded down, on one of these an old fort was to be seen.—This plain contained eight or nine hundred acres; was uninterrupted, in its whole extent, by any enclosure or houses, (save two small ones on the river bank); and was covered with a low growth of green weeds: the cool breeze blew gently over it; and there was much beauty in the place.—Looking back, over the canal and lake, we saw the city of Tampico, now above us—the buildings rising on the side of the hill like terraces, one over another.

As we marched out on the plain, away from the city, and towards the old fort on the hill, at the extremity of the plain the advance were halted: the infantry came up behind us. The three regiments were then marched square off to the right, which soon brought all down to the edge of the river again, upon the bank of which they halted and encamped; our regiment being the farthest from the city, Colonel Haskell's next, and Colonel Campbell's nearest, not being far from the canal and bridge. Here we had a splendid place for a camp:—The lovely river was on one side, with vessels and steamboats coming by and returning; the city was in full view; the plain was large enough for several thousands to drill and parade upon; the hills were near; and old ocean himself was but five miles off, and in view.

Only two inconveniences we found:—One was, that all the water in the river was somewhat salt, and our drinking water had to be brought from a large circular wooden cistern, above ground, on the canal, near the bridge, about half a mile from our regiment.—This cistern was kept full by many Mexicans, who were continually employed, with large boats filled with hogsheads, in going up the river, to the fresh water, filling these, bringing them back, and discharging their contents into the cistern;—to do this, bringing their boats into the canal, close to it. From this, it was drawn off into our buckets, as we wished it.

The other was the want of wood.—Upon first encamping, we collected all the loose drift wood that the winds and waves had thrown upon the shore, close to us. This, although soaked with salt water, and covered with barnacles, (a small seashell that adheres in numbers to all wood and other objects exposed in salt water), yet burned well after the sun and wind had dried it. After this was gone, we had to go with the wagons to the hills, towards the mouth of the river, to obtain any kind that we could get, with more labour than ever before;—yet, during our stay at this encampment, we always found enough.

There was not a particle of shade here, but at this season of the year, though sometimes very hot, the sea breeze kept the air at a pleasant temperature.

Here, now, we were comfortably placed at the city of Tampico, the second commercial town in the republic of Mexico, three hundred and twelve miles from the capital, near the mouth of the river Panuco, in the midst of as lovely a country as is to be found on the globe; and here we were furnished with every comfort, every convenience, that soldiers in a foreign land could expect or ask for.—Provisions of every kind, used in the army, were abundantly issued to us;—oats, corn, and hay, for our horses, as much as they could eat;—and our duty, during our stay here of forty days, was light, being principally drills and parades; which, though keeping us continually employed, and often tiresome, yet were by no means hard.

The course of the journal, from day to day, along, will be interrupted, and only written at intervals, during this stay of forty days; for the course of one day was often so much that of the day preceding, that the repetition of the same scenes would be tiresome to the reader. —The next chapter will be devoted to a description of the scenes that, met our observation at Tampico; chapter 3, bringing up the operations of the other divisions of the army, happening in the meantime; and we will commence chapter 4 with our departure from Tampico for Vera Cruz, still farther to the southward, and at this time in the possession of the enemy.

Note.—The Mexicans do not use chewing-tobacco, but are continually smoking. Their government turns this habit of the people to a means of revenue. The cigars used in the country, are all made in the government establishments; and sold at the same price everywhere. If any tobacco is found upon the premises of any person, save of those who sell it for the government, called *Estanques*, the delinquent is punished with a fine of five hundred dollars, and one year's imprisonment. The government contracts every year, with a merchant, for the quantity they want.

He contracts with certain *haciendas* to raise this amount, which is done, and no other person in the nation is allowed to raise a single plant. The *Estanque* of every town is appointed by the government; and is under bond and security, for the faithful payment of the proceeds of the *puros* (large cigars), and *cigarros* (small ones), that the governor forwards to him, from time to time. The *Estanque* furnishes other shops with cigars, and allows them to sell, on his own responsibility; these are called *Estanquillas*. The *Estanque* makes returns monthly to the governor, reserving six per cent., for his pay. Besides, no note, deed, or bond, is valid in Mexico, without it is written upon paper stamped with the seal of the government (*papel sellado*). The price of this is placed at from a quarter of a dollar to two dollars and a half per sheet, according to the instrument to be written; and no one can sell it but the *Estanque*.

CHAPTER 2

Camp Scenes

February 4th. We had been now at Tampico a week, had become well acquainted with its position, appearance, &c., and we will endeavour to give the reader a correct idea of it. We have mentioned the old fort on the hill, at the farther extremity of the plain from the camp, and the course toward the mouth of the river. From this fort is a fine prospect.—The author sketched two views from it, which are presented. (See pictures p.68/69.)

This, called Fort Andonega, stands on a high eminence, looking down on the plain, river and lake, and commands the city. In the first view, reader, imagine yourself standing on this old fort, looking towards the south-west.—As you see in the picture, the wall is in front of you; this wall is of stone and cement, and is about eight feet thick, eloped off on the top. Over the wall, you look down on a tangled mass of small timber and vines; a little brook runs round in there, and then flows under the base of the hill on which you are, and continues on to the river below; beyond the thicket of brush-wood, you see the smaller lake, which has been mentioned; a long canoe, with a sail, is upon it, having come through the canal.

Over the lake, on the hill, you see the city.—You observe that it falls off from the centre, down to the river, on the left. At the right extremity of the city you observe a tall building, with a flag over it. It has been turned into a fort, and has artillery mounted on its flat roof, though the pieces are not to be perceived at this distance.—To the right of that, you see a large building; that is the military hospital; built and used as such, by the Mexicans, and appropriated by our forces to the same purpose. The road from the interior, by which we entered the city, comes in there. To the right of that, is the *campo santo,* or cemetery, with its stone walls and lofty gate. There is another to its left, but it is concealed from view by the hospital. Nearly between you and the cemetery, and not far from the edge of the lake, you see a new fort, with a flag above it; it is yet unfinished, and has been before mentioned. To the right of these, and farther up, you see the tents of part of General Shields' brigade.

Now, reader, could you be on the top of the building with the flag upon it, or at the cemetery, or on the top of the hill, anywhere there, you would see below you, on the other side, the river, the mouth of the lake, both widely spread out with the beautiful islands spoken of, and lovely channels between.

You would see far over these, still onward, a blue range of hills, in the distance; and could you be across the waters, and upon those hills, then you could look down on the vast expanse of lake Tamiaqua, an inland sea, in extent, that runs far to the southward, and is separated from the Gulf of Mexico, by a high, long, range of hills. Its wide inlet communicates with the Gulf, far to the southward, beyond this range, near the mouth of the Tuspan River; but over all its shores, as well as up to the Panuco River, General Cos, with his Mexican army, holds possession.

On the left of the picture, from Fort Andonega, you see first, part of the extensive plain, which has been described, and on the farther extremity of which the Tennessee brigade, under General Pillow, is encamped; the tents of the first regiment of which can be seen. Those of the second, are still farther to the left, and nearer, in the bend of the river, and our regiment in the same bend, still nearer. You perceive that the long skirt of low timber extends up to the left from the main body, and is between the lake and the plain; its extremity conceals the canal, which there runs from the river to the lake. It also hides from view the bridge over this canal. There is a new fort there, made by our forces, which is also concealed; beside, an old circular one of the Mexicans, now nearly torn to pieces.—Beyond the camp you see the river, that flows round from the other side of the city; over the lower part of which can be seen the numerous masts of the vessels there at anchor. A large flag can be seen over this part of the city. It is on the flag-staff in the *plaza de Camercio,* or the lower *plaza,* adjoining the river. Beyond the vessels, and over the river, concealed by numerous islands, is Pueblo Viejo, or old Tampico, the former city, a very old place. This new city of Tampico has sprung up in late years; the population settling here on account of the better harbour.

Now, reader, from the picture and the description of it, you have a correct idea of the situation of Tampico; and, having sufficiently observed the position of the city, and all the prominent objects about the exterior of it, turn slowly round to your left, and in imagination see the plain below you, the remainder of the camp of the Tennessee brigade, and the river, which comes nearer to you than before, while the high, forest-covered banks opposite, are pleasant to view, from the peculiar freshness of their green.

Turn completely round, with your back to the city, and then the other picture is before you. First you look upon the area of the small fort in which you stand. Three Mexicans are there, smoking their *cigarros,* and talking of the steamboat which is towing up the brig in the river. In the fort, on the right, and front, you observe the stone platforms, on which formerly stood the heavy pieces of artillery, which bore down upon the river. On the left, is a building, now decaying, with the tiles nearly gone from its roof; it was used for the barracks of the garrison, and when our naval forces first took the city, in November last, it was occupied by marines from the ships of war; then, the former name of the fort, Andonega, was abolished, and it was now called Fort Conner, in honour of the commodore.

The marines held it until the arrival of the land forces; when, with much ceremony, the possession of the city and all the forts, was handed over, by the naval officers, to those of the army.—By

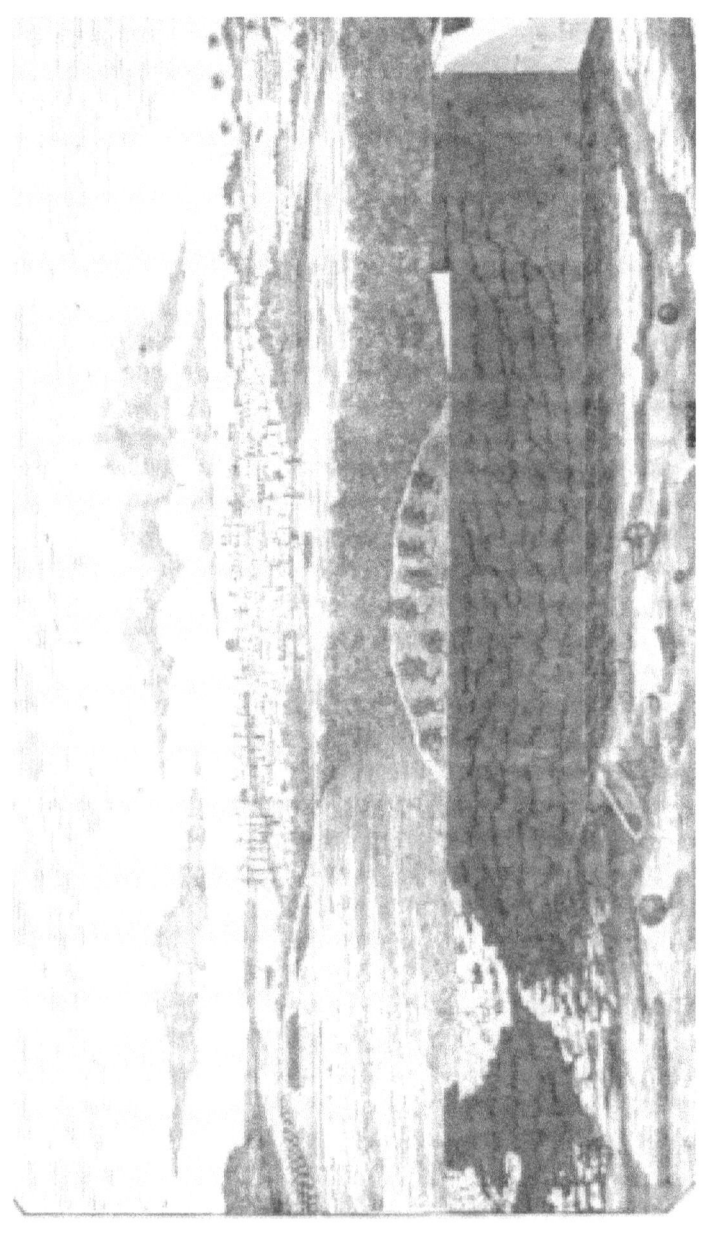

City of Tampico from Fort Andonega

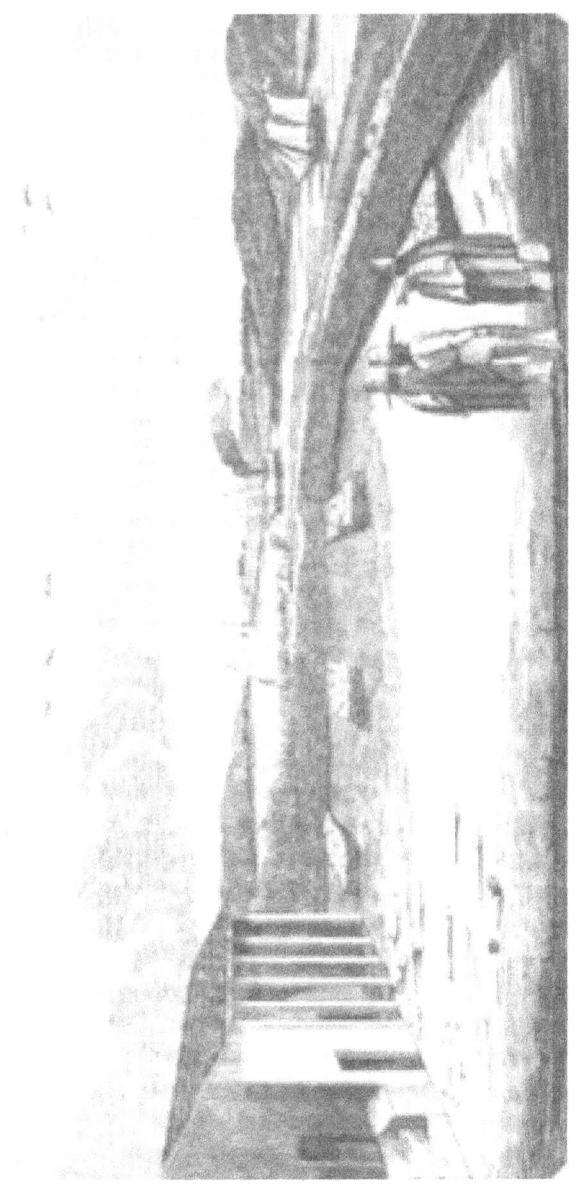

Mouth of Panuco River from Fort Andonega

the last, this has not been occupied, for no attack is feared from sea.—On the left of the picture, can be seen three stone steps they ascend to a fine, smooth platform, the former walk of the officers of the garrison; the magazine, also, was in this elevation.

Over the broken wall in front, you observe a hill covered with bushes: that hill is the final resting-place of many soldiers of our own, and of the other regiments of our brigade. The graves are on that part of it seen beyond the corner of the house.—From the front of the picture round to the right, you perceive the smooth plain spread out, not so wide as above; on it, in the distance, is the wagon train of the brigade;—beyond this, is the river—a schooner is going out, and a steamer is towing up a brig. Down the river, you see another small schooner, going out;—beyond her, you perceive the mouth, the old forts, and the pilot houses;—these are about four miles distant. You observe two large ships lying off; several more are out there, but not in view:—they draw too much water to come over the bar.—Still beyond them, are the waters of the Gulf.—On the right, are the hills of green before mentioned, though, in many places, plains strike off from them; but these cannot be perceived in the view.

Having observed this scenery towards the mouth of the river, turn again to the view of the city on the other hand. You perceive the large flag in the lower part of it, before spoken of as being over the *plaza de Camercio*; and as that is the most busy part of Tampico, we will commence the description of the city there : imagining yourself at the foot of that tall flag-staff.

You are in the centre of the large square.—The flag-staff is placed in a circular pedestal, quite large, being near twenty feet in diameter at the top, and of six steps, (between four and five feet), in height; all of stone, and beautifully finished. It is said here, that this was intended for the base of a statue of Santa Anna; but our forces have applied it to the use of furnishing a firm foundation for the large staff supporting the flag of the United States. The steps, which run all the way round, are excellent seats;—ascend two or three, and let us seat ourselves, and look upon the lively scene before and around us:—The square is finely paved with small flat stones, with *radii* or diverging lines (made by these set on edge) running from this circular elevation to every part of it. It is separated from the width of the streets that join it, by a row of handsome, tall, cemented, square stone pillars.—On the back and two sides, you see the crowd continually passing to and fro, with many wagons, many *burros*, and more pack mules. The buildings around the square, you see, are of two lofty stones, with handsome fronts;—stores are in all the lower stories.

The stores around, you will notice, have odd signs over their doors. One has a large sun over it, with the inscription "*Ti-Enda del Sol*" (the store of the sun); another, with a crescent, and "*La Luna,*" (the moon); another has a comet painted out, with "*El Cometa,*" another a white horse, with "*El Cabal-Lo Blanco;*" another a palm tree, with the same inscription, "*La Palma*;" and so on, according to the taste of the owner.—Almost everyone has such a representation.—These signs are so placed for the convenience of *peones, criados,* (house servants), and others who cannot read.—If you step over into one, you will notice a great variety of articles, and in very many of them a bar with wines to sell; for, by the general's orders, they can sell nothing stronger;—but ask for some "strong wine;" the Mexican will understand you, and with much politeness hand you out a glass of the strongest sort of brandy; but ask him if he has any brandy, he shakes his head and his fore finger before his face:— "*No hai, Señor; 'brandy' no se vende"* (has got no brandy to sell); though he has just handed you a glass, and will hand you another if you ask for "strong wine."

Mexican Liquors:

In Tampico were plenty of French and Spanish wines, brandies, and cordials for sale, beside their own Mexican liquors, of which there were one or two distilleries, fitted like our own, in the city. The principal Mexican liquor, as has been said before, that is used over the whole republic, is *pulque*. When a maguey plant, (see picture, Ch. 1 p. 49), is coming to maturity, *i. e.* preparing to blossom, which it does but once, and which takes place at from sixty to even a hundred years of age, according to the soil and elevation, a large excavation is made in the side of the stem, to the hollow within, the bottom of which is like an acorn cup.

The juice of the plant, that would have fed the tall blossoms, distils from the wounded leaves into this cup, and is dipped out twice a day; a good plant yielding, daily, from three to four gallons. It is of a sweet taste when taken out; requires no preparation, but is set aside. The second day it is partly fermented, and is somewhat like metheglin in taste; the third day, the fermentation is complete, and it then is about as strong as hard cider; has a peculiar smell, something like tainted meat, and is drank in great quantities by the Mexicans, and sold in the market places and shops of the towns; often coloured, to make it attractive to the eye. (At Vera Cruz, the *pulque* sellers coloured it of many tints). The soldiers, generally, did not like it; though they would have drank it, had it been stronger; but it was not sufficiently so for them to overcome their repugnance to the odour of it.

From this *pulque* a strong liquor is distilled, called, in this section, *aguardiente*, though this term signifies all strong liquors, meaning, literally, "strong water," equivalent to the Indian's "fire water." *Muscal*, a very strong, peculiar liquor, which has been several times mentioned, is made of the wild maguey, which is not so large as the other. The plant is crushed, and, when fermented, the whole is distilled. The method of distillation in the interior of Mexico is rude. A row of copper kettles is set, usually within the adobe walls of the house; beneath the kettle, and opening on the outside of the wall, are the arches for the fires.

Each kettle has a double or hollow head, for the steam to ascend into it, through a hole in the bottom, the edges of which are raised. There is no still worm for condensation, but a stream of water is brought along in a trough above, and a spout of it, dashing down on the copper head of each kettle, cools and condenses the steam within, and the liquor so obtained, being prevented from running back into the kettle by the raised edge of the hole within, issues from a little stopcock in the side, into the receiving vessel. So much for a Mexican distillery in the interior.

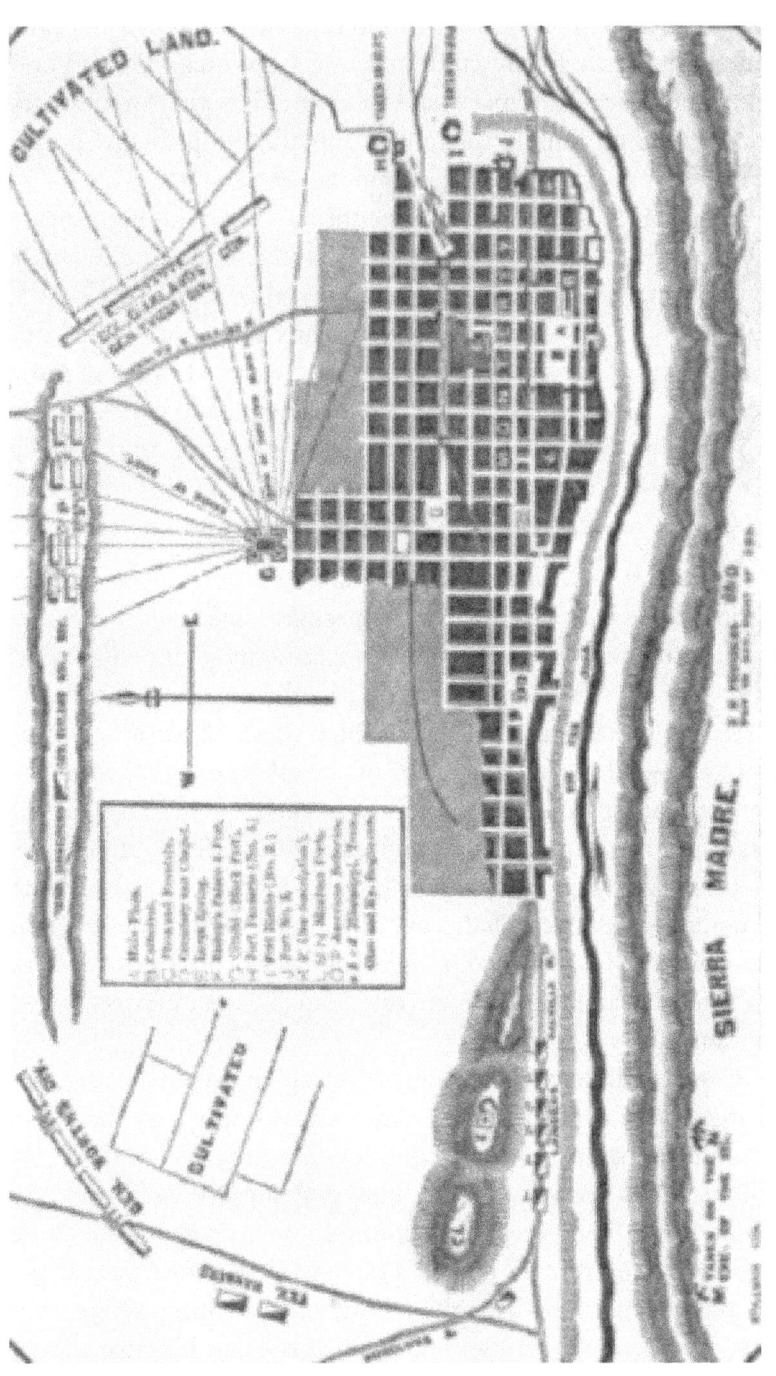

Plan of Monterey

In some parts of the republic, especially about the city of Parras, in the interior, west from Monterey, (see map previous page), the grape is extensively cultivated, and large quantities of good wine and brandy are made, and much used by the Mexicans, as are the foreign liquors spoken of; but still, the principal drinks come from the maguey, *pulque*, and *muscal*.

After being tapped, that plant continues to yield the quantity mentioned, each day for about four months, although there may not be a drop of rain during that time; it then dies in the centre; but as it decays toward the outside, many little ones spring out at the roots of the enormous leaves. These are set out, and grow freely. They are sometimes arranged as a fence, and neither horse nor ox dare attempt to pass them. He who sets out maguey plants, does it for the next generation, for the chances that ever he will see it yield, are a hundred to one against him.

In these stores, they have a much better idea of exposing their goods to the best advantage for appearance, than our merchants have, with equal stocks on hand. One little thing you will notice: no store is without its *brasero*, or pan for coals, on the counter, at which to light the cigars, which these Mexicans are ever smoking.—There are little ones of cut tobacco, wrapped in paper, and sold in bunches of forty-eight each. These cigars are not larger than a ten-penny nail, and smoke but a few moments;— they are called *cigarros*. A larger kind are all of tobacco, somewhat like ours;—they are called *puros*, and are sold in bunches of eight or sixteen.—The tobacco of the country is of a superior quality for smoking, and the puros are often equal to our highest priced Havana cigars.

Observe these two Mexicans, meeting on the square; they are strangers to each other; one is smoking; is stopped by the other, who, in the most polite manner, touching his *sombrero*, asks for a light; this is answered by the first, with a grace that would do honour to a Frenchman, by handing him his *cigarro*, at which he lights his, then returns it with a bow, while the former receives it, stepping back with another bow, and touching his *sombrero* also, as if expressing his sense of obligation, that his cigar should be returned to him; and the expression of *muchas gracias, Señor*, is given, as they separate.—That is a fair sample of their politeness and easy ceremony, even among the lowest class, upon all occasions. (If the parties are of unequal rank, the inferior takes off his hat, and holds it in his hand, while the other is lighting).—They are faithless and treacherous,—will rob, steal, and even murder, upon every favourable occasion; but still, in all their intercourse with you, and with one another, they are exceedingly polite and accommodating.—Enter one of their houses, and everything they have, seems to be at your disposal; and they often disoblige themselves, to accommodate you. They will give you freely, any information in their power; and seem to take a pleasure in so doing.—Singular traits of character to be united in the same persons; but so they are.

Those Mexicans have gone across the square; let us continue our observations. In front, towards the river, and obstructing part of the view of that, from the flag-staff, you see a long, one story building, with a *piazza* roof, standing out, under which are some pieces of cannon and several men crowded around the windows.—Upon looking closely, you observe they are bringing *tortillas* from the market-place near, bread from the bakeries, and other provisions, and handing them in through the gates, to those inside. This building is the guard-house. The men there, have been placed in for various reasons: some have been fighting, getting intoxicated, &c.; some have refused to do extra duty, imposed upon them for being absent from rollcalls or drills, and have been marched up here; some have thought themselves ill-used, by their company officers, and have told them so, and being cursed in reply, have returned oath for oath, with good interest, and have been confined here for insolence, and insubordination. Some have thoughtlessly strolled off from camp between the intervals of duty, without a permit in writing, and have been placed in here, by some sergeant of the guard, who has met them in the town, &c., &c.

Let us now leave the observation of the guard house, and the men there confined, and from the flag-staff walk a few steps to

the upper portion of the square, on the river, to the right.—
Here is a jabbering, busy scene; all over the pavement, far and
near, crowded upon each other, are numbers of Mexicans; men,
women, boys, and girls; each one with a small square mat of
palm-leaf, or rushes, spread out, on which they are seated, cross-
legged; before each one, is something to sell, mostly eatables.—
One has before her a number of little piles of sweet potatoes,
cooked; each pile to sell for *un real*; another has a pile of *mies*
(*pron. mice*), corn, on his mat, and is on his knees, with his little
square measure of *media almud*, to sell it full, for *dos reales* (twenty-five cents); another has upon his mat a large pile of red peppers (*chilli*), without which, these Mexicans could not live.

Another has a pile of onions (*cebollas*) and garlic (*ajo*); while
another has several baskets of the finest oranges (*naranjas*), five
for a *media* (six and a quarter cents); another has many pineapples, from *un real, un media*, to *dos reales* each. Another, has
nothing on her mat but a large heap of *frijoles* (beans), but she
gets many customers; another has several cabbages (*repolios*), and
she is busy in calling the attention of all to them.—Another has
a large heap of bananas, at a *media* for a bunch of about a dozen,
each the size of a common cucumber.

Here was a row of a dozen little girls, all with their *rebosos* drawn over their heads, seated on their mats, with, before
them, large piles of *pan a dulce*, or sweet bread, in fancy forms,
looking nice and clean; while opposite them, are several old
women, ugly as sin, each with a large earthen pot, over a charcoal fire; the steam comes from the vessels, in which are stowed,
layer upon layer, little parcels of a composition made of chopped
pork, mashed corn, and red peppers, called *tomales*. Each one
is wrapped in a piece of plantain leaf, and is not, in size, two
mouthfuls; many stop to buy, and eat these little morsels, hot
with steam and pepper.[1]

Near these are several rough-looking *rancheros*, with large rab-

---

1. In other cities these tamales are wrapped in corn-shucks. They are much prized by the population, and are eaten when quite hot. All who have heard the vendors, will remember their continual cry of '*tomales calientes*.' (hot *tomales*).

bits, *peccaries*, a species of hog, of an iron-gray colour, with stiff, sharp, bristles, and very lean, called by them *cochino del monte*, or hog of the woods. They have, too, many raccoons, rather different from ours, partridges, squirrels, and any number of ducks.—Another is beyond, whose whole stock consists of a few dozen *huevos*, or eggs.—Some have little chocolate cakes and balls, of a superior quality; while others have chocolate and coffee ready to drink.—Here is a *ranchero* who has made up a number of *sombreros*, from palm-leaf, now offering them for sale; while another has some *lariats*, or hair ropes, for horses.—The whole pavement, from the square down to the water's edge, is covered with these mats, with various articles; while, through the whole, a crowd of Mexicans are stepping round, and many American soldiers, attracted by the continual bustle and jabber over the whole ground; such a noise is there, that one could hardly hear himself speak.

From the square, you see down the paved slope to the water's edge, where are many large boats at the shore, with their bows on, and crowded against one another. Near them, directly in front, is the short wharf, at which lies a steamer and another vessel; while out in the stream lay many brigs, schooners and steamers, while boats are continually going and returning from these to the wharf, bringing their cargoes of grain, provisions, ammunition, wagons, &c. Many enormous piles of all these, save the ammunition, (which is immediately taken away), are on the pavement at the head of the wharf, the cart-men and wagoners taking these away, and the sailors and labourers landing them, make much noise; but it is but little to that made by the Mexican boatmen in their long canoes, to the right of the wharf, for some distance up and down the river.

Let us pass down to them, carefully stepping about amid the mats of vegetables, &c., in our way, and finding some difficulty in getting through the busy crowd among them.—As we come near the boats, a dozen of the boatmen, thinking that we wish one, to take a sail for pleasure, are around us, each one jabbering as fast as he can speak about the beauty and speed of his boat, while pointing to it; another jabbers as fast, and says that the boat of the first is *mui malo,* (very poor), and his is *mucho bueno,* (very good);—they get hold of you, and each one, by every means, endeavours to induce you to employ him.—But, refusing them, let us look at their boats:—These are quite long,—some thirty feet or more; are dug out of a solid trunk of a tree;—some are mahogany, but the most are of a species of cedar, that grows abundantly in the borders of the large lakes which join this river; and for such an extent of country around does this canoe navigation extend, that there are great numbers of them made.—Almost everyone has a short mast and low sail, that, in a light breeze, skims them swiftly over the water.

Some of these here collected are passenger boats, and are waiting for hire; but the most have come from up the Panuco River, or from far up the Carpentero Lake, beyond Altamira, or from the large lake called Zapote, on the other side of the river, with vegetables and fruits of all descriptions, which grow in the torrid zones, to sell.—Some of them are entirely loaded with oranges;—lemons are of too little value to bring in.—You may go out here in the country a few miles, and off from the road, pick up any quantity of them under the trees. Before this, we had got plenty of them.

Other canoes are loaded with bundles of green twigs, and leaves from the *ohalita,* or fodder tree, which are sold here in great quantities, to feed horses with.—It appears singular that horses should be fed on such fodder as the green leaves of a large tree, but they eat it with avidity; though we have never seen this fodder used anywhere else in Mexico, save here.—There are several of these boats thus loaded, and many are buying their bundles of fodder.

Let us walk up further.—Here are four boats that have just come up from the mouth of the river with *tortugas,* turtles, and *pescado,* fish. Look at these turtles:—There is one that will not weigh less than seven or eight hundred pounds, and several others that will weigh from four to six hundred. They are of enormous size, and there are plenty of them on this coast.—See that little Frenchman looking at one of the smaller ones, and hear how the Mexican fisherman praises it, and how many gestures are used on both sides during the trade. The Frenchman keeps an eating house a little back of the square, and wants to furnish his customers.—The whole scene of these noisy boatmen, joined with that mentioned by the others, is interesting, and time runs rapidly on while walking round among them.

Let us return to our position at the flag-staff.—By referring to the picture, as taken from Fort Andonega, you perceive that the city rises back from this flag-staff, to the outer skirt on the interior, at the military hospital there seen.—Let us go back in this direction.—In the first place, by a considerable ascent, we go up a pretty street, in a parallel direction with the river, and one square back from it. This street, like all the rest, is well paved, and has side-walks of flag stones.

No stores are in it; but on either hand are dwelling houses, with their stone walls joining each other along;—where apart, they are connected by a high garden wall. These buildings are well made and lofty, but have a bare, somewhat gloomy appearance, from their fortress-like manner of construction, with a heavy door opening inward to the interior court, and but few windows; these are projecting and iron barred, so as to give the ladies (for there are many females in Tampico deserving that appellation) a chance to look out up and down the street.—You will observe that the gutter is in the middle of the street, and that both sides slope down to it, instead of our custom of having one on either side.

As you pass these buildings, you will hear the sound of several pianos in the houses, and see at the windows many quite pretty women, though a little dark in complexion; but that, with their black hair and eyes, only heightens their beauty.

Proceeding up this street two squares, you come on the left, or towards the river, to the house occupied by General Patterson, as the military headquarters.—A large flag is suspended over the door above, by a cord, which crosses the street to the large building opposite.—These two buildings are the corners of the next cross street, that runs directly from the river bank, here high and bluff, back down to the principal *plaza*, and then on directly through the city, coming out near the lake seen in the view.

As this house, occupied by General Patterson, was one of the best style here built, we will enter it, and observe its construction.—You perceive that there are windows on either side of the arched doorway;—these are of large panes of glass, but have the usual iron bars without;—the doors are stout and ornamented. Above the door and each window, the large space of the arch is filled with panes of glass, each in segments of the half circle, of which these form a part. These panes are of coloured glass;—one is red, another green, another orange, another blue, another yellow, and so on round the half circle;—the mellow light from these gives a beautiful tinge to the objects within.

We enter into the first large room;—the floor is of square marble slabs, each about eighteen inches wide;—one is black, the succeeding one white, like the squares on a chequer board;—in the centre is a large black marble star.—Heavy ornamental pillars support the ceiling above, which is lofty, and adorned with rich stucco work;—the walls have, round the tops, the same.—They are not papered, but white and smooth.—The smaller room, on the right, is finished in the same manner.

The larger room, in the rear, is also finished in the costly style of the first, with as large a door, opening out into the spacious court, at the further side of which, are the stone stables, which these people in the cities always have near their houses, and sometimes, (as at Vera Cruz), in the lower story, where they reside above.—The whole building, costly and splendid in appearance,—has a cool, but to us, accustomed to our kind of houses, a cheerless, bare, appearance. This house is owned by the former collector of the customs at this place, who now has lost his situation and his profits, since our forces have taken possession of the city, and a new and much lower rate of duties is levied upon goods.

Leaving this house, and turning to the right, we will follow down the cross street before mentioned, towards the principal *plaza*. The first object that you will perceive, is a number of Mexicans at work repairing the pavements, under the direction of an overseer, or *alcaide*.[2] As they seem to labour in a constrained manner, you will see, as we come nearer, that some of them are confined by a chain.—They are the criminals condemned by the *alcaldes* to labour on the streets, for petty crimes. You will perceive that the *alcaide* has a sword, and several rods with it.

Here, as in other cities, that we have taken, the course of justice with the population continues undisturbed. The guard of our soldiery overlooks the whole, and keeps order among the Americans. Our government, of course, is only military, though, as will be mentioned, shortly after this time, our commanding officers took part of the civil authority, and endeavoured to show these people something of the manner of trial by jury; a thing wholly unknown in their laws. Along this street, we see the same continuous course of mingled population on the side-walks. Here knots of Mexican *peons*, in their uncouth dress; there, gentlemen, in that more dashy; beyond, American soldiers, continually passing, or stopping to converse; officers, in couples, or threes. In the body of the street, is a long *atajo* of mules, just come in from the country; observe each patient animal, heavily packed, as he follows steadily along, after his predecessor.

Let us pass along, glancing in at the numerous stores; not so large on this street, as on the *Plaza de Comercio*; still you see the lofty shelves, covered with goods, earthen-ware, crockery, and every article that elsewhere you can purchase.

You see many women buying. Observe that one drawing her *reboso* more closely over her head, as she steps out; notice her walk, she seems to step so lightly, still with such ease and dignity, or, as some call it, "with a queenly tread;"—they all walk so. But here, up the side-walk, comes one in whom you can better observe it. She is returning from "mass;" is of the higher class; she

---

2. The *alcaide* is an inferior officer of police, who has charge of the prison in every town, particularly responsible to the *ayuntamiento* of the town.

looks as "neat as a pin;" her *reboso* is fine, and richly ornamented, and fits to her head and shoulders, as closely as a cut garment. As she comes near, look at her fan; it is of the "open and shut" kind; she carries it in her hand, although the day is not warm; hear with what a peculiar rattle, she throws it open and closes it.

They have a variety of motions with the fan, for their sweethearts and friends: one to attract and permit, another to repulse and deny, &c. Look at her foot, so small and well turned; her form fine; her features regular; complexion olive; pretty mouth and white teeth. But notice the glances of her eyes, are they not attractive? They seem to show her whole soul. There is no coldness in her look. Turn, and look at her walk, as she has passed by; is it not "queenly," sure enough? But do not look at her too long, for you might have no relish for the next objects to which the author would draw your attention.

This is no other than four patient *burros* (jackasses), that while you have been gazing at the beautiful *señorita*, have been shaking their long ears close to your elbow; one is elevating his head and tuning his throat for a sonorous bray; while another is stretching out his nose, endeavouring to reach a piece of orange peel, which is near your feet. They have each an open box on either side of them, which are connected above their backs. In each box are two kegs of ten gallon size, so that each *burro* has four of them on his back. They are filled with water; and the industrious owner (*aguador*, or water-carrier), has been four or five miles up the river this morning, with them, filled each keg, and now is round supplying his customers with that article so necessary; and this is the only way in which the city is furnished; the water of the wells not being good, and there being no aqueduct. The furnishing of water gives employment to many *aguadores*; and in every street we will meet them, with their *burros*. Every carrier has a little bell, with which, at the gate of a mansion, he makes his arrival known.[3]

---

3. In Matamoras, the water was taken up from the river, in barrels with iron hoops. Each barrel, when full, was bunged up, and a pin being in the centre of either head, with a hide rope attached to them; the barrel was thus drawn, rolling over and over, by a *peon*; no *burros* being used for that purpose; but here they do all the work.

Nor is this all that these *burros* are used for; they will carry anything; and more tractable and patient animals cannot be found; and their character certainly has been very much abused among us, by making their name the very personification of stupidity and stubbornness.

But here come some more of them; you see they salute these water-carriers with a loud bray, which polite attention is immediately answered, and then all are still, and take no more notice of each other, than though they had not met.

These, just coming, you observe are loaded with little bags of charcoal; which is here used entirely, or almost so, for cooking. Little grates, not more than four inches square, being their means of raising a heat for cooking; that is, in these fine houses; in the others, they cook on the ground.

Hear how lustily that sooty fellow calls out carbon, (charcoal), through the streets.—We have mentioned before the coal-pits from whence he comes. But look again; there is an odd sight. Do you see that *ranchero* coming up behind the coal drivers, leading a fodder stack? It follows him closely; it is tall, bulky, and sweeps the ground, yet falls not, and passes along without exciting any surprise in the patient donkeys around; but the horse of that cavalry soldier seems about to break his neck with fright at the stack, which slowly pursues its way.

Walk round it:—you observe that it is tied together with a small rope; and is well shaped. Lift the leaves that brush the ground, and stooping, peep under:—the mystery is solved; you see the hoofs of a patient *burro* under there. Again walk round, and you cannot see a trace of him, head, body, tail, feet, or ears, which always are the most prominent objects in this animal. [4]

Here comes three more donkeys, loaded with the green leaves of the *ohalita*, or fodder tree. You observe the street is continually busy and crowded with the mixed multitude. Let us go on towards the *Plaza de Armas*, or the principal square.

---

4. There are, near every Mexican city, many persons who make a living by the aid of three or four burros. These bring loads of wood on their backs, or coal, or sand, or anything that may be needed, the *burros* picking up their own scanty living. The men are called *burreros*, literally, jackass men, referring to their manner of business.

Upon arriving at the corner, you see the square before you, surrounded by good buildings, mostly two stories;—the principal church stands on the opposite side, and the tower, (which, in the picture, can be observed), is furnished with a large clock, after our own style; but it strikes the hours on a heavy bell, and the quarters on a lighter one.—The interior of that church is not so rich as those before described.—You observe the whole area of the unpaved square before you is taken up by large piles of wagon bodies, axles, wheels, bows, and tongues, and many men are engaged in placing them together. Nothing here engrosses your attention much, save the same mixed throng passing back and forth.

Let us step over the *plaza* towards the church:—On the corner we see a building where already, in full operation, are a company of American actors, engaged in carrying on the "American Theatre;" and pretty well they do also, and obtain each night crowded houses, and make much money.—Back of this is a large building, formerly occupied for public instruction, as the sign over the principal door declares; but now it is used as a hospital.

Let us pass the sentinel on duty, at the gate at the end of the building, and, entering the yard, go round among the small interior buildings occupied by Dr. Wright, and several assistant surgeons, nurses, guards, and other attendants.—Upon entering the main building, you perceive rows of neat bedsteads, each with a covering of raw hide, stretched up and down either side of the long room, on every one of which is a sick soldier. Some are improving, and in a day or two will be able to take the fresh air in the pleasant yard, where, as we came in, we might have observed several pale looking men seated around.—Others are growing worse; one out there has just died;—see with what a look his next comrade turns his weak eyes towards the corpse, not knowing but he may go next.—Another there is being bathed in warm water, and the surgeon is applying mustard plasters to him, endeavouring to keep up his circulation; but it appears as though it was in vain, for the life is nearly out of him now.

Observe how still it is in here, although there are so many sick and so many attendants.—See this other surgeon, who goes from cot to cot, examining, and giving to the nurses directions for each.—At the upper part, the attendants are coming down from one to another, with tin cups of soup and slices of fresh bread, to give to those who can eat.

Here, sitting upon the side of a bed, you see a weather beaten soldier, who, with the tears standing in his eyes, is watching the convulsive movements of the death-like countenance of his sick comrade and mess-mate, over whom, perhaps, when both left their native state to serve their country in the field, he promised the parents, brothers or sisters of that comrade, to watch and to assist. Now he is fulfilling his promise; but the hand of death is on the youth.

Let us turn away from this mournful stillness, and out of this place of sickness and death, and again emerging into the street, find ourselves in the bustle of life.—We hear the music of a full band at the head of a detachment of soldiers, swelling fully out the inspiring strains of "Hail Columbia"; and the music, so enlivening, drives away all melancholy thoughts.—Let us stop at the corner of the *plaza*, and admire the precision of military movement with which they pass along.—They are part of the Alabama regiment.

They have gone, and we will continue our course along up the hill, towards the outskirts of the town, and the military hospital, already noticed in the picture. In this part of the city we will observe that the buildings become smaller, being mostly of but one story. The gardens are many, with ornamental trees growing in them. We observe but few stores, or shops of any kind; for this part is occupied principally for dwellings.

Here and there is a *panaderia*, or bakery, which bakes fine bread, and is, in every respect, like our establishments of the baking order, save that these not only bake for the living, but also, occasionally, for the dead.—they, however, do not have much appetite, and are only fed once a year; this refers to a singular custom, or remnant of an old Indian superstition, which in nearly all of Mexico, has been like other similar ones, incorporated into their present religious belief; and, by the lower classes, is scrupulously observed.

On All Saints' Day (first November), the bakeries not only issue their daily amounts of bread for the living, but bake up a number of white, hard loaves, of a peculiar shape, being circular, like large rings, with a raised top, which is pinched up into hundreds of little prominences; these loaves are called *rosca de los muertos,* or rusks or loaves for the dead.

Singular as it may seem, the lower classes buy these, and put them up in their houses, for the sustenance of the souls of their deceased friends and relations; and they will tell you, in a serious tone, that such souls had ate such a part of it in one night! The loaf remains in the same spot, until the souls have eaten it; *i. e.,* the mice, crickets, and roaches have consumed it.

The souls are not fed again until next year, on All Saints' day, when, if not forgotten, they get more loaves! In what part of the world can a more singular exhibition of the darkest superstition be found? And what is more singular, is, that such an idea is not removed by the priest; but, like many other rites and ceremonies of the ancient Mexicans, this too, has remained, and presents a curious instance of a most ridiculous heathen ceremony incorporated by the descendants of those heathens, into the Christian religion they profess.

Upon arriving at the military hospital, we find great exertions making, to place this part in a situation to resist an attack from the interior; wide, deep ditches are dug, and heavy embankments thrown up. The small fort near the margin of the lake is nearly finished; at all of these we notice many men at work.

Having taken this walk through the busy city of Tampico, we will return along its streets, turning corner after corner, until we arrive again at the *Plaza de Comercio,* at the starting point, the flag-staff; thence we come along the river, seeing only the same bustle, but meeting with many more wagons, employed in transportation of stores, for different brigades, encamped around the city. Passing the outskirts of the small houses, we leave the city. A few steps bring us to the canal, bridge, and new fort; crossing the bridge, on which we find many soldiers, we come out on the plain; on our right, and far extended to the front, lies the camp of our brigade, along the river; and at this, having spent the day in the observation of the town, we bid you, reader, good night.

Saturday, February 6th. General Pillow's brigade, as well as all the others, were now subjected to severe and continual drilling. Every day, the plain in front was enlivened by large bodies of troops, in their various exercises. The regiments of infantry now moved in solid phalanx over the plain; then rapidly deployed in long lines, re-formed in columns, charged, threw themselves in hollow squares, &c., &c.

The artillery swept by them, at a rapid rate, whirled round, the horses were detached, cannon aimed, and in one minute after the first check of speed, the light cloud of smoke arose from the gun, and the ball went crashing through a large target, about a third of a mile distant from them, at the foot of the hill on which is the old fort. Again, in another moment, the horses were attached, the riders up, and away went the piece to another position, at full speed, and as suddenly whirled, unlimbered, aimed, and fired.

The howitzers, in the same rapid manner, threw shells into the old fort Andonega, which loudly exploded there. It was only occasionally, that either the artillery, cavalry or infantry fired, in these drills.—The evolutions, and practice of loading, &c., were gone through with, continually; but the firing, almost always, was imaginary; for we had no ammunition to throw away.

The large bodies of the two battalions of our cavalry, can be seen, sometimes, coming on, at a rapid trot, in solid masses; then, suddenly wheeling, they open to the right and left, in detachments, and long imposing columns; sometimes they move slowly, then again, the volumes of dust, suddenly rising, as it were, with the whirlwind, shows the charge; the dust obscures them; far ahead, they emerge from it, rein up, and by companies, turn, and double upon, and among, each other, in a thousand ways; yet there is no confusion, no mistakes, by any. The roll of drums, the shrill sound of the fifes, and the clear notes of the cavalry bugles, and the deeper music of the regular bands, fill the air with martial strains. Sometimes these are silent, then, all in concert together. The varying scene goes on continually;—the sunny plain every day presents the same striking martial appearance, ever varying, but still the same: parade upon parade, drill upon drill, at intervals, from sunrise to sunset.

Sometimes many small squads, each under its officer, are practising the manual of arms, &c.; then the plain is covered with companies, each acting singly; then again larger bodies, battalions, are moving independent of one another; then, in the afternoons, each regiment is carrying on, under the command of its colonel, its regimental manoeuvres; then again the whole brigade is acting in concert, under the general;—the whole appearance is such as can only be witnessed in the performances of an army in the field. The beauty, variety, and precision of movements, never can be seen in parades and reviews at home;—they can only be executed by bodies of soldiers who for months have made it their business.

And now, while, from time to time, we speak of the camp and scenes around it, the reader will bear in mind this principal martial view, accompanied by the music, continually going on over the area of the plain before the camp, save for a few intervals, of a Sunday or two, and during the severe blowing of the northers.—At daylight, at seven, a. m., at eleven, a. m., at three, p. m., and at five, p. m., the principal drills and parades take place, and, save at meal times, the plain never is bare.—The weeds, which grew upon it on our arrival, are all trampled down, and it is level as a floor.

February 17th. This was a most lovely day; and the sun shone pleasantly on the beautiful river, on the green hills opposite, on the city in the distance, on the camp and the plain.—It was warm, pleasant, bright and still. Before the sea breeze rose, not a breath of air was stirring;—and every sound was distinct. The flags over the city, and those on the lofty masts of the shipping near it, drooped motionless from their staffs;—the screams and chattering of the numbers of parrots, of brilliant plumage, in the forests opposite the camp, came with distinctness across the calm surface of the water. Upon the river, here and there, were long canoes, the paddles of which, now and then dipped in the surface, glided them quietly on; while the little undulations from their movements caused the rays of the morning sun to dance, as it were, on its bosom.

Below was a vessel, which, for the want of the slightest wind, had let go her anchor, to retain her in the same position, while her white sails were still stretched above, courting the renewal of the breeze. The crew were leaning over her sides, gazing out on the camp that was spread before them.

The city and the camp were still.—In the former, the bells calling the people to "mass" had ceased their tones, and in the latter, the drums, the fifes, the bugles, and the instruments of the bands were all silent: for, a wonder, Sunday had been recognized, and there was no drill, no parade, no movements.—The long line of succeeding infantry sentinels, that extended in front of the entire brigade, at regular intervals, from the bridge on the left, towards the town, down to the bend of the river, on the right, seemed as if struck with the stillness and beauty of the scene before and around them, and were motionless also.—They leaned on their muskets, at their posts along, from space to space.

Now, reader, while all is thus reposing, let us turn our attention to the tents, and see at what the boys are engaging themselves; for, at all times when they are at leisure, their occupation and movements are about the same, and a glance at this leisure day, shows for all.

Let us walk round in the cavalry regiment.—The horses are still; tied with their long lariats;—they seem dozing in the pleasant sun.—At the line of tents nearest to us, you observe the captain's marquee, with a crowd around it, sitting on the bales of hay and bags of corn, that have been sent for the use of the company.—They are engaged in conversation with respect to our next probable movements.

At the first tent in the line we will stop and look in.—We see a couple of the men sitting down in the little space, amid carbines, swords, pistols, blankets, &c., engaged in writing letters on pieces of barrel heads, which are placed across their knees.—They have obtained their sheets of paper from the officers, (to whom, every quarter, a quantity is allowed by the government), and are busy; being prompted by seeing so many vessels arriving and departing from the United States, and also by receiving letters from home. Two of their mess-mates are on the sides of the tent, on their blankets, asleep, and appear very comfortable.

Leaving them, another step or two brings us to the second tent.—The flap is closed, and the tent is, as it were, shut up. Let us open it, and enter:—There is but one man within, and he is mending his bridle;—the whole bottom of the tent is filled with baggage and arms.—In comes a comrade, who, in a low voice, asks him if he has got anything. He nods. "Hand it out, then." He drops his bridle, and reaching over, pulls out, from under the blankets, a bottle of brandy, and sells the other a dram, for a bit; but it is done in a very quiet manner, for it is contrary to the regulations of the camp.

Liquor the soldiers would have; and they worked many schemes to be able to obtain it At Victoria, where no spirituous liquors, save *muscal*, could be procured, many of the soldiers made a profitable business by buying it from the Mexicans, (who are fearful, on account of the prohibitory commands of our general, to sell it to us by the small quantity), and with a canteen on their sides, and a little cup in their pockets, were ready, when one raised his finger, to step round a corner, or into some courtyard, and pour them out a drink for a real, or bit. These "travelling groceries," as the soldiers called them, could be met in any street. The officers would pass by them, as they strolled about, never suspecting anything of the kind. So, in spite of all restrictions put upon them, the soldiers would manage to get their drams.

And so it is here, in Tampico. By order of General Patterson, severe punishment has been inflicted on the barkeepers, both Americans and Mexicans, in the town, for selling spirituous liquors. But our soldiers buy it from the Mexicans in quantities, and bring it into camp, and silently sell it to their comrades in their tents. Every morning you may see men walking silently and carelessly up the lines, and then suddenly diving into a tent; all is still there, but lift the flap, or the door, and you can see the vendor pouring, from an old black bottle, a dram into a mug; the soldier lays his bit on the blanket, drinks the liquor, wipes his mouth, lifts the flap and goes out, as if nothing had happened The bottle is put away again in the corner of the tent, under the pile of arms and loose blankets, and the vendor walks out too, until another silent customer gives him the wink. Brandy, *muscal*, *aguardiente*, or some other spirituous liquors, they will have.

At the third tent, we find some of the boys asleep, and a couple cooking behind it;—they have been up in town and bought some beef and vegetables, and having borrowed a camp-kettle from another mess, are trying their hand at making soup, for a rarity. They have got some light bread from the bakery, some pepper, and several little articles, and they seem as much engaged in making their soup as though it was to be of immense advantage to them.

You will smile to see what value they set upon it; but if you had been through the hard times that they have, and were in their position now, a dish of hot soup would appear to you to be indeed a luxury.—There are two more of the men there who do not belong to that mess, and with each one of these they have struck a trade:—One is to get them an armfull of wood, for which he will have to go at least a mile, and bring it on his shoulder;—the other is to go to the cistern at the canal, a half a mile, and bring back a bucket of water for them: for these services, they are to get a cup of soup a-piece; and both think they have made good trades, and start immediately to perform them.

At the next tent, crowded at its door with bags of oats, are, within, several seated on a blanket, playing "old sledge," while another has got a novel, which has been read about the camp until it is hardly readable, and is passing away the time in deciphering it.

At another tent, the fire is kindled, and a chap is pounding coffee with the muzzle of his carbine, and is quarrelling all the time with his mess-mates about the cooking, declaring that it is not his day in turn, &c., and swearing that hereafter he will cook for himself alone, &c., &c. In this tent are the mess-mates, some of them asleep, others endeavouring to mend up their uniforms and other clothing, and keeping up the dispute with the one who is cooking.

In the next, you see a water bucket, with a full supply of water, and a pan of fried pork, and hard bread, to which the boys of the mess are about to apply themselves for a dinner.

In the succeeding tent, a general cleaning of arms is going on; for one of the mess has been lucky enough to get hold of a little sweet oil, and all of them are availing themselves of the opportunity; and with much conversation, and many tales to one another, they appear to pass the time very pleasantly.

In the next one are many collected, to hear a man who is telling amusing tales, and many a loud laugh comes from there.—After he is done, another sings a song in high glee. Let us peep in:—They have got several bottles of brandy cherries, and they insist upon our taking some of them.—

(These are procured from the sutler, who, as he is not allowed to sell spirits, thus evades the restriction, and his brandy cherries go off like hot cakes).

We will go on.—At the next, we see more writing letters, sewing, &c., and several at a game of *euchre*. At the next, we find all engaged in a general dressing and cleaning up, having had their clothing returned from the Mexican washerwomen, who have made it look new.—They are evidently much pleased with their change in appearance.—In front of this tent, as well as of several others that we have passed, down the line, you observe many of the men spending much time and pains in rubbing and currying their horses; and in the meanwhile they are talking to them, and patting them, and so accustomed have the horses become each to his rider, during the long march, that he knows him as far as he can see him, and will express it by neighing, and if loose, will come up to him. A horse could not be driven from near the camp, and it takes them but one feed to learn them their particular place; and, if turned loose, they will each come to it at night.—These men are devoting their leisure time to the attention required by their horses, and they could spend it in no better way.

Let us look for a moment upon this group in the next and last tent, busily employed at a game of poker. The tent is not much larger in area than that which is covered by a double bedstead, about eight feet by ten. In this little place, covered with blankets on the bottom, are now nine persons.—At the back is a pile of carbines, cartridge-boxes, swords, holster pistols, &c.;—on the side are two of the mess-mates, stretched out and wrapped in their blankets, trying to sleep; but they can scarcely do it: for, crowded upon them, set the chaps at poker.—A green blanket serves them for a table.

There are five at play, and everyone busy. Grains of coffee, called checks, ranking as *picayunes* each, are on the blanket before them.—Nearest is a small man, with a quick, restless eye, who shuffles and deals off the cards with the sobriety of a senator.— Hear him quickly say, as he throws down a couple of grains, "I bet two checks; what will you do, Sam?"—see with what eagerness they all look on, as they compare their hands, and the highest rakes down the heap

And so they go on for hours;—the same scene and words.
"I pass,"
"I bet a check."
"I see your check, and go three better."
"I go four blind."
"I call you."

With little dispute, occasionally, about putting up their "antics;" with sometimes a loud laugh from the winner, and then a muttered exclamation from a loser, who, thinking he had held the best hand, had bet freely upon it, and then found, to his disappointment, that another held a better one.

We have now passed down one line of tents, or one company; each company in the regiment, and each one of the regiments of the brigade, will be found engaged in nearly the same ways. It is so all over the camp. Let us now look along the shore of the river, near to which our walk down the line of tents has brought us.—Here, we find seated on the low bank, many groups of men, who are looking on the beautiful scene before them, of the peaceful river, with the vessels passing up and down; for the sea breeze now gently blows, though the surface of the water is yet unruffled.

They are watching the porpoises, who throw their large backs out of the water, blow, and then disappear. An enormous turtle occasionally appears.—Passing along, we see other men, catching crabs, in the shallow water; these are very numerous, and with a short pole, a line with a piece of meat on it, and little dip net, one man catches from twenty to thirty in an hour.[5] Others we see, walking the shore, apparently in thought; though there are not many of these, most having laid aside the task of thinking, as a continual job, to be taken up on their return home.—Now, reader, we have given you a sample of the crowded camp, when in a state of rest and quiet. Of course, we have not mentioned all particulars, but enough to furnish you a definite and correct idea of the way in which we employ our time when off duty; and knowing it upon one day, you know it upon all.

Monday, February 8th. As mentioned, in the note appended, our company, G, after spending half the night in cooking provisions, and preparing forage for a three day's cruise, against General Cos, to assist the wrecked Louisianians,[6] had marched to town, and upon the reception of the news of their safety, had returned to camp. One of the principal attractions in a soldier's life, is the total uncertainty of the future, even for an hour; no

---

[5] Besides these sea crabs, which were fine eating, the whole plain was covered with the holes of the land crab; these were not fit to eat, but were a curiosity to our men. They were of a blue colour, the body somewhat larger than a hen's egg, long claws, and the way they could "scud it," sideways, over the ground, to their holes, when pursued, "wasn't slow."

calculation is made; no thought is taken; we wait for orders, and are ready to execute them., of whatever kind they may be. One soon gets tired of making any plans for the future, save for the time when again he shall arrive at home; and all feel, with regard to themselves, that this is so uncertain, that those plans are few. When a definite order is delivered, we know immediately what to do; but that order may be countermanded, and we return to our former state; so that we think but of the moment, and let the future take care of itself. This absence of all care, is certainly, what at home, in busy life, is never experienced; and in whatever light those at home, who never tried it, may view it, it proves to us very pleasant.

One is peculiarly fitted to enjoy the present, and the days pass lightly away. It was on this account, that all were continually so full of sport; even the foreheads of many that had, when first they joined the army, a contracted appearance of thought, now seemed relieved, appeared smoother, and their countenances were brighter. If difficulties and hardships came, they endured them while remaining; but they had not suffered them in anticipation; and of the troubles of life generally, those of anticipated evils make up no small proportion.

On this day was a difference of scene, from that expected; for the author, as well as all his company, had received orders to go on a hard march, and attack the enemy; but that march had only been a pleasant little ride into town and back; and the rest of the day he spent in company with Captain Sneed, and two or three others, in a delightful little excursion, in a sailboat, down the beautiful river (as seen in the second picture), and over the bar, [6]out into the wild waves of old ocean; passing the day very agreeably, and returning as the sun was declining in the west.

On this day, in Tampico, much anxiety was felt for the safety of four companies of the Louisiana regiment, under Colonel De

---

6. From this point, which is the left hand one seen in the view, at the mouth of the river, Tampico bar stretches across the mouth from N. W. to S. E.; the depth of water on it, is about ten feet. The position of this bar, is, according to the nautical charts, 22 17' north latitude, and 98 24' west longitude.

Russey, who had been wrecked a few days before this, in the ship *Ondiaka*, some thirty-five or forty miles south of the mouth of this river. General Patterson, as soon as the news of the wreck came to hand, dispatched to their relief, a steamboat by sea; and by land, forty dragoons, a full *atajo*, or sixty pack mules, with five day's rations for the four companies; and, for the officers, sent fifteen saddle-horses. A report reaching us the next day, that the detachment were about to be attacked on the beach, by General Cos, who had a considerable force to the southward, at Tuspan, but farther from the wreck than we were, General Patterson ordered one company from our regiment, and one company of infantry, from Colonel Campbell's, to march on the following morning.

Our company, G, was ordered by Colonel Thomas, this evening, to be off by daylight. Everyone jumped at the chance. We were ready, mounted, and marched into town, with the company of infantry; but as we were about to enter the steamboat, to be set across the river, the other boat, which had been sent out the day before, came puffing in, and landed some officers, who reported the detachment safe, and on its march for this place. All anxiety was at once relieved in the city and camp; and we were ordered back, by the general. The same day the command arrived safely, and in good condition. No one had been lost in the wreck, for the ship did not go to pieces; and after the gale abated, they had but little difficulty in getting ashore,

They were warmly greeted by all; they appeared as brothers, from the interest felt in their safety, for the few days back But a shade was thrown over the general relief, by the announcement that the march had been made with such precipitancy, that all the sick unable to keep up, were left along, from time to time, to fall into the hands of the enemy; who treat all such with no mercy.

The condemnations of their colonel, by his officers and men, for this precipitate march, and abandonment of the sick, were neither few nor low; and the same feeling, from them, was imparted to all others through the different camps; which feeling, on the fourth day afterwards, was increased, by the appearance of the sick men; who had slowly dragged themselves on, up the sea-beach, until they arrived at the mouth of the river, and following that up, had come opposite our camp, and waved their hats on poles; which being perceived, was made known to General Pillow, who immediately sent boats for them. They were much exhausted, still sick, having had nothing to eat for the whole time, save some sea-fowls, which they had shot. One was suffering from a large blister, which had been placed upon him before he was abandoned.

The alarm of being pursued, they pronounced untrue, for they had not seen a hostile Mexican after being left. When asked about their ammunition (of which, in excuse, it had been said, that the detachment were out), they showed their cartridge-boxes with a good supply. Many men, with indignant expression of countenance, crowded around the poor fellows, as they came ashore. While the boat landed the first, the others made their appearance; and, to our great joy, we found that all were safe.

Tuesday, February 9th. We have lost three men, by death, while here encamped: M. Brady, of Captain Gillespie's company, who died two or three days since; C. S. Rungan of Captain Evans', died day before yesterday; and Sergeant J. A. Smith, of Captain Marshall's company, died yesterday. They were buried under the hill, seen in the picture, near the old fort. There were many dying in town, at the hospital. The climate and air, although very pleasant to the senses, do not appear to agree with many of our men; and sickness, when taken, is unusually fatal few seem to recover, when severely attacked. Probably the change of air, experienced in our coming down from the mountains so elevated, to the lower coast, has a deleterious effect upon their constitutions. A man is here not sick long; he dies or recovers in a short time.

The weather now, is extremely hot; and the direct heat of the sun, before the sea-breeze rises in the morning, is compared, by many, to that experienced in standing a few feet off from a log fire. The heat of the direct rays certainly is intense. While men perspire freely, they do not appear to be affected by it; but if one gets a little cold, and his perspiration is checked, he is thrown into a high fever immediately; and then, as the numerous deaths show, the chances are against him.

Wednesday, February 10th. Last night, we lay down in our crowded little tents, without covering, suffering much on account of the extreme heat; but before morning, a norther burst down upon us, and the air became immediately very cold, and the wind came up the bend of the river, careering with power. When we turned out to roll call, it required an extra blanket upon our shoulders, to keep us comfortable. The parade following, was extremely unpleasant on the plain, from the strong wind and clouds of dust; our horses, being chilled, were almost unmanageable; we galloped round, formed lines, columns, files, platoons, &c., and were heartily rejoiced to be released at last, and get into our tents for shelter.—The river was lashed into breaking waves, that dashed upon the shore near us, with a continual tumult. In the afternoon, the wind blowing still stronger, Captain Sneed, and many of the men rode down to the mouth of the river at the beach, to old ocean in its majesty, when his billows, chased and driven by the strong, keen blasts bursts in thunder on the shore. The rolling mountain waves, as they dashed in, excited the astonishment of all.

Ingram, the philosopher mentioned before, went with them to observe the scene. Ingram, thin-visaged and lean in his person, rides a tall frame of a horse, equally lean, with sunken eyes, hip-bones and ribs standing out in relief against his tight hide, his hair standing every way.—It is a wonder to all that he has lived so long, or survived the labours of the campaign. This tall, raw-boned frame, Ingram calls Rosinante; and surely, from Cervantes' description of *Don Quixotte's* steed, there are many points of resemblance between the two.

Rosinante has been unable, for some time, to carry his master, being afflicted with general weakness, tightness of hide, contraction of the stomach, and skinned upon the prominent ridges of the backbone; but in the two weeks he has remained here, having had twelve quarts of oats a day, has somewhat recruited, though the philosopher declares he could eat thirty-six, and says that he would fatten if he had that quantity,—and probably he might upon that:—but he is so old that his teeth are all out, and he swallows both corn and oats without mastication, and nothing but a large amount of forage could at all fatten him. He has been assisted in his general state of health, by large doses of *nux vomica*, administered to him by his master.

The philosopher rode him on parade today, for the first time since our arrival here; and, after parade, went down with the party to the sea beach. The waves, as before said, were rolling far up, and the party would follow a retiring wave, and then, suddenly turning their horses, retreat at full speed from the next one, which came in at a rapid, threatening rate, towards them; and, escaping its fury, follow that out when returning, and again retreat from the next angry billow that advanced.

The third wave that followed was of larger size, and all save the philosopher escaped it; he thought, that by making Rosinante rear up as the wave came, he would plunge over it;—and he reined him up, stuck the spurs to him, and charged the curling billow, that threw up its foaming crest far above the rearing Rosinante, and far above the philosopher's head, as well as above his previous calculations, and broke down upon them all with power; knocked off the rider, and covered him up in the foam, sending him far away from Rosinante, who, with saddle and bridle, was rolling over and over in the billows.

The wave retreated;—both horse and rider, now far separated, endeavoured to rise.—The next billow broke down and rolled them over and over again;—the next served them in the same way; but both, at last, nearly exhausted, obtained foothold, and got out, with the salt water running in streams off of them.—Rosinante held down his head, and mustered strength to shake his bones;—the philosopher, dripping and-exhausted, got upon him, and they took a "beeline" for the camp.

Friday, February 12th. A little excitement helped us out this day.—It was caused by some Mexicans, who were endeavouring to swim a large drove of several hundred cattle, across the river, about two miles below our camp, to drive them down to the Mexican General, Cos.—On account of the lakes above, they were forced to cross here. It was a bold move; but in the night they had succeeded in crossing about half of them, before it was known to our generals. Several companies of our regiment were ordered to saddle up, and while part went down on one side, the steamer conveyed the others across the river, and they passed down on that side;—the whole drove was captured.—The drovers and *peones*, some twenty-five in number, were taken prisoners, and they, together with about forty pack mules, brought up to town.

Saturday, February 13th. During the time we had been here, but few crimes were committed;—scarcely any murders, or stabbing, so common near Matamoras and in the valley of the Rio Grande.—These people were a better sort than those of the frontier. Our generals wished, as before said, to learn them something more than they already knew about our customs; and wished to introduce among them the form of trial by jury, a thing they never heard of.

An opportunity about this time offered.—An American citizen was killed by a Mexican.—The murderer was apprehended; a judge, sheriff, and clerk, were appointed by the general; and the criminal court of Tampico opened its sessions, to the utter astonishment of the old administrators of justice, the *alcaldes*. The panel of jurors was summoned, and a trial took place in due form. The Mexican was convicted, and sentenced to be hung; but evaded that part of the business, by escaping from confinement.

The whole proceedings of this new court caused much merriment among the men; more especially when the sheriff was most busily enquiring for Mr. Locks, of the Tennessee cavalry, whom he had summoned, the previous evening, as a juror. Each one could direct him to the whereabouts of Mr. Locks:—he was in such a store, nearby, or around such a corner;—everyone had just seen him; and the poor sheriff was run nearly down, in looking for him. He must have supposed that Mr. Locks was hard to find;—and so he was, for he was often hunted, but never found, as far as we ever heard. As his name became so known to the regiment, we will speak of him in the following note:

"Locks and Cogle":

Locks was a queer fellow, and cut up more rustles, shines, and capers, than all others in the company and regiment; and we will introduce to the reader this chap "Locks," and his relative, "Cogle," of the Kentucky regiment of Cavalry, and relate a few of their numerous *peccadillos*. Both are fictitious characters; and Locks was first heard of in our regiment, and Cogle in the Kentucky, as long ago as when both were encamped near Memphis, in Tennessee.

Colonel Marshall, of that regiment of Kentuckians, was strict and positive in his orders, and all firing of guns in the camp, among other things, was forbidden; and the officer of the day was instructed to take all offenders against this order into immediate custody. Some of the men, full of fun, contrived and carried out the following scheme, to annoy the officer. Several went into the woods, at the lower part of the camp, and one discharged a gun, and immediately disappeared among the bushes; the others remained on the spot, strolling around; presently, the officer came down in a hurry, and wished to know who fired that gun.

They told him that a chap named Cogle had done it, and then cleared himself. He asked to what company he belonged; they directed him to one, where they had left a man, to tell him that Cogle belonged to another; where, also, he was to be sent to the third, and so on. He hurried on, from company to company; sometimes Cogle was here, and sometimes there; one had just seen him in a certain tent; there they told him he had gone to the next, until, after a weary search, the officer reported that Cogle fired the gun, but was not to be found.

When the regiment arrived at Little Rock, one of the soldiers committed a crime, for which he was placed in prison; a number of his companions, disguising themselves, forced the jail in the night, and released him. This transaction greatly incensed the colonel, who offered a reward for the ringleader of the party, and his associates. The jailer, too, was indefatigable in his endeavours to recognise them in the regiment; but, among the multitude of strange faces, was unable so to do. A party of the soldiers, who had been into town, on a frolic, and who had run dry of the means to get anything more to drink, met the jailer in the street, and told him, that if he would treat them, they would inform him who was the leader of the crowd that forced the jail; that they regretted much the whole transaction, and that, moreover, he must keep the source from whence he obtained the information entirely secret.

This he promised gladly; and he treated the party to punches and juleps, as much as they could carry, with what they had taken before. They then informed him, that Cogle was the man who got up the plan of attacking the jail, and that he had headed the crowd; but that they did not know to which company he belonged. The jailer hastened to Colonel Marshall, who had fretted and fumed about the matter, threatening vengeance against the offender.

When the jailer gave him the information he had received, the colonel immediately made out an order for Cogle's arrest; and the provost-marshal commenced the search for him. He was directed from company to company; from tent to tent; into town, at certain groceries, and out of town to other places; till the poor provost was heartily tired out, and had to give up the chase. Cogle was not yet caught.

When the regiment arrived at Washington, Arkansas, they remained there seven days; and Cogle was still at his tricks. The colonel had a bill presented to him by one of the citizens of the town, for butter, eggs, hams, and market vegetables, bought for him by his servant "Cogle," the day previous. The colonel declared that Cogle was not his servant, that he had heard of the man, but had not yet been able to recognise him.

When the regiment arrived at Port Lavacca, two of the soldiers walked out from the camp, and one shot a goat, belonging to a Frenchman, who resided nearby; and his comrade went to the Frenchman and told him of the fact, and condemned Cogle for it, in the most unmeasured terms. The Frenchman was very "wrathy," but expressed himself under "*de mos* great obligations" to the informer, treated him plentifully to good old brandy, and immediately laid his complaint before Colonel Marshall, demanding redress. Strangely, but from the amount of business on his hands, the colonel had forgotten Cogle; and in a few moments, the provost-marshal had in hands an order for his arrest, and was looking for him; but, of course, the search was vain; and he, as well as the colonel and the complaining Frenchman, found that "Cogle" was the personification of "nobody." The Frenchman got no satisfaction for the loss of his goat, and left the camp amid the shouts of "Cogle!" "Cogle!" to his extreme annoyance.

About this time, there arrived at Lavacca thirty of our regiment, who had been sick at Memphis, and left there; and who now came round by water. They were under the command of Lieutenant Seaman, and were encamped near the Kentuckians. Some of the men of the regiment, too, had been sent ahead, and arrived there seven days before us. Lieutenant Anderson, of our own company, went with them; and they all remained in Seaman's little camp. The Kentuckians, in the mean time, shifted their camp, five miles lower down.

Seaman's men became tired of their salt pork; and some went hunting, but had no success; returning, they came near this same Frenchman's place, and seeing, in the prairie beyond, a fat yearling, they shot it, and brought the meat to camp; and it was soon distributed among the messes, and was in the kettles, boiling for dinner. The Frenchman soon "smelt the rat," and came down to their encampment, and examining the kettles, saw the meat; and looking at the unskinned legs and hoofs of the yearling, discovered that it was the missing one.

He went up to the lieutenant's tent; Lieutenant Seaman was absent, but Lieutenant Anderson was there, reading. The sides of the tent were looped up, to allow the fresh sea-breeze to pass through; and Hamilton, an old negro, who cooked for Seaman, was busy about his dinner without, and to him the Frenchman began talking, in a rapid and vociferous manner, about his "pull his leetle plack pull! and who killed his pull? and he vould have satisfaction for his plack pull," &c.

He attracted Anderson's attention, who asked him what he wanted.

"I vants satisfaction for my pull, my leetle plack pull; for I have anoder plack pull, and next year I vill have a yoke of pulls!"

Anderson, knowing that the bull had been killed, told him to name his price, and he should be paid.

"No, no," said the Frenchman, "I sall have no pay! I vants no pay for my leetle plack pull; I vants satisfaction; I vant him who kill my plack pull to be punish; for I have anoder leetle plack pull, and next year I vill have a yoke of plack pulls; I vants satisfaction who kill my pull?"

Anderson told him it was Cogle, of the Kentucky regiment, not dreaming that he had ever heard of Cogle. The name struck the Frenchman all aback; throwing up his hands, and turning short on his heel, he shook his head, saying bitterly, "G—d d—n Cogles! I knows him before; he kill my goat!" off he went, and came back no more.

What Cogle is in the Kentucky regiment, "Locks" is in ours. All missing articles, when inquired for, are found to be taken by Locks If mischief is done, and looked into, Locks is found at the bottom of it; and many have been the searches after him, and many a threat has been made against him, by those who have been trying to hunt him up, being directed back and forth continually.

"Who took my bridle, last night?" shouted the sergeant, early one morning, when preparing to saddle up for the day's march.

Far down in the line came up, repeated several times, "Locks got it."

"G—d d—m—n Locks," was the reply. A soldier broke by the guard; information was given by the sentinel, and the offender's name was found to be Locks; and much search was made to find him out, but he had disappeared.

A man lost his blanket coat, when intoxicated, as far back as the Trinity River, in Texas: one of our company found it, and wore it. About a month afterwards, when we were encamped near Victoria, Texas, the owner, having seen it upon him at a distance, about supper time, came into camp to inquire after it. Lieutenant Anderson told him that Locks had it, and that he was cooking his supper at the sixth fire down the line.

Daniels, an old soldier of the Florida war, who belonged to that mess, was cooking; was, as usual, crabbed and cross as a snapping-turtle, especially when cooking over the hot fire; with his butcher-knife in his hand, and, with his sour looking phiz, he appeared like a malicious spirit, brooding on revenge. He was in his worst mood; the sweat rolled off his face, and, as he stood looking at the frying meat, he appeared as though he would swallow meat, fryingpans, and a few of the burning coals, for a trifle.

The owner of the coat approached, through the bushes, pretty near him, but did not much like his appearance, and stopped. Some of us followed in the thicket, to hear the noise, which we knew was coming; (for, in our company, to call a man Locks was a quick insult; for it was to accuse him of numberless petty thefts, and little rascalities).

Looking on for a moment or two, the man, in quite a subdued tone, said, "Mr. Locks, will you step this way, if you please?"

We were silent, biting our lips. Daniels heard him, but, as the man was nearly behind, did not notice it, not knowing that he was addressed; but continued grasping his long knife, and looking savagely in the fire.

He called again, a little louder—"Mr. Locks."

Daniels, casting his eyes up, saw the man, standing at a respectful distance; and, to his surprise, too, saw that he was looking at him, with his hand raised, beckoning for him to come there.

"Mr. Locks," as he caught his eye, "step this"—

"G—d d—m—n your half-made soul," shouted Daniels, jumping towards him with his knife, "do yon call me Locks?"

The man, retreating, held up his hand,—"Mr. Locks, you

have got my coat"

This made Daniels ten times more furious than ever. "You say I have stolen your coat, you d—m puppy."

The man endeavoured to apologise, but to no effect; for, in his alarm at the storm he had raised, he kept repeating "Mr. Locks," and "his coat," and Daniels was furious; and we had quickly to interfere, to stop the storm.

"You had better be getting away from here," shouted Daniels to him, as we held him from pursuit The man took him at his word, and cleared. He came next day and got his coat, from another the one who had found it

The adjutant of the regiment, one hot day, upon the march, in the heat and dust, was suffering for the want of eatables and water. At the head of the column, he was directed to Locks, a little down the lines, who, he was told, had a plentiful supply of cold beef, bread, &c., with a large gourd of water. Riding down the lines, he inquired industriously for Mr. Locks, and was directed by everyone down farther, until he was in a fair way to arrive at the rear of the column; and would have done so but for a young Irishman, who burst into a loud haw-haw, when inquired of, and informed the adjutant that he was after a fictitious character.

Corporal Rhoton, of our company, a young man of fine disposition, but sometimes, irritable when joked too hard, a few days since in town, got rather high, from the effects of a bottle of brandy cherries, and came to camp in that way. After carrying on sport for some time, to the amusement of all, he stretched out his blanket, and lay down to rest One of the regular soldiers, in the meantime, came into our camp to find clothes to wash (following that in all his leisure time, at the cistern, by the canal).

Our men told him that although they had no articles of clothing to wash at that time, that Lieutenant Locks had many, and directed him up the lines, to seek him. Some others showed him Rhoton, on his blanket, as the man he was looking for. Looking at him, as he lay with his eyes shut the soldier exclaimed, that Lieutenant Locks was like some of his officers, pretty essentially drunk. Rhoton, hearing this, opened his eyes, and seeing that he was the one referred to as Locks, sprang up and made at the regular, who then called on his legs to do their duty; and they done it well, for he was gone quickly; neither did he ever return to get Lieutenant Locks' clothing. A day never passed, but that Locks was called upon. He was accused of all mischief, and often condemned and cursed most bitterly by those in search of him.

Saturday, February 13th. A pleasant day, but cool; for the wind was still from the north. The drills were short, and many devoted the day to strolling around, in city and camp.—Many went up into the city, to seek at the post-office, here established, letters from home. The author went for the same reason, as well as to pick up any items of news, that might have been received, as to our future movements;—but no letters had arrived for many days; and as to news, there was none.

Nothing could be known until General Scott arrived, and no one knew where he was, save that he was on the coast somewhere.—The cool weather had induced all the Mexicans, walking in the streets, or crowded in the markets, to closely wrap themselves in their *horongos* and *serapes*; and they appeared as cold as our people at home would do in a snow-storm. There were just as many of them, however, on the edge of the square, seated around, with their wares and provisions to sell, as before, and they made as much noise.

One thing was not mentioned about these little traders, that in such numbers are found in every Mexican town, which is, the taxes that they have to pay.—Not a load of wood on a jackass, not a little trifle of charcoal, not a dozen bunches of fodder, a basket of oranges, a pig, quarter of beef, a few pineapples, or a bag of red pepper, or anything else enters a Mexican town without a corresponding little duty being exacted on it, and must be paid at the entrance.—These people are taxed in every possible shape and manner.

This morning, a full supply of all articles sold here was brought in; the ugly old hags, with the hot *tomales* steaming in their pots, were squalling out their *tomales calientes!* more often than before;

and they had many customers, to whom the hot bits went well in the cold air.

Every Mexican that we met, as we passed him, had the same expression, with his arms under his blanket, holding that up to his neck, and muffling it around his mouth and chin, with his eyes and nose just seen between the large fold and his wide-brimmed *sombrero*,—"*buenos dias, Señores; hace mucho frio!*" (it is very cold) and, with a shiver, he passed on.

The band of regular musicians were making the *plaza*, this morning, resound to the swells of their notes, and they appeared to sound more clearly than usual; though, at all times, they play in a most excellent manner, and their music is so attractive to the population, that every calm, pleasant evening, when they take their station on the circular stone elevation around the flag staff, the square is crowded for an hour by the Mexicans, both male and female, to hear the inspiring strains. From such continual practice, they become very expert, and the people seem to forget, even, that they are part of a hostile force that have taken possession of their beautiful city.

Whatever position these regulars fill in the service, they do it in a first rate manner, devoting all their time to that one thing.—They march well, drill well, and fight well;—though, in the fighting part, the volunteers who were in the field had shown themselves to be, what was not expected, fully equal to them; and, in some of the regiments, equal in drill and parade;—though a volunteer, here, in every little matter of ceremony, will not be bound down, as a regular is obliged to be.

A regular soldier, who follows it for a livelihood, in peace and war, in garrison and in camp, has need for only so much brains as will enable him to stand erect, keep his clothing and tent clean and neat, and his arms bright; to enable him to go through the common evolutions, and to understand the common words of command, without explanation; to handle the musket, sword and pistol quickly; and just language enough to ask for his allowance of eatables and whatever else he may need to satisfy his appetite, and to be able, when out of hearing of his officers, to swear freely. If he has any more brains or language than is sufficient to answer these purposes, they are of no value to him; for he never will be permitted to use them.

What induces men of intelligence to enlist in this life for five years, and then enlist again for as many more, we cannot tell, without it is that they get plenty to eat and drink, and comfortable clothes to wear, without thought or care to themselves; the labour of thinking, they are never obliged to do. Money they cannot make, their wages being so small, a private of infantry, seven dollars per month; dragoons, eight; no hope of promotion above the rank of a sergeant can they have, for graduates of West Point, cadets, step in above as lieutenants, and fill all higher grades. No matter what bravery, what qualities of a soldier may be exhibited in a private, still he is to be kept under, in subjection to the youngest cadet, to whom he dare not speak, without he has business, and he never can cope with him in rank.

It was cold comfort in town this day, for there were no fires; they never using them, save for cooking; and we returned to camp, and wrapped in our blankets, lay down in our tents to read, or sleep; which last as usual came very quickly to us, whenever stretched out. We were not disturbed until the drums, fifes, and bugles called us to the three o'clock parade, which (thanks to the norther), was but a name today; for hardly were the regiments paraded on the plain, when all were dismissed again; and soon our horses were unsaddled and fed, and we again in the tents, out of the blasts, which drove the angry waves, of the heretofore peaceful river, in a continual dashing roar, on the shore near us, and at one time threatened to make us *vamos* for a more elevated situation.

Thursday, February 18th. Times had gone on for the last week as before; all were getting impatient to move, to go ahead. It had been for several days, the only inquiry in the camp, when will General Scott arrive? where shall we next go? Everyone seemed anxious to be off. (Some, the most impatient, the author remembers, seemed hurried on by their destiny, as the movement for which they were so anxious, was the last;—they found their graves at Vera Cruz and Cerro Gordo). Last night the whole army was elated, by the intelligence that General Scott was at the mouth of the river; and this morning they were gratified by seeing him come up on the steamer. The camp of our brigade, being the first at which he would arrive, each of the regiments were drawn out on the river's bank, and, as the steamer passed, fired a salute; as he arrived at the town, the artillery thundered out a louder welcome.

As there was no secret in our future movements, we soon learned all that was doing. We found that General Worth had been detached from General Taylor, and, with his division of regulars, was embarking, at the mouth of the Rio Grande, for Vera Cruz; and we learned that the nine new regiments from home, which we had heard were ordered out by the president, had arrived on the coast; but the ships on which they came were lying at Lobos Island, some forty or fifty miles down the coast, waiting for the whole army to be collected, for a grand descent upon Vera Cruz and the castle of San Juan de Ulloa. Every arrangement made by General Scott towards this great end, was now drawing near to completion.

Saturday, February 20th. There being many vessels here, not in the employ of the government, yesterday, all such were chartered to assist in the transportation of the army. And this done, General Scott issued orders to all the other generals and colonels, to prepare their troops for an immediate embarkation. General Twiggs' division of regulars, first; second, General Pillow's Tennessee brigade; third, General Quitman's brigade; fourth, General Shields' brigade; then the artillery.—Every movement now, in camp, was made with the greatest activity.—A large fleet of ships appeared off the bar, to take the troops. No sooner was the order issued, than General Twiggs' division struck their tents, and marched through town, across the plain in front of us, and passed to the mouth of the river, where they encamped for the night, ready to go on board the four large ships, that lay there to receive them, on the next day.

Sunday, February 28th. General Twiggs' division having all been embarked, and put to sea for Anton Lizardo (an anchorage near Vera Cruz), going by the way of Lobos Island,—and General Scott also, having gone,—General Pillow's brigade, to which we belonged, was in turn next; but a violent norther came on, and the ships were obliged to put to sea, for safety; and thus, the embarkation was interrupted.

Some of them having arrived this day, the other two Tennessee regiments struck their tents, and were, by the steamboats, taken down to the ships. Our regiment were compelled to remain, none of the horse transport vessels having arrived. We disliked this very much; but it had been foreseen; and a day or two previous to this, General Pillow had addressed our regiment, and told us, that there was a scarcity of vessels, and gave us our choice, if vessels to convey our horses did not arrive, whether we would remain with them at Tampico, until such vessels should come, or whether we would leave our horses, to be brought on as soon as possible, and go on ourselves, and serve in the siege of Vera Cruz, on foot.

He told us, that every man might vote for himself; that if a man did not like to leave his horse, he might remain; and that those who were willing to serve on foot, should go; that those who wished to go upon those conditions, would march to the left, and those to stay, to the right.—At the word march, the whole regiment, in a body, turned their horses to the left thus voting to go, and serve on foot—save one man.—General Quitman's brigade came in to embark next; General Shields' to follow.—Reader, while waiting for our own turn, let us attend, in the next chapter, to the operations of the other divisions of the army, during January and February, 1847.

Marriage *Ceremonias* in Mexico:

There is no country where marriage ceremonies are more imposing and obligatory, and yet where those obligations are generally so little binding, as in Mexico. We will speak of the marriage of the higher class, which covers all the less expensive and showy mode of the lower. The law requires the man to be twenty-one years of age. the lady eighteen, and both members of the Catholic church. When a young man sees a *señorita* with whom he "falls in love," it is unnecessary for him to say anything to her about it; for the parents of the lady have the whole matter to dispose of, and do not much consult her feelings. The young man goes to their house, and, without any preliminary, solicits their daughter in marriage.

The matter is immediately considered; his wealth, standing, &c., weighed; and if he have these qualifications in sufficient degree, the bargain is at once concluded. The lover now called *el novio* proceeds to the priest, the curate of the *parochia*, and makes known his intentions. The curate goes to the house of the maiden, and informs her that she is applied for, and by whom. She may or may not have previously heard of it. lie requires her certificate of baptism.

This has been committed to her years before by her parents, and has been carefully kept; for without it, she has learned when a child, that she never could marry. She immediately produces this, and the curate, by perusal, learns her name and age. She is now called *la novia*. The curate returns to the *parochia* sends for the young man, the *novio* shows him the baptismal certificate of the *novia*; then demands his own, which is produced. All, so far, is right. But if he has been born elsewhere, the curate demands of him the certificate of the priest of that place, that he is a *saltero* (a single man).

This may be hard to get, on account of distance, ice.; and then the difficulty is obviated by obtaining a *dispensa* from the bishop, which costs as high as that functionary thinks the *novio* is able to pay. That certificate obtained, or thus avoided, the *notno* and *novia* are informed that all is right, and that the ceremony of marriage will be performed in the *parochia*, after publishing the same there for three consecutive Sundays; (this publication may be avoided, by the *notno* buying of the bishop another *dispensa* for the purpose).

Two other young persons are now needed, (the same as are familiarly called, in our western country, the waiters); these are the young man *compadre* attendant on the bridegroom; and young lady *eemadre*, the bridesmaid. All is ready. The party, attended by friends and relatives, go to the *parochia*. The *novia* and *novio* confess their sins to the priest, receive absolution, and partake of the holy sacrament; and then must immediately be married, before they sin again.

The *novio* and *novia*. the attending *compadre* and *comadre*, advance to the altar, and kneel upon the step. The priest comes out, preceded by four church boys in their robes. One bears a lofty cross, called *cruz alto*; another swings the censer of holy burning incense, the smoke of which diffuses itself around; the other two each bear a rich double candlestick, with two lighted candles. The parties rise to their feet. The ceremony is precisely like that of the Episcopal church; the ring is always used.

This ceremony through, they leave for their home; but, at three o'clock the next morning, reappear at the church the married lady dressed in black. Her husband kneels by her, and over them both is thrown a black mantle called a *manquerno* (yoke); the attending *compadre* and comadre also kneel, and both hold up lighted candles, while mass is said.

This holy *funeion* not only binds the marriage ceremony upon the *novio* and *novia*, but. together with that, throws the waiters the *compadre* and *comadre* into a state of relationship with one another, not so near as brother and sister, but nearer than cousins; so that they can never after marry each other, without an especial *dispensa*.

This relationship is always afterward claimed. The parties, after mass, rise; the *compadre* hands to the bride twelve pieces of silver or gold: these she gives to the priest as a *don* (gift); each one represents an apostle. Beside this, the regular fees are sixteen dollars and a half; and in addition to this is a compensation for the *cruz alto* (high cross), of from twenty to one hundred dollars, or more, according to the wealth of the parties; and still, added to the expense, is a quantity of small coins, to be thrown by the *compadre* among the crowd of *peones*, 4c., at the doorway.

For the poor people, the *cruz bajo* or low cross is used; many of the higher ceremonies dispensed with; and the priest receives but the regular fees—16½ dollars.—All married couples must attend mass, and be covered with the *manquerno* three several times

CHAPTER 3

Operation of the Divisions

In this month of February there had been much fighting in Mexico, with the other divisions of the army: there had been but little in January. Some fighting had taken place in the conquered province of California, during the month of January, as well as in the preceding month— December; for, when General Kearney arrived there, from Santa Fe, with his hundred dragoons and two pieces of artillery, instead of finding it tranquil, as he expected, to his surprise he found that the enemy, under General Flores, had risen and retaken the country, save two or three seaport towns; and the first reception that the gallant general, with his little band, met, was an attack from a much superior Mexican force, on December 6th, near San Pascual.

In the severe contest that ensued, he came off victorious, with a loss of twenty killed, and fifteen wounded; and, on the 12th December, he entered the town of San Diego, then in the possession of the naval forces. Commander Stockton adding five hundred marines to his force, he, in a short time after this, marched against *Pueblo de los Angeles*, where was the main force of the Mexican insurgents. These he defeated in two engagements one on the 8th, and the other on the 9th of January; and thus regained the whole country.—He assumed the chief command of the conquered province on March 1st, and its tranquillity was no more disturbed.[1]

---

1. General Kearney was succeeded in command of California, on the 1st of June, 1847, by Colonel Mason, first dragoons, United States' army.

Beside this insurrection in California, one had broken out in another quarter, New Mexico. After General Kearney had left for California, and Colonel Cooke's battalion and Colonel Doniphan had gone to the southward, Colonel Price was the military commander of the province. He had under his command near two thousand men, consisting of his own regiment of cavalry, also one battalion of four companies of mounted men, under Lieutenant-Colonel Willock, and two companies of infantry, under Lieutenant-Colonel Angney, one company (Fischer's) artillery, (all of which troops were from Missouri), and three companies, regular dragoons, under Captain Burgwin.—This force, mostly mounted, was scattered in different situations, throughout those parts of the province where grazing for their horses could be found.

An insurrection was planned by Señores Ortiz, Charvez, and General Archulette, against the Americans.—This plan, which was to make a general rise at midnight, on December 19th,—afterwards postponed to Christmas eve, the 24th,—was discovered on the 21st, and prompt measures adopted for its prevention.—The leaders, however, escaped, and planned another, which was executed on the night of January 19th; but, on account of the watchfulness of the different detachments, although the rising, save in the city, was universal, was but partly successful.—Governor Bent and several of his officers, being in the valley of Taos, at the town of San Fernando, to the north of Santa Fe, fell victims to it, being brutally massacred.—Twenty others, also, in the different detachments, were killed in the separate attacks. The Mexican population immediately flew to arms, for, as yet, they had not tried their strength with *"los Americanos,"* having, at first, quietly surrendered.

On the 23rd, Colonel Price, at the head of four hundred men, and four pieces of artillery, marched against the body of the insurgents, who, with a force of fifteen hundred, had posted themselves on the strong heights, at the village of Canada. On the 24th, a spirited action, of an hour and a half, began by cannonade, and ended by a charge, which sent the routed foe in every direction over the hills, with the loss of thirty-six killed, and some two or three hundred wounded:

> Report of killed and wounded at Canada, January 24th, 1847:
>
> Infantry battalion, commanded by Captain W. Z. Angney.
> Killed—Private Graham; Wagoner G. M. Smith, (volunteered to fight).
> Wounded—Private John Pace, slightly; 1st Lieutenant Irwin, severely, through the leg.
> Lieutenant Dyer's battalion, artillery.
> Wounded—Sergeant Caspers, slightly; Privates Aulman, severely, in the ankle; Murphy, severely, in the knee; Meagre, severely, in the arm.

The insurgents fell back farther to the north, up the river, to the pass of Emboda, and took a very strong position.—Captain Burgwin now had joined Colonel Price, with two companies of dragoons and another field piece, and the augmented force marched against the enemy, and a detachment under Captain Burgwin charged upon them, in a narrow gorge, and completely routed them, with the loss of twenty killed and sixty wounded:

> Killed and wounded at the battle of El Emboda, under Captain Burgwin, January 29th, 1847.
> Killed—Private Papin, of St. Vrain's company of Santa Fe volunteers.
> Wounded—Dick, Governor Bent's servant, severely.

The insurgents fell back still farther to the north, and prepared to make a desperate stand at San Fernando de Taos, where Governor Bent and others had fallen victims to the massacre. The enemy were not allowed much interval in fighting, for, although the snow lay deep on the mountains to be crossed, the victorious force toiled over them on the 1st and 2nd of February, on the 3rd entered San Fernando, and immediately marched against the neighbouring Indian town, El Pueblo, where the insurgents were posted in a strong church, and two other buildings like pyramids, the walls of which were almost impenetrable to cannon shot.

The battle commenced that afternoon, ceased at night, and was renewed on the 4th; and the enemy, after a severe engagement, were wholly defeated and subdued, with a loss, on this day, of one hundred and fifty-two killed, and between three and four hundred wounded; American loss, fifty-four killed and wounded,—among the latter, mortally, was the gallant Captain Burgwin—One of the under leaders of the rebellion, Mortayo, was taken here, and, in a day or two, hung at San Fernando:

> Killed and wounded at Pueblo de Taos on the 4th February, 1847
> Regiment Missouri Volunteers, and U. S. Dragoons.
> Company D, Captain. S. H. McMillen. Wounded—Captain McMillen, slightly, in the head; Privates R. C. Bower, severely; Henry Fender and George W. Thompson, dangerously; Robert Hewett, George W. Howser, and Wm. Ducoing, slightly.
> Company K, Lieutenant White. Wounded—Captain James W. Jones, severely; Sergeant Alfred L. Caldwell, mortally, (since dead); Private James Austin, mortally, (since dead).
> Company L, Captain Wm. Y. Slack Wounded—Second Lieutenant John Mansfield, slightly; Privates Jacob Moon, severely; Wm. Gillem, slightly.
> Battalion of artillery, Lieutenant Dyer, U. S. ordnance. Wounded—Privates Berlfed and Jod, severely; Kohne, slightly, and some others slightly, not reported.
> Battalion of infantry, commanded by Captain W. Z. Angney. Killed—Sergeant Hart. Wounded—Lieutenant Vanvolkenburgh, (since dead); Sergeants Ferguson and Auall, severely.
> Company G, U. S. Dragoons, commanded by Captain Burgwin. Killed—Sergeant G. B. Ross; Privates Brooks, Beebe, Levrey and Hansucker. Severely wounded—Captain Burgwin, (since dead); Sergeant J. Vanroe, twice; Cor-

porals Engleman and J. Linneman; Privates S. Blodget, S.W. Crain, R. Deits, G. F. Sickenburgh, J. Truax, (dead), Hagenbaugh and Anderson. Slightly wounded—Beach, Hutton, Hillerman, Walker 1st, Schneider, (dead), Shay, and Near. Company I, 1st Dragoons. Wounded—Bremen, slightly Company M, Captain W. C. Halley. Wounded—Samuel Lewis, slightly Company N, Captain Thomas Barbee. Wounded—First Lieut T. G. West, slightly; Privates J. H. Calaway, John Nash, and John G. Lights, all slightly.

At the same time that these events were going on, to the north of Santa Fe, Captain Hendley was to the east, at Bagas, with two hundred and fifty men. With eighty-five, he attacked the village of Mora, where three hundred of the insurgents had posted themselves. He defeated and dispersed these, killing twenty-five, wounding fifty, and taking seventeen prisoners; but lost his own life, falling on the field.

Thus, in a short space of time, by these energetic and decisive movements, did Colonel Price and his officers quell the serious rebellion; and the province of New Mexico was again quiet, in the hands of the American forces.

While these battles had been fought with the insurgents in New Mexico and California, others, between larger forces took place, farther south. One of these had been fought by Colonel Doniphan, with the first Missouri regiment, and its auxiliaries of the second, at Sacramento, near Chihuahua; and we will now follow up the movements of this gallant body of men, from the time at which we left them, at the close of the year 1846.

Then, they had, after the battle of Brazito, taken possession of the town of El Paso, on the Rio del Norte. Colonel Doniphan was now placed in a very difficult situation. He had been ordered to report to General Wool, at Chihuahua; but that officer had, on account of the difficulties of the route, abandoned that purpose, moved to the south, and joined his forces to those of General Taylor. This was, for some time after their arrival here, unknown to the Missourians; who now, at this little town on the

Rio Grande, were shut out from all knowledge of home, or of any operations of the war, save those that they themselves had carried on.

They were now placed in the heart of an enemy's country, with the general, to whom they were ordered to report, far in the south—near a thousand miles, by the winding mountain roads; and between them were large tracts of desert country; then again, large sections thickly populated, all hostile, and unsubdued; and not only many small towns on the way, but the city of Chihuahua had to be taken—a strongly fortified place of twenty thousand inhabitants; and all this would, if the march was undertaken, have to be done by a small force, little over one regiment, cut off entirely from all succour.

For many days, with the gallant commander and his brave men, all was uncertainty and doubt. Contradictory rumours from the enemy followed the previous report.—The utmost vigilance could not prevent the departure from town of persons for Chihuahua, who carried to the enemy there a full account of the state and strength of this regiment.—Captain Reid's company having been out on a little scout, a few miles down the river, on returning, met three Mexicans, well armed, who had succeeded in leaving town; he apprehended and searched them, and found upon them, letters from one of the principal priests of El Paso, giving information of the condition of their force, their probable intention to march to the south; and also making the most extravagant and false assertions, of their cruelty and barbarism towards the inhabitants of El Paso.

The men were immediately taken back to the town, and the priest arrested; together with another, whose letters were found of the same kind, and both were placed in confinement.—In the mean time the Mexicans at Chihuahua having ascertained the strength of Doniphan's command, and knowing also that there were no reinforcements for him behind, and also knowing that General Wool had abandoned the idea of marching from the southward against them; and having, at the city, a force of four thousand five hundred men, and thirteen pieces of artillery, wished much to draw Doniphan into the march against them, confident of annihilating his force; and to this end, published in the Chihuahua papers, that General Wool was on the route, with a heavy force, and within a few days' march of the city, and contrived that this report should be circulated at El Paso, followed by another, in a few days, that the city was taken by him.

These reports came to El Paso, but shortly they were contradicted, by an American, who had escaped from Chihuahua; who informed Colonel Doniphan, that General Wool was not there, and that, moreover, from all they could learn, that he was not coming; that the most current report in Chihuahua, was, that General Santa Anna was marching against him and General Taylor, with twenty thousand men.

This information gave to all a desire to go onward. A council of officers was held, and although it was universally pronounced hazardous in the extreme, yet all were in favour of going.—More than the loose report, before mentioned, they knew not; had not heard where the generals were, but only knew that they were to the southward; had just learned through Mexicans, of the battle of Monterey; but knew not of the capture of Saltillo, and the country on the Rio Grande, although these events had taken place months before; in fact, only knew that the war continued to exist, by the continued belligerent attitude of the Mexicans around.

This regiment having made a campaign against the Indians, having already passed through the greatest hardships, and travelled two thousand miles, nearly all of which was unknown to the public at home; and being still far out, alone, surrounded by vast mountains, and tracts of wilderness, clothed in skins, like savages; without any of the scant conveniences even of soldiers, were still willing and eager to advance through unknown districts, a distance they knew not how far, except that it could not be less than a thousand miles, in which they were sure of meeting a formidable enemy, four times as strong as their own force, that they knew had been mustered for the purpose of meeting that of General Wool; and beside that, they knew that the strength of the city of Chihuahua was ready to oppose their progress, beside many other inferior towns. In the face of all this formidable array, they were willing and anxious to go.

But the officers of this command, though, as said, willing and anxious to go, yet decided not on it; determining to leave it to the men, who must endure the toil and pain together with themselves, of this arduous undertaking, if determined upon.

It might be thought that the movement was the only one the regiment in their advanced situation could make, to extricate themselves. But this was not so. —Colonel Doniphan had received orders to report himself to General Wool at Chihuahua; but he had now found that that general was not there, nor had he been within six hundred miles of that place.—His orders, therefore, were at an end; and as a commander of a separate division of the army, and more especially, as placed beyond the reach of orders, his control of his force, and powers of using his discretion, were equal to those of a general. The road back to Santa Fe was open — he could fall back with honour to himself and command.

The regiment, with its auxiliaries, having now, in addition to Lieutenant-Colonel Mitchell's escort of ninety-three men, been joined by Captain Weightman's company of artillery, of six pieces, and one hundred and seventeen officers and men, under the command of Major Clark, from Santa Fe, where they had been sent for, after the battle of El Paso;—numbered now, in all, nine hundred and twenty-four men. They were drawn up, under arms, in the *plaza* of El Paso, and the deliberation of the council of officers was made known to them.

They were reminded of their already arduous campaign; of the contemplated route, and its length, and the renewed privations and hardships to which they would be exposed;—of their battle already fought; of the certainty of one with a much larger force, if the advance was made of the strongly fortified city of Chihuahua; and, on the other hand, that the route to return was open; and then told that the decision was, by the officers, left to them.

A few moment's pause was made, and the order given for everyone who was willing to go, to step to the front. In an instant, with a quick, free step, the whole moved out;—to go was the unanimous, unhesitating resolution.—The conduct of this detachment, under these circumstances, needs no comment.

After the march was thus decided on, nothing remained to do. save to get ready for it, which was done in a day or two; and, on the 8th day of February, after having remained in El Paso forty days, the troops and artillery, accompanied by their trains, (and three hundred and fifteen wagons of traders, who had thus far come with them from Santa Fe, arriving at El Paso from time to time, during the stay of the regiment there, and who now proceeded on towards Chihuahua.

Many of these wagons had been under the protection of the troops from Missouri, halting in Santa Fe while the troops were on the Indian expedition, and afterwards coming down the Rio Grande),—crossed the river, and pursued the march to the southward, travelling along the river forty miles, over a sandy road, when they entered a *Jornada*, as the Mexican term is for a long extent of country destitute of water.—This was mostly through a winding valley among the mountains; there was plenty of grass, but no water for its whole extent, over seventy miles. This was accomplished in three days and nights;—the suffering the last day was intense among men and animals; many of the latter died.—The road through this was good.

At the evening of the third day, they arrived at ponds of water; next day encamped at noon, at a good spring on the road,—a warm, clear spring was on a hill near, and still another very large one was about two miles from camp,—plenty of fine grass around. That night they marched thirty-seven miles, through the next *Jornada*, and encamped in the morning on a lake of good water.

A large number of Apache Indians, foes to the Mexicans, inhabit the mountains around here.—The scouts, continually kept out, met with some of these; but the Indians were friendly, and gave them some important information with regard to the Mexican force ahead.—This *Jornada* now being passed, the troops and train got on better.

The distance from El Paso to Chihuahua is above three hundred miles. Continuing the march until the evening of February 25th, at about fifty miles distance from Chihuahua, the force halted at a fine spring; and the interpreter, Kirker, a man well acquainted in the country, with his party of twelve men, who had been employed all the route from El Paso as scouts, and had been ahead to reconnoitre, returned, and reported that a force of about fifteen hundred men were drawn up at *Encinillas*, the country seat of Don Angel Trias, at that time governor of the state of Chihuahua.

This seat was about twenty-five miles ahead. These troops appeared to the scouts, as though prepared to make a defence; for, as said before, they were perfectly aware of the strength and condition of the American force, and had received, from time to time, accurate information of its advance; not liking to try the prowess of "*los Americanos*," by themselves, the Mexicans retreated the next morning; and on the evening of the 26th the troops came up to the houses, but there was no enemy.—The next day, the 27th, the force came within thirty miles of the city, to Sanz.

The scouts coming in, had reported the enemy in great numbers, strongly entrenched on a hill in the valley ahead.—Now everyone prepared himself for the battle on the morrow; for, from this encampment, that of the enemy had to be reached next, as there was no water between.—On the morning of the next day, February 28th, the command were early roused, and their breakfasts disposed of, lines formed, and all on the move by sunrise.

The long train of three hundred and fifteen traders' wagons, beside some sixty, belonging to the detachment, were brought up in four parallel columns, so as to be more easily defended; they could well travel that way, for the road lay down a pretty valley, unbroken, and they could occupy a wide space; high and naked mountains were on either side.—As the force to be met was so far superior in number, the dispositions of the march were made with the utmost care. Two hundred of the men rode in front of these columns of wagons; the remainder, with the artillery, were stationed between these columns, which hid them from the view of the enemy.

In this broad, compact, and regular body of wagons on the outside, horsemen in the front and rear, horsemen and artillery within the spaces of the columns, the whole a sort of moving fortification, fully sufficient to protect the small body of men from the charge of the enemy's cavalry, the whole moved down the valley; which spread out, open, nearly level, with no trees or brush to obstruct the view.—A party, commanded by Major Clark, of the artillery, was sent forward to reconnoitre; when within three miles, the enemy's camp was plainly in view. As the solid, extended body of the Americans, of the four parallel columns of wagons, and force between, and ahead, and in the rear, slowly and steadily advanced, the enemy prepared to receive them.

Across the valley, which so far had been level, rose in front, a crescent-shaped hill, with the hollow side to the north, and flat on the top, with the eastern part, or to the left, as the force came from the north, higher than any other. This hill was about sixty feet in elevation above the surrounding plain: and one point of it was close to the mountains, on the left, and the other point came round by the mountains on the right, about a mile further up the valley than the left extremity, but as said before, it was not so high.

The road upon which the Americans were passing, proceeded directly down the valley to the foot of the hill in front, crossing there a little stream that runs around the hill to the east; it here divided, one fork of it rising the hill, passing directly over its centre, and down on the other side to another stream, which it crossed, and then passed directly on towards Chihuahua. At this last stream was a fort, called Sacramento. The other fork of the road wound to the left, round the base of the hill, following down the bed of the little stream, and joining the first on the other side of the eminence; but this road had been rendered impassable, by strong barricades across the bed of the creek, and by the guns of the forts above it, on either hand.

This was so completely arranged for defence, in order to force the Americans, as they advanced, to take the direct road over the hill; upon the top of which, on a wide area, they had constructed their main fortifications, bearing upon and commanding the road; though to these were added a succession of others, above all; for over this creek, as said before, was a mountain; on an eminence of this, called Cerio Frijoles, was a strong fort, the fire of which bore down on the road in front, and completely commanded and rendered impracticable, the passage along the bed of the creek.

This fort was the enemy's right, and was protected by the inaccessible mountain in its rear. On the west, or opposite from this, the long part of the crescent hill came farther up the valley; between this and the mountain on that side, called Cerro Sacramento, was the second or larger stream mentioned. This was called the Rio Sacramento, and flowed along down between the mountain and the western horn of the hill, and then turned round the base of that hill, and crossed the valley, running to the eastward. On this mountain of Sacramento, over the river, a large fort formed the enemy's left; this fort was elevated, sweeping the whole hill below, and, like the other, it could not be taken in rear.

As the road over the hill was the only one now that the Americans could pass, the enemy had built two forts, one on each brow of this, and twenty-seven redoubts, at little distance from each other, in a parallel line to the road as it crossed the hill, where their whole force could be under cover.—Their cavalry was drawn up before the redoubts, and faced the road.

Here, then, on this strong position, on the hill and entirely across the valley, from mountain to mountain, with strong forts on either extremity, forts and redoubts all along these, the enemy was drawn up, consisting of twelve hundred cavalry, from Durango, Chihuahua, and Vera Cruz; twelve hundred infantry, from Chihuahua, and three hundred artillery, with ten pieces of brass cannon and three carriages, each mounting three *culverins*, (a small long gun). This force of twenty-seven hundred men was well armed, the cavalry with lances, *escopetas*, and sabres, the infantry with muskets and bayonets, and the artillery with the same and swords.

Besides this array, there were fourteen hundred and twenty irregular troops, armed with indifferent guns, lassos, lances, and long cane knives.—These were protected by the regulars and redoubts:—in all, a force of four thousand one hundred and twenty men. These were under the command of General Jose A. Heredia, assisted by General Garcia Conde, who had planned the entrenchments, and who commanded the cavalry; Governor Trias, and colonels and other officers in proportion to the force.

Against this formidable array on the heights, were in the plain below a little force of nine hundred and twenty-four men, with six pieces of artillery, and encumbered with a heavy wagon train. But every man of this force was a host in himself;—cut off from all resource or retreat, with a cruel and notoriously perfidious enemy before them, the alternative was literally victory or death.

This force advanced in full view of the enemy, until within fifteen hundred yards of them, when, pushing the two companies of the advance ahead, the column of wagons and troops turned from the road to the right, and soon making a passage over the first stream, called the Arroyo Seco, the battle commenced about three, p. m.

The following graphic account in relation to it is extracted from the report of Major Clark, commanding battalion of artillery, to Colonel Doniphan:

"Further I have the honour to report that the battalion of artillery under my command, composed of one hundred and ten men and seven officers, with a battery of six pieces of artillery, were, on the morning of the battle, directed to form under the direction of Captain Weightman, between the two columns of merchant and provision wagons, being thus masked from the view of the enemy. In this column my troops continued the march to within about fifteen hundred yards of the enemy's most advanced position; our direction was then changed to the right, and the column having crossed the Arroyo Seco, within reach of the enemy's fire, rapidly advanced towards the table land between the Seco and Sacramento.

"At this time the enemy was perceived advancing from his entrenchments, to prevent our seizing upon those heights; but, by a rapid movement of the battery, it was quickly drawn from its mask, and seizing upon a favourable position, protected in the rear, by a marsh, from the attack of a large body of the enemy's cavalry ascertained to be hanging on our rear, it was formed, and at once opened fire upon the enemy's cavalry, rapidly advancing upon us.

"At this moment, his charging column was about nine hundred yards distant, and the effect of our strap-shot and shells was such as to break his ranks and throw his cavalry into confusion. The enemy now rapidly deployed into line, bringing up his artillery from the entrenchments. During this time the line was preparing for a charge, my artillery advancing by hand and firing. The enemy now opened a heavy fire of cannon upon our line, mainly directed upon the battery, but with little effect.

"Lieutenant Dorn had his horse shot from under him by a nine-pound ball at this stage of the action, and several mules and oxen, in the merchant wagons in our rear, were wounded and killed, which, however, was the only damage done. The fire of our cannon at this time had such good effect as to dismount one of the enemy's pieces, and completely to disperse his cavalry and drive him from his position, forcing him again to retire behind his entrenchments.

"For a short time, the firing on either side now ceased, and the enemy appeared to be moving his cannon and wounded, whilst our line prepared to change our position more towards the right, for the purpose of occupying a more advantageous ground. Our object being soon gained, the order to advance was given, and immediately after I was directed to send the section of howitzers to support a charge upon the enemy's left. I immediately ordered Captain R. F. Weightman to detach the section composed of two twelve-pound mountain howitzers, mounted on carriages constructed especially for field prairie service, and drawn by two horses each these were commanded by Lieutenant E. F. Chouteau and F. D. Evans, and manned by some twenty men, whose conduct in this action cannot be too much commended.

"Captain Weightman charged at full gallop upon the enemy's left, preceded by Captain Reid and his company of horse, and after crossing a ravine some hundred and fifty yards from the enemy, he unlimbered the guns within fifty yards of the entrenchments, and opened a destructive fire of canister into his ranks, which was warmly returned, but without effect. Captain Weightman again advanced upon the entrenchment, passing through it in the face of the enemy, and within a few feet of the ditches; and in the midst of a cross-fire from three directions, again opened his fire to the right and left, with such effect that, with the formidable charge of the cavalry and dismounted men of your own regiment, and Lieutenant-Colonel Mitchell's escort, the enemy were driven from the breast-works on our right in great confusion.

"At this time, under the heavy cross-fire from the battery upon Cerro Sacramento, I was advancing with our battery of four six-pounders, under Lieutenants Dorn, Kribben and Labeaume, upon the enemy's right, supported by Major Gilpin on the left, and the wagon train, escorted by two companies of infantry, under Captain E. J. Glasgow and Skillman, in the rear, when Major Gilpin charged upon the enemy's centre, and forced him from his entrenchments, under a heavy fire of artillery and small arms; at the same time, the fire of our battery was opened upon the enemy's extreme right, from which a continued fire had been kept up upon our line and the wagon train.

"Two of the enemy's guns were now soon dismounted on their right, that battery silenced, and the enemy dislodged from the redoubt on Cerro Frijoles.

"Perceiving a body of lancers forming, for the purpose of out-flanking our left and attacking the merchants' wagon train under Captain Glasgow, I again opened upon them a very destructive fire of grape and spherical case shot, which soon cleared the left of our line; the enemy vacating his entrenchments and deserting his guns, was hotly pursued towards the mountains beyond Cerro Frijoles, and down the Arroyo Seco to Sacramento, by both wings of the army, under Lieutenant-Colonel Mitchell, Lieutenant-Colonel Jackson, and Major Gilpin, and by Captain Weightman, with the sections of howitzers.—During this pursuit, my officers repeatedly opened their fires upon the retreating enemy, with great effect.

"To cover this flight of the enemy's forces from the entrenched camp, the heaviest of his cannon had been taken from the entrenchments to Cerro Sacramento, and a heavy fire opened upon our pursuing forces and the wagons following in the rear. To silence this battery, I had the honour to anticipate your order to that effect, by at once occupying the nearest of the enemy's entrenchments, twelve hundred and twenty-five yards distant; and notwithstanding the elevated position of the Mexican battery, giving him a ploughing fire into my entrenchments, which was not defilated, and the greater range of his long nine- pounders, the first fire of our guns dismounted one of his larger pieces, and the fire was kept up with such briskness and precision of aim, that this battery was soon silenced, and the enemy seen precipitately retreating.

"The fire was then continued upon the *rancho* Sacramento, and the enemy's ammunition and baggage train, retreating upon the road to Chihuahua.—By this fire, the house and several wagons were rendered untenable and useless.

"By this time, Lieutenant-Colonel Mitchell had scaled the hill, followed by the section of howitzers under Captain Weightman, and the last position of the Mexican forces taken possession of by our troops, thus leaving the American forces master of the field. Having silenced the fire from Cerro Sacramento, our battery was removed into the plain at the *rancho*, where we gained the road, and were in pursuit of the enemy when I received your order to return and encamp within the enemy's entrenchments for the night.

"From the time of first opening my fire upon the Mexican cavalry, to the cessation of the firing upon the *rancho* and battery of Sacramento, was about three hours; and, during the whole time of the action, I take the utmost pleasure in stating that every officer and man of my command did his duty with cheerfulness, coolness, and precision, which is sufficiently shown by the admirable effect produced by their fire, the great accuracy of their aim, their expedition and ingenuity in supplying deficiencies in the field during the action, and the prompt management of the pieces, rendered still more remarkable from the fact that I had, during the fight, less than two-thirds the number of cannoneers generally required for the service of light artillery, and but four of the twelve artillery carriages belonging to my battery harnessed with horses, the remaining four carriages being harnessed to mules of the country."

So ended the Battle of Sacramento.—The field was strewed with the dead and dying. The enemy lost over three hundred killed, four hundred and odd wounded, seventy prisoners, all their artillery, ammunition, baggage wagons and provisions, some six thousand dollars, and an immense number of horses, mules, cattle and sheep in the plain below. It was a complete victory and dispersion; nothing was saved by the survivors of the enemy, save the trifle of eight rounds of artillery ammunition that was secreted by a servant in the mountains.[2] Of the American force, strange as it may appear, exposed so long to a fire of artillery and small arms, only one was killed, three mortally wounded, and seven others more slightly.

The victorious army encamped on the battle-ground that night; and, having fought hard, slept well.—Another battle was expected at the city, on the following day. On that morning, a

---

2. See dispatch of General Heredia, *March 2nd, 1847.*

detachment, under Lieutenant-Colonel Mitchell, commenced their march; but. as they approached the city, they were met by some American citizens, who had been residing there, and who, having been for some time in prison, were released this morning.

They informed Colonel Doniphan, that no resistance would be made in the city; that all there was consternation and despair;—that the most exaggerated accounts of the prowess of the Americans had been circulated by the routed army, in their flight through, the night previous.—The detachment having marched in without opposition, Colonel Doniphan, on the next day, followed; took possession of the city in the name of the American government, and occupied the buildings around the *plaza* as the barracks for the troops, while he took his residence in the palace of Governor Trias; from the flag-staff of which, the American flag waved out over the large city of Chihuahua.—

Here were found abundance of supplies. The sheep and cattle they had taken, furnished meat in abundance. Many of these were exchanged with the citizens, for fine, large, and fat hogs. Vegetables were plentiful. A good flour mill supplied them with that article; and, in everything, the army lived well. A full supply of fine water was brought by the aqueduct into the city, and flowed from the fountains in the squares.

Having now established himself in Chihuahua, and having heard that generals Taylor and Scott were surrounded by the powerful army of Santa Anna, and being anxious, in such a case, to assist them, by marching to their relief, Colonel Doniphan soon sent Collins, one of the interpreters and scouts, with an escort of thirteen men, through to General Wool, at Saltillo, to report his progress, and obtain orders.

This small party proceeded through the long route of about seven hundred miles, without molestation, save at the town of San Sebastian, one hundred and twenty leagues from Chihuahua, where they stopped at evening. When about to go, the *alcalde* of the place asked Collins to step into the house again, which he did; and he then demanded of him, in a threatening manner, if he had a passport to travel through the state. Collins—who had been an old trader among these people, spoke their language fluently, and understood their customs told him that he had a passport, and led him out to see it. At the door, he pointed to his thirteen men, dressed in skins, with long beards, that the razor had not touched for months, and remarked to the Mexican that those were his passports, and told him how many shots they had each; every one of this party having, in addition to his gun, holster pistols, sword, and revolving pistols;—and then, telling the *alcalde* that it would be dangerous work for any Mexicans to interrupt them, mounted his horse, and all proceeded.

The next night they encamped; and, while getting their supper, were overtaken and surrounded by between one and two hundred Mexicans, who had collected at San Sebastian, and pursued after them. The Mexicans remained at a distance, and not a shot was fired.—The party finished their suppers; and, every man leading his horse, walked on, until they gained the base of a mountain.—The Mexicans, remembering the field of Sacramento, fell back from before them; and, the party then mounted, and rode all night.—They understood, on their return, that this force was waiting for the arrival of a larger one coming, before they would attack; but, when that arrived, the party was gone.—The Mexicans prepared to attack them on their return, but this was frustrated by their additional strength.

In less than fifteen days they reached Saltillo, and reported themselves to General Wool. That general was astonished beyond measure, when he heard, for the first time, of the battles of Brazito and of Sacramento: of fourteen hundred men, with a piece of artillery, discomfited by a little over five hundred, taken unawares; and of more than four thousand, strongly entrenched, with a train of artillery of ten pieces, defeated and totally routed, with great loss of men and camp equipage, by this same body, then a little more than nine hundred strong;—of the great length of the march they had made, through a wilderness of mountain and prairie, without supplies of any kind; and, more than all, to find that this force—of which these fourteen hardy, rough looking men, were a sample—were in quiet possession of the large and fine city of Chihuahua, for the capture of which, originally, his whole command, of nearly three thousand five hundred men, with abundance of supplies, had been fitted out; and the force, now at six hundred miles distance, understanding that Taylor and himself were surrounded, now sent to him, offering him assistance;—the whole appeared more like a fable of olden time, than like the reality of modern warfare.

After reading the dispatches, he again looked at the men, in their rough appearance, and dress of skins, and asked, still half-seriously, who they were? where they came from? and under the flag of what nation were they fighting? &c., &c.[3] —We will leave this force in possession of the city of Chihuahua, engaged, about this time, in making a treaty with the state authorities; the result of which was, an agreement on the part of those authorities to abstain, hereafter, from all participation in the future actions of the war; and to allow the entrance of American traders into their state, on payment of the customary duties, and to protect them in disposing of their goods;—and, on his part. Colonel Doniphan, in consideration of those agreements, promised to withdraw his troops from the city. (It is but justice to the authorities of Chihuahua to state, that they have faithfully fulfilled this treaty).—We will now turn our attention to the army of General Taylor, and its operations during this eventful month of February.

When General Scott arrived at the Rio Grande, on the first of January, as has been before mentioned, he instantly sent his dispatches to General Taylor (then on his way to Victoria), directing him to return to Monterey, with a small portion of the troops he had, and ordered the main body, under Major General Patterson, Brigadier-Generals Twiggs, Pillow, and Quitman, to go on to Tampico. The march of these has been described.

---

3. To those readers who would wish a more extended notice of all the operations of this gallant regiment, as well as of those of General Kearney, in California, and Colonel Price, in Santa Fe, the author would recommend *Colonel Doniphan's Expedition*, a new and interesting work by J.T. Hughes of the first Missouri regiment.

He also sent dispatches to General Worth, at Saltillo, who there had just been reinforced by the army of General Wool, to leave that post in the command of the latter general, and, with his whole division of regulars, to march to the Rio Grande, and thence transport his troops to Matamoras, preparatory to embarking them for Vera Cruz, in conjunction with the large force that should embark for the same point, from Tampico, and those of the new levy of nine regiments, that were arriving from the United States, and collecting at Lobos Island, south of Tampico. Dispatches were also sent to General Butler, commanding the reserve through the valley of the Rio Grande, and whose headquarters were at Monterey, informing him of the arrangements.

These dispatches to each, altered all the arrangements previously made. General Patterson marched to Tampico;—General Taylor returned to Monterey;—General Worth, with his division, left General Wool in command of Saltillo, and marched with celerity towards the sea-coast.

There had been indications, for some time before this, of an attack, by Santa Anna, upon the advanced position of Saltillo, preparatory to a grand movement, which that general was contemplating, the object of which was, with his powerful army, to overrun and reconquer the whole valley of the Rio Grande, and annihilate our small force there.—One alarm had already been given, of his approach, and General Taylor had begun his march, to assist Worth, when it was rendered unnecessary, by General Wool's army coming in from Parras.

Now, General Worth left, in obedience to the command of General Scott.—General Wool's force not being strong enough, in case of an attack, General Butler, from Monterey, dispatched, to reinforce him, the Kentucky regiment of cavalry, Colonel Marshall, the second Kentucky infantry, Colonel McKee, the second Indiana regiment, Colonel Bowles, the third Indiana regiment, Colonel Lane, and Webster's artillery, all under Brigadier General Lane.

In the meantime, reports of the advance of the enemy continually increased; and were at last made certain.—Scouts had been, by General Wool, sent out in every direction; but all had been uncertain, until on the night of the 22nd of January, a combined reconnoitring party, of forty men and officers, of the Arkansas cavalry, under Major Borland, and thirty-seven of the Kentucky cavalry, under Major Gaines, were surrounded, and subsequently captured by three thousand Mexican cavalry, under General Miñon, at the *hacienda* of Encarnacion, sixty miles south of Saltillo, on the road to San Louis Potosi (see map).

This general had made a forced march of nearly one hundred miles, to surprise them; which he did, aided by the darkness and storm of the night—. The whole command had just returned from a position thirty miles nearer General Miñon's position, and ninety from Saltillo, and had not been able to find a trace of the enemy; and were now on their return march to camp, and in the evening, had halted for the night at the *hacienda*.

Although not the slightest probability of an attack was apprehended, yet the customary vigilance was pursued, and their sentinels were regularly placed.—General Miñon, who was an able officer, had been in their rear on their return march, all day, unknown to them; and at a late hour coming up, he placed his army around the *hacienda*, at the distance of about half a mile, in each direction, and wholly without the hearing of the sentinels, in the furious wind and cloudy darkness; and in this position quietly awaited the morning, which, by its first dawn, should reveal to the Americans their situation.

These were, as may well be imagined, astonished at their position; surrounded by such an enemy, which had appeared so suddenly; but they were by no means intimidated.—The swelling, exulting music of the Mexican forces, who, with their glistening arms, belted them in as it were, rose clearly, on every side of them; and was answered immediately, by the unwavering notes of defiance from the single bugle of the undaunted American cavalry.

Though small in force, and outnumbered, forty to one, these Kentuckian and Arkansas horsemen were eager for the strife; and with the utmost alacrity all belted on their arms, turned to their noble steeds, and were ready for the conflict. Their gallant commander read in the face of every man, the determination of victory or death.—But General Miñon was too able an officer to expose his men to the sure aim and strong arms of these cool-hearted and determined men, whose spirit of resistance was borne to his ears by the tones of their bugle, while already he had them in his power; and so, while his heavy body of lancers, in solid and glittering array, slowly approached the *hacienda* on one side, a bearer of a white flag came bounding from his lines on the other, stating to the Americans the number of their force, the uselessness of resistance, and then offering honourable terms of surrender.

The number of the Mexicans looked large, but the American officers did not believe the Mexican report, and all the soldiers wished to fight it out.—General Miñon sent in a Mexican officer of the same rank, as a hostage, while Major Gaines went out into the Mexican army, and satisfied himself of their force; then returned, and as it was but throwing away every life to resist, they surrendered, upon condition of being treated as prisoners of war; and they were marched immediately to the southward. About the same time, another scouting party of the Kentucky Cavalry, of seventeen men, under Captain Heady, were surrounded and taken.

Thus were nearly a hundred men lost; but though they were captured, their object was gained, and the result was, to the American army, of the highest importance and advantage for by the escape of Captain Henrie, one of the prisoners, and his return, the force of the enemy, and the certainty of his advance, became at once known to General Wool who instantly sent a dispatch to General Taylor, which reached him just after he had arrived at Monterey from Victoria. He immediately, with his column that had returned from Victoria with him (Colonel Davis' Mississippians, Captain Bragg's artillery, and Colonel May's dragoons), marched on to Saltillo, and proceeding by the hacienda of Buena Vista, encamped the whole army, save a garrison for Saltillo, at the base of the Agua Nueva Mountain, twenty miles from the latter place, and on the road that Santa Anna's army would be obliged to come. Here he waited to give that general battle, for his approach was now sure.

The time, to the 21st of February, was devoted to preparing for the approaching combat; the passes in the neighbouring mountains were all examined, to secure the advantages for a battle-ground. The position at Buena Vista, twelve miles back towards Saltillo, which had been selected by General Wool, was examined by the engineers, and found to be the best calculated to withstand the attacks of a powerful force; and to this, on the 21st of February, as the scouts gave notice that the enemy was at hand, the army fell back; arrived there in the evening, and immediately commenced the preparations for the battle.

Let us turn our attention to the previous movements of the enemy; for, as soon as Santa Anna knew (by the reception of the dispatch from General Scott to General Taylor, taken at Villa Grande, by the death of Lieutenant Ritchie,) of the disposition of the American forces, and saw that the valley of the Rio Grande was defended but by a small number, he put his army in motion for the north, towards Saltillo, after sending a strong brigade of cavalry, under General Urrea, across the mountains from San Luis, by Tula, to proceed through Victoria, Villa Grande and Linares, to the vicinity of Monterey, and thus be in General Taylor's rear, to cut to pieces anybody of American force that might escape the defeat which he was confident, from his superior forces, of inflicting on "old Zack." General Urrea pursued his march on the eastern side of the mountains, and arrived near Monterey at the same time that Santa Anna came on the west of the mountains, near Saltillo.

On the 20th of February, Santa Anna arrived at the *hacienda* of Encarnacion, thirty miles from Agua Nueva. There he sent General Miñon, with twelve hundred cavalry, (so stated by Santa Anna; by General Taylor computed to be two thousand), round the mountains to the right, with instructions to get on the rear of General Taylor, and take possession of the *hacienda* of Buena Vista; and as he (Santa Anna) drove the Americans through the pass, to fall upon them.—General Miñon set out on this expedition, and on the next day Santa Anna' a force moved on, and encamped on a plain called De la Guerra, nine miles from Agua Nueva.

At daylight on the 22nd of February, his army was again in motion, and moved on to force the pass of Agua Nueva; but, to his astonishment, no one was found there: for the American army had fallen back to the *hacienda* of Buena Vista the preceding day, save the Arkansas Cavalry, Colonel Yell, which remained at the old camp to observe the movements of the enemy; and a few miles farther, the Second Kentucky, Colonel McKee, with a section of artillery, halted at the *rancho* of Encantada, to support Colonel Yell, should he be attacked; and still farther back, on the battle ground of the next day, the first Illinoisans, Colonel Hardin, to support them both, if driven in.

On that day, too, the greatest activity had been used in removing all the stores, provisions, &c., from Agua Nueva; in the night, all having been done, Colonel Yell's regiment, (his pickets having been driven in by the Mexican army), and Colonel McKee's came in, accompanied by the Kentucky Cavalry, Colonel Marshall, and the First Dragoons, who had been sent out to support them.—General Taylor, in the meantime, accompanied by the Mississippi regiment, Colonel Davis, Bragg's and Sherman's batteries of artillery, and Colonel May's dragoons, proceeded back to Saltillo, to make preparations for the defence of the city against an attack of General Miñon, and with the same force was returning, the next morning, to Buena Vista, when the enemy appeared in front at ten, a.m.—A view of the battle ground may be seen in the sketch overleaf.

The view[4] is there taken from the north-east part of the ground, and of course fronts to the south-west. Although, in a view, the position of the various columns cannot be so par-

---

4. For this view of the battle ground of Buena Vista, the author is indebted to the politeness of Lieutenant Gray, adjutant Third regiment, Ohio, by whom it was drawn upon the ground, a few weeks after the battle. The camp of General Wool, in the foreground, is not precisely correct in its lines, having been placed on from recollection; but as it represents the camp after the battle, the difference is immaterial.

ticularly laid down as on a plan, yet, reader, you can obtain a clearer idea of their movements. You are, as it were, looking on the ground before you;—you see the pass, the *hacienda*, the mountains, and the elevated plain, or plateau, upon which so many brave men fell. In front, you see the camp of General Wool, as it was in a few days after the battle. On the left, rises the high, rugged mountain, on which the battle commenced on the evening of the 22nd, and recommenced on the morning of the 23rd. Our light troops are positioned along the lower part of the mountain and attacking column of the Mexicans.

Across the plain, not seen in the picture, are several deep ravines, running from the mountain out towards the *hacienda*. The elevated top of the plateau is seen, so often mentioned in the battle. Beyond this, about twelve miles in the distance, is the tall mountain of Agua Nueva;—it is double.—Nearer on the right of the picture, you observe the range of mountainous hills that bound the plain on that side.

The position of the troops, during the battle of the 23rd, only express the general position of each regiment, for during the engagement they were advancing or falling back, and changing position continually, though generally operating over the same ground.

The Washington battery is stationed at the pass;—at a breast-work to the right of the battery are two companies First Illinoisans.—also in position during the night before the battle were Bragg's battery and the Second Kentucky;—one hill was occupied on that morning by the First Illinoisans:—another was occupied by the Second Kentucky, when first coming into action;—The Second Illinoisans took up position at the same time. The position of Second Indianans on the plateau was where the heavy Mexican column first made its attack; —The Kentucky Cavalry, The Riflemen,(Kentucky, Arkansas, Indiana, and Illinois), Colonel May's dragoons and Captain Pike's squadron Arkansas Cavalry, and the remainder Arkansas Cavalry are all positioned—The Third Indiana and Mississippi regiment are attacking the enemy in the centre—the *hacienda* of Buena Vista

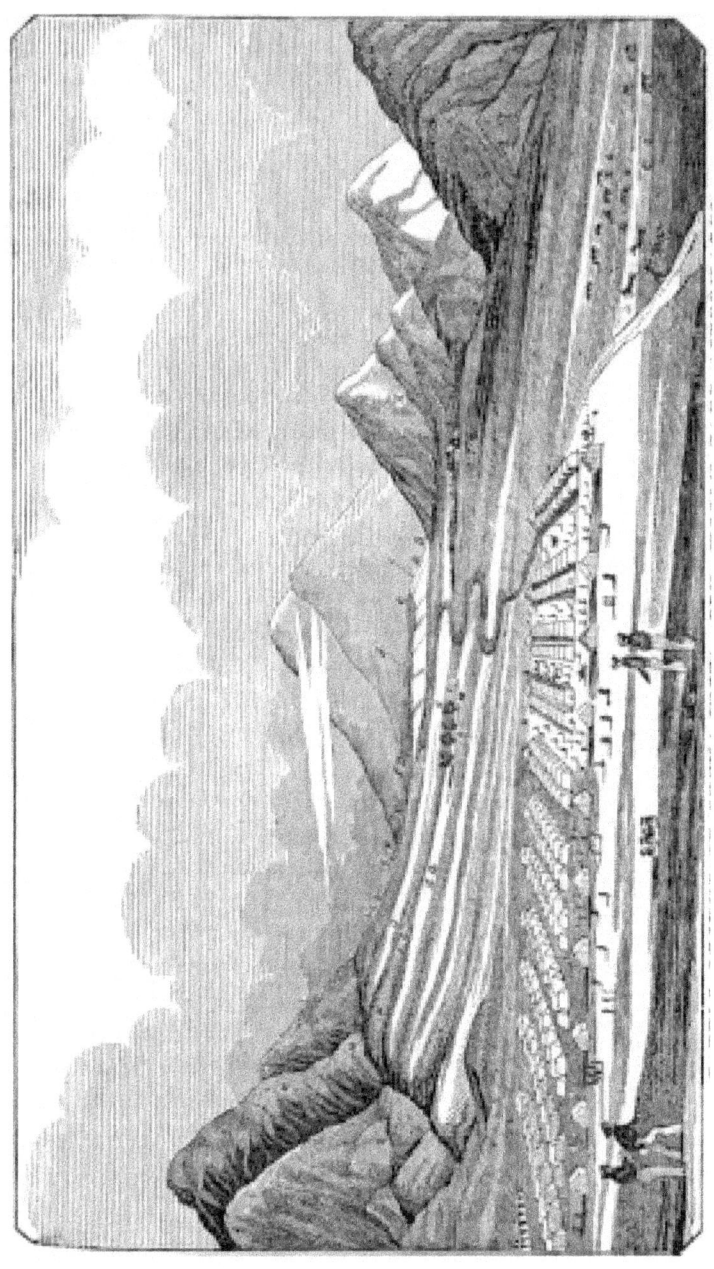

Battle Ground of Buena Vista

is also shown.

Coming round the base of the mountain, and on the plain is the position of General Pacheco's column, three thousand infantry, a large body of cavalry, and four pieces artillery. After turning the American left, they came round to the rear, were checked by the Mississippi regiment, and fully repulsed by the Mississippi, Third Indiana, part of Second Indiana, Arkansas and Kentucky Cavalry, May's dragoons, and Bragg's and Sherman's batteries artillery.

A Mexican battery was established after the column had gained its position;—General Ampudia's body of Mexican troops were positioned on the 22nd, and the larger body of those of General Lombardini on the 23rd. A heavy Mexican battery was positioned beyond the plateau and pass.—The heavy column under General Ampudia attacked the American right;—The final and heaviest attack of the Mexican army was directed over the plateau. This was under the command of General Perez, and was composed of the division of General Pacheco, now retreated, General Ampudia, and all the reserved forces of the Mexican army.—It was checked by Captain O'Brien's artillery, with the loss of his guns; repulsed by the Second Kentucky, First and Second Illinois, Bragg's and Sherman's artillery, assisted by the Mississippi and 3rd Indiana regiments, and Washington's battery. The battle commenced shortly after the arrival of the enemy; and as "old Zach." who fought the battle, has written the plainest account of it, we will give it in his words:

> Headquarters, Army of Occupation.
> Agua Nueva, March 6, 1847

Sir:—I have the honour to submit a detailed report of the operations of the forces under my command, which resulted in the engagement of Buena Vista, the repulse of the Mexican army, and the reoccupation of this position.

"The information which reached me of the advance and concentration of a heavy Mexican force in my front, had assumed such a probable form, as to induce a special examination far beyond the reach of our pickets, to ascertain its correctness. A small party of Texan spies, under Major McCulloch, dispatched to the *hacienda* of Encarnacion, thirty miles from this, on the route to San Luis Potosi, had reported a cavalry force of unknown strength at that place. On the 20th of February, a strong reconnaissance, under Lieutenant-Colonel May, was dispatched to the *hacienda* of Heclionda, while Major McCulloch made another examination of Encarnacion. The results of these expeditions left no doubt that the enemy was in large force at Encarnacion, under the orders of General Santa Anna, and that he meditated a forward movement and attack upon our position.

As the camp of Agua Nueva could be turned on either flank, and as the enemy's force was greatly superior to our own, particularly in the arm of cavalry, I determined, after much consideration, to take up a position about eleven miles in rear, and there await the attack. The army broke up its camp and marched at noon on the 21st, encamping at the new position a little in front of the *hacienda* of Buena Vista. With a small force, I proceeded to Saltillo, to make some necessary arrangements for the defence of the town, leaving Brigadier General Wool in the immediate command of the troops.

Before these arrangements were completed on the morning of the 22nd, I was advised that the enemy was in sight, advancing. Upon reaching the ground, it was found that his cavalry was in our front, having marched from Encarnacion, as we have since learned, at eleven o'clock on the day previous, and driving in a mounted force left at Agua Nueva to cover the removal of public stores. Our troops were in position occupying a line of remarkable strength. The road at this point becomes a narrow defile, the valley on its right being rendered quite impracticable for artillery by a system of deep and impassable gullies, while on the left a succession of rugged ridges and precipitous ravines extends far back towards the mountain which bounds the valley. The features of the ground were such as nearly to paralyse the artillery and cavalry of the enemy, while his infantry could not derive all the advantages of its numerical superiority.—In this position we prepared to receive him.

Captain Washington's battery (4th Artillery) was posted to command the road, while the First and 2nd Illinois regiments, under Colonels Hardin and Bissell, each eight companies, (to the latter of which was attached Captain Conner's company of Texan Volunteers), and the 2nd Kentucky, under Colonel McKee, occupied the crests of the ridges on the left and in rear. The Arkansas and Kentucky regiments of Cavalry, commanded by Colonels Yell and H. Marshall, occupied the extreme left, near the base of the mountain, while the Indiana brigade, under Brigadier General Lane, (composed of the 2nd and 3rd regiments, under Colonels Bowles and Lane), the Mississippi Riflemen, under Colonel Davis, the squadrons of the 1st and 2nd Dragoons, under Captain Steen and Lieutenant-Colonel May, and the light batteries of Captains Sherman and Bragg, 3rd Artillery, were held in reserve.

At eleven o'clock, I received from General Santa Anna a summons to surrender at discretion, which, with a copy of my reply, I have already transmitted.(Seen at end of account). The enemy still forbore his attack, evidently awaiting for the arrival of his rear columns, which could be distinctly seen by our lookouts as they approached the field. A demonstration made on his left, caused me to detach the 2nd Kentucky regiment and a section of artillery to our right, in which position they bivouacked for the night.

In the meantime, the Mexican light troops[5] had engaged

---

5. These, about fifteen hundred in number, were under the command of General Ampudia and Colonel Baneneli, This day they only were near the base of the mountain, not so high as the upper part, which position they took during the night, and from which, (being reinforced to the number of two thousand five hundred, under General Lombardini), they commenced the battle on the 23rd.

ours on the extreme left, (composed of parts of the Kentucky and Arkansas Cavalry, dismounted, and a rifle battalion from the Indiana brigade, under Major Gorman, the whole commanded by Colonel Marshall), and kept up a sharp fire, climbing the mountain side, and apparently endeavouring to gain our flank.

Three pieces of Captain Washington's battery had been detached to the left, and were supported by the 2nd Indiana regiment. An occasional shell was thrown by the enemy into this part of our line, but without effect. The skirmishing of the light troops was kept up, with trifling loss on our part, until dark, when I became convinced that no serious attack would be made before the morning, and returned with the Mississippi regiment and 2nd Dragoons to Saltillo. The troops bivouacked without fires, and laid upon their arms.

A body of cavalry, some fifteen hundred strong, had been visible all day in rear of the town, having entered the valley through a narrow pass east of the city. This cavalry, commanded by General Miñon, had evidently been thrown in our rear to break upland harass our retreat, and perhaps make some attempt against the town, if practicable. The city was occupied by four excellent companies of Illinois Volunteers, under Major Warren, of the First regiment. A field work, which commanded most of the approaches, was garrisoned by Captain Webster's company, 1st Artillery, and armed with two twenty-four pound howitzers, while the train and headquarter camp was guarded by two companies Mississippi Riflemen, under Captain Rogers, and a field-piece commanded by Captain Shover, 3rd Artillery. Having made these dispositions for the protection of the rear, I proceeded, on the morning of the 23rd, to Buena Vista, ordering forward all the other available troops. The action had commenced before my arrival on the field.

During the evening and night of the 22nd, the enemy had thrown a body of light troops on the mountain side, with the purpose of outflanking our left; and it was here that the action of the 23rd commenced, at an early hour. Our riflemen, under Colonel Marshall, who had been reinforced by three companies under Major Trail, Second Illinois volunteers, maintained their ground handsomely against a greatly superior force, holding themselves under cover, and using their weapons with deadly effect.[6]

About six o'clock, a strong demonstration was made against the centre of our position, a heavy column moving along the road.[7] This force was soon dispersed by a few rapid and well-directed shots from Captain Washington's battery. In the meantime the enemy was concentrating a large force of infantry and cavalry under cover of the ridges, with the obvious intention of forcing our left, which was posted on an extensive plateau[8] The Second Indiana and Second Illinois regiments formed this part of our line, the former covering three pieces of light artillery, under the orders of Captain O'Brien;—Brigadier General Lane being in immediate command. In order to bring his men within effective range, General Lane ordered the artillery and second Indiana regiment forward.

The artillery advanced within musket range of a heavy body of Mexican Infantry, and was served against it with great effect, but without being able to check its advance. The infantry ordered to its support had fallen back in disorder, being exposed, as well as the battery, not only to a severe fire of small arms in front, but also to a murderous crossfire of grape and canister, from a Mexican battery on the left. Captain O'Brien found it impossible to retain his

---

6. These troops, under Colonel Marshall.
7. The position of these troops, was concealed by the "pass." They were under General Ampudia.
8. This column of troops, which attacked the 2nd Indiana, and the 2nd Illinois, was commanded by General Pacheco; consisted of three thousand infantry, accompanied by nearly two thousand cavalry and four pieces of artillery, which were placed in battery. The brunt of opposing this heavy force, from their position, fell on the 2nd Indiana regiment and Captain O'Brien's artillery.

position without support, but was only able to withdraw two of his pieces, all the horses and cannoneers of the third piece being killed or disabled. The Second Indiana regiment, which had fallen back as stated, could not be rallied, and took no farther part in the action, except a handful of men,[9] who, under its gallant colonel, Bowles, joined the Mississippi regiment, and did good service, and those fugitives who, at a later period of the day, assisted in defending the train and depot at Buena Vista. This portion of our line having given way, and the enemy appearing in overwhelming force against our left flank, the light troops which had rendered such good service on the mountain, were compelled to withdraw, which they did, for the most part, in good order. Many, however, were not rallied until they reached the depot at Buena Vista, to the defence of which they afterwards contributed.

Never have troops been more abused by public opinion, (controlled and directed by letter-writers from the army), than have these 2nd Indianans; and although a court of inquiry afterwards investigated fully the matter, and came to a far different opinion than that thus sent back to the United States, still many are under a misapprehension with regard to them. From their position, they were forced to withstand the principal weight of General Pacheco's heavy columns of infantry and cavalry, and were further exposed to the cross-fire of grape and canister from the Mexican battery of artillery. Pacheco's troops were fresh, for it was the first assault, and confident of victory from very numerical force.

The 2nd Illinois, under the gallant Bissell, were some distance to the right of the Indianans Colonel Marshall's force of dismounted cavalry, and infantry riflemen, were to the left, and on the mountain, closely engaged with the far greater force of General Lombardini. Thus placed, the second Indiana stood its

---

9. "From one hundred and fifty to two hundred." See proceedings of court of inquiry, published at Saltillo, *May 3rd, 1847*.

ground, although suffering so severely from the enemy in front, and their battery on their left. Retreat was never thought of by them while with coolness they loaded and fired; not once or twice, but delivered, in that position, twenty-one volleys round, in the meantime losing thirty-two killed and thirty-six wounded.

Colonel Bowles, seeing his men falling in such numbers before the shower of musket balls, grape, and canister, sweeping through them, he, himself, unadvisedly and unfortunately ordered the regiment to "cease firing and retreat" But still they stood, unwilling to go. He repeated the order, before it was obeyed; and then the left, in obedience, began to retreat, followed by the right, who were still firing. But the colonel, having thus most unfortunately broken up the line, and sent them on retreat, with no place designated to re-form, and with the tremendous fire of the enemy behind them, had got them into a situation from which he could not extricate them.

Confidence was gone. The order to retreat, earnestly given from him, conveyed to the minds of every one that he despaired of maintaining his ground; and it was, in fact, equivalent to an order for every man to save himself. They believed the battle lost, not from fear, but on account of the order so given and repeated. There was no time now for explanation; the mischief had been done; the impression forced on the men; and the fire of the enemy was in the ear. The court of inquiry, after patient investigation, pronounced this movement of Colonel Bowles to proceed not from cowardice, (for he fought most gallantly all the day afterward, in the ranks of the Mississippi regiment), but from an ill-judged motive of expediency, to save the lives of his men. Such was the retreat of the 2nd Indianans.

Reader, judge of them impartially; place any other regiment, even of the oldest regulars, in their situation put them before a well-armed and fresh force, of ten times their number, in front, and on their flank an active battery sending grape and canister in showers through them, and then, after standing in the face of such a force, in the heat of the battle let them hear their own colonel, to whom they look for all commands, loudly calling to them to retreat, and repeating it, and the idea will flash on every soldier's mind, that the day is lost, and that everyone is to retreat for himself.

This was a battle of volunteers, and no regiment engaged in it had before been in one, save the Mississippi, which had done such good service at Monterey. The regiments stood their ground and fought with such bravery for ten hours, against the legions opposed to them with such heroic firmness resisting the concentrated attacks from morn till night, that praise of them is idle; to look at their conduct excites not only admiration, but astonishment.

Colonel Bissell's regiment, (2nd Illinois), which had been joined by a section of Captain Sherman's battery, had become completely outflanked, and was compelled to fall back, being entirely unsupported. The enemy was now pouring masses of infantry and cavalry along the base of the mountain on our left, and was gaining our rear in great force.

This 2nd Illinois regiment acted, during the entire day, in the most gallant manner. As the 2nd Indiana retreated, and the heavy column of the enemy advanced upon the ground which had been occupied by it, this regiment fell back from its position, two or three hundred yards.

This movement was performed in the face of the enemy, as it would have been on parade being faced about, marched the distance, and again faced to the front. They received several volleys here, then advanced nearer, and engaged the main body of the enemy for thirty minutes, suffering severely. Their gallant colonel drew them off to the right, and attacked, with the 1st Illinois and 2nd Kentucky, the left of the enemy; afterward was in the last charge of the day against the enemy column; and took the colours of the Guanajuata regiment, after hard fighting.

The loss of this regiment was more severe than that of any other. It had one captain, nine lieutenants, thirty-seven non-commissioned officers and privates killed, and three captains, four lieutenants, and sixty-seven non-commissioned officers and privates wounded. Two companies of this regiment, under Major Trail, Captains Leman's and Woodward's, fought on the mountains, and on the left, at and near the *hacienda*; and two more were detached for the defence of Saltillo.

At this moment I arrived upon the field. The Mississippi regiment had been directed to the left before reaching the position, and immediately came into action against the Mexican cavalry which had turned our flank.

This regiment, under Colonel Davis, leaving two of its companies at Saltillo, accompanied General Taylor on that morning to the battlefield. On the way they heard the artillery, which assured them that the battle had commenced; and they hastened on, arrived, and immediately, unsupported, advanced against the heavy victorious column of the enemy, which, more than four thousand strong of cavalry and infantry, had turned the American left. The regiment took a position, and opened a volley when near the enemy; and continued, although suffering severely, to advance with such deadly fire upon the column, that it fell back, and a column of cavalry were sent round to attack the fearless Mississippians in the rear; but, in crossing around to do this, they were received with such a destructive fire from the rifles, as wholly to disperse them with much loss.

The regiment re-formed, and, joined by the 3rd Indiana and a piece of artillery of Bragg's battery, under Lieutenant Kilburn, again attacked the heavy column, and forced it to retire toward the mountain; but, coming in the range of a battery of the enemy, they fell back, and were charged upon by the whole body of Mexican cavalry.

Forming its line as these came up, with the third Indiana, they received the lancers with such fatal volleys as immediately to force them to fall back; and, shortly after, with the aid of other troops, the whole column, was forced to retreat. In the severe and bloody final charge of the whole Mexican force under General Perez, on the high plain, the Mississippians were of the greatest service reaching the ground opposite, and pouring a destructive fire into the enemy's flank, as he endeavoured to force the position; and when the head of the column had come near to Bragg's battery, the fire was so severe that the enemy's right was immediately broken.

Most nobly did the regiment and it's gallant commander, who was wounded at the first fire, sustain, through the day, the reputation of their State. Many brave men fell in its ranks; loss, forty-two killed and fifty-one wounded. Number of men in action, three hundred and forty-one.

The 2nd Kentucky regiment and a section of artillery under Captain Bragg had previously been ordered from the right to reinforce our left, and arrived at a most opportune moment. That regiment, and a portion of the 1st Illinois under Colonel Hardin, gallantly drove the enemy, and recovered a portion of the ground we had lost. The batteries of captains Sherman and Bragg were in position on the plateau, and did much execution not only in front, but particularly upon the masses which had gained our rear. Discovering that the enemy was heavily pressing upon the Mississippi regiment, the 3rd Indiana regiment, under Colonel Lane, was dispatched to strengthen that part of our line which formed a crotchet perpendicular to the first line of battle. At the same time, Lieutenant Kilburn, with a piece of Captain Bragg's battery, was commanded to support the infantry there engaged. The action was for a long time warmly sustained at that point—the enemy making several attempts, both with infantry and cavalry, against our line, and being repulsed always with heavy loss. I had placed all the regular cavalry and Captain Pike's squadron of Arkansas Horse under the orders of Brevet Lieutenant Colonel May, with directions to hold in check the enemy's column, still advancing in the rear along the base of the mountain, which was done in connection with the Kentucky and Arkansas cavalry, under Colonels Marshall and Yell.

In the meantime our left, which was still strongly threatened by a superior force, was further strengthened by the detachment of Captain Bragg's and a portion of Captain Sherman's batteries to that quarter. The concentration of artillery fire upon the mass of the enemy along the base of the mountain, and the determined resistance offered by the two regiments opposed to them, had created confusion in their ranks, and some of the corps attempted to effect a retreat upon their main line of battle. The squadron of the 1st Dragoons, under Lieutenant Rucker, was now ordered up the deep ravine which these retreating corps were endeavouring to cross, in order to charge and disperse them.

The squadron proceeded to the point indicated, but could not accomplish the object, being exposed to a heavy fire from a battery established to cover the retreat of those corps. While the squadron was detached upon this service, a large body of the enemy was observed to concentrate on our extreme left, apparently with the view of making a descent upon the *hacienda* of Buena Vista, where our train and baggage were deposited. Lieutenant Colonel May was ordered to the support of that point, with two pieces of Captain Sherman's battery under Lieutenant Reynolds. In the meantime the scattered forces near the *hacienda*, composed in part of Majors Trail's and Gorman's commands, had been to some extent organized under the advice of Major Monroe, chief of artillery, with the assistance of Major Morrison, volunteer staff, and were posted to defend the position.

Before our cavalry had reached the *hacienda*, that of the enemy had made its attack, having been handsomely met by the Kentucky and Arkansas Cavalry, under colonels Marshall and Yell. "

These two regiments, Kentucky Cavalry, Colonel Marshall,

and Arkansas, Colonel Yell together with the few regular dragoons under Colonel May, during the battle on the 23rd, had most severe and laborious services to perform They had had no rest on the previous day, the 21st, or even on the 20th; nor until after the battle was finished on the 23rd, was there any cessation of their exertion.

The Rifle battalion of each, dismounted, in conjunction with that of the 2nd Indiana, fought on the mountain side, during the afternoon of the 22nd, and, reinforced by the Rifle battalion of the 2nd Illinois, commenced here the glorious action of the 23rd. When General Pacheco's heavy column, had succeeded in turning the American left, these detachments retired to the plain, and there kept up their exertions. The mounted companies had continually their utmost endeavours to make, in repelling, with the other regiments, the onward march of this column; and in these heroic and successful efforts, they lost many of their number, and among them Colonel Yell, the brave and talented commander of the Arkansas troops. He fought at their head, and was killed in the charge, not far from the trees.

Loss of Kentucky Cavalry, killed and wounded, sixty-one. Loss of Arkansas, killed, wounded and missing, fifty-three.

The Mexican column immediately divided—one portion sweeping by the depot, where it received a destructive fire from the force which had collected there, and then gaining the mountain opposite, under a fire from Lieutenant Reynolds' section, the remaining portion regaining the base of the mountain on our left. In the charge at Buena Vista, Colonel Yell fell gallantly at the head of his regiment; we also lost Adjutant Vaughan, of the Kentucky cavalry—a young officer of much promise. Lieutenant Colonel May, who had been rejoined by the squadron of the 1st Dragoons, and by portions of the Arkansas and Indiana troops, under Lieutenant Colonel Roane and Major Gorman, now approached the base of the mountain, holding in check the right flank of the enemy, upon whose masses, crowded in the narrow gorges and the ravines, our artillery was doing fearful execution.

The position of that portion of the Mexican army which had gained our rear was now very critical, and it seemed doubtful whether it could regain the main body. At this moment I received from General Santa Anna a message by a staff officer, desiring to know what I wanted. I immediately dispatched Brigadier General Wool to the Mexican general-in-chief, and sent orders to cease firing. Upon reaching the Mexican lines, General Wool could not cause the enemy to cease their fire, and accordingly returned without having an interview. The extreme right of the enemy continued its retreat along the base of the mountain, and, finally, in spite of all our efforts, effected a junction with the remainder of the army.

During the remainder of the day, General Miñon had ascended the elevated plain above Saltillo, and occupied the road from the city to the field of battle, where they intercepted several of our men. Approaching the town, they were fired upon by Captain Webster, from the redoubt occupied by his company, and then moved on towards the eastern side of the valley, and obliquely towards Buena Vista. At this time, Captain Shover moved rapidly forward with his piece, supported by a miscellaneous command of mounted volunteers, and fired several shots at the cavalry, with great effect. They were driven into the ravines which lead to the lower valley, closely pursued by Captain Shover, who was further supported by a piece of Captain Webster's battery, under Lieutenant Donaldson, which had advanced from the redoubt, supported by Captain Wheeler's company Illinois volunteers. The enemy made one or two efforts to charge the artillery, but was finally driven back in a confused mass, and did not again appear upon the plain.

Santa Anna, in his account of this battle, lays all the blame of his want of success at the door of General Miñon; for that general, he says, was ordered to charge upon the American force on the left, instead of doing which, he contented himself with remaining all day in position between Buena Vista and Saltillo, and in making an unsuccessful demonstration on the latter place. General Miñon, on the other hand, maintains to the effect that his instructions from General Santa Anna were for him to take position where he did, and fall on the "Yankees," after Santa Anna had driven them through the pass; and he maintains that he exactly performed his orders, save as to cutting down and annihilating said "Yankees;" which failure resulted only from the fact that General Santa Anna was not able, with all his force, to drive them through the pass towards him.

 In the meantime, the firing had partially ceased upon the principal field. The enemy seemed to confine his efforts to the protection of his artillery, and I had left the plateau for a moment, when I was recalled thither by a heavy musketry fire. On regaining that position, I discovered that our infantry (Illinois and 2nd Kentucky) had engaged a greatly superior force of the enemy—evidently his reserve—and that they had been overwhelmed by numbers. The moment was most critical. Captain O'Brien, with two pieces, had sustained this heavy charge to the last, and was finally obliged to leave his guns on the field—his infantry support being entirely routed. Captain Bragg, who had just arrived from the left, was ordered at once into battery. Without any infantry to support him, and at the imminent risk of losing his guns this officer came rapidly into action, the Mexican line being but a few yards from the muzzle of his pieces.

The first discharge of canister caused the enemy to hesitate; the second and third drove him back in disorder, and saved the day. The 2nd Kentucky regiment, which had advanced beyond supporting distance in this affair, was driven back, and closely pressed by the enemy's cavalry. Taking a ravine which led in the direction of Captain Washington's battery, their pursuers became exposed to his fire, which soon checked and drove them back with loss.

The last great struggle of the day was now about to be brought on. The attacking column of General Ampudia, on the right, had been repulsed by the rapid and destructive discharge of Captain Washington's battery. The column of General Pacheco, on the left, after partial success, had been driven back by the Mississippi, Third Indiana Infantry, Arkansas and Kentucky Cavalry, Colonel May's dragoons, Bragg's, Sherman's, and Kilburn's artillery, and the miscellaneous force at the *hacienda*. The centre column, under General Villamil, had been repulsed by the 1st and 2nd Illinois, and the Second Kentucky, aided by Captain O'Brien's and others' artillery.

Thus, the three separate charges upon different portions of the American position, although desperate and bloody on both sides, had failed, and the dead and dying covered the hard fought field. In this last charge, the whole power of the Mexican army was to be brought to bear upon the American centre.

While this lull in the storm of battle was taking place, during which the artillery, only, on both sides, belched forth their opposing thunders, Santa Anna was, with the greatest activity, throwing his columns together for this grand charge. General Ampudia's column was united to those of General Pacheco and General Villamil, and to this force were added all the fresh troops of the reserve; the whole was placed under the command of General Perez; and the vast body came down like an avalanche, on the elevated plain.

> In the meantime, the rest of our artillery had taken position on the plateau, covered by the Mississippi and 3rd Indiana regiments, the former of which had reached the ground in time to pour a fire into the right flank of the enemy, and thus contribute to his repulse. In this last conflict, we had the misfortune to sustain a very heavy loss. Colonel Hardin, 1st Illinois, and Colonel McKee and Lieutenant Colonel Clay, 2nd Kentucky regiment, fell at this time, while gallantly heading their commands.

This gallant 2nd Kentucky regiment, whose loss in killed

and wounded was most severe, was engaged through the day, in conjunction with the two Illinois regiments, upon the elevated plateau. On the evening of the day before, it had been ordered from its first position, in rear of Washington's battery, to accompany and support Bragg's battery, to the extreme right. Here they remained on their arms during the night, and at the commencement of the action of the 23rd, at daylight, they crossed to the centre, and took position in the battle on the plateau. A most enthusiastic ardour in the regiment was manifested throughout the long-contested conflict.

Loss of the regiment during the day, forty-four killed, fifty-seven wounded, one missing.—total, 102.

No farther attempt was made by the enemy to force our position, and the approach of night gave an opportunity to pay proper attention to the wounded, and also to refresh the soldiers, who had been exhausted by incessant watchfulness and combat. Though the night was extremely cold, the troops were compelled for the most part to bivouack without fires, expecting that morning would renew the conflict. During the night, the wounded were removed to Saltillo, and every preparation made to receive the enemy, should he again attack our position. Seven fresh companies were drawn from the town, and Brigadier General Marshall, who had made a forced march from the Rinconada, with a reinforcement of Kentucky cavalry and four heavy guns, under Captain Prentiss, 1st artillery, was near at hand, when it was discovered that the enemy had abandoned his position during the night.

Our scouts soon ascertained that he had fallen back upon Agua Nueva. The great disparity of numbers, and the exhaustion of our troops rendered it inexpedient and hazardous to attempt a pursuit. A staff officer was sent to General Santa Anna to negotiate an exchange of prisoners, which was satisfactorily completed on the following day. Our own dead were collected and buried, and the Mexican wounded, of which a large number had been left upon the field, were removed to Saltillo, and rendered as comfortable as circumstances would permit.

On the evening of the 26th, a close reconnaissance was made of the enemy's position, which was found to be occupied only by a small body of cavalry, the infantry and artillery having retreated in the direction of San Luis Potosi. On the 27th, our troops resumed their former camp at Agua Nueva, the enemy's rear guard evacuating the place as we approached, leaving a considerable number of wounded. It was my purpose to beat up his quarters at Incarnacion early the next morning, but upon examination, the weak condition of the cavalry horses rendered it unadvisable to attempt so long a march without water. A command was finally dispatched to Incarnacion, on the 1st of March, under Colonel Belknap. Some two hundred wounded, and about sixty Mexican soldiers were found there, the army having passed on in the direction of Matahuala, with greatly reduced numbers, and suffering much from hunger. The dead and dying were strewed upon the road, and crowded the buildings of the *hacienda*.

The American force engaged in the action of Buena Vista is shown, by the accompanying field report, to have been three hundred and thirty-four officers, and four thousand four hundred and twenty-five men, exclusive of the small command left near and in Saltillo. Of this number, two squadrons of cavalry, and three batteries of light artillery, making not more than four hundred and fifty-three men, composed the only force of regular troops.[10]

The strength of the Mexican army is stated by General Santa Anna, in his summons, to be twenty thousand; and that estimate is confirmed by all the information since obtained. Our loss is two hundred and sixty-seven killed, four hundred and fifty-six wounded, and twenty-three missing.

---

10. Volunteers: officers and men in battle of Buena Vista, 4,420; loss in killed, 263; wounded, 371; missing, twenty-one. Regulars: number of officers and men, 493; loss in killed, seven; wounded, fifty-five; missing, three.

Of the numerous wounded, many did not require removal to the hospital, and it is hoped that a comparatively small number will be permanently disabled. The Mexican loss in killed and wounded may be fairly estimated at one thousand five hundred, and will probably reach two thousand. At least five hundred of their killed were left upon the field of battle. We have no means of ascertaining the number of deserters and dispersed men from their ranks, but it is known to be very great.

Our loss has been especially severe in officers, twenty-eight having been killed upon the field. We have to lament the death of Captain George Lincoln, assistant adjutant-general, serving on the staff of General Wool—a young officer of high bearing and approved gallantry, who fell early in the action. No loss falls more heavily upon the army in the field than that of Colonels Hardin and McKee, and Lieutenant Colonel Clay. Possessing in a remarkable degree the confidence of their commands, and the last two having enjoyed the advantage of a military education, I had looked particularly to them for support in case we met the enemy. I need not say that their zeal in engaging the enemy, and the cool and steadfast courage with which they maintained their positions during the day, fully realized my hopes, and caused me to feel yet more sensibly their untimely loss.

I perform a grateful duty in bringing to the notice of the government the general good conduct of the troops. Exposed for successive nights, without fires, to the severity of the weather, they were ever prompt and cheerful in the discharge of every duty, and finally displayed conspicuous steadiness and gallantry in repulsing, at great odds, a disciplined foe. While the brilliant success achieved by their arms releases me from the painful necessity of specifying many cases of bad conduct before the enemy, I feel an increased obligation to mention particular corps and officers, whose skill, coolness and gallantry, in trying situations and under a continued and heavy fire, seem to merit particular notice.

To Brigadier General Wool my obligations are especially due. The high state of discipline and instruction of several of the volunteer regiments was attained under his command; and to his vigilance and arduous services before the action, and his gallantry and activity on the field, a large share of our success may justly be attributed.—During most of the engagement, he was in immediate command of the troops thrown back on our left flank. I beg leave to recommend him to the favourable notice of the government. Brigadier General Lane (slightly wounded) was active and zealous throughout the day, and displayed great coolness and gallantry before the enemy.

The services of the Light Artillery, always conspicuous, were more than usually distinguished. Moving rapidly over the roughest ground, it was always in action at the right place, and the right time; and its well-directed fire dealt destruction in the masses of the enemy. While I recommend to particular favour, the gallant conduct and valuable services of Major Munroe, chief of artillery, and Captains Washington, 4th Artillery, and Sherman and Bragg, 3rd Artillery, commanding batteries, I deem it no more than just, to mention all the subordinate officers.

They were nearly all detached at different times, and in every situation exhibited conspicuous skill and gallantry. Captain O'Brien, Lieutenants Brent, Whiting, and Couch, 4th Artillery, and Bryan, Topographical Engineers (slightly wounded), were attached to Captain Washington's battery. Lieutenants Thomas, Reynolds, and French, 3rd Artillery (severely wounded), to that of Captain Sherman; and Captain Shover, and Lieutenant Kilburn, 3rd Artillery, to that of Captain Bragg.—Captain Shover, in conjunction with Lieutenant Donaldson, rendered gallant and important service in repulsing the cavalry of General Miñon.

"The regular cavalry, under Lieutenant Colonel May, with

which was associated Captain Pike's squadron of Arkansas Horse, rendered useful service in holding the enemy in check, and in covering the batteries, at several points. Captain Steen, 1st Dragoons, was severely wounded early in the day, while gallantly endeavouring, with my authority, to rally the troops which were falling in the rear.

Captain O'Brien, a gallant officer, lost three cannon during the day; and the possession of these enabled Santa Anna, in his flowing dispatch, to conceal his terrible defeat, by claiming a victory. The first one was lost in the attack on the plateau by General Pacheco. from the fact that the horses and cannoneers were all killed or disabled, so that it could not be brought off. The other two were lost in the main and last attack on the centre, by the whole disposable Mexican force under General Perez. Captain O'Brien sacrificed these guns by intention; keeping the enemy in check by them, until the other artillery and infantry arrived, and the regiments of infantry concentrated, pouring a deadly fire on the massive column.

The situation of the artillery is not placed in the picture, for, save the battery, they were continually back and forth, over the whole ground, during the day. The battery of Captain Bragg discharged about two hundred and fifty rounds of round shot, grape and canister; the other batteries nearly the same. The infantry regiments discharged from seventy to ninety rounds of cartridges per man, during the same time.

> The Mississippi Riflemen, under Colonel Davis, were highly conspicuous for their gallantry and steadiness, and sustained, throughout the engagement, the reputation of veteran troops. Brought into action against an immensely superior force, they maintained themselves for a long time, unsupported, and with heavy loss, and held an important part of the field until reinforced. Colonel Davis, though severely wounded, remained in his saddle until the close of the action.—His distinguished coolness and gallantry at the head of his regiment on this day entitle him to

the particular notice of the government. The 3rd Indiana regiment, under Colonel Lane, and a fragment of the 2nd, under Colonel Bowles, were associated with the Mississippi regiment during a greater portion of the day, and acquitted themselves creditably in repulsing the attempts of the enemy to take that portion of our line. The Kentucky cavalry, under Colonel Marshall, rendered good service dismounted, acting as light troops on our left, and afterwards, with a portion of the Arkansas regiment in meeting and dispersing the column of cavalry at Buena Vista.

The 1st and 2nd Illinois and the 2nd Kentucky regiments served immediately under my eye, and I bear a willing testimony to their excellent conduct throughout the day. The spirit and gallantry with which the 1st Illinois and 2nd Kentucky engaged the enemy in the morning restored confidence to that part of the field, while the list of casualties will show how much these three regiments suffered in sustaining the heavy charge of the enemy in the afternoon.—Captain Conner's company of Texas volunteers, attached to the 2nd Illinois regiment, fought bravely, its captain being wounded and two subalterns killed.[11] Colonel Bissell, the only surviving colonel of these regiments, merits notice for his coolness and bravery on this occasion. After the fall of the field officers of the 1st Illinois and 2nd Kentucky regiments, the command of the former devolved on Lieutenant Colonel Weatherford, and that of the latter on Major Fry.

This 3rd Indiana was, on the morning of the 23rd, stationed not far in rear of Washington's battery, save two companies of rifles, who, in command of Major Gorman fought on the mountain under Colonel Marshall. Major Gorman also had two rifle companies, of the 2nd Indiana. This 3rd regiment, under Colonel Lane, fought, during the day, principally on the left, with the

---

11. The loss of this gallant company of Texans was very severe, in proportion to their numbers, being fourteen killed, two wounded, and seven missing. Well did the little body maintain the reputation of their state throughout the day.

other regiments here engaged, against Pacheco's strong column, and at the last heavy charge, together with the Mississippians and the rallied part of the 2nd Indiana, moved rapidly to the plateau, and by their destructive fire hastened the enemy's retreat.

The conduct of this regiment was of the most spirited character. The repulse of the heavy column of lancers in the morning, by these and the Mississippians, was among the most brilliant exploits of this day of continued astonishing achievements of valour and constancy. Although much exposed for the whole day, the loss of the regiment was not very severe; being nine killed, and fifty-six wounded.

The coolness and intrepidity of this 1st Illinois, under their heroic colonel, could not be excelled. During the night of the 22nd, six companies of it, under Colonel Hardin, occupied the hill, C, and two companies, under Lieutenant Colonel Weatherford, were stationed to the right, to protect Washington's battery there. Two other companies had been detached, under Major Warren, to hold, with other troops, the possession of the city of Saltillo.

When Colonel Hardin led his command, upon the plateau, to take a part in the tremendous action there going on, he commenced his gallant operations by a spirited charge of bayonets upon a heavy body of the enemy, in which killing and wounding great numbers of them he drove them in confusion back over a deep ravine they had crossed. Though this regiment, like the 2nd Illinois and 2nd Kentucky, with which it fought during the day, was exposed continually to a most terrible fire, and many of its men were wounded, yet none were killed until the last concentrated effort of the enemy; but in this, as in the subsequent pursuit, they suffered much.

They captured the colours of the Mexican corps from the city of San Luis Potosi. Loss of the regiment during the day, thirty killed and twenty-five wounded.

Regimental commanders, and others who have rendered reports, speak in general terms of the good conduct of their officers and men, and have specified many names;

but the limits of this report forbid a recapitulation of them here. I may, however, mention Lieutenants Rucker and Campbell of the dragoons, and Captain Pike, of the Arkansas cavalry, upon whom the command devolved after the fall of Colonel Yell; Major Bradford, Captain Sharpe, (severely wounded), and Adjutant Griffith, Mississippi regiment; Lieutenant Robinson, *aid-de-camp* to General Lane; Lieutenant Col Weatherford, 1st Illinois regiment; Lieutenant Colonel Morrison, Major Trail, and Adjutant Whiteside (severely wounded) 2nd Illinois regiment, and Major Fry, of the 2nd Kentucky regiment, as being favourably noticed for gallantry and good conduct. Major McCulloch, quartermaster in the volunteer service, rendered important services before the engagement, in the command of a spy company, and, during the affair, was associated with the regular cavalry.—To Major Warren, 1st Illinois Volunteers, I feel much indebted, for his firm and judicious course while exercising command in the city of Saltillo.

The medical staff, under the able direction of Assistant-Surgeon Hitchcock, were assiduous in attention to the wounded upon the field, and in their careful removal to the rear. Both in these respects, and in the subsequent organization and service of the hospitals, the administration of this department was everything that could be desired.

"Brigadier General Wool speaks in high terms of the officers of his staff, and I take pleasure in mentioning them here, having witnessed their activity and zeal upon the field. Lieutenant and *Aid-de-camp* McDowell, Colonel Churchill, inspector general, Captain Chapman, assistant quartermaster, Lieutenant Sitgreaves, Topographical Engineers, and Captains Howard and Davis, volunteer service, are conspicuously noticed for their gallantry and good conduct. Messrs. March, Addicks, Potts, Harrison, Burgess and Dusenberg, attached in various capacities to General Wool's headquarters, are likewise mentioned for their intelligent alacrity in conveying orders to all parts of the field.

In conclusion, I beg leave to speak of my own staff, to whose exertions in rallying troops and communicating orders I feel greatly indebted. Major Bliss, assistant adjutant-general, Captain J. H. Eaton and Lieutenant Garnett, *aids-de-camp,* served near my person, and were prompt and zealous in the discharge of every duty. Major Munroe, besides rendering valuable service as chief of artillery, was active and instrumental, as were also Colonels Churchill and Belknap, inspectors general, in rallying troops and disposing them for the defence of the train and baggage. Colonel Whiting, quarter-master-general, and Captain Eaton, chief of the subsistence department, were engaged with the duties of their departments, and also served in my immediate staff on the field.

Captain Sibley, as assistant quartermaster, was necessarily left with the headquarter camp near town, where his services were highly useful. Major Mansfield and Lieutenant Benham, engineers, and Captain Linnard and Lieutenants Pope and Franklin, topographical engineers, were employed before and during the engagement in making reconnaissances, and on the field were very active in bringing information and in conveying my orders to distant points. Lieutenant Kingsbury, in addition to his proper duties as ordnance officer, Captain Chilton, assistant quartermaster, and Majors Dix and Coffee, served also as extra *aids-de-camp,* and were actively employed in the transmission of orders. Mr. Thomas L. Crittenden, of Kentucky, though not in service, volunteered as my *aid-de-camp* on this occasion, and served with credit in that capacity.

Major Craig, chief of ordnance, and Surgeon Craig, medical director, had been detached on duty from headquarters, and did not reach the ground until the morning of the 24th too late to participate in the action, but in time to render useful services in their respective departments of the staff.

I respectfully enclose returns of the troops engaged, and of casualties incident to the battle.

I am, sir, very respectfully, your obedient servant
"Z. Taylor, Major General U. S. A. Commanding,
To the Adjutant General of the army,
Washington, D. C."

Summons of Santa Anna to General Taylor.

You are surrounded by twenty thousand men, and cannot, in any human probability, avoid suffering a rout, and being cut to pieces, with your troops; but as you deserve consideration and particular esteem, I wish to save you from a catastrophe, and for that purpose give you this notice, in order that you may surrender at discretion, under the assurance that you will be treated with the consideration belonging to the Mexican character; to which end you will be granted an hour's time to make up your mind, to commence from the moment when my flag of truce arrives in your camp. With this view, I assure you of my particular consideration.

God and Liberty. Antonio Lopez de Santa Anna
Camp at Encantada, February 22nd, 1847.
To General Z. Taylor, commanding the forces
of the United States.

Headquarters, Army of Occupation,
Near Buena Vista, February 22, 1847.

Sir: In reply to your note of this date, summoning me to surrender my force at discretion, I beg leave to say that I decline acceding to your request.

With high respect, I am, sir,
Your obedient servant,
Z. Taylor, Major General U. S. army com'g.
Señor General D. Antonio Lopez de Santa Anna,
Commander-in-chief, La Encantada.

And so ended the battle of Buena Vista, in which the volunteer troops had shown themselves equal to veterans;—and they established the truth, that it is not discipline alone that makes the soldier, but that the heroism of the heart, the pride of character, the self-reliance, and the love of country which the volunteers pre-eminently possessed, are most valuable qualifications on the battle-field.—The loss of these volunteer regiments is given in notes below, from the official reports.

Mississippi Regiment—Killed and Wounded.

Colonel Jefferson Davis was wounded through the foot, just below the ankle, while on horseback, charging upon the enemy.

Wilkinson County Volunteers.

Killed—B, G. Pwiberville, Thomas H. Pitley, Wm. H. Wilkinson, Seaborne Jones.

Wounded—Lieutenant C. Posey, very slightly; Solomon Nowman, James M. Miller, G. H. Jones, W. Spurlock, W. A. Lawrence, J. W. Donnelly, slightly.

Tazoo Volunteers.

Killed—Sergeant W. Ingram, C. C. Sullivan.

Wounded—Captain Sharp, Henry Clark, W. H. Stubblefield, severely; Sergeant D. Hollingsworth, Steph. Stubblefield, R. G. Shocks, slightly; George Brooks, mortally.

Raymond Fencibles.

Killed—Lieutenant F. McNulty, J. S. Bond, J. N. Graves, W. Seay, R. E. Parr, J. M. Alexander, R. Feltz, G. A. Cooper.

Wounded—R. S. Edwards, severely; J. Hammond, P. Russett, P. Sinclair, W. G. Harrison, H. A. Neely, slightly.

State Fencibles.

Killed—Sergeants Wm. Philips and James Langford, Corporals Frank Robinson and Joseph Revell, Robert Jayce, William Sellers.

Wounded—Richard Clauds, A. Puckett, severely; John Kennedy, Isham C. Lord, Robert Fox, James Waugh, slightly.

Marshall Guards.

Killed—Sergeant G. Anderson, Henry Trotter, John S. Branch,

A. Collingsworth, John Peace.

Wounded—Sergeant P. Martin, John Hedthpeth, severely; T. O. McClanahan, T. D. Randolph, John Bass, slightly.

Vicksburg Southerners.

Killed—Wm. Couch, Richard Eggleston, James Johnson, John Preston.

Wounded—Sergeant Howard Morris, James W. Conn, severely; Sergeant Wm. A. Scott, Corporal J. McLaughlin, Samuel C. Suit, J. N. Collier, John Barnes, L. H. Stevens.

Vicksburg Volunteers.

Killed—Lieutenant R. G. Mooned, Fletcher Harrison, P. Raridon, Jacob Block.

Wounded—Thomas White, dangerously; Wm. Winans, S. Edwards, Henry Lowell, severely; Dr. S. D. Carson, A. Henman, slightly.

Lafayette Company.

Killed—Sergeant B. Hagan, Corporals James Blakeley and M. Butler, Stephen Jones, Enos Garrett, P. Doniphan.

Wounded—James Bigley, arm lost; J. G. Simpson, Wm. Courtney, James W. Morriss, severely; Lieutenant J. P. Stepford, J. F. Malone, slightly.

The Tombigbee and Carroll Companies were left in charge of the camp.

Recapitulation.	Killed	Wounded
Wilkinson county volunteers	5	7
Yazoo county volunteers	2	7
Raymond Fencibles	8	6
State Fencibles	6	6
Marshall Guards	6	5
Vicksburg Southerners	4	8
Vicksburg Volunteers	5	6
Lafayette Company	6	6
Total	42	51

Kentuckians Killed and Wounded.

Kentucky Cavalry—Killed.

Adjutant—E. M. Vaughan.

Lillard's company—Sergeant D. J. Lillard; privates Lewis Sander and A. J. Martin.

Price's company—Privates J. D. Miller, B. Warren.

Milam's company—Privates J. Lesion, John Sander, John Ellingwood.

Shawhan's company—Corporal J. A. Jones; Privates D. P. Rogers, W. McClintock, J Pomeroy.

Beard's company—Privates A. G. Morgan, C. Jones, Wm. Twaits, N. Ramsey, H. Carty and W. W. Bates, Corporal.

Pennington's company—Privates H. Danforth. J. G. Martin, E. Houston, J. M. Rowlin, John Ross, E. F. Lilley.

Clay's company—Private Thomas Weyest.

Heady's company—Private C. B. Thompson.

Marshall's company—Private C. B. Demit

Commissioned officer, one; non-commissioned officers, three; privates, twenty-five—total twenty-nine.

Wounded.

Captain—John Shawhan.

Shawhan's company—Privates Wm. Snodgrass, J. S. Byram, W. C. Parker, J. M. Vanbook, George H. Wilson, James Warford, C. H. Fowler.

Heady's company—2nd Lieutenant J. H. Merrifield, Sergeant S. Marratin.

Clay's company—3rd Lieutenant J. M. Brown, Corporal James Scooley.

Price's company—2nd Lieutenant Thomas Conn, Privates John H. Cleverlan, Samuel Evan, Joseph Murphy and Will Herndon.

Lillard's company—Privates John Walker, B. Spencer, E. W. Ruson, and Thos. Scandelt.

Milam's company—John Reddish. B. F. Price, J. K. Goodloe.

Pennington's company—Privates J. S. Jackson, Thomas Brown, L. Help.

Marshall's company—Private H. E. Brady.

Beard's company—Privates Charles Sheppard. J. Sheppard, M. B. Callahan,—Lerasay.

Commissioned officers, four; non commissioned officers, two; privates twenty-six.—total, thirty-two.

Second Kentucky Infantry.—Killed.

Colonel Wm. R. McKee, Lieutenant Col Henry Clay, Jr.

Company A,—Mosse's—Privates Whitfield Smith, A B. Crondowens.

Company B,—Chambers—4th Sergeant Henry Wolf; Privates Major Updike, Wm. Blackwell, L. B. Bartlett

Company C,—Thompson's—1st Sergeant S. M. Williams. Privates Robert M. Baker, W Booth, Wm. Burks, John Moffit.

Company D,—Fry's—4th Corporal Peter Trough. Privates Joseph Walden, Harvey Jones. Wm. Harman.

Company E,—Cutters—1st Corporal J. Q. Carlan; Drummer, Martin Raudebaugh. Privates Hiram Frazer, John H. Harkins, Richard McCurdy, Hercules Snow.

Company F,—Willis's—Captain W. T. Willis. Private Harry Trotter.

Company G,—Daugherty's—Privates John A. Gregory, Joseph R. Ballard, Willis Vest, Jesse J. Waller.

Company H—Joyner's—2nd Sergeant Joseph King, 3rd Sergeant John M. Dunlop. Privates Wm. Rhann, John Williams.

Company I—Turpin's—1st Sergeant Henry Edwards. Privates John J. Torron, Abram Goodpaster.

Company K—McBrey's—Privates Jas. Layton, Wm. Brand, James Johnson, David Davis Arthur Thacker, John W. Watson. Wm. P. Reynolds

Illinoisans Killed and Wounded.

Second Kentucky Infantry.—Wounded.

Company A—2nd Lieutenant E. L. Barber, slightly; Sergeant John Minton, do. Privates Elza Morris, Samuel Wallace, Robert Winlock and James Barnett, all slightly.

Company B—1st Corporal Sandford Mayhall, mortally; Private Benjamin O. Branham, severely; James Williams, W. S. Bartlett and Ameal Brea, slightly.

Company C—Adjutant 2nd Lieutenant Wm. T. Withers, severely; 3rd Corporal C. C. Sneadlay, slightly; 3rd Sergeant John Wheatley do.; Privates Edward Benton, James Cahill, John Crawford and Marion Davidson, slightly; Woodson Hendron, mortally; W. D. Purcell, slightly.

Company D—2nd Corporal J. Craig, slightly; Privates H. Burdin, mortally; P. Humbleton, Allen S. Montgomery and Henry Vanfleet, severely.

Company E—4th Corporal John Jennison, Privates Thomas Welch and John S. Vaudiver, severely; Privates Jasper Honk, Wm. Park, David Walker and Isaac Yelton, slightly.

Company F—Privates John Hunter, severely; Thomas J. Bruner, slightly.

Company G—Assistant Adjutant 2nd Lieutenant Thomas W. Napier and Privates Wm. Stinger and Thos. Hughes, severely; M. A. Devanport, slightly.

Company H—Sergeant J. Ward, mortally; Corporal H. Craig, slightly; Privates F. Oak, mortally; F. Fox, Wm. Dalley, R. Holden, J. Willington and G. Simmons, slightly.

Company I—Privates J. Redmon, E. McCulloh and W. Blowett, slightly; E. S. Cahill, mortally.

Company K—Sergeant W. Lilliard, severely; Privates B. Perry, do.; W. Waford, mortally; G. Leavy W. Howard and J. Montgomery, slightly.

Missing.—Private Jackson Catlett.

Recapitulation.—Staff. two; killed, forty-two; wounded, fifty-seven; missing, one—Total, 102.

Grand Total.

Killed and wounded in cavalry regiment	61
" " 2nd Infantry	102
Kentuckians killed and wounded at Buena Vista	163

First Regiment of Illinois Volunteers.

Killed—Colonel: John J. Hardin. Captain: Jacob W. Zabriskie. First Lieutenant: Bryan R. Houghton. Principal Musician: Austin W. Fay. Privates: Company B, Francis Carter; Company C, Merrit Hudson; company D, Augustus Canaught, John Emerson; company E, Silas Bedell, Henry H. Clark, William Goodwin, James J. Kierman, Randolph R. Martin, Greenbury S. Richardson, Samuel W. Thompson, Charles Walker; company H, Elias C. Mays, Matthew Dandy, William Smith, Thomas J. Gilbert, John White; company K, John B. Bachman, Ingharat Claibstottle, Conrad Burrh, John Gable, Aaron Kiersted, Joseph Shutt, William Vanklehnrker, George Pitson.

Wounded —Privates: company D, Michael Fenton, badly; Jas. T. Edson. slightly, Francis Quinn, slightly; Potter Clemens, slightly. Company C, Corporal: Patrick Mehan, badly. Private: Jas. Robins, slightly. Company D, Sergeant: John C. Barr, badly. Private: Albert Kershaw, badly; company E, Watson R. Richardson, badly; William Stevenson, badly; company F, Job Brown, slightly. Second Lieutenant: Hezekiah Evans, slightly. Company H, Privates: Jackson Evans, slightly; William Roe, slightly; Daniel Penser, badly; company K. Geo. Sinek, slightly; Frederick Rekow. badly. First Lieutenant: John L. McConnell, slightly. Privates: Robins, slightly, serving with company B, 4th artillery, Washington's battery; Brown, slightly, do., Richardson, do.; Ralco, do.; Duff, do.; McLean, do. Phillips, do.

Indianans Killed and Wounded.

Second Regiment Illinois Volunteers.

Killed—Captain: Woodward. Lieutenants: A. B Rountree, Fletcher, Ferguson, Robbins, Steel, T. Kelley, Hartleson, Atherton. Price. Privates: company A, William Kenyon; William L. Smith. Corporal: company C, Hibbs. Privates: Woodling, Patton, Therman, McMichel; company E. Gable; D. O'Conner; company H, Lortz; Couze, Cruesman, Schoolcraft; company I, Lear, Davis, Cook, Bradley, McCrury, G. Clark. Hogan, Squires; company K, Abernathy, W. M. Jones, Bonner, Kinsey, S. C. Marlow. Robert

Marlow, Wilkes, Ragland, W. S. Jones; company G, Jenkins, Hill. Company B, First Sergeant: Faysoux. Privates: Emmerson, Kizer, Durock, Crippen.

Wounded—Captains: Coffee, Baker. Lieutenants: company B, John A. Pickett, Engleman, West. Adjutant: Whiteside. Sergeant: company A, J. W. Farmer. Privates: Auldridge, Barnet, Bird, Cooper, Cheek, Dempsey, Hatchings, J. T. Lee, Mansker, Pate, G. W. Rainy, Robins, White. Sergeant: company C. Brown. Privates: Burke. Bryant, Clarage, Early, Feake, Foills, Fletcher, J. N. Nolland. Montgomery, Ricketts, Maxwell, H. C. Smith, Van Camp, Dwyer, Tidd, Fisher; company E, Hill, Riley, Robinson, Wright; company H, Bordaux, Irridges, Felameir, Funk, Gerhard, Ledergerber, Ranneberg, Talbot, Traenkle, Uppman. First Sergeant: company I, Reid. Privates: Henkler. White, Murmert, Fisher, Kell, Strong, McMurty, Warcheim, Hiltoman; company K, G. T. Montage, Hamilton, Hoge, Kelley, R. Marlow, John Ragland, N. Ramsey; company G, Wiley, McLain; company B, Scott, Goodale. Quartermaster Sergeant: Buckmaster. Sergeant Major: Ketter.

Missing Privates: company H, Mellen, Sinsel; company G, Messinger.

Company Texas Volunteers.

Killed—First Lieutenant: Campbell. Second Lieutenant: Leonard. Corporals: Voort and King. Privates: Clark, Donovan, Donohoe, Forche, Hazes, Godvin, Finney, McLean, Klinge and Lagston.

Wounded—Captain: Conner. Private: Freaekind.

Missing Sergeant: Donop. Corporal: Brand. Privates: Gillerman, Bruno, Miller, Smith and Larlg.

Indiana Volunteers Brigade Staff.

Wounded—Brigadier General Joseph Lane, slightly.

Second Regiment Indiana Volunteers.

Killed—Captains T. B. Kinder and Wm. Walker; 2nd Lieutenant Thomas C. Parr; Sergeants. McHenry Dozier, company E; Privates Francis Bailey, Chas. H. Goff. Warren Robinson, and A. Stephens, company A; John Shoultz, J. Lafferty, A. Massey, D.

McDonald, and J. T. Hardin, company B; M. Lee, W. Richardson, and J. H. Sladen, company D; W. Akin, and J. B. D. Dillon, company E; H. Matthews and J. H. Wilson, company F; H. Draper, R Jenkins, and T. Price, company H; R. Havritt, and H. M. Campbell, company I; J. C. Higginbotham, A. Jenkins, G. Chapman, O. Lansburg, E. Wyatt, T. Smith, and J. Teasley company K.

Wounded—Captains W. L. Sanderson and John Osborn, both slightly; 1st Lieutenants S. W. Cayce, and J. Davis, both slightly; 2nd Lieutenants H. Pennington, D. S. Lewis, J. Moore, and J. A Epperson, all slightly; Sergeants A. H. Potts, company D, J. Carathers and V. Vestal, company F, and P. D. Kelse, company G, all slightly; Corporals E. Macdonald, company B, and D. C. Thomas, company D, both badly; Corporals A. B. Carlton, N. B. Stevens, and J. Bishop, company F, all slightly; Corporals T. Rawlins, company G. slightly, and H. Wilson, company H, severely; Musician A. M. Woods, company D, slightly; Sergeant E. Blalock, company G, badly; Private T. Goen, company F, slightly; H. Mulvany. M. Queen, and J. McMillon. company G, all slightly; W. Adams, W. Bencfiel, R. Colbert, and V. Swain, company H, all severely; J. Ingle, A. Smith, and W. D. Wier, company H, slightly; N. Rumley, company I, badly; G. McKnight and G. Wilhart, company K, slightly; A. C. Farris, company K, badly.

Arkansas Troops Killed and Wounded.

Missing—Privates J. Brown and J. H. Harrison, company B; W. Spalding, company D B.. Hubbard, company I.

Third Regiment Indiana Volunteers.

Killed—Captain J. Taggart; Privates, company A, J. M. Buskirk, W. B. Holland, D. J. Stout; company C, J. Armstrong; company D, W. Hueston; company F, D. Owens and W. C Good; company G, J. Graham.

Wounded—Major W. A. Gorman, slightly; Captains J. M. Sleep and V. Conover, slightly Corporal R. K. Nelson, company A, slightly; Privates, company A, J. S. Levo, severely, W. G. Applegate, J. Y. Davis, J. W. Pullim, and J. Knight, slightly; Corporal J. Gringrich, company B, slightly; Privates, J. Faulkner, dangerously H. Hind, jr., H. C. Hoyt, D. Conroy, and T. H Bowen, slightly;

company C, J. Voight, dangerously, P. Lain, M. Cole, F. Aubke, A. Armstrong, J. Orchard, and G. Miller, slightly; Corporal R. Torrance, company D, slightly; Privates T. Gustin, severely, J. Hinkle, J. Rochat, P. Bright, and A. Merrill, slightly; Corporal E. Weddel, company E, severely; Privates, J. Brown, and M. Mathis, severely, S. Fred, J. G. Arter, and S. Stuart, slightly; company P, J. C. Burton, seriously, O. Dyer, J. Inskeep, D. Hunter, D. Coughenower, H. C. Riker, and Corporal J. S. Wilson, slightly; company G, J. Meek, seriously, E. Mace, J. Patterson, and J. Cain, slightly; company H, R. Benson, and J. Kelley, severely; Sergeant W. Coombes, company I, mortally; Private M. Connway, slightly; Sergeants R. McGarvey, company K, severely, S. P. Turney, slightly; Privates J. Hervey, seriously, M. Gray and Y. Foster, slightly, S. Bradley and S. Lefollet, severely

Arkansas Cavalry.

Killed—Colonel Archibald Yell; Captain Andrew R. Porter; Corporals R. M. Sanders, W. Gomberlin, and D. Stewart; Privates Wm. Phipps, H. Penter, J. H. Higgins, G. W. Martin, J. B. Pelham, J. Ray, W. Robinson, D. Hogan, P. Williams, A. Teague, H. Wynn, and T. C Rowland.

Wounded—1st Lieutenant Thos. A. Reader; Sergeant-Major B. F. Ross; Sergeants J. D. Adams, slightly, G. Y. Latham, Z. D. Bogard, and H. L. Hamilton; Corporal M. L. Poplin; Privates M Kelley, B. F. Nicholson, W. B. Scarcy, Joseph Penter, C. Taylor, L. McGruder, J. F. Allen, M. Graham, D. Logan, A. C. Harris, J. Wilmouth, Franklin W. Brown, O. Jones, slightly, E. McCool, J. Williams, L. B. Beckwith, J. Ray, L. A. Twronski, W. Turner; J Biggerstaff, W. Gibson, R. Arnold, and J. Lowallen, slightly; J. Johnson, and C. Sullivan.

Missing—Privates L. Settle, Jos. Green, George Norwood, and M. Parker.

Regulars—General Staff.

Killed—Captain Geo. Lincoln, Assistant Adjutant General.

Wounded—First Lieutenant Henry W. Denham, Engineers, and Brevet 2nd Lieutenant Francis T. Bryan, Topographical Engineers, slightly.

First Regiment Dragoons.

Wounded —Captain Enoch Steen, severely; privates, company E, Holloway and Anderson, severely, and Sherrod, slightly; company A, Lanning and Sweet, severely, and Waggoner, slightly.

Second Regiment Dragoons.

Wounded—Brevet Lieutenant Colonel C. A. May, severe concussion; Private W. F. Erbe, company E. severely.

Third Regiment Artillery.

Killed—Private Christian F. Walhinger, company C.

Wounded —Sec. Lieutenant Samuel G. French, severely; company C, Corporal Robert Garns, severely, privates Wm. Hudson, severely, Jacob Weyer, slightly; recruit Jesse Gormer, 3rd Infantry; company E, Ord. Sergteant Bowning slightly, Corporals Wolf and Boyle, severely, Tischer, musician, supposed mortally, Livingood, artificer, severely, privates Bel., dangerously, Fisk, Kemp, McCray, Levier, Kollisher, and Gillam, slightly, Smith and Kelsey, severely, Shane, mortally, McDonnell, dangerously.

Missing—Privates Marcus A. Hitchcock, company C, Youngs and Morgan, company E.

Fourth Regiment Artillery.

Killed—Company B; privates Holley, Weekly, Kinks, and Doughty; Green, recruit, 3rd Infantry.

Wounded —First Lieutenant J. P. J. O'Brien, slightly; company B, Sergeant Queen, and Lance Sergeant Pratt, slightly; privates Puffer, mortally, Hannams, Beagle, Berrier, Floyd, Baker, Tharman, Brown, Birch, Butler, and Clark.

Recapitulation.

Volunteers	Killed	Wounded	Missing	Total
1st Mississippi Rifles	21	51	21	93
1st Illinois	30	25		55
2nd Illinois	47	74	3	124
Company Texas	14	2	7	23
Indiana General Staff		1		1

2nd Indiana	32	36	4	72
3rd Indiana	9	56		65
2nd Kentucky Foot	44	57	1	102
Kentucky Cavalry	29	32		61
Arkansas Cavalry	17	32	4	53
Regulars—General Staffs		1	2	3
1st Dragoons			7	7
2nd Dragoons			2	2
3rd Artillery	1	21	3	5
4th Artillery	5	15		20

Total Volunteers, killed, wounded, and missing   649
Total Regulars, killed, wounded, and missing   57
    Grand Total of killed, wounded, and missing   706

Santa Anna, satisfied that he could not conquer General Taylor, called a council of war at Agua Nueva, to which he had retired after the battle, and it was by that unanimously determined to abandon the plan of operations which had been commenced, and retreat to the south and towards San Luis Potosi; which was immediately done, not, however, until an exchange of prisoners had been effected.

Leaving that general, with his shattered and disorganized army, marching back, let us for a moment turn to the operations of General Urrea, who, as before stated, had been sent up on the east side of the mountains, to attack the American forces near the valley of the Rio Grande, and to act in the anticipated pursuit of the routed Americans of General Taylor's army.

General Urrea reached the main road from Monterey to Camargo, near Marin, about the 22nd instant, and joining forces with the notorious Canales, attacked a wagontrain of one hundred and ten wagons, loaded with provisions, &c., for the army; and some three hundred pack mules, belonging to merchants. The detachment, of about thirty Kentuckians, under Lieutenant Barbour, who guarded this train, were surrounded by numbers and taken prisoners; the train was captured, fifty of the teamsters massacred, and the wagons burnt; the remainder of the wagoners escaping to the mountains.

On the 23rd, Urrea attacked Lieutenant Colonel Irvin's command of 2nd Ohioans, at Marin, but retired from before the town on the morning of the 25th on the approach of Major Shepherd, from Monterey, with three companies of the First Kentucky regiment, under Captains Triplett, Bullen, and Kearn, two companies of the First Ohio regiment, under Captains Bradley and Vandever, and a detachment of Kentucky Cavalry, under Lieutenant Patterson, with two pieces of artillery, who came to the relief of Colonel Irvin, and the reinforced detachment returned towards Monterey.

On the 26th, Urrea, attacked Colonel Morgan, of the Second Ohio regiment, who, with two hundred men, was also going on to Monterey, where, all the troops that could be spared from the various garrisons in the valley of the Rio Grande were ordered to concentrate.—This attack was made with vigour, and kept up with spirit. Lieutenant Stewart gallantly dashed forward, through the enemy, and overtook Lieutenant Colonel Irvin, who immediately turned back with two companies,—Captain Bradley, First Ohio, and Captain Kearn, First Kentucky,—and the action terminated in the repulse of Urrea, with a loss of about sixty. American loss, four killed, and a few wounded. Among the killed was Captain B. F. Graham.

After this, on Sunday, March 7th, General Urrea with one thousand six hundred men attacked, near Ceralvo, the detachment of Major Giddings, first Ohio, who, with a force consisting of three companies first Ohio, under captains Bradley, Armstrong and Kenneally, two companies of First Kentucky regiment, under captains Howe and Fuller, and a body of Arkansas Cavalry, under Lieutenant Thompson, with two pieces artillery, under Lieutenant McCarter,—in all two hundred and sixty men,—was escorting a train of one hundred and fifty wagons, and also the bearers of General Taylor's dispatches, from Monterey to Camargo.—The attack was made with vigour by a much superior force, and was continued for two or three hours before Urrea was repulsed.—From the great length of the train, the enemy were enabled to entirely surround the rear-guard, and summon them to surrender; but this summons was disregarded.—Urrea was repulsed, with a loss of forty-five killed and wounded. Loss of the detachment, seventeen killed, and forty wagons taken.— (The mules becoming alarmed at the firing, were unmanageable, and rushed in among the Mexican forces on either hand; hence their loss).—Major Giddings, the morning after this gallant action, entered Ceralvo,—and, for the want of ammunition, his ammunition wagon having been one of those that the frightened mules carried among the Mexicans, and which had been set on fire by them, was compelled to wait until the 12th, when Colonel Curtis, at the head of near twelve hundred men, the 3rd Ohio regiment, and a part of the new Virginia regiment, came up from Camargo, by whom he was supplied, and resumed his march.

Colonel Curtis continued on towards Monterey; came in sight of the enemy; halted, and prepared for battle. But at this time Old Zach himself was coming down the road from Monterey, with the dragoons, Kentucky Cavalry and Bragg's battery. Urrea found himself in an unpleasant situation, and immediately retreated to the southward by the route he had come.

If Colonel Curtis had not halted, he would have forced Urrea to have fought either with him or with General Taylor; but of that he was not aware at the time, and knowing Urrea's force to be some three thousand men, he wished to be fully prepared. With Urrea's retreat, the valley of the Rio Grande was again free from the enemy.

Santa Anna continued his retreat to San Luis, thence to the city of Mexico, having induced the population to believe that he had gained a great victory over General Taylor. He found the principal parties in Mexico engaged in another revolution.— He stopped this; united all; roused their enthusiasm, and that of his army, and great rejoicings took place throughout all Mexico on account of his victory.

Having now given an account of all the fighting that had taken place in the winter, we will close the chapter and again return to Tampico, where, at the end of chapter 2 we left the troops of General Scott embarking for Vera Cruz; and with the embarkation of our regiment, we will commence chapter 4, ending this only with the remark, that propositions of peace, in the meantime, had again been made by the United States' Government, through Señor Atocha, and rejected by the Mexican. Señor Atocha had been conveyed to Vera Cruz, in the revenue cutter *Forward*; had landed under cover of a flag of truce, on February 9th he proceeded directly to the city of Mexico with his dispatches; arrived there on the 13th, and laid them before the Mexican Government.—He was, on the next day, ordered to leave the city, and, near Jalapa, to await a reply; which, in a few days, was sent to him, being a decided negative.—He left Vera Cruz on the 26th, and embarking again on the *Forward*, hastened back to Washington.

List of the troops of Santa Anna's army, as they left San Luis Potosi, to attack General Taylor, as given in the Mexican journals of the day:

January 26, 1347 the Sappers and Artillerists, with 19 guns of heavy calibre	630
January 29 1st, 3rd, 4th. 5th. 10th and 11th regiments of the line, and 1st and 2nd light troops	6,240
January 31 4th light troops, mixed, of Santa Anna. 1st Active of Celaya, do. of Guadalajara, do. of Lagos, do. of Queretaro, do. of Mexico	3,200
Total, departed from San Luis	10,090
Troops which General Parrodi conducted from Tula, with three pieces of heavy calibre, with their munitions	1,000
Cavalry on the march	6,000
Artillery "	250
Division under General Mejia	4,000
Grand total of troops sent against General Taylor	21,340

CHAPTER 4

Amusements at Sea

March 8th. Nothing of interest had occurred during the few days that we have dropped the regular accounts of the journal. Some of the regulars, induced by the promises of the Mexicans, had deserted, and also one of our men had done the same. This scamp's name was Hill.—He joined the regiment at Matamoras, and was a member of Captain Goodner's company. He has been mentioned before, in this work, as an interpreter. He was thought by many to be the same Hill who is so highly spoken of by Waddy Thompson as favoured by Santa Anna.[1] Captain Newman's company, of our regiment, had made a scout into the interior, beyond Altamira, after these deserters, and overtaken four of them, belonging to the artillery, bringing them back to town, where they were confined for trial.

The force designated to remain as the garrison of Tampico, was composed of part of the Louisiana regiment, stationed at the fortifications at the upper part of town, near the military hospi-

---

1. There was something mysterious about this young man from the first. He was always anxious to obtain information with respect to the troops, and at every town he made an immediate acquaintance with the *alcaldes*, which his intimate knowledge of the Spanish language enabled him to do. In his unguarded moments he had communicated, from time to time, the facts that he had for many years resided in Mexico; that a wealthy *Don* had adopted him for a son that he had resided at the cities of Mexico, Puebla, and San Luis Potosi; and his general conduct left no doubt, after he had deserted, that he had been with us only as a spy. He wore off an officer's coat, thus making it appear to his former friends, the Mexicans, that he had held an office with us; and we afterwards heard that Santa Anna, on his return, gave him a captaincy.

tal, and the Baltimore battalion, which was at the lower part, at the canal bridge, and three companies of regular artillery, near the *plaza*. The troops of the different brigades had been leaving as fast as vessels arrived, and now it was our turn, though as the horse transports had not come, we were to go as foot soldiers.

March 9th. This was a busy day with our regiment. In the morning, early, the bugles called each company into line; the rolls were run over, and eight men were selected from each company to remain with, take care of, and accompany the horses when they should be embarked;—the remainder were ordered to put up their saddles, bridles, horse-blankets, sabres and holster pistols securely, and mark them, to be placed in boxes and sent with the horses.—Each man of the regiment took with him his rifle, or carbine, and cartridge-box, only.

Breakfast was soon over, and now came much preparation; much inquiry for the men detailed to remain; each requesting and imploring these to take good care of their horses left behind; their long-tried steeds, who, for thousands of miles, had safely borne them thus far in the campaign.

At ten, a. m., the companies were formed, the tents were struck, and with our little baggage, we took our march into town. Arriving there, we remained in the square by the market a few moments only, and then marched down to the wharf and entered the surf boats prepared for embarking and disembarking the troops;—each boat would carry sixty men.[2] These were then rowed off to the steamboats, that lay ready to receive us. The first battalion was soon on board, crowded and jammed together. The one that company G was on was a propeller, and moved along slowly, though with much puffing and noise.—Both boats got up steam, and started down the river together.

We soon came opposite to our camp; the crowd of horses was there, though but few tents were left only those for the men remaining. These collected together in groups on the shore,

---

2. These were sent from the United States, especially to embark and disembark the hoops; were of peculiar construction, and very large. For view of one, see frontispiece, "canal in castle."

and raised a shout as we passed, which we returned;—every man looked for his own horse on the bank, and gazed at him, as on we passed for the bar.—The other boat passed us on the river, and got out much before us; and while she was making her way to the distant ships, that lay far out, almost on the very horizon, we only had come near the bar, and began to feel the waves a little as they rocked us. In a short time we were over it, and our little steamer, puffing and blowing, rolled and pitched in the breakers, and many of the men, who were crowded so thickly upon her decks, became dizzy with the motion, and their faces were pale with sea-sickness, while they held on to the rigging.—Our vessel made more noise than ever, but went so slow, that how she had ever reached the coast of Mexico, became a wonder to us.

The other steamer had all the men she carried, with their baggage, on the ship before we came near her, and had commenced the return; but in half an hour we came up also, near to her as she lay at anchor. She was the *Essex*, of Boston, a noble vessel, of eight hundred tons burden. She was high above the water;—her lofty masts and lengthy spars were in perfect trim and order; her numerous ropes were drawn in straight lines. She had been freshly painted without, and her colour was bright. She rolled gently at her heavy anchors, in the swell that came in from the Gulf.

Our little steamer came along side of her, and made fast, and the men commenced climbing up her sides.—The baggage and arms were passed up, and in half an hour everything was on board, and the crowd of men were looking strangely at every object around them, not knowing which way to move.

The sailors of the ship were engaged in getting the baggage and arms down on the lower deck, and in showing our men their berths, all arranged for them; but many were so confused with the strange scene around them, the long rolling of the ship, and the busy movements of the seamen, that they found all their baggage removed and piled up below, before they were aware of it.

The ammunition was placed in the magazine, the deck cleared up, and everything put in order. There were four companies of us now on this ship, with their officers, the remaining company of the first battalion, Caswell's, having gone before. The second battalion went on board the ship *Desdemona*, lying about a mile from the *Essex*. Four other ships lay at anchor within a mile around, having on board the 4th and most of the 3rd Illinois regiments.

March 9th. Last night, the ship rolled heavily on the waves; and it was difficult for our men, crowded together, to pass one another, up and down the hatchway ladders, or to walk the unsteady foundation, either on the upper or lower deck. They turned pale and sick, especially below, where their heads were rendered giddy, by seeing everything, apparently, move around them. Blankets were thickly spread on the upper deck, each with an occupant, vomiting, and thinking he was about to die.—

When offered breakfast, they refused it, with a shake of the head, indicating extreme disgust. They wished themselves on land; and would, when up, lean on the bulwarks, and gaze most wishfully on the low coast they had left, and which was visible in the distance.—The other ships, in the offing, were rolling and pitching in the same way; and on looking at them with a spy-glass, we saw many on their crowded decks, leaning over the bulwarks, and "casting up their accounts." Sea-sickness is most unpleasant, and many think they will surely die from it.—One man on board was declaring, last night, that he could not possibly live till morning; but still he is alive, and a little better. It never killed anyone yet; but, on the contrary, is said to be highly beneficial.

The steamboats have been bringing off, this forenoon, the second battalion of our regiment, to the ship *Desdemona*, mentioned yesterday. Colonel Thomas and Major Waterhouse are with them; while Lieutenant Colonel Allison is in command of us; though, at the present time he cannot command himself, being laid up in his state-room with seasickness.

The day was calm until noon, when a little breeze from the

south-east sprang up; and to our gratification, the captain of the ship gave the order to heave up the anchor.—"Man the windlass!" shouted the first officer of the ship, a burly, weather-beaten, humorous-looking, old sea-fowl, with a voice like a speaking-trumpet. "Man the windlass!" shouted the second officer, a younger tar, as he heard the order.—"Aye, aye, sir," "aye, aye, sir," answered the sea-men, as they seized their handspikes, and jumped to it; and it was soon slowly revolving, bringing in the heavy chain cable, the clanking of which on the deck was pleasant to us all, for it told us that we were about to proceed to sea.

Soon the ponderous anchor was broken from its hold on the bottom; then came the orders, "Hoist the jib!" "loose the topsails!" and while some of the seamen did the first, others ran nimbly up the shrouds, and soon sail after sail, above and below, were hoisted, sheeted out, and exposed their wide surface to the breeze, which filled them; and the large ship, under her press of canvass, leaned over to the wind, and gathered way through the billows, which broke and parted at her bows.

The anchor was now brought up to its place, and we stood out to sea.—The decks were cleared up; the loose ropes, that had been used in "getting her under weigh" (as the sailor's term is, for raising the anchor, spreading the sails, and putting the ship in motion to the breeze), were coiled up. The seamen took their stations, and all was at once reduced to the sea regulations, of order, form, and discipline.

Two of the other ships got under weigh, at the same time. The ship *Sharon* was a little later than ourselves, in getting her anchor up; and as we passed her, the troops, with which she was crowded, gave us three cheers, to which we heartily responded.

In an hour we had lost sight of the land, and the scene was but the blue of the sky above, and the darker blue of the water below and around.—The waves now were larger, and the ship rolled more; and many that had hitherto been well, became sea-sick, and came up on deck, unable, from their giddiness, to remain below. Those who were sick at the anchorage, now became worse; and those who were well, sought their berths, and laid down to sleep.

March 10th. Early this morning, all crowded upon deck, each one wishing to see the sun rise from his bed of distant waves, and to breathe the fine air of the sea, after having been crowded in the confined atmosphere below, only relieved by the draft of freshness brought by the wind-sails, so arranged as to send a current down.

Many of those sick yesterday are getting better, and are eagerly inquiring for coffee, bread, meat, &c.; while some look worse than ever. They appear to feel most melancholy, as they lie upon their blankets upon the deck.—With those who are well, the greatest good humour and sport prevails; they have many odd remarks to make at the new scenes presented to them.

When the seamen are engaged in their duties and passing to and fro amid the lofty rigging, our men look up at them and often call out to them, with some queer expression, which is highly amusing to the old tars. The captain of the ship is indulgent towards their capers, and laughs heartily at the droll remarks. Captain Welch was solicitous for the comfort and convenience of all; and seeing many with nothing to engage their attention, he brought to them all the lighter reading of his library, and distributed histories, novels, and romances, with a liberal hand.

March 11th. This day we have had light winds from the southeast, ahead, and we have stood out into the gulf, and back towards the coast; and this evening, are about twenty miles from the Island of Lobos, where our colonel has orders, discretionary, however, to report to the officer in command.—The wind is very light, almost calm; and the lofty ship rolls, and the sails flap against the masts and rigging, with a short, irregular motion, most disagreeable to those who are sick; who wish, from their hearts, that she would keep still a single moment.

The day has passed away pleasantly with all others. Many are enjoying the light breeze, who were yesterday laid up in their berths. The bulwarks, or sides of the ship, and the topgallant forecastle, or small, high deck at the bow, have been crowded with men, leaning over the side, observing the blue water passing behind, or extended in its vast expanse, bounded only by the distant horizon, with here and there the figure of a ship, so far off that they looked only like pillars of white; or else watching the flying-fish, which sprung from the water, with their wings outspread, and dashing along the undulating surface, disappeared as suddenly as they rose or they crowded up the lower rigging, to catch a view of a huge shark, that rolled his body at intervals, above, the waves, displaying the large fin on his back, as he slowly moved along, as if conscious of his power; now coming near us, and then receding; while his attending pilot-fish approached, and examined everything thrown from the ship.

Some were much interested at the frolics of a large number of porpoises, that gambolled around the ship, leaving us with extraordinary speed, and returning as swiftly, crossing and recrossing each other amid the foam at the bows, then again dashing away, full of life; in each successive appearance they were greeted by a shout from the crowd. Little birds, blown off from the land, that had kept upon their fluttering wings until nearly exhausted, came to us to rest, and save themselves, alighting on a rope, or on any person's head.

The men caught a small shark, and he, for a time, took their attention.—His broad, shovel-shaped nose; his eyes, standing so far on the sides of his head; his skin, rougher than sand-paper; his singular tail, and his mouth far under his head, with his sharp teeth, rendered him an object of curiosity. One after another turned him over and over, and at last some of them, with "Bull Killer" and "Skin Horse" at the head, determined to eat him; which they did, amid the jeers of the others, declaring, however, that he was first rate.

Many listlessly threw themselves on the decks, and laughed and chatted quietly for hours.—Towards evening, all was a burst of fun and frolic. One of the men turned orator, and mounting on the elevated hatches amidships, gave a long harangue to the listening crowd.—Went into a description of his past life;—then branched off into an account of the difficulties and inconveniences to which all ardent lovers of liberty, equality, and social drams, were subjected to in the campaign, &c.

Then changing his ground, he discussed the questions of the tariff, the distribution of the public lands, the annexation of Texas, and the present war; then assured his audience that he came to the war for the same reason as did many of the officers, not from any particular love for fighting, but to be able, hereafter, to gain popularity; said that in this he should succeed; that he was sure of being sent to the legislature of Tennessee when he returned, and from there was equally certain of going to congress;—that then he should do much for his native state.—

But his main effort should be the extermination of the abuses existing in the present system of distilling liquors; a martyr in the cause of which, he said, he believed he should yet yield up his life. He exhorted all the men to fight bravely when they arrived at "Peter Cruz," as he called it, and not, by cowardice, to disgrace their mothers;—he said that for his part, he should fight well, and then he was sure of being cordially received by his patriotic old mamma when he returned; and that after the first congratulations had passed, the old lady would say to his younger brother, "Here, John, take the jug and run quickly down to the store, and get a gallon of the best whisky for Zed: for he used to love it mighty well before he went to the wars, and I reckon he loves it yet."

This speech lasted for an hour and a half; and such a flow of words, and often eloquence of style, had the speaker, (a man of great natural talent and rare ability), that the deck was crowded with listeners, both officers and men, who, with loud laughter, cheered him continually during its delivery.

At sunset, the barometer in the cabin fell rapidly, and fearing the approaching change of weather that it indicated, Captain Welch ordered the topsails closely reefed, the jib hauled down, the top-gallant sails furled, and the main-ail clewed up, bringing the ship under short sail; but, as yet, there was no indication in the sky of any change.

Friday, March 12th. Last night, at one o'clock, a norther came down upon us, verifying the prediction of the truth-telling barometer. The sails were filled, bellying to the blast, and the ship drove on through the waves, which soon rose high, curling and breaking in foam. With the wind on her quarter, under short sail, she ran till morning, at ten miles an hour. Her motion of rolling and pitching now became more violent, and, urged by the wind, driving the foam from her bows, she rose upon a wave and dashed forward and downward, as it passed by and broke ahead.

She rolled, and rose up on the next, as it came on, again to plunge forward and settle down for a moment in the trough of the sea; while the wind blew with a rustling, whistling, moaning noise—now increasing in shrillness and intensity, as the ship rose high on the crests, and then lessening for a moment, as she settled in the troughs. The men, as they came up from below, could not walk forward or aft, save by catching at the ropes, the cooking-places, water casks, &c.; and they looked around, dizzy and bewildered.

The centre of the ship, between the fore and mainmasts, was occupied by the long-boat first; and in front of that was the galley, or house of the cook, containing a large cooking-stove, copper kettles, &c. On each side of the long-boat, were two wooden frames, or large fire-places, lined with brick, with a grate of iron across;—these were for the soldiers to cook, divided into their different messes.—Now the men, crowded round these, caused much merriment to the seamen, as they endeavoured to make coffee, and cook their pork.

Every surge of the ship sent them back and forth in a body, against one another;—from the fireplaces and casks, on one side, in a moment they were heavily thrown against the bulwarks on the other.—Some were grumbling, some laughing, and some swearing—especially those who slipped on the deck, as the ship pitched, and came down, with heels up, and elbows in the water that ran about in the scuppers; their coffee-pots were upset, and their bread and meat were sliding round on the deck.

It was a job for them to go even to the water casks; they

caught hold of one another, and of the rigging, and seized their chances, between the rolls and pitches, to jump along three or four feet, to catch again; many were at the sides, holding on, and looking wistfully and sourly at the cooking places:—these wanted their coffee, but they thought it more than it was worth, to try to make it at such a time as this; though the seamen glided along, at their various occupations, without difficulty: for it was their own life, and habit enabled them to step as securely on the unsteady deck, or on the ropes of the lofty yards, and masts above, as our men would on their native hills and mountains.

After those who had succeeded in getting their breakfast had finished it, and those who had not, had satisfied themselves with dry crackers, raw fat pork, and cold water, they retreated to their berths, to forget, in sleep, the unpleasantness of their present situation.

The wind blew strong from the same quarter all the day, the same scene continuing until about four o'clock, when the gale began to lull, and the billows somewhat to subside; and the motion of the ship became more easy, though at times violent— occasionally throwing a half dozen men from one side to the other; or some unlucky wight, who had stepped on the upper part of the ladder to descend to the lower deck, from his foothold, sending him down the steps, bumping on each, to the deck below, on which he was invariably sprawled out, greeted in his coming by shouts of laughter, with all kinds of exclamations, from the numbers around themselves safely stowed away in their berths, there secure, and not being willing to venture out of them.

The wind continued to lull, till, at sunset, the ship became steady enough for all to come above, where they amused themselves much until after dark, when they turned in again;—and now, having got well of sea-sickness, they had a time of sport, singing, laughter, jokes and mimicry, in the darkness below.

Saturday, March 13th. We continued to run, having last evening tacked ship to the south-westward, under easy sail. In the distance were two ships, and a brig, standing on the same course with ourselves. This morning the wind was from the north, but was light. At eight o'clock, we saw the land on the starboard bow;—at eleven, having stood in nearer, we found that we were directly opposite Alvarado, thirty-three miles south-east from Vera Cruz. We came in near enough to see the fort with the spy-glass, and the flag-staff on it, and the road which led over the hills into the town, and a large dark, waving mass of Mexican troops, apparently cavalry, upon it. The town itself was concealed from our view.

This place has been twice attacked by our squadron, but not taken; the vessels not being able to get over the bar.—The view of the coast was clear and distinct, for a long distance, to the south-east and north-west. To the south-east was visible the summit of the mountain Tuxla said to be an active volcano.—In the distance, to the north-west, was the point Anton Lizardo.

As soon as our position was ascertained, the ship was braced sharp up to the wind, and stood to the north-east the other vessels followed our example. After standing out some hours, she was put upon the other tack; and, coming in sight of the coast again, at six, p. m., we found that we were directly north of Alvarado, ten miles; but now, to our astonishment, the norther, which we had thought breathing its last, sprung up again in power, and blew so hard that this was no place for us, for the land lay directly to leeward; and the captain put the ship directly out to sea, on a north-eastern course.

The wind blew stronger in the course of the evening, and whistled shrilly through the rigging;—the ship pitched and rolled in the sea that was raised.—All of our men went below early to their berths. The gale increased as the night drew on; blew more furiously after dark;—a heavy sea arose, and the driving ship laboured hard;—the caps of the waves broke over her.—Towards morning, the close- reefed maintop-sail, with a loud report, burst from its bolt-ropes; another, however, was quickly sent up, which stood out the gale.

March 20th. Another week had our noble ship been driving about, tossed by the tempestuous winds, and unable to reach her desired port. We had fallen in with the ship *Desdemona*, on which was our second battalion, and with several other vessels, all endeavouring to make the port of Vera Cruz. The norther had driven us all far southward, and the wind, though it had lulled away, still blew from the former quarter; our efforts to beat against it were almost unavailing.—Our men lined the sides and deck of the ship, in listless impatience to arrive at the scene of conflict.

At one o'clock, a. m., to our great joy, the north wind had entirely ceased, and a light breeze sprung up from the south-east, which was favourable to us. The ship was immediately put on the course for the coast, and sheet after sheet of sail was spread on her lofty masts. The other ships, which were scattered for miles around, on the distant horizon, did the same, spreading all their canvas to the favourable wind. After sunrise, the bows and lower rigging of the ship were crowded with our men, straining their eyes over the vast expanse of water ahead, to catch a glimpse of land; but hours passed without a word being heard from them.

At eight o'clock, an old salt, belonging to the ship, who had followed the sea for forty years, came up on the fore-castle deck, looked a moment, and then discharging a huge quid of tobacco, hitching up his duck trousers, and half rolling himself round, so as to face the quarter-deck, called out, in a loud voice, "Land O!"

The sound brought every man to his feet.

"Where away?" shouted the chief mate, who was near the cabin.

"Two points on the starboard bow," growled out the old seaman.—But still we could not see the least trace of it, during half an hour's nearer approach.

The low, blue coast then became visible, but it was enveloped in mist, and only partially discernible. The ship still continued to approach directly in towards it; and, after a while, flashes could be perceived, to light up the mist, at regular intervals. Now, with great interest, all strained their vision to bring something more in view.—In another half hour, the heavy booming of cannon could be heard.

At ten o'clock, we had approached so near as to hear distinctly the reports, and shortly after, the fog dispersed, and revealed the scene, in the clear sunlight, most beautiful and intensely interesting.—Before us, and to our right, in the distance, was the heavy castle of San Juan de Ulloa; it was wrapped in clouds of white smoke, that rolled away from above its large extent; the bright flashes darted out from its bastions, and the Mexican flag waved gracefully above it.

Between the castle and ourselves, the expanse of water, within the reefs which were close to us, was calm and tranquil; to the left of the castle, and beyond it, was the city of Vera Cruz, with its numerous domes—and spires, in full and distinct view; in its extent, surmounted by so many of these it appeared to be a beautiful place; and wholly unlike any city we had ever seen. The left side of this was also obscured by the volumes of white smoke, which gracefully rose over and among the spires and domes.

To the left of the city and castle, the coast was a succession of low sand-hills, which appeared bright in the morning sun; they run far off to the southward, losing themselves on the distant horizon. Near these, to our left a little, but yet in front, was a large fleet of our vessels of war and transport-ships; their forest of tall masts, so closely standing together, were surmounted by gay flags and streamers.—They were lying just out of effective reach of the guns of the castle.—Still farther to the left, and almost opposite to us, was the more distant anchorage of Anton Lizardo, where many ships were lying.

On the north of the city and castle, the low range of sand hills extended in the distance, until lost to the view.—Two small islands, and several reefs, or shallow places of coral rock, on which the waves were breaking sullenly, lay between us and the anchorage, which now we were steadily nearing. Of our army nothing could be seen; being all hidden by the sand-hills, at the left of the city. But as we came nearer, we could observe its position, from the clouds of smoke and dust, raised there by the exploding bomb-shells, that were thrown from both castle and city. We heard their reports, nearly equal to those of the artillery that sent them; but no answering cannon could be heard from our forces.

In coming into the harbour, the whole view presented to the eye was most interesting, and rendered exciting by the continued cannonade. It was of one of those scenes which, at first view, strike the mind of the beholder with such a vivid and distinct impression, as will ever afterwards impress it upon his recollection.—While all, crowded on the ship's bows, bulwarks, and in the rigging, were gazing at this extensive view, their eyes wandering from object to object, we were steadily drawing near; sail after sail was furled, and shortly after, the ship moved in among the crowded fleet at Sacrificios Island; the anchors were let go, and she swung round to her heavy chains; the sails were all furled, and the voyage was ended.—Every man was ordered to collect his arms and baggage, and be ready to leave the ship at a moment's notice.

Shortly we were approached by a small four-oared boat, in which was the harbour-master, who, as he came alongside, informed the captain, that on account of the use of the surf-boats, we could not be landed until the morrow; and observing the impatience of the men at this, told us, that there had not yet been anything done, in the way of answering the fire of the city and castle; that eleven days before, on Tuesday, the 9th instant, all the troops then here, about seven thousand, had landed at once, in magnificent style; but that the continued norther, which had kept us at sea, had prevented the landing of the cannon and mortars necessary; and that it would yet be two days before these could be planted, to begin operations.

Informed us, that General Worth's division had taken position nearest to the harbour; that General Patterson's was next, back of the city, and that General Twiggs' was at the water's edge, on the other side; and that the city was thus completely invested, and the trenches were made within eight hundred yards of the walls.—Told us that the remainder of our brigade, 1st and 2nd Tennessee, together with the 1st and 2nd Pennsylvania, and General Quitman's, the South Carolina, Alabama, and Georgia, and the Rifle regiment, had so far, done the skirmishing and fighting, driving the Mexicans within their stronghold; and that the 2nd Tennessee, under General Pillow, after charging up a steep hill, on a large body of Mexicans, in the rear of the city, as they drove them off, found themselves on the top in full view, and within a short range, of the city walls and batteries; they planted their flag, and in answer to their three loud cheers, they received the first fire of the Mexican batteries of the city, which had since been kept up.—That a continuous storm of balls and shells, from the city and castle, swept like hail, over our lines; but, from the troops being hidden in the trenches, the loss of life on our part as yet was small.

He spoke in the highest terms of the generalship of Scott, of his masterly plans, the exactness with which he worked them out, and their effect in saving the lives of his men.—Said the city and castle were doomed: with such a general as Scott, and such men as he had,—that fall they must; that now, with ourselves and the other troops in the harbour there were about thirteen thousand five hundred men under his command.—He then took his leave, warning the captain to look out for the renewal of the norther, for the extraordinary clearness of the atmosphere indicated that the furious wind was not yet done. The barometer, in the cabin, told the same tale; so the ship was moved into a better position, under shelter of the small island of Sacrificios, and both anchors dropped, and a great length of the heavy chains given out.

We now had leisure to observe the scene around us; and the bulwarks were crowded with men, looking round at the large fleet of vessels; among which were several British, French, and Spanish men-of-war, and several steamers; our own fleet of vessels of war,—numbers of large ships, from which many boats were passing back and forth, with troops, cannon, mortars, ammunition, shells, shot, provision, &c., landing them on the beach, to the left, about a third of a mile distant.

This beach, for a mile up its extent, or until it came within reach of the guns of the castle, which was about two and a half miles in front, was lined, under the sand hills, with tents, occupied by the quarter-master's men, and temporary store-houses, for the protection of the articles landed. The whole length was covered with piles of these stores, and was crowded with men. When brought near to the vision by a spy-glass—which revealed upon it a most busy scene—it appeared like the *levée* of a vast commercial city.

The continued cannonade from the castle drew our attention to that fortification, and we observed a large vessel lying under the protection of its guns; on inquiry, we found that she was a French *barque*, which had run the blockade, delivering to the castle a full cargo of excellent powder and shells; and was now awaiting her chance to get out without capture. Many a curse had been bestowed upon her by our naval officers and men; but she was now in a situation in which they dared not interrupt or approach her.

The island of Sacrificios, near us, too, was an interesting object: for upon it the Spaniards, under Cortez, first landed, more than three hundred years since, when about conquering the empire of Mexico.—Here they found that human victims were yearly offered in sacrifice to the heathen gods of the Mexicans;—hence they gave the present name, Sacrificios, to the island. A heathen temple was on it then, and, of late years, several subterranean apartments have been found in its little extent, and many curious sculptured specimens of earthen and stone ware, manufactured with great skill by the ancient Mexicans, and used in those sacrifices of men, have been brought to light.

After night had set in, we remained upon deck to witness the light, flashing continually from the guns of the city and castle, and the brilliant red glare of the Congreve rockets that rose, passed over, and exploded; but at length, wearied, we retired below to sleep.

Sunday, March 21st. We had gone below last night at a late hour, and having the information we had received to converse upon, we did not immediately retire to our berths. Many of the men sat in groups on the lower deck, with their candles giving a flickering light upon the tiers of rough berths in the middle of the ship, and on either side, in which, in rows above each other, many had gone to rest;—the ship being quiet and still on the water, for the first time since we had come on board. Before we dispersed to our berths, the norther again rushed down in power from the open sea upon the coast, city and fleet.—The ships swung around to its force, and the furious wind soon raised a heavy sea, which, notwithstanding the protection of the island and reefs to seaward, ran so high as to give all the heavy vessels much motion.

The wind increased through the night, and on coming on deck in the morning, a wild scene was before and around us, far different from that of the day before. The wind was coming in from the open sea, and the mountain waves, rapidly following each other, were dashing in a terrific manner on the reefs, which protected us from their violence. The water about these appeared white with foam.

On the reef to the seaward was the wreck of the French *barque*, that, last evening, had been so quietly lying under the guns of the castle. She had endeavoured to get out, but being chased by the steamer *Hunter*, ran aground; the steamer also shared the same fate, as well as a schooner that had endeavoured to come in. The crew of the *barque* were in a most perilous situation, for she was a total wreck;—every mountain billow dashed over her broken frame;—her deck was ripped off; her foremast and mainmast were gone;—from her mizzenmast was flying a signal of distress, their flag at half-mast. The French man-of-war immediately, in the violent gale, sent boats to rescue the crew, who, in the intervals between the waves, could be seen with the spy-glass hanging to the timbers.

"Served her right," said the captain of our ship, as he took his spy-glass from his eye; "but," continued he, "they can well afford to lose the ship, after making as much as they have by running the blockade."

"But, captain," said one of our officers, as he took the glass and directed it towards the wreck in the distances, "her money was probably on board of her."

"Oh no!" replied he; "they were not so foolish as to risk the loss of that; probably they have sent it off by the British mail steamer, which our government, perhaps too fearful of offending John Bull, have allowed to run back and forth continually during the blockade."—And so we found it afterwards:—the vessel was lost, but the money was safe.

In the fleet of vessels around us, every exertion had been made by each to hold on during the stormy night; most of them, like our own, had done so; but three had parted their chains, and had gone ashore, where they now lay, with every wave dashing over them. On one, which had filled with water, were the seamen in the rigging, and a crowd of men on the beach, endeavouring to rescue them,—which was finally accomplished, with the loss of two lives, as we afterwards learned. A beautiful white-bottomed brig had gone on bows foremost, and was hard up on the sand.

In the distance, in front, the firing from the castle continued unabated, but the wind was so furious, and so moaned and whistled in the rigging, and the dashing surf on the reef was accompanied with so loud a roar, that both combined prevented us from hearing a single report of the heavy artillery. The smoke from each discharge blew away in an instant, instead of lingering in graceful volumes above it, as on yesterday.

No more artillery or stores could be landed, for the boats were not able to come to the fleet;—many of them were thrown up by the gale on the beach:—so, seeing no prospect of being landed this day, and knowing, that in such a wind, nothing was doing on shore, we contented ourselves with watching the furious war of the elements, and the deadly strife of men visible above it. Listlessness no one could feel, with such a grand scene, upon so magnificent a scale, as that now presented to them.— The lofty mountain of Orizaba, near an hundred miles distant in the interior, could be seen overlooking all, by its white top of snow.

During the whole forenoon the scene continued of furious winds, with a clear sky; of rapidly chasing waves within the reefs; of rolling vessels riding out the gale; of the beach, lashed with foam; of the heavy surf of the sea thundering upon the reefs to windward and upon the shipwrecked vessels, and of the cannonade from the castle and city. In the course of the afternoon the wind began to abate, and the boats to run, although it was still dangerous for them; but the necessity for cannon, mortars, shells and shot, was pressing on shore.

The flag was hoisted at our foremast head, in token that we were ready to go, but it was so late that no boats came for us; and so, disappointed, we again went below, and endeavoured to pass away the time as easily as possible. With our ships of war was much ceremony and firing salutes during the day, on account of change of commanders—Commander Perry taking the place of Commander Conner. Night came on, and with it the brilliant scene of rockets and bomb-shells from the enemy,

Monday, March 22nd. This morning the wind was from the south-east, and the boats had been passing to and fro from daylight, and the greatest activity was seen among them and on the beach, which was, for its long extent, almost black with the crowds of soldiers, seamen and labourers, at their various duties Early in the morning, to our great joy, we saw four of the heavy surf boats, each manned by twelve seamen, coming towards us and the *Desdemona*, near, on which was our Second battalion.

They came alongside, and sixty of us went at a time, in each, towards the beach, where, when we struck the sands, we leaped into the water, holding up our guns, and soon stood upon the shore amid the crowd, close by the stranded vessels.—The boats made other trips, and in an hour or two the whole regiment had left the two noble ships that had so safely brought them, and were again on the land, in the midst of a noisy, apparently confused, extensive scene, up and down the beach, which can be imagined, but not easily described.

During the time occupied by the boats, as they returned to

the ships for the remainder of the regiment, we that had landed threw ourselves on the sands, and, interested in the busy scene around us, passed the time pleasantly, awaiting their return.—The waves threw up many articles from the wrecked *barque* on the reef; pieces of her timbers and furniture were scattered along the shore.

Seeing a large object floating about in the billows, some of the men stripped off and swam to it, and found it to be a hogshead of wine.—With a whoop they announced their prize, and many jumped into the water, and it was soon rolled ashore, the head knocked in, and a merry, noisy crowd of us gathered around it. Every canteen near was filled; and every one had a draught of the fine liquor that the waves had thrown up, as if to "treat" us on our landing at Vera Cruz.—A cask of porter soon followed, but that was taken possession of by the officer of regulars stationed near.

Then came another object, and they dashed in for that. On getting it out, it was found to be a box of shoes. These were sold by the rescuers at twenty-five cents per pair. They were gone quickly.—Something else was seen, and the swimmers buffeted the rolling surf, and brought to shore a couple of boxes of ground pepper, in papers. The pepper was found to be but little injured. This was distributed *gratis* among the messes.—Broken kegs and rolls of butter, mixed with sand, came up; but, on account of the sand, not much attention was paid to it.

Some "cute" chaps, however, silently collected it. and at night, placing it in camp-kettles, melted it; the sand —which was clean—sunk to the bottom, and they had plenty of first rate butter: a great rarity.—These were pronounced "smart," by their comrades.—Many other things came; and, after the regiment had gone, some of the regulars dashed in, and, in place of a box of goods, brought out a dead man—one of the shipwrecked seamen.

The regiment had landed upon the beach. It was formed and marched up to the encampment of General Pillow's brigade, in the investing lines, to the rear of the city; leaving a small guard, to protect the tents and baggage remaining. On this guard the author was detailed; and, there being nothing to do, he easily obtained the opportunity to stroll around.—And now, reader, will you, in imagination, accompany him?

In the first place, you stand on the flat, sandy beach, which, from the breaking waves on the right, (as you look up toward the city), is about one hundred yards in width, to the base of the fantastic shaped sand hills on the left.—These, by the wind, are thrown up like snow-drifts, in every shape and form, from fifty to two hundred feet high. They run parallel with the beach, all the way up towards the city; and the whole extent of this, thus bounded, is crowded with busy life.

Near us are the vessels which have been driven ashore.—They are endeavouring to get off, having all sail backed to the wind; and heaving at their anchors, placed out in the deep water.—You observe, to the right, the harbour spread out; the large fleet at anchor; the busy boats, going and returning; the horse transports, throwing horses and mules overboard:—these are swimming ashore, and are caught by men stationed along, up and down the beach.—On the distant horizon you perceive many vessels, which are coming here, and departing hence.—On the left, you see nothing but the bare sand hills, and the camp of a company of infantry—the picket guard in this direction.

In front you witness such a crowd and bustle, for a mile or more, that you can make nothing of it: so in that direction we will walk; but first notice that the beach, after stretching up that distance in a straight line, takes a sweep off to the right, and then all of it is bare; for in this course it comes directly under the range of the guns of the castle, which you see still further up. There are no tents or men upon it there, save, in the distance, three horsemen, which you observe going up with a white flag.

Do you notice, that on the heavy battlements of the castle, the firing has ceased?—the smoke rolls away from it, and a corresponding white flag is run up on the staff, near to the national ensign. You observe, too, that the firing ceases from the city, and all is still.—The bearer of the flag is Captain Johnson, of the engineers; he is accompanied by a bugler, to sound a parley, and an interpreter. He is bearing from General Scott a summons to General Morales, (shown below),the Mexican commander, to surrender the city, the castle he asks not for; but proposes, if the town is surrendered, not to fire on the castle, provided that it does not fire upon the city. It is not known what effect this summons will have; as General Morales is said to be a brave and accomplished officer; but we will soon find out.—As it is now about two o'clock, p. m., and the officer carrying the flag has instructions to return within two hours, and will not be back in less than that, let us pursue our walk.

Summons of General Scott to General Morales.

Headquarters of the army of the United States of America

Camp Washington, before Vera Cruz, March 22, 1847.

The undersigned, Major General Scott, General-in-Chief of the Armies of the United States of America, in addition to the close blockade of the coast and port of Vera Cruz, previously established by the squadron under Commodore Conner, of the Navy of the said States having now fully invested the said city, with an overwhelming army, so as to render it impossible that its garrison should receive succour or reinforcement of any kind; and having caused to be established, batteries competent to the speedy reduction of the said city he, the undersigned, deems it due to the courtesies of war, in like cases, as well as to the rights of humanity, to summon his Excellency, the Governor and commander-in-chief of the City of Vera Cruz, to surrender the same to the arms of the United States of America, present before the place.

The undersigned, anxious to spare the beautiful city of Vera Cruz from the imminent hazard of demolition, its gallant defenders from a useless effusion of blood, and its peaceful inhabitants, women and children, inclusive, from the inevitable horrors of a triumphant assault, addresses this summons to the intelligence, the gallantry and patriotism, no less than to the humanity of his Excellency, the Governor and commander-in-chief of Vera Cruz.

The undersigned is not accurately informed, whether both the city of Vera Cruz and the Castle of San Juan de Ulloa, be under the command of his Excellency, or whether each place has its own independent commander, but the undersigned, moved by the considerations adverted to above, may be willing to stipulate, that if the city should, by capitulation, be garrisoned by a part of his troops, no missile shall be fired from within the city, or from its bastions or walls, upon the castle, unless the castle should previously fire upon the city.

The undersigned has the honour to tender to his distinguished opponent, his Excellency the Governor and Commander-in-Chief of Vera Cruz, the assurance of the high respect and consideration of the undersigned,

  [Signed]   Winfield Scott,

After passing the stranded vessels, and the landing horses, we see the stores of all kinds, large piles of corn, oats, bread, pork, &c., are being taken off by the wagons, to the commissary's and quartermaster's stations. We notice a hundred or two drowned horses that are washed up by the waves; these were from a wrecked transport, off the harbour. We observe landing, great numbers of ten inch shells, which the seamen and labourers are rolling up on planks, laid along down to the water;—look at these shells; they are round and hollow; have one circular hole in them; by looking into that, you perceive the solid iron is nearly two inches thick;—lift the shell,—can't do it well—too heavy.

Observe what a pile of them are here;—beyond, what quantities of cannon shot. You see about fifty men carrying from the large boats square copper boxes of powder, up to the magazine, which is rudely built of rough plank at the base of the sand hills.

Here are several mortars landing; you observe that they are short and very heavy; set on a stout timber bed; their mouths are slanting up, and you can almost stand in one; look into it,—it is very thick and strong; it has a chamber below for the powder. They are hoisting one of these cumbrous, destructive pieces, upon a heavy wagon frame, and in the night it is going up to the trenches, to be placed in position.—Lying beyond, are four Paixhan guns; each one weighs two or three tons;—see how heavy, how large; the balls they carry weigh sixty-eight pounds each, and a crashing they make, when they strike;—here is a large pile of these shot. These cannon are to go up to the batteries also.—Here are large piles of wagon-bodies, axles, tongues, and bows, and hundreds of men are fitting them together, for they are all wanted now.

Farther up, we witness crowds of seamen, naval officers, quartermaster's men, and soldiers, all at work, as quickly as they can spring to it, in the landing and taking care of so many heavy articles, all needed immediately.—There are a number of men fitting upon the mules the new harness, which, in boxes, is near in large quantities.—Here stand a row of wagons, loaded with the heavy shells, to start after dark for the trenches; there, powder-wagons, the same; here a row of mules, packed with barrels of bread, tents, and mess-bags, are quietly going on towards the camp, around the city.—There come a drove of wet mules, just landed, dashing along, and driven towards the yard, which is farther up.

Along the beach are many small boats from the men-of-war and the transport-ships; many landing sutler's goods, &c., and men are taking them up to the store tents, that are thickly stowed one to another, under the sand hills, each with a crowd of men around, buying. High and dry, here and there, you see the huge form of one of the surf-boats, which the storm drove up. There are thirty, or more, of these so placed; and as they are all wanted, and nearly all injured, you observe gangs of ship-carpenters knocking and banging away at each.—Up a little further, brass cannon and howitzers are landing, and the soldiers are attending to them as they come.

Officers, both army and naval, wagon-masters, quartermasters and commissaries, mounted, and on foot, are in the scene, giving orders, &c.—Let us look into one of the sutlers' large tents, and see the style in which he has to stow his goods;—all in confusion, boxes upon boxes, around, and above his head, leaving a little area in which he stands to sell.—You have to keep a look-out every moment, or you will be run over, in the busy scene; the noise of so many operations going on, confounds you.—What a jabbering, cursing, commanding, shouting, and noise mingles from the long extent of the beach, and is drowned in the heavier roar of the waves.

You may travel much, reader, but it will be a long time before you see such a noisy, active, various, crowded scene as that on the beach below Vera Cruz now. Look around upon it up and down: you see land and water; you observe ships, brigs, schooners, steamers, launches, surf boats, long boats and small boats; you perceive artillery, munitions of war of every kind, stores of all sorts, wagons, mules, and horses; you witness officers, soldiers, seamen, sutlers, wagoners, ship carpenters, wheel-wrights, labourers, and loafers, crowding, winding and turning among one another, and between and about the high piles of stores, shells, cannon balls, goods, &c., &c., from the brink of the dashing waves to the sand hills.—Look again, for it is worth seeing.

Passing on, after a long walk, we come up to the head of the busy scene, and to the point where the beach takes a long turn off to the right, going towards the castle and city. It will not do to go further upon it, for we might get our heads blown off, if the firing re-commences: so we will turn to the left, along the road which has been made among the sand hills, towards the camp.—The sand now is deeper, and hard to travel through.

The marquees of the quartermaster and commissary departments are standing thickly on each side of the road, and the bare hills are thrown up like huge snow drifts above them. Around, in the little valleys between these, some of which are covered with short grass, are the camps of that portion of the troops that are near General Scott's quarters; which are over the next sand hill, to our left.—The road is crowded with soldiers, labourers, seamen, horses, mules and wagons, going to and returning from camp; and there are many loose *burros*, whose owners have fled from our neighbourhood, and these are left to pick up their living;—they are caught and rode by the sailors, who cut a queer set of capers upon them.

Let us leave the road, and turning to the right, climb up the huge sand hill and look around. As we go up, you observe our tracks far behind us, appearing precisely as though they were made in snow; and you see the surface of the hill is blown into thousands of little ridges and waves, like those that the wintry storm at home piles up on the snow-drifts.

Arrived at the top of the hill, a beautiful and extensive view presents itself. Before us is the city; on the right of it, the castle; between us and the city, is the succession of sand hills, which, however, there, are mostly overgrown with musquit bushes. On our right, we see the beach we have left, the fleet at anchor, the islands of Sacrificios and Verde, and beyond them, sweeping around the castle in front, the broad blue gulf. The castle is quiet, and the white flag of truce is still flying from above it. The city is silent also;—no smoke is seen no report heard.—Our trenches, that run along between the city and ourselves, cannot be discerned, being concealed by the musquit *chaparral* on the hills intervening;—not a living person can be seen in that direction, though the trenches are full of soldiers, artillery and infantry, of General Worth's division.

None of our camps can be seen from this height; they are all in the valleys and among the hills behind us, and stretching round to our left, until General Twiggs', the farthest advanced, is upon the edge of the water, to the north-west, and the city is thus completely invested;—no one can go in or come out, save foreigners, who have been allowed, until today, to leave the city and go on board the men-of-war of their respective nations. But today, General Scott has stopped that privilege, of which few have availed themselves; the greater number, with the consuls of England, France, Prussia and Spain, at their head, believing that the city is so strong and well armed that we cannot take it, and that the heavy stone buildings are impervious to bomb-shells;

and if we should attempt to carry it by storm, that we would be cut to pieces:—and in this last they were not far wrong.

In the city before us, and around the walls in the heavy forts, are nearly five thousand men, besides the inhabitants, well armed, with near two hundred cannon and mortars; and in the castle to the right are more than a thousand men, with more than two hundred heavy cannon and mortars, with plenty of water and provisions, they say.

But see:—down comes the white flag which has been flying on the castle, and we see the horsemen, with the flag of truce, coming back along the beach.—What can be the answer to the summons?—Look at that white smoke that darts out from the city wall, followed by the thundering report: see the ball throwing up that cloud of dust near the trenches.—That gives us the import of the answer. See another from the same fort, and shortly another; but none are directed towards the horsemen, who, with the white flag, come rapidly down towards us;—they dash along the beach, by the base of the hill, and, taking the road by which we left, a few moments' gallop brings them to the quarters of General Scott.

Let us look back over the hill, towards those.—Hardly a moment has elapsed, before another horseman leaves there at full speed does not, like the others, go up the beach.—He has no flag.—He comes to the foot of the hill, and passing around it and among the others, is lost to our view, as he moves directly towards the trenches. Let us look; he undoubtedly carries the order to re-commence firing, for several mortars are there ready.—Every moment seems an age of suspense. That single battery of the city is still in operation, and its balls plow up the earth.

But see:—from the tangled distant growth of *chaparral* between us and the city, a large volume of smoke shoots up and rolls out; another, and still others follow. Hear their stunning reports, together with the noise of the shells, as they pass over into the city. The first few burst in the air;—their sharp peals are like sudden claps of thunder.—The city opens from all the batteries in reply. Witness the volumes of smoke rising from the castle, and the booming of artillery is incessant.

Turn around to the right;—see, gracefully approaching, five slender schooners on the water, and with them two steamers;—they take their positions. They are what is called the *Mosquito* Fleet, and each one carries heavy guns, (Their position, taken this evening, is placed on the right of the picture p.227). See the smoke rising from them;—how rapidly they fire.

Now, a grand scene is before us.—Seven large mortars and four six-inch *cohorns*, smaller, but destructive, from the trenches or batteries Nos. 1, 2, and 3, are at work, and seven heavy guns from the *Mosquito* Fleet; while so many are opening in reply from the castle and city, that we cannot keep the account. But the iron storm of shot and shells, bursting, ploughing, and throwing up clouds of sand and dust, far and near, are doing but little damage to our troops or batteries, for they are all in the long narrow trenches, under the ground.

Scott has not, in his arrangements, allowed any detachment to expose itself to the destructive fire that would so quickly annihilate them. Every advance near them has been made by digging at night, like moles, unseen, slow, but sure.—See the shells from the fort in the city, nearest the harbour, burst round the vessels.—Here is an officer who is directly from General Scott's quarters. He informs us that General Morales sent back a reply to General Scott, refusing to surrender the city, and stating his determination to defend it to the last.

Reply of General Morales to General Scott's Summons.
[Translation.]
        Vera Cruz, March 22, ,1847.

The undersigned, commanding general of the free and sovereign state of Vera Cruz, has informed himself to the contents of the note which Major General Scott, general-in-chief of the forces of the United States, has addressed to him, under date of today, demanding the surrender of this place, and castle of Ulua; and, in answer, has to say, that the above named fortress, as well as this place, depends on his authority, and it being the principal duty, in order to prove worthy of the confidence placed in him by the government of the nation, to defend both points at all costs, to effect which he counts upon the necessary elements, and will make it good to the last; therefore, his Excellency can commence his operations of war in the manner which he may consider most advantageous.

The undersigned has the honour to return to the general-in-chief of the forces of the United States the demonstrations of esteem he may be pleased to honour him with.

      God and Liberty.
      (Signed)   Juan Morales.

To Major General Scott,
General-in-chief of the forces of the United States, situated in sight of this place.

His action he has now commenced in good spirit.—The scene is such that you could remain and gaze with interest unabated for hours; but night is approaching, and the author must return to his post. Let us descend the hill to the road;—there we learn that Captain Vinton, commanding the batteries, was killed a few moments since, by one of the enemy's shells.—Turning to the crowded beach, we find it still busy as before, though now it is near dark. Three heavy mortars are hoisted on the wagon frames, and these, with the wagons containing shells, are about starting out for the trenches, as they cannot now be seen in their approaches there.

Following the beach down, as we came up, through the multitude, who seem to forget that there is any such thing as rest at night, we at last come to the stranded vessels, and near them are the guard fires, made of pieces of the wreck washed ashore. Will you, in imagination, stay with us longer?—If so, sit down on the sand around the fires, and take with us a tin cup of hot coffee and a piece of hard bread, with a piece of fat pork.—We would offer you more, if we had it.

Gaze around: how wild and dark is the scene;—the troubled waves dash at our feet, and sparkle in their foam: the roar of their breaking is continual. The wind is cool, coming off the water.—See how many lights are visible in the crowded fleet of vessels to our right, and what a number more are up the beach.—Observe how singularly our camp fires light the sails of this brig, that is ashore so nearby us that her bowsprit is almost over us.—What a ghastly flickering they throw around, and illumine the rough faces of the men who are seated about you.—Are we not a hard looking set, with our long *moustachios* and longer whiskers, and rough garbs, illumined by so wild a light?—But your attention is drawn away from these things, which, although strange and interesting, cannot keep your eyes from the magnificent scene that is still going on towards the castle and city.

Observe the bright flashes there, as they for the instant light up the battlements of the castle, and render the heavy volumes of smoke above it luminous against the surrounding darkness. See the same from the vessels: one instant by the light you perceive the whole outline of the vessel, her masts, and spars, and smoke, and then all is dark, but again illumined; above the whole, describing long arcs of circles high in the air, see the bomb-shells rising over and falling, shown in their courses by the fuses, which twinkle like bright red stars.

Observe that flash; notice the shell thus rising;—count seconds: one, two, three, four,—it is still rising,—five, six,—it takes its long sweep,—seven,—it is coming down,—eight, nine,—it has fallen.—How heavily must that iron mass of a hundred pounds have fallen from such a height as that. But look, the flash of the explosion brings out in view, for an instant, the domes and spires among which it descended.—The report you cannot distinguish from the mingled roar of the whole. Several shells, from both sides, are in the air at the same moment; and, in their high sweeps, they cross each other in their lines of light.—After gazing at the scene, you may turn from it; yet you will be drawn to look again.

But the night wears away, and on the cold beach around you, the soldiers, spreading their blankets, and wrapping themselves up in them, seek repose, careless of the morrow's fate.—This sleeping on the wet sea-beach, with the cold wind upon you, and with a single blanket only, for. bed and covering, with the dashing waves at your feet, and the reports of artillery to lull you, you will not choose; and as the author is obliged to take it so, and from continued exposure it comes easy, too, he bids you, reader, goodnight.

Saturday, March 23rd. Will you again accompany the author during the day? for in the various and important events, so rapidly taking place, it is difficult to keep up with them; and now, every day is an age in the life of one who sees them.—From the same spot we left last night, on the beach, look with him around you;—the cannonade and bombardment have kept their continual thunder for the whole night, until about an hour since. The landing of shot, shells, powder, cannon, and stores, has not ceased; fatigued men have been replaced by fresh ones, and all is yet going on.

Another vessel has arrived, during the time, with thirteen additional mortars, and quantities of shells, which are landing.—Now there is a quiet in the storm of war; the scene around is beautiful and grand. The castle and the city are noiseless; the little fleet, that have done such service during the night, have hauled off from their position, and are resting, as it were, near the heavy ships of war. The batteries are also quiet.—The sun rises from his ocean bed, and his rays brighten up the magnificent stone buildings of the city and the imposing battlements of the castle; the Mexican flag, of green, red, and yellow, floats in the morning air from the lofty staffs above them; while from every mast in the crowded fleet, the stars and stripes flow out in the light breeze.

The mountain of Orizaba, with its lofty, snow-capped summit, is distinctly visible inland; but this only foretells the renewal of the norther, notwithstanding the calmness of the scene at present.—The scene is beautiful of nature's quiet, but it is soon to be broken; for, see, the signal flags are run up on the commodore's ship. These are responded to by the *Mosquito* Fleet, of the seven small vessels; which immediately move out, and fall in a line opposite the castle, and about a mile from it.—It is a dangerous position.—Look at them, as gracefully they lay, each with its large flag waving above.—There goes the smoke; and again, again, and again; the loud reports reverberate along the sand hills, in the still, morning air.

Their shells burst in and about the castle, but that seems to notice them not.—"A little puppy, barking at a bull-dog," says a volunteer, seated on the sand, and with us watching them.—Still they fire, and are enveloped in their smoke; now a slight wind takes that off over the water.

But look! all along the battlements of the castle, dart out sheets of flame and clouds of smoke;—around the vessels the water is thrown high, in perpendicular columns of dashing spray; how thickly the balls fall near them; but the vessels are so small, that, at the distance, they are hard to hit; amid the terrific hail of iron that is pouring upon them, they still keep up their fire.— The batteries open on the land, and throw their shells into the city. The three mortars, that went out last night, are added to those in operation before. The peals of all are continual; the ten-fold number of cannon along the city walls, reply in their thunders; and in the immense volumes of smoke that rise from all, and hang over and among the domes, the destructive scene closes in.

But observe, one of the schooners ceases her fire; the steamer goes to her, and making fast, tows her rapidly away. She is badly struck; see, her mainmast totters.—You look round, at the splendid fleet of frigates and sloops of war, with the line-of-battle ship, *Ohio*, at their head, and each with their heavy guns protruding in bristling rows from their sides, and with gay streamers from their tall masts, and you ask why they do not go to the relief of the little vessels that are in such a dangerous situation.—They know better than to do it.

The castle is not now as it was when the French, by accidentally blowing up one of its magazines, took it, when it was already almost dismantled. Then its powder was so poor, that the shot would not go through the sides of the ships; only nineteen of its guns were in a condition to be worked, and the garrison were all unprepared for an attack: but that catastrophe had learned them a lesson; and having had the whole summer to prepare, they have now put the impregnable fortress in its proper state. Its guns are good, its powder excellent, its garrison strong, and it is folly for our large vessels to approach it.—See, the signal of recall is hoisted on the commodore's ship, and the little flotilla haul off as fast as possible;—they have had enough, and will not try it again.

As the guard of our regiment are now going up to the camp, let us follow; leaving, for the present, the beach at this point, and passing up through the busy crowd, to the road, striking off in that to the left and winding among the bare sand hills, upon which not even a bunch of grass can find root;—passing over these, and through the little valleys between, we come to hills of thick *chaparral*, through which the road has been cut, and a mile and a half distance from the beach, brings us out to a plain, upon which is a winding lake of shallow water; at the extremity of this plain from the town, directly towards which it runs, is the old, ruined castle of Malibran; and in the rear of this, we find our regiment encamped, with some of the 2nd Tennessee and Illinois infantry.

In a building near, are the headquarters of General Patterson. (A view of this old ruin may be seen p.221).—We find that most of our regiment have been hard at work all the night, in hauling the sixty-eight pounders, from the beach, through the sand and over the hills, to a new work, called the Naval Battery, or battery No. 5, which is erecting in the *chaparral* on a hill, not far from the city walls; of the construction of this, the Mexicans, as yet, are not aware; it will play heavily upon them, for it is to mount six guns, three of them being sixty-eight, and three thirty-two pounders.

The men, after their work, are stretched out in their tents asleep, unmindful of the continued cannonade, that is thundering upon the air. Some few are on the old ruins, looking with interest upon the smoke-enveloped city, which is before them, up the plain; though the general will not let many show themselves at a time, lest they should provoke the cannon balls of the enemy, for we are directly under their fire.—We find that a prisoner was taken this morning, who says, that during the night our shells were most destructive within the city. And now, reader, the author can accompany you no farther today, not knowing at what time the regiment, or part of it, may be called upon for more active service.

At noon, on this day, according to the indications in the morning, the norther sprung up again, and blew with great force; throwing the sand in the trenches, blinding the eyes of the artillerists, more than the gunpowder smoke from the mortars, and impeding the operations much; almost stopping the work on the new batteries, Nos. 4 and 5.

It also raised the waves in the harbour so high, and dashed them so on the beach, as entirely to stop the passage of the boats, and the landing of mortars, shot, and shells; and, for the want of the latter, the mortars, which had thrown them so incessantly into the city during the night and the forenoon, were now obliged to slacken their fire. This falling off seemed to encourage the enemy, who, from the castle and every fort, fired with renewed energy;—for the norther was not at all inconvenient to them, being at their backs, and the high buildings of the city broke its force; neither was there any sand within the walls, to trouble them; but without, it rolled in driving clouds into the trenches.—The smoke of the combat now was blown off as it issued from the mouths of the cannon, and all was clear above the city and castle.

As the excitement of the army, daring the whole day and the previous night, had been highly raised, they were now, even to every soldier, fretted and displeased at the slow, languid manner in which our batteries were obliged to fire, for the want of shells, and on account of the furious driving sand; and at the rapidly of the discharges of the enemy's artillery, so cheered by the depression of ours. In the mean time, the storm increased, drove many of the surf-boats upon the beach, and entirely stopped the busy scene there, before described; prostrated the sutlers' store tents, and sent all the labourers over the sand hills, for shelter.

Night drew on, and still the norther continued unabated;

the castle and the forts of the city were lit up by the continual discharge of their artillery; and the numerous shells seemed to ride out towards us, borne on the careering tempest; while only occasionally did our opposing shells rise up, and, breasting the wind, fall over from their long sweep into the city.

After dark we had an alarm of an attack in the rear, as we had had the night before; and as we knew that there were some two thousand lancers nearby, there was much bustle and preparation made to receive them; but the alarm proved false.—About nine o'clock, our shells set fire to some of the buildings within the walls, and they burned with a lively flame, fanned by the stormy wind, and gave out a bright light, that glared on all the buildings, domes, and spires above, bringing them into strong relief against the dark sky beyond, and, with the lurid flashes of the artillery below, presented a scene of terrific grandeur.

Then the fire burned down, and only black smoke arose from it, and all was gloomy and dark, save the flashes of the guns. We turned away from the strong blasts, in which we had been standing, gazing at the grand appearance, and, chilled through, sought our tents, where, thickly stowed to one another, and wrapped in blankets, we became comfortable, and lay quietly listening to the rushing wind and the ceaseless roar of the cannon, and dozed quietly off to sleep, when suddenly came an order from General Pillow, for four companies of the regiment to march to the beach, and drag up one of the sixty-eight pounders, for the naval battery.

We passed down, and by the long rope attached to the heavy timber wheels, under which hung the weighty piece of artillery, we tugged and pulled, and, in our endeavours, sweat and blowed with it, as we passed over the sand hills up to the camp, and then on to the battery, which, by the roundabout way we had to go, was nearly three and a half miles. It was the toughest sort of work; and, as we approached the place of the battery, had to be done in the stillest manner possible, to avoid discovery; the bushes concealed the place from the view of those in the city.

By hard labour we got it there late in the night, and it was soon hoisted upon its carriage, and stood with its four companions, with their long black muzzles projecting through the embrasures in the embankment, which was thickly laid tip of bags filled with sand; the sides of the embrasures were covered with raw hides.

One more gun was lacking, which had been brought, by another detachment, as far as the camp at Malibran, but as the morning approached, it was stopped for the present; its carriage and plank platform, like the others, were ready for it, and we regretted that it could not be brought on; for by General Scott's orders, not a shot was to be fired from the whole battery, or the least indication of its existence given to the Mexicans, until every gun was in position; for this battery, when known to them, from its elevated position would draw upon itself a heavy fire.

It was to be manned entirely by seamen from the navy, which had furnished the guns, though detachments from the brigades of Generals Pillow, Shields and Quitman, had erected the battery.—The naval officers and seamen were impatient for the other gun; for, without it, the battery would have to remain silent during the next day; and they had already brought the shot and ammunition.—So busy and hard at work had we been during the night, that we had scarcely noticed the firing, which from our side had almost ceased, and from the enemy had greatly slackened; nor had we perceived, till our task was accomplished, that the norther had spent its strength, and was now dying away.—Leaving the battery, with its five guns in position, in charge of the seamen, we were dismissed an hour before day, and finding our way back in the darkness to Malibran, we quickly stretched ourselves in our tents, and were soundly asleep.

Wednesday, March 24th. The fire, which had been slackened off before daylight, as mentioned, was renewed by the enemy with vigour, and all his batteries were served with great rapidity, and shot and shell fell in showers over our lines. Our own, though keeping up the fire, did so slowly, for want of shells; but every one of these fell within the city, and did fearful execution, as we learned from some deserters who escaped from there last night.—The naval battery being much needed, and the ammunition for it, as said before, being ready there, while that of the mortars was scarce, and the only remaining gun to be mounted in it being at Malibran, in, front of the quarters of General Patterson, General Pillow, after examining the road, determined to run the risk, and take the gun to the battery in open day; being urged to it, by the slackening fires of the mortars, and the vigorous cannonading of the enemy.

This was a hazardous undertaking; for, after proceeding over the hills about three-fourths of a mile, the way lay for several hundred yards, up along the side of the level railroad, in view of, and directly in front of one of the forts of the enemy, on the walls, the guns of which could bear directly down the road, and rake it for a mile.—General Patterson, seeing the risk on one side, and the advantage, if successful, on the other, simply repeated to General Pillow the order of Scott, that the guns should be carried during the night, and remarked to him, that if he undertook it, that it would be on his own responsibility.

Pillow, after noticing that the battery to which he would be exposed was almost constantly enveloped in smoke, from its rapid firing, and as the wind had ceased, judging that such a movement as he contemplated, would not be thought of, or watched for by the enemy, determined to carry it into execution; and, ordering out a heavy detachment, the gun was taken over the hill to the railroad. Now came the trying time; the road was level; steep hills of *chaparral* were on one side of it, and the railroad on the other, and immediately in front, in the city wall, was the dreaded battery.

The detachment, with the gun, rapidly advanced up the road; the battery continued discharging its cannon at the trenches on the right, and still the clouds of smoke settled over it; once or twice this smoke blew away, so that it was clear for a moment; but the enemy there not dreaming of so bold a move as an advance uncovered, up the railroad, paid no attention to the view of it.

Again the battery was enveloped, as the gun advanced; it

reached the road to the right, up the hill; turned into it; was concealed by the *chaparral*; was undiscovered, safe, and soon at the battery, to the great joy of the brave naval officers and the seamen, who had given up all hope of opening the fire of the work until the morrow.—It was soon placed in position; the *chaparral* in front, on the brow of the hill, was quietly cut down, and, to the astonishment of the Mexicans, so elated at the slackening fire of the mortar batteries, this opened its six pieces, with a terrific and well-directed discharge of its heavy shot; which, especially the sixty-eights, made the stones and mortar fly from the buildings and walls—they crashed through blocks at a time, and a different aspect was placed upon the day.

All the Mexican batteries, that could bear, immediately turned their fire upon the new and destructive work; which, now under the command of Captain Aulick, second officer of the naval force, sent the heavy shot with such effect among them.—This it kept up for the remainder of the day; in the afternoon, under the command of Captain Mayo. In a short time after it opened, four sailors within it were killed, two badly wounded, and Lieutenant Baldwin slightly. The dead were taken off, down to Malibran.(see picture p.221)—The battery was much torn to pieces by the shot of the enemy.

The storm having now subsided, the landing of shot, shell and mortars was resumed with spirit; and all the afternoon the beach presented the busy scene before described, and the utmost efforts were made to supply the mortar batteries, Nos. 1, 2 and 3, under the direction of Colonel Bankhead, called Worth's batteries, with shells, so much needed by them.

At eleven o'clock a. m., our shells set fire to some buildings in the city, and dense volumes of black smoke arose on the air, contrasting with the white volumes from the artillery below, along the walls, and increasing the grandeur of the scene.

The Mexicans fought with great gallantry and bravery; their artillery was served in such a way as to excite the admiration of our officers, who universally remarked that it could not possibly have been better done; and the only reason that their powerful fire was not more destructive among us, was the most excellent arrangement of Scott, for the defence of the men.—They tore the heavy embrasures of the naval battery, at which only they could get a chance, completely to pieces. The fire from that battery had been directed much against a fort opposite to it, called St. Barbara,—by our men called the "red fort," from the colour of the buildings behind it.

The Mexican flag above this fort was cut down by a ball.— Our troops in the battery and trenches stopped firing for a moment, and raised three cheers all along, the sound of which rose above the bombardment. The Mexican officers and soldiers jumped down on the outside of their fort, seized their flag, and, amid the heavy balls that again flew among them, held it to its place until it was lashed.—This gallant act excited the astonishment of our men.

The fort to the eastward of it, or to the right as we face the city from the south, called by us, from its position "the railroad fort," fired most accurately. One gun, a twenty -four- pounder, was known by its peculiar sharp report, and the artillerists so managed it, that the balls, rapidly following one another, struck the naval battery, entering the embrasures, and never missing farther than two or three feet. Our men called it "spiteful," and named it the "spit-fire."

Another fort still farther to the east, along the walls, called by our troops the "white fort," was close by the "Gate of Mercy," or principal entrance of the city; (for a view of part of this fort, see plate of "Gate of Mercy,"). It was very active, and had not suffered much; the naval battery not having any opportunity to pay its respects to it, having enough to do to answer the fire of the forts of St. Barbara and the "rail road fort."

A mortar was between these two forts, by itself, and threw shells without intermission, sometimes at the trenches, sometimes at the naval battery, and sometimes over towards our camps at Malibran. One of its shells fell directly into the narrow trenches, about two o'clock, and stopped under the mouth of a mortar which had just been loaded, and its heavy shell lifted into it; instantly exploded, wrapped the mortar in flame, ignited its charge, thus sending its shell high in the air, to fall into the city; in the same instant tearing the heavy mortar, which could not have weighed less than two thousand pounds, from its firm timber bed, breaking the strong iron clamps that confined it, and sending the whole into the air out of the trench, and forty feet back from it.—Most fortunately, the exploding fragments of thick iron passed up, instead of horizontally in the trenches, thus saving the lives of scores of men.

Some of the small pieces mortally wounded one man, and severely three others,—several slightly. Lieutenant Arnold who commanded the mortar, that thus, after doing its duty, by a continual fire for two days and nights, (beginning on the afternoon of the 22nd), had most unceremoniously been thrown out of the trenches,—narrowly escaped with his life, and was left without a gun.

This was but an ordinary example of the force of an exploding shell, but they are much more destructive, when falling in a confined place—such as the interior of a building. What, then, must have been the effect in the crowded city, into which, though the firing last night and this day had been slow, the mortars have, in these forty-eight hours, thrown over two thousand of the ponderous missiles. These, from their high sweeps aloft, have descended with irresistible force on the stone tops of the buildings, passing through them and all the floors, and exploding below;—or else falling into the streets and crowded squares, spreading death and destruction among soldiers and inhabitants, men, women and children, in one common sweep.

But that is not all—for the *Mosquito* Fleet has thrown in over a thousand more;—not so heavy, but yet averaging sixty-two pounds each; and most destructive are they in explosion and powerful in force, in their descent from their high elevations, in which they appeared almost to touch the lower clouds. And not only these, but the naval battery, this day, so far, has thrown nearly three hundred sixty-eight pound and thirty-twos, direct shot, which have produced a terrible effect.

Ruins of Malibran, near Vera Cruz

Yet there is not the slightest appearance of surrender or slackening of the enemy's fire.—With a strong and efficient garrison, a massive built city, and the best fortifications in, around, and near it, on the continent of America; with a most complete and heavy armament, and the utmost abundance of material of war they seem determined to carry out the promise of General Morales, to defend the place to the last; their flags yet wave out in defiance, supported by their ceaseless artillery.—They have probably fired about five cannon or mortars to our one; or, during the two days, so far, near fifteen thousand shot and shells, besides an enormous number before our batteries commenced. The plain and the hills are covered with balls and fragments of shells, and the ground is torn, blown, and plowed up in every direction. The awful, constant roar of this artillery, and the sublimity of the scene, the reader can hardly imagine.

Fort Santiago, on the water's edge, is a fine work, and its guns are most excellently managed. The magnificent castle in the distance belches forth its thunder, and sends its heavy shells over the lower part of the city, into our lines, without intermission.

Now, reader, leaving this thunder of the artillery and gathering volumes of smoke, to relieve our minds, let us turn our attention to the more quiet scenes of camp at Malibran, represented in the picture (p.221). This old building that you see, still strong in its ruins, was once a splendid place. It was constructed more than two hundred and fifty years since, by a Spanish count;—was occupied by his descendants, as a palace, for several generations; then went to ruins, and so remains.

The walls, which surrounded the grounds, are now broken;—some of them can be seen in the picture. That in the foreground, that runs around the lake, is nearly entire; it has several round holes in it, which are earthen jugs set in: for, to help out in the material of building, in this section, the former inhabitants set rows of jugs, each filled with earth, in the walls, and plastered them around with mortar and stone, and from their shape and situation, they were strong and firm. Now, many of them are broken into, and the sand has run out.

The water in front is part of the lake, which extends back towards the city; for, in this picture, we are supposed to stand upon the wall, which ends in the water, with the city behind us.—Several sentinels are standing around the building; in the ruined arches of this are yet perfect stone rooms;—these are the quarters of several of the officers. On the top of the ruins rises a singular and large species of ivy, which grows like a tree, finding no earth for its roots, which insinuate themselves in every crevice of the stone, and run up and down the sides of the ruin, within and without, clinging with great tenacity.—The dead and wounded are brought in from the batteries, which, are pealing away behind us.

On the hill, to the right, are the tents of some infantry companies, while behind the building, and on the left, crowded together, are those of our regiment, and two companies of the second Tennessee. On the little hill over the tents, are a number of our men looking above our heads in front, at the bombardment. The top of the old ruins would be crowded with these also, but General Patterson has forbidden the men to go up there, because they draw the shells of the enemy, who are ignorant, as yet, that this is his headquarters. These are in the building to the right, but little of which can be seen. The muskets of a company are stacked before it, and a sentinel is on post by them. On the left of the picture is an officer, coming at full speed from the headquarters of General Scott, bearing orders to General Patterson.—Two sailors are riding little *burros* that they have picked up, and are exciting much sport.

In the camp, the men are variously employed:—most of them are now up, having been asleep at times during the day, exhausted by the hard labour of last night and the night before, in the batteries.—Parties of them have been out towards the interior; have had a skirmish with a scouting party of Mexican lancers in our rear, and repulsed them, killing some few, and now have returned, loaded down with fresh beef that they have killed, and vegetables from the gardens of the *ranchos* around, from which the families have fled; they are engaged in cooking, and have entirely forgotten the horrors of the bombardment that is raging, and are laughing, joking, telling tales, and enjoying themselves finely.

They were just now interrupted by one of the larger shells thrown from the city, which came with a loud noise, and caused them to dodge about the tents in an amusing manner; but the falling shell burst in the lake, and the pieces flew, amid the smoke and mud, with sharp, long, singing sounds, far on every side, but fortunately touched no one.

Some stop and appear serious for a moment, as they look at the mangled dead that lay under the arch of the buildings. One had a horrible appearance, that struck them particularly;—he was a stout, muscular man, of perhaps forty years of age. A cannon ball from that excellent gun, with keen report, that has been mentioned, had entered the embrasure, striking him fairly on the right breast, tearing a terrible hole through him, and taking his lungs through his back.—He was dead in an instant.—His countenance had an expression of mortal agony upon it;—his blear eyes gazed upward.—The wound was obscured with dirt and sand; his hands were clenched, and his bloody hair streamed back.

Two, that lay immediately along side of him, however, had smiles on their countenances, and one appeared to be in a sleep, with pleasant dreams, if we might so express it: for he was not mangled or torn.—He was neatly dressed, was young, of fine form and handsome countenance. A small piece of a bursting shell had entered his head, above his ear. He had bled but little, and died so quickly, that the laugh that he was giving utterance to, excited by an odd remark of his comrade, as they were assisting to fire the heavy cannon, was yet depicted on his countenance.—That comrade, too, had the same expression, as he was killed at the same instant; but he was most horribly mangled:—one piece of the shell had taken off the back and side of his head; the brain was all out of the bloody skull, and sand was stuck thickly within, while the long hair that covered the remainder was stiff with blood and dirt.—Another piece had struck his right shoulder in front, and had torn and mangled the shoulder, arm, breast, and ribs, in a hideous manner. The long strips of skin, of bloody, hanging flesh, of white sinews, ends of bones, and protruding vitals, with the torn clothing among them, and sand within him, was revolting to the eye; and the laughing features seemed to mock the terrible, mangled expression of death.

The batteries of the enemy increased in rapidity about sunset, and kept up vigorously; and, after dark, ours began to answer them more rapidly, for they had shells on hand; and, as large trains of wagons now went to them, conveying part of the immense quantity that had been landed during the day, after the cessation of the norther, there was no fear of their exhausting the quantity; and they fired freely, with a continual roar.

Another fire was kindled by the explosions in the city, and burnt with brilliancy; in and around the flame, our bombs came down from the long sweeps, in which their courses had been traced by the twinkling fuses, and brilliantly, with sullen roar, exploded in the midst.

At nine o'clock, p. m., the fire of the forts and batteries of the enemy had slackened, and shortly after ceased; and a sally of the garrison being expected, more troops were thrown into the trenches;—but the cessation proved to be from another cause:— four foreign merchants came out with a flag of truce from the foreign consuls in the city to General Scott, requesting a truce and suspension of firing, to enable the subjects of the powers of England, France, Spain, and Prussia, to leave the city with their families, &c.;—the city was becoming too hot for them; and their opinion was altering with respect to the efficiency of the bombardment. We now heard definitely of the terrible destruction within the walls.

No answer was returned this evening by General Scott to this application, but every arrangement was made for carrying on the bombardment. Large quantities of shot and shells were landed from the fleet during the night, and the wagons were engaged during the same time in taking them to the batteries.

Detachments of our regiment, and others, were occupied nearly the whole night, in repairing the damage done to the naval battery during the day, and in mounting the guns at a new battery, No. 4, which was between No. 5 and the mortars. These guns, two sixty-eights, Paixhans, and four twenty-fours, were all got ready, and amply supplied with ammunition; and, at a late hour, the men detailed to work, after having filled and placed up two thousand bags of sand, returned to camp, and threw themselves down to sleep.

Thursday, March 25th. Early this morning General Scott sent back his answer to the communication of the consuls of England, France, Spain and Prussia, which he received last night. (See below.) As this was a decided refusal to their request, no delay was made in the progress of the bombardment. The fire had slackened off during the night on both sides; but directly after daylight, General Worth's batteries, 1, 2, and 3, mortars and *cohorns*, (smaller mortars), commenced the fire with great rapidity, having now plenty of ammunition and shells. The new battery, No. 4, finished last night, opened in fine style, and fired most rapidly, while the naval battery, thoroughly re-fitted, was not behind, in pouring its heavy shot with the others, upon the devoted city. Already had great distress arisen within the walls.— Those who were at work in the darkness, on the naval battery, spoke, this morning, of the continual shrieking and wailing that rose from the city, on the stillness of the night, after the firing had ceased; but now that distress rapidly accumulated: for three shells to one, and double the shot, were going in.—Ten large mortars, six smaller ones, six sixty-eight pound cannon, three thirty-twos, and four twenty-fours, were served in the most rapid and efficient manner.

Answer of General Scott to the Foreign Consuls:

Headquarters of the army of the United Sates Camp Washington, before Vera Cruz, March 25th, 1847. The undersigned, Major General Scott, &c., &c., had the honour to receive (late last night) the memorial signed

Vera Cruz During the Bombardment

by the consuls of Great Britain, France, Spain, and Prussia, in the city of Vera Cruz, requesting that the undersigned would grant a truce sufficient to enable the consuls and the subjects of those powers, together with Mexican women and children, to leave that city, now under a close siege and blockade.

The undersigned deeply regrets the lateness of this application, for up to the 22nd instant, the communication between the neutrals in Vera Cruz and the neutral ships of war, lying off Sacrificios, was left open, mainly to allow the neutrals an opportunity to escape the horrors of the impending siege, of which the undersigned gave to the consuls every admonition in his power.

In respect to a truce, it must be evident, on reflection, that the undersigned cannot grant one, except on the application of the governor or commander-in-chief of Vera Cruz, accompanied by a distinct proposition of surrender. In the meantime, the siege will go on with increased means and rigour.

That the unavoidable distress of the women and children in the besieged place had deeply engaged the sympathies of the undersigned, before one shot or shell had been fired by him in that direction, he begs to refer to the accompanying copy of his summons, addressed the 22nd instant, to his Excellency the governor and commander-in-chief of Vera Cruz. His Excellency chose to consider the castle of San Juan de Ulua, as well as Vera Cruz, to be included in that summons, and expressed his confidence in his ability to make a successful defence of both.

The undersigned has the honour to tender to the consuls of Great Britain, France, Spain, and Prussia, the assurance of his high respect and consideration.

    (Signed)   Winfield Scott.
To Messrs. Gifford, Gloux, Escalente,
and D'oleive, &c., &c., Vera Cruz.

All the Mexican forts redoubled their energies, and from

castle and city shot and shells were thrown in immense quantities. The scene became intensely interesting.—The air was filled with missiles; the roar of so much ordnance in operation was deafening, nor was there the slightest intermission.

On this morning fatigue parties were set to cutting brush and making fascines, or bundles, with which to fill the ditches, in the final storming of the forts and city, with which General Scott intended to close up the combat, if the city surrendered not.—All that were off duty crowded upon the sand hills, far and near, to view the scene, such as they had never before witnessed.—The day was warm and pleasant, and the air clear.—To get a good view, the author, with several others, proceeded towards the beach, turned to the left among the sand hills before he reached that; crossed several of these, and stopped on the top of one from which the best view could be obtained of the whole scene; and there was sketched the picture.

Imagine yourself, reader, on this hill at this time, and the whole, though in the distance, and partly obscured by smoke, before you: but you can see enough of it: you are east of the city, and about a mile from it. The lines showing the course of the shells are imaginary: for, in the day time, the shells themselves could not be seen, and in the night, could only be perceived by the twinkling of their fuses. You see the steamer *Vixen*, and one of the small schooners of the *Mosquito* Fleet, in the position they occupied on the afternoon of the 22nd, when the bombardment commenced; the other steamer, and four schooners, are still farther to the right.

You observe the water battery of the castle; and, on the left of that, the castle itself in the distance, a vessel is out far beyond it. She is going around to General Twiggs' position, which is out of view to the left of the picture;—the water there comes round in a bay, and this vessel, to get to them with provisions, &c., is forced to go far off, to avoid the guns of the castle.

On the left extremity of the castle is the light house, which is high;—on the opposite quarter is an upper building:—the flag-staff rises there, with the Mexican flag upon it. You observe that the fire of shells is kept up from the main castle, and from the water battery also.—The strength of the whole has been alluded to.

There is a shallow bank or reef of coral rock, which makes out from the right of the water battery some distance, called the Gallega shoal; this prevents vessels from approaching it in that direction.—The vessel that you perceive, is beyond the extent of that. The castle is about one thousand yards from the city.—The water that you notice between them, is deep enough for the largest men-of-war; and, in times of peace, the whole space is filled up with vessels.

To the left of the castle, and nearer to you, at the south-eastern corner of the city, you see the fort of Santiago, with a flag above it;—this is strong, and the guns of it are now busy. To the left of that is another flag, at the custom house. To the left of this, and nearer to us, is the commencement or eastern extremity of the trenches; and the cemetery, with its chapel in the centre.

General Worth's mortar batteries, Nos. 1, 2 and 3, are in the trenches, which run parallel with, and close to the walls of the cemetery, beyond them. The volumes of smoke arising from these obscure the city. To the left of this is the smoke of the new battery, No. 4, which has been mentioned as finished last night. Farther to the left is the naval battery, sending out its peals and volumes. also here is the Mexican fort of St. Barbara; over No. 4 is the "railroad fort;"—the "white fort" is near the tall spire in the centre of the view.

To the left of the picture, between you and the naval battery, is part of the plain upon which the surrender of the Mexican arms afterwards took place, and at the lower part of this is the lake spoken of. In the foreground, you witness a detachment of infantry, going to the batteries.—You observe the hills of sand, some of which are bare, and some covered with *chaparral*.—Many of the men, that are off duty, are standing on the sand hills, gazing at the scene, while the castle has honoured them with the presentation of a thirteen inch bomb-shell, which has fallen on the little plain before you, close to that group of men, who were going to join their comrades on the hill, but who are now running away from the shell which has come among them; one is endeavouring to scramble up the steep side of the opposite sand hill.—You perceive no troops, save those going to the trenches; for these in the latter, and in the batteries, are all concealed from your view.

You can obtain a more correct and definite idea from this engraving, of the position and appearance of Vera Cruz at this time, than you could from a dozen pages of description; and from this same hill can also have a definite point in your mind, from which to judge of the position of the camp and fleet, not laid down in the picture: for, as you stand upon this hill and face the city, the sea is to your right hand, and the island of Sacrificios, the busy beach, and the fleet of ships laying off from it, is also to your right, as it were over your shoulder,—partly behind you. Directly in your rear, among the hills, are the camps of General Worth's division, and General Scott's headquarters. Behind you yet, and over your left shoulder, are the numerous valleys, in which are encamped the division of General Patterson, or the brigades of generals Shields, Pillow, and Quitman;—these go far off to the left; and beyond them, and on the left of the city also, is the camp of the division of General Twiggs, extending to the water's edge, at a little place called Vergara.

On the beach, between you and Fort Santiago, over the hill is a small point, concealed from your view, called Punta de Homos; and is the place where, afterwards, the capitulation was signed by the American and Mexican commissioners.—Now, reader, you have a correct idea of the situation of the city, castle, trenches, cemetery, batteries, fleet, beach, positions of troops, &c., &c.

The unabated fire of the batteries and mortars, and the forts and castle, continued for the whole day, and the scene was terrific;—no change took place until 3, p. m. Many were killed and many wounded in the trenches;—and among them, Midshipman Shubrick was instantly killed in the naval battery, by a round shot;—within the city the destruction was most terrible.

At that hour, an alarm was raised of an attack in the rear, by a large body of Mexican lancers, who repulsed Colonel Harney, with his dragoons, and one company of our regiment of cavalry, Captain Caswell, who had attacked them; and that officer, in command, now sent in to General Scott for reinforcements and artillery, stating the force of the enemy to be two thousand men, with two cannon. General Pillow was ordered to detach a force from his brigade, which was immediately done, by sending four companies of the first Tennessee Infantry, under Colonel Campbell, four of the second Tennessee, under Colonel Haskel, and four companies of our own, dismounted cavalry, and two pieces of artillery, under Lieutenant Judd.

And now, reader, as the author has to go with his company, he will leave you for the present, to witness the bombardment, by which the city is suffering every moment, in a terrible manner, remarking only, that the foreign consuls, that so treated with contempt the previous warnings of General Scott and chose to remain in the city and take their chance, and who sent the flag of truce last night, are now in a most uneasy position, and are endeavouring to induce General Morales to surrender the place, sending him, this evening, the answer they received this morning from General Scott, accompanied by the communication given in the note below.

Copy of Safeguard.

General Scott, a week before the bombardment commenced, sent to each of the consuls a "safeguard," as, in such cases, is authorized by the articles of war. The copy of one of these safeguards is here given:

Whosoever belonging to the Armies of the United States, employed in foreign parts, shall force a safeguard, shall suffer death.—55th Article of War.

Safeguard. By authority of Major General Scott, General-in-Chief of the armies of the United States, the person, the family, and the property of the French Consul, residing in Vera Cruz, his house, and its contents, are placed under the safeguard of the army of the United States. To offer any violence or injury to them is expressly forbidden; on the contrary, it is ordered that safety and protection be given to him and them in case of need.

Done at the headquarters of the army of the United States, this 13th day of March 1847.

      Winfield Scott.

By command of Major General Scott.

H. L. Scott, A. A. A. G.

Address of the Foreign Consuls to General Morales.
The undersigned, Consuls of the different foreign powers near the Mexican government, have the honour to address the general commanding the state of Vera Cruz, a copy of the reply which they have received from General Scott, commanding in chief the army of the United States of the North, to the request which they made to him for a truce, to permit their respective countrymen, as well as the Mexican women and children, to leave the city of Vera Cruz.

More and more afflicted by the disasters which this place has suffered during three days of bombardment, and desiring to accomplish, to the end, the duties of humanity imposed on them by the mission which they have received from their governments, and by their own personal feelings, they beseech General Morales to have the goodness to interpose to General Scott his support to a request so reasonable as theirs.

They have the honour to renew to His Excellency the Commandant, General Morales, the assurances of their respectful consideration.

  (Signed) T. Gifford, Consul
       of Her Britannic Majesty.
      A. Gloux, Consul of France.
      F. G. De Escalente, Consul of Spain.
      Henry D'oleive, Consul of His Majesty
       the King of Prussia.

We had an exciting and quite interesting fight this afternoon.—

In the morning, Colonel Harney, with the dragoons under Captain Thornton, and Captain Gaswell's company of our regiment, under the immediate command of Major Sumner, was ordered by General Scott to the southward, it being reported that a large force of the enemy were near us. The gallant colonel and his command fell in with the enemy at a stone bridge over a lagoon, called Puente de Moreno, and a fight ensued; but as the force of the enemy was large, and their position too strong for him, reinforcements were sent for. We marched out at a quick pace, partly across *chaparral* hills, and then across small prairies, about nine miles, and went immediately into action, up and down the bank of the lagoon in the *chaparral*, and commenced firing at the bridge.

The dragoons were drawn up in the rear. The firing became very sharp; but, from the thick *chaparral*, together with the smoke, concealing our men, was not very effective upon us; but the balls cut the twigs and branches over and among us at a great rate, whistling loudly. The artillery fired grape shot at the fortifications that the enemy had thrown across the bridge, and after some twelve or fifteen rounds, knocked it down, and the order was given to charge; and then, with a wild yell, that resounded far and near, we rushed towards the bridge in an irregular manner, the men of the three regiments becoming all mingled together.

The enemy retreated, run, broke, *vamosed*,—the lancers going at full speed up the road, and the infantry taking the thick *chaparral* in every direction. Some were overtaken and killed; and we pushed on in a trot after the main body of lancers. The dragoons being brought up by Captain Thornton, passed by, overtook them, and killed many more.

After four miles' chase, we were halted by General Patterson, who seemed to be in his right element, and extremely pleased with the spirit and conduct of the troops. He took off his hat, as he rode by us, after the pursuit was done, and, carried away by his enthusiasm, raised himself in his stirrups, and, as he swung his hat around, called out, "Hurrah for Tennessee!" which compliment, of manner and expression, from him, who commonly was so stern and silent, was immediately responded to, with three loud cheers for General Patterson.—He rode along, with an approving remark to each company as he passed it.

It was nearly dark when we commenced the return to the camp before Vera Cruz, about thirteen miles distant. The *ranchos* on the road, near the battle-ground, were all deserted.—The men took from them the chairs, blankets, &c., and, as the inhabitants were hostile, fired the buildings, as they returned. The dead were brought in across horses, and the wounded on litters.

Killed and Wounded at Madeline Bridge.

Killed James H. Nicholson, corporal of company F, in action at Puente de Moreno, March 25th; Hopkins, Private, company H, 3rd Artillery, same place and time.

Wounded Lewis Neill, 3rd Lieutenant, Adjutant; Joseph Marshall, Private, company B; Jones, do., 2nd Dragoons, severely; Hugh Gavin, Private, Captain Cheatham's 1st Tennessee, slightly; M. Foy, W. Ailes, Privates, company A; D. Vann, do., company C; G. Woodly, do., company H, 2nd Tennessee, slightly; Thomas Young, guide, slightly; W. T. Gillespie, company B, Lewis Geisele, company C. John Smith, company K, Privates, 2nd Dragoons, slightly.

We had lost but few, and killed some fifty or sixty of the Mexicans,—Would have killed more, had they fought longer; but they had enough, and could not stand the wild charge.

Thus ended the spirited little battle of "Madeline Bridge," as it is called, or of Puente de Moreno; and here we are back, in fine spirits, but exceedingly exhausted. It was nearly midnight when we reached the camp. We found our batteries firing slowly, while those of the enemy were all silent. And so, reader, as we are about to throw ourselves down to sleep, we bid you good night.

Friday, March 26th. At two o'clock this morning, the batteries recommenced upon the city; but only a few guns were fired from the enemy in reply to the numerous shells that rose, passed over, and fell within, more rapidly than before, several new mortars having been added to those in operation yesterday.

Another norther came down upon us, immediately after the firing commenced. This gale blew with more violence than any which had preceded it.—It whistled across the hills and plains, deadening the noise of the mortars.—As soon as it was light, the fatigue parties were again set to work, making fascines and scaling-ladders for the final assault;—but, directly after sunrise, a flag of truce came from the city gates. The order to cease firing was sent to the batteries, by General Scott.

We now found, what we were confident of yesterday, that the bombardment had been productive of the utmost desolation within the walls, tearing the buildings to pieces, and sweeping hundreds,—soldiers, citizens, women and children—into a common grave.—We learned that the destructive effects, sometimes of a single shell, had been tremendous:—that one had fallen, crashing through the stone side of a building, and exploded within, where a meeting of the citizens was being held, and killed and wounded scores of them in one bloody pile.—That the distresses of the citizens and private families could not be described;—that whole families had perished by a single shell, that, in the same instant, by its explosion, had tumbled in the floors, roofs, stone and mortar, of their shattered mansions, upon their mangled bodies.

That there was safety nowhere; that the heavy stone roofs, so much relied upon, were futile in defence: for the ponderous shells, from their height, had burst down through, crashing to the ground;—that they had torn up the pavements, sending stone and iron in destructive showers through the streets.—That the churches were not safe;—that the altars of these, around which the frightened women had collected to pray for deliverance, had, in some instances, been the places where they were torn and mangled by the shells, that, loaded with destruction, crashed through the roofs. That the round shot were terrific in effect, but the shells, from their falling in every part of the thickly crowded city, were far more so.

That last evening, so terrible had become their situation, the citizens united with the foreign consuls in application to General Morales, and the soldiers to the same added their requests, being unable to stand longer against the murderous fire.—That, driven to desperation, part of the garrison formed in the night, on the outside of the city walls, to attack the batteries that were so destructive to them; but not enough, to be successful, could be induced to join it, as they were well aware that the trenches were strongly defended, though the men therein could not be seen.

General Morales, not wishing to surrender, and to save his word, under colour of sickness, resigned his command during the night, and thus devolved it upon the next officer, General Jose Juan de Landero, who, at this early hour, hastened, by a flag of truce, to stop the horrors that were recommencing.—By this flag he sent the letter seen in the note below.

General Landero to General Scott.

I have the honour of transmitting to Your Excellency, the exposition which has this moment been made to me by the *Señores* Consuls of England, France, Spain and Prussia, in which they solicit that hostilities may be suspended while the innocent families in this place, who are suffering the ravages of war, be enabled to leave the city, which solicitation claims my support; and considering it in accordance with the rights of afflicted humanity, I have not hesitated to invite Your Excellency to enter into an honourable accommodation with the garrison, in which case, you will please name three commissioners, who may meet at some intermediate point to treat with those of this place upon the terms of the accommodation.

With this notice, I renew to Your Excellency's attentive consideration,

God guard Your Excellency, &c.

On account of the sickness of the commanding general,

  [Signed by]   Jose Juan de Landero

The batteries remained silent, but everything was in preparation for a renewal of the fire.—The storm was now raging with the utmost fury, and many of the vessels in the fleet at Sacrificios were unable to hold to their anchors; and as their chains parted, they went ashore on the beach.—Twenty-seven ships, brigs and schooners were thus ashore before night, with the waves dashing over them. This wind blew with such a hurricane force that no boat could float in the tremendous surf;—even the line of battle ship, Ohio, that lay proudly moored at the head of the fleet, was forced to send down all her upper masts and yards, and she appeared almost dismantled.—In consequence of this violent gale, the commander-in-chief found it impossible to communicate with the commodore of the naval forces, as he wished to do upon this application of General Landero; and, after waiting some hours, he appointed his commissioners, and sent to the Mexican general the answer seen in note. The time for a reply was restricted to thirty minutes.—Now was there the utmost curiosity in every regiment and company, to know what was going on; and even at every tent, the only subject of inquiry or remark was concerning the passing flags of truce, and present events.

General Scott's reply to General Landero.
Headquarters of the army
of the United States of America.
Camp Washington, before Vera Cruz, March 26, 1647.
The undersigned, Major General Scott, General-in-Chief of the Armies of the United States of America, has had the honour to receive a communication on the part of His Excellency the Governor and Commander-in-Chief of Vera Cruz, signed by the Señor General Landero, in which it is proposed to the undersigned, that he [the undersigned] should appoint three commissioners to meet an equal number to be appointed on the part of the city of Vera Cruz, to treat of the surrender of that city and its dependencies, on terms honourable to the garrison of the same.

The undersigned, not doubting that the proposition was made in good faith, has promptly given orders to all his batteries to suspend their fire upon the city of Vera Cruz, which cessation of fire will be continued, unless after a delay of thirty minutes, any Mexican battery shall continue or renew its fire upon the batteries or the lines of the army before Vera Cruz.

The undersigned hastens to name, on the part of the United States of America, three commissioners generals Worth and Pillow, and Colonel Totten, Chief Engineer, all of the said army to meet an equal number of commissioners to be appointed by competent authority, to treat of the surrender of the city of Vera Cruz and its dependencies, on terms honourable to the garrison. And the three commissioners named above will, in that delay, repair, under a flag of truce, to Punta de Hornos, there to await the arrival of the corresponding commissioners on the part of Vera Cruz.

It is expected by the undersigned that the commissioners will proceed, at once, to treat of the business jointly submitted to them, without unnecessary interruptions, and that the. negotiation will be concluded early in the present day.

The undersigned has the honour to tender to the *Señor* General Landero the assurances of his high consideration and respect

    [Signed]   Winfield Scott.

Generals Worth and Pillow, and Colonel Totten, proceeded up the beach to the buildings at the point Punta de Hornos, under the guns of Fort Santiago. In a short time, three Mexican officers, with another white flag, issued from the lofty arched gateways of that fortress, and approached the same spot. Many polite salutations now passed, as though the parties had been most intimate friends for their whole lives, and only lived to be agreeable to each other.—The Mexican officers brought out General Landero's reply to General Scott, which is placed below.

General Landero to General Scott.

Vera Cruz, March 26th, 1847.

In virtue of your Excellency's having accepted the proposition for an accommodation, which I made in a dispatch of this date, and in conformity with a reply which I have just received, 1 have the honour to inform you that I have named, on my part, Colonels Don Jose Gutierrez Villanueva, Don Pedro Miguel Herrera, and Lieutenant Colonel of Engineers, Don Manuel Robles to whom I have committed competent powers to arrange the said accommodation, having the honour to add herewith a copy of said powers.

I renew to your Excellency the assurances of my high consideration.

God and Liberty.

[Signed]　　Jose Juan de Landero.

The preparation for the assault still went on. The landing and transportation of shells, shot and powder, was stopped on account of the norther, which drove the waves in furious breakers over nearly the entire beach; and, so sudden and strong was its effect, that immense quantities of stores were overflowed and spoiled.—In camp, we crowded in our firmly pinned tents, to avoid the cold wind; and thus the remainder of the day passed.— The commissioners returned at evening, not having come to any agreement, save to meet again in the morning.

Saturday, March 27th. This was a lovely morning:—the norther had ceased, and the sun shone pleasantly. Everything was quiet in the city, batteries, and camp.—The commissioners met again at Punta de Hornos, and the entire day was spent in their deliberations.—Let us, therefore, reader, take a look into the trenches—pursuing our walk from the sand hill, in the foreground of the picture, across the hills and valleys towards the cemetery, or *campo santo*, as the Mexicans term it.

As we pass over the hills, and come near, you are astonished in seeing how the ground is torn up by cannon shot and bomb-shells: the large balls lay thickly scattered around.—Many holes, each of size sufficient to bury a horse, are blown out, by the explosion of the shells that there descended. Large and small fragments of these shells are scattered everywhere about. The Mexicans have thrown shot and shells enough to kill a hundred thousand men and yet, so skillfully have our movements been directed by the generalship of Scott, that our loss is very small.—We approach the cemetery—pass around the left hand corner, and enter the enclosure through the lofty arched gateway.

On going in, we are struck with the appearance of destruction there exhibited: the walks and the graves are torn up, and skulls and bones are scattered around, by the numberless shells thrown here from the city and castle; the enemy thinking that part of our force was within it. The walls of brick, plastered over within and without, are riddled with so many large holes, that it was useless to attempt to count them; and the brick and mortar from these, had been driven over the whole ground.—Here is an entire shell, whose fuse did not ignite the charge;—it is in the ground, and you see but little of it.

The chapel, which is in the centre of the cemetery, is about forty feet square, with a brick dome, also plastered. You see this chapel in the picture.—Around the building is a wide, raised platform, of chequered marble, enclosed by a light balustrade of masonry, which is mostly torn to pieces; the marble slabs are broken and thrown up by the shells.—Within the chapel we observe a fine sculptured structure of white marble; it is broken, and covered with the mortar and pieces of brick that have fallen from the dome above, and the sides of the house, as the cannon shot have coursed through it again and again. The large door of the chapel, towards the city, has over a dozen cannon shot holes in it.

The marble floor is covered with rubbish; and the wardrobes for the funeral trappings and dresses for the priests, are splintered into thousands of fragments.—The eastern wall of the cemetery, or the right hand one seen in the picture, is of such thickness as to be divided into four rows of cells like ovens, above each other, on the same plan as is adopted in New Orleans.—In these cells are the bodies of the more wealthy placed.—You observe that the cannon shot, coming slanting from the city, have opened the ends of many of these, and left the corpses and skeletons exposed. It is not a pleasant sight to view them.—You perceive that they were buried in their ordinary clothing.

Do you notice that pair of feet, with boots on, sticking nearly out of the hole made by a cannon ball that ranged along, opening a dozen or more of these sepulchres?—Many of the soldiers are peeping about in the cemetery, and looking into these cells; but the sight of death, or his mementos, are nothing to them:—hardened, careless, and indifferent by habit, the appearance of dead men produces no more effect than that of so many dead animals.

Hear that dare-devil, humorous looking volunteer, as he calls out to another:"I say, Bill, don't you believe these chaps thought the resurrection day had come, when that 'ere cannon ball raked open their holes? D—n—d if I don't think they were getting ready to sing, 'Hark! from the tombs.'"

So little is human life valued by the older soldiers, that no one is affected by these sights.—Some, of the new regiments that have just come out, walk round, and appear serious; but they, too, will be equally careless after a while. But let us look at the marble slabs that close the vaults which have not thus been rudely broken into. We see that many of them are finely sculptured. Observe this one, of black marble, on which life is represented as a fragile vase of beautiful flowers—Death as a wolf, who jumps upon it; and it is falling over, to be crushed under his tread.

Having seen enough of the interior of the *campo santo*, let us go out by the gate by which we entered, and a few steps bring us to the farther wall, under which run the trenches.—Here are piles of balls and shells lying on the edge of them , and near are several small brass *cohorn* mortars, which have the English crown upon them, and the letters G. R.—*Geargius Rex* (King George).

These were taken at the surrender of Burgoyne, during the revolutionary war, and are yet good as ever; and, after being used in the last war, against their former masters, are sent here to fight Mexicans with.—Look into the trench: it is six or seven feet wide—eight or nine where the mortars are placed. You perceive the embankment is thrown towards the city; and, in the deep trench thus sheltered, you do not wonder that the troops have been so secure.

Look along in it:—you see it full of infantry, seated, patiently awaiting the issue of the negotiations for a surrender. You observe the numerous black mortars on their beds, ranged along, with the match-rope slowly burning by each: and piles of loaded shells are near; while the artillerists are leaning on the destructive pieces, chatting and laughing, ready, at any moment, again to send the ponderous missiles into the city.—Let us go down into the trench: it is quite a jump; and now we are in among the crowded men.

Look at this mortar before us, which, firmly placed in its bed, is on a platform laid down for its support; its muzzle slants upward. Take out the wooden mouth-piece, and you see the shell lying in there: it is heavy, and required two men to lift it in. You perceive that four small wedges are placed around it, so that it does not press tight to the interior of the mortar; for, if it did, the fuse, which is on the upper side, would not catch as it went out; but the wedges causing a small space to be left, the flame from the charge wraps around the shell as it is sent out, and fires the fuse, which burns as it goes.

You observe that the fuse plug is of wood, large enough to fill the hole in the shell, being about an inch and a half thick at the larger end, and tapering to an inch; being, when whole, about nine inches long; it has a small hole drilled lengthwise through it.

This hole is filled with the fuse combustible, which is black and hard—appearing something like the lead in a pencil; and is about as large as a common pencil itself. The tapering plugs are marked into inches and tenths, so that they may be accurately sawed off to the length they are required to burn.

If the shells are to go but a short distance, a small quantity of powder is put into the mortar, and the fuse is cut off in proportion; so, for a greater distance more powder is added, and the fuse is left longer. So well have our artillerists done this, that of the thousands of shells[2] they have thrown into the city, very few have burst before they had crashed through the buildings; and almost every one, then, has immediately exploded.—Let us pass to the mouth of this magazine near, which is a deep hole in the trench, covered with a slanting double roof of plank and timber, upon which are three tiers of large bags, filled with earth or sand, to protect it from the bombs of the enemy.

Near the magazine door, in which set the powder-men, are a number of shells, loaded, with their fuses driven in them. These men inform us that they filled every shell with three pounds of first-rate powder, and that the mortars were at first loaded with two and a half pounds, to send the shells to the walls; then two and three-quarters, three, three and a half, three and three-quarters, and at last four pounds were used for a charge; and that these different charges were used at the same time, in order to distribute the deadly missiles over the city,—thus bringing all within it into the same terrible condition.

Turning to the left, we follow along the crowded trench, and, working our way by the mortars, shells, and through artillerists, and supporting infantry, we soon come to battery No. 4. We find no shells here, but abundance of the heaviest kind of shot;—the

---

2. Shot and shell thrown into the city of Vera Cruz, during the bombardment, on the evening of 22nd, the 23rd, 24th, 25th, and morning of 26th March, 1847: Worth's Batteries, Nos. 1, 2, 3, 4.

3000 ten inch shells	99 lbs. each,
500 round shot	25 " "
200 eight inch howitzer shells	68 " "
Navy Battery, No. 5.	
1000 Paixhan shot	68 lbs. each.
800 round shot	32 " "
Musquito Fleet.	
1200 shot and shell, averaging	62 lb. each.
Making in all, 6,700 shot and shell, weighing	463,600 lbs.

large cannon stand on the high platform, with their muzzles sticking out of the embrasures towards the city, into which they have already vomited so many destructive missiles.—We find the artillerists here ready to renew the firing; the infantry are stretched out, some asleep, others engaged in conversation, wondering whether they will have another chance at the city.

When leaving this battery, we pass still farther to the left; we come out of the trenches on the plain; crossing that, as well as the railroad, we ascend the hill, on the top of which is the naval battery.—This hill, like many of the others, is covered with a species of musquit, of which the sharp thorns are several times as large as the twigs on which they grow; and they are so singular, that the author has placed below a drawing of a small twig, bearing them.

After climbing the hill, and working through the thorny *chaparral*, we arrive at the naval battery.—Here, too, the heavy cannon were all loaded and aimed, ready to fire the moment hostilities may be recommenced. The seamen that man this battery are in groups around, as are the supporting infantry. The sailors are having much sport to themselves, and wish that the "bloody Mexican land-lubbers," as they call them, may hold out a little longer, to give them a chance; (for this battery has a change of seamen every twenty-four hours, and those now at it have not

TWIG OF MUSQUIT

had an opportunity of firing).

The naval forces which had been so long before this place had, during the bombardment, manifested the greatest desire to have a part on shore, and this battery had therefore been assigned to them; it was manned in turn by detachments from the vessels. These vessels of war now before the city were

Ship of the line	*Ohio*, Captain Stringham,	74 guns
Frigate	*Raritan*, Captain Forrest	44
	Potomac, Captain Aulick,	44
Sloop	*Albany*, Captain Breese,	20
"	*John Adams*, Commander McKinney,	20
"	*St. Marys*, Captain Launders,	20
Steamer	*Mississippi*, Commodore Perry,	10
"	*Princeton*, Commander Engle,	9
"	*Spitfire*, Commander Tatnall,	8
"	*Vixen*, Commander Sands,	8
Brig	*Porpoise*, L. Commander W. E. Hunt,	10
Storeship	*Relief*, Lt. Commander Bullus,	8
"	*Supply*,	8
"	*Fredonia*	8
Steamers	*Petrita, Hunter,* and *Scourge,*	

Schooners (musquito fleet) *Bonito, Petrel, Reefer, Tampico,* and *Falcon,*

We notice that the battery is much torn to pieces: for, from its situation, being so high and exposed, it has drawn many of the shot from all the forts, and well has it answered them. On its opening, the Mexican batteries directed most of their fire at it, for nearly the whole day;—but this had been foreseen, and it had been made very strong.

From this we can look directly into the town; but nothing appears there to be in motion, save the bodies of Mexican soldiery, who are parading about to the strains of their martial music, or else thickly crowded in the shattered forts, busy in repairing them with bags of sand; but the battered buildings above and around them cannot be so repaired; they present, when viewed with the glass, an appearance of utter destruction.

And now, reader, we have endeavoured to give a particular account of the batteries, as well as of the occurrences of the siege, though thousands of circumstances accompanying it must, for want of space, pass unrecorded. At five, p. m., the capitulation was signed by the commissioners, and we learned that the city was to be given up on Monday, the 29th.—the terms on which the city and castle were surrendered are given in the note below.

Punta De Hornos. (without the walls of Vera Cruz), Saturday, March 27, 1847

Terms of capitulation agreed upon by the Commissioners, *viz.*:

Generate W. J. Worth and G. J. Pillow, and Colonel J. G. Totten, chief engineer, on the part of Major General Scott, General-in-Chief of the armies of the United States, and Colonel Jose Gutierrez de Villaneuva, Lieutenant Colonel of Engineers, Manuel Robles, and Colonel Pedro de Herrera, commissioners appointed by General of Brigadier Don Jose Juan Landero, Commander-in-chief of Vera Cruz, the castle of San Juan de Ulloa, and their dependencies, for the surrender to the arms of the United States of the forts, with their armaments, munitions of war, garrisons and arms.

1. The whole garrison or garrisons to be surrendered to the arms of the United States, as prisoners of war, on the 29th inst., at ten o'clock, a. m.; the garrison to be permitted to march out with all the honours of war, and to lay down their arms to such officers as may be appointed by the general-in-chief of the United States' army, and at a place to be agreed upon by the commissioners.

2. Mexican officers shall preserve their arms and effects, including horses and horse furniture, and to be allowed, regular and irregular officers, as also the rank and file, five days to retire to their respective homes, on parole, as hereinafter prescribed.

3. Coincident with the surrender, as stipulated in Article 1,

the Mexican flags of the various forts and stations shall be struck, saluted by their own batteries, and immediately thereafter the forts Santiago and Conception, and the castle of San Juan de Ulua, occupied by the forces of the United States.

4. The rank and file of the regular portion of the prisoners to be disposed of, after surrender and parole, as their general-in-chief may desire, and the irregular to be permitted to return to their homes. The officers, in respect to all arms and descriptions of force, giving the usual parole, that the said rank and file, as well as themselves, shall not serve again until duly exchanged.

5. All the materiel of war, and all public property, of every description, found in the city, the castle of San Juan de Ulua and their dependencies, to belong to the United States; but the armament of the same (not injured or destroyed in the further prosecution of the actual war) may be considered as liable to be restored to Mexico by a definite treaty of peace.

6. The sick and wounded Mexicans to be allowed to remain in the city with such medical officers and attendants and officers of the army as may be necessary to their care and treatment.

7. Absolute protection is solemnly guaranteed to persons in the city, and property, and it is clearly understood that no private building or property is to be taken or used by the forces of the United States, without previous arrangement with the owners, and for a fair equivalent

8. Absolute freedom of religious worship and ceremonies is solemnly guaranteed.

    [Signed in duplicate.]
        W. J. Worth, Brigadier General
        Gid. J. Pillow, Brigadier General
        Jos. G. Totten, Colonel and Chief Engineer
        Jose Gutierrez de *Villanueva*
        Pedro Miguel Herrera
        Manuel Robles

Captain Aulick, appointed commissioner by Commander Perry on behalf of the nary, (the General-in-chief not being able, in consequence of the roughness of the sea, to communicate with the navy until after commissions had been exchanged), and being present by General Scott's invitation, and concurring in the result and approving thereof, hereto affixes his name and signature.

J. H. Aulick, Captain U. S. N.

Headquarters of the Army of the United States, Camp Washington, before Vera Cruz, March 27, 1847.

Approved and accepted:

Winfield Scott.
M. C. Perry.
Commander-in-Chief of U. S. Naval Forces
in the gulf of Mexico.
Vera Cruz, Marzo 27, 1847.

Aprobad y aceptado:

Jose Juan de Landero.

March 28th. We have endeavoured to find out the loss of the Mexicans within the city, during the terrible bombardment, but it is not known to themselves; of course it can never be definitely ascertained by us. Their calculations of it vary from twelve to fifteen hundred.—our own loss, killed and wounded, during the regular operations of the siege, falls a little short of eighty, all told. The names of those that fell at Puente de Moreno have before been given. The list of the others is listed below.

LIST OF KILLED AND WOUNDED AT THE SIEGE OF VERA CRUZ.

Under General Worth.

Killed J. B. Vinton, Captain 3rd Artillery, on the 22nd March; John Huffner, Private, company B. 2nd Artillery, 26th March; Nicholas Burns, Private, company B, 24th March;———, musician, 21st March.

Wounded James Foster, Sergeant, company G, 3rd Artillery, March 23rd, severely; W. B. Hunt and Emile Voltarat, Privates, company B, 2nd Artillery, 24th March, slightly; Adolphe Malhe, John Golding and Wm. Henderson, Privates, company D, 2nd Artillery, 22nd March, the two last named slightly, the other his left arm shot off; Ernest Krunse, Owen Boote. William Carthage,

Joseph S. Hayden and Archibald McFadger, Privates company F, 2nd Artillery, the first on the 20th and remainder on the 24th March, slightly; Martin Dignant, Private, company G, 2nd Artillery. 22nd March, slightly; S. D. Schuetzenback, Private, company A, and Edward Fleming, Private, company I, 8th Infantry, 23rd March, slightly.

Under General Twiggs.

Killed Wm. Alburtis, Brevet Captain 2nd Infantry, March 11th, by a cannon ball; Wm. R. Blake, Sergeant company F, 4th Artillery, March 15th; Robert T. Cunningham, Private, company A, Mounted Riflemen, March 11th.

Wounded W. B. Lane and Edward Harris, Sergeants, company D, Mounted Riflemen, March 24th, severely; John Teluna, Private, company E, Mounted Riflemen, March 24th, severely; Frederick Warren, Private, company C, Mounted Riflemen, March 24th, slightly; Henry Niell. slightly, and Thomas Weller, severely, Privates, company B, Mounted Riflemen, March 11th; John Rose, Musician, company B. 1st Artillery, severely; James Stephen, Private, company F. 4th Artillery. March 14th, severely; Spencer, Corporal, company D, 2nd infantry, March 11th, severely.

Under General Patterson.

Killed John Miller and Gothlet Reip, privates, company G, 1st regiment Pennsylvania Volunteers, the first on the 17th, and the latter on the 20th March.

Wounded Lieutenant Colonel J. P. Dickinson. South Carolina regiment, severely; Private Ballad, severely, privates Coke, D. Phillips, and Hickey, slightly, all of South Carolina regiment; Q. M. Sergeant B. F. McDonald, severely, Sergeant Jos. King, slightly, Privates T. J. Scott, severely, Henry Lanbeck, slightly, John G. Eubank, severely, all of Georgia regiment all on 11th of March; Sergeant John Henson, company E. 1st Pennsylvania regiment, March 9th, slightly; Privates O. Burden. Wm. Vandenbark, and Andrew Keamer, company I, Jas. Stevens, company J, all of 1st Pennsylvania regiment, Private Fry, company D, 2nd Pennsylvania regiment all on 11th of March, slightly; Private Mark Fose.

company A, 2nd Tennessee regiment, 25th March, slightly; Private John Hubbard, company A, 1st Tennessee regiment, during bombardment, slightly; Sergeant R. Williamson, company C, 1st Pennsylvania regiment, 11th March, slightly; Private Daniel Harkins, company A, 1st Pennsylvania regiment, (on picquet). slightly.

In addition to these, were killed on the 28th, of the New York and Pennsylvania regiments Reverend W. H. T. Carnes, Robert Jeff, George W. Miller, Benjamin Fane, Hardin, William H Kearney, and several others, whose names are not ascertained, were lassoed, shot, stabbed, and all horribly mutilated, by the enemy.

Beside those mentioned, there were, also, Midshipman Shubrick and fifteen seamen of the navy, killed and wounded.—With so little loss of life amid such terrible and long-continued discharges of artillery, has General Scott thus taken the city of Vera Cruz and the strong castle of San Juan de Ulloa, that even now, on the ground, we are surprised at the result. Most anxiously are all throughout the camp waiting for the approach of tomorrow, which shall place us in possession of these formidable strong-holds.

March 29th. This has been a day of triumph to the American army, which will long be remembered by every one whose fortune it was to witness the imposing scene.—The morning was calm and tranquil, the sky clear, and the sun rose in unusual splendour; not a breath of wind was there even to display the flags, with which the shipping was decorated, or those which hung over the castle and forts of the city. No sound could be heard from within the walls. Our batteries and trenches were still manned with their full number of troops and seamen, and the guns remained loaded.

At an early hour the drums were beat in the encampments of Worth's and Patterson's divisions, and all their troops mustered to take part in the ceremonies of the approaching surrender.—The author, to obtain the best view of the whole, left the camp and took his position on the naval battery; which, though a little distant from the plain below, on which the Mexican army were to march, yet commanded a fine prospect of the city, the castle beyond it, and the fleet at Sacrificios, as well as the whole extent of the plain from the city walls, back as far as Malibran.—The different regiments, with their colours flying, moved upon the ground about nine o'clock, and formed in two long lines, facing each other, a mile or more in length. At the head of these lines, about half a mile from the walls, were placed the rocket and howitzer company, under Captain Talcott, with its six small field pieces, so as to rake the foreground, incase of any treachery; the matches were lighted, and the men were ready for such an event.

The mounted dragoons were drawn up in the rear of Worth's line, and a large detachment of seamen from the navy were near. The music bands of the army were at their stations, but were wholly silent.—The view of these large bodies of troops, thus placed, was in itself of much interest.—General Worth was conspicuous at the head of his column, from his brilliant uniform and long, waving plume.—The sea-breeze shortly began to blow gently, and the numerous banners floated gaily in it.—At ten o'clock, precisely (according to the terms of the capitulation), a single light volume of smoke burst out from the castle, and rolled off over the water. The report announced that all was ready. Immediately the Mexican bands within the city struck up their loud music, and with drums, fifes, clarinets and bugles, swelled the concert.

As they finished, the fort of Santiago commenced a salute of artillery, in honour of the Mexican flag still waving above it. As the last cannon of this was fired, the flag was hauled down, and at the same moment descended all the others, which had been flying at different points above the city. The gates were thrown open, and the head of the Mexican army emerged therefrom, accompanied by loud music, and battalion after battalion swept out under their banners; they appeared soldier-like, as they moved towards our lines, with shouldered muskets and free step, while the rays of the sun glanced upon their bright arms. Their movements were made with precision and concord. Their officers paid the same attention to these, as though they had been on parade. Some of the regiments were clothed in brilliant uniforms of green, trimmed with red; others in blue, trimmed also with red; others in light dress, nearly white, with red pompoms; and, taking them altogether, they made a much more imposing display than did the same number of our troops in their plain blue.

First came the column of regulars; then followed the National Guard. Crowds of women came out, loaded with baskets, children, household furniture, and almost every other conceivable article. These camp-women, thus burdened, followed contentedly, and seemed more like the slaves than the companions of the soldiers. They waited on them, bringing them water, &c. Most of these were by no means attractive in their appearance, although some were indeed handsome in countenance, and with good forms.—The platoons of regulars moved on with a free step, to their music, and coming to the space between our lines, were halted, wheeled into line, and, at the command, stacked their muskets regularly, and hung over them their bayonet-scabbards and cartridge-boxes; their numerous colours, drums, and musical instruments, were alike placed down; and then, at the renewed order, the disarmed platoons moved off and gave room for other columns and other bands, which still were pouring from the city gates.

This scene continued for two hours, during which no music. but that of the Mexican bands could be heard. Not a word was said by the American troops to the disarmed bodies, as they passed down the lines towards Madeline. After the army came a miscellaneous crowd of citizens, officers, priests, and camp-women; wounded and sick soldiers; and in the throng were carts, each drawn by three mules abreast, containing the women and children of the officers; also, *literas*, a kind of covered box, with shafts each way, supported by a mule before, and another behind; in these were entire families.

Other carts were loaded with various articles, and many mules were packed with bulky bundles. None of these things were interrupted, but all were allowed to pass without hindrance;—every soldier had something besides his full knapsack; and every camp-woman was loaded like a mule. The officers themselves were on fine steeds, splendidly caparisoned. One officer seemed to have much money, for it took four soldiers to carry the litter containing it upon their shoulders. Every officer retained his sword; and one company of soldiers, in number about forty, marched down the lines with their muskets shouldered, not stopping to stack them.

They, by previous arrangement, had been permitted to retain these, in order to guard a gang of convicts, who had been confined in the castle, and were now taken with them.—Toward the last of the long procession came a body of dismounted lancers, dressed in their uniforms of green. These laid their *escopetas* and lances on the ground, and in regular order followed after the dense crowd that had preceded them.—On the countenances of the soldiers, notwithstanding the firm step and martial bearing, with which they swept down the plain, could be seen an undefined expression of doubt and anxiety, especially as they came before the artillery of the rocket and howitzer company, which bore upon them, looking threateningly.—A bare sketch of the vast crowd that continued to pour out from the gates, is all that can be given in this compass to the reader.

The officers generally were fine-looking men, of light complexion, and exceedingly polite in their manners; saluting our generals with their drawn swords, as they passed. The soldiers were of every grade of colour.—When the rear of the conquered army had emerged from the gate, three companies of the 3rd and 4th regiments U. S. artillery, with their field-pieces and colours, commenced the march for the gate, without music, passing along the column of Mexicans, who with shouldered arms were still advancing. They soon arrived there, and passed through; one company going down to take possession of Fort Santiago, the other to the castle.

Shortly after, the whole of the Mexicans laid down their arms, and the throng of stragglers that followed, had passed on.—As yet not a sound of music had been heard from our lines. Our troops were motionless, and a few moments of suspense took place.—All eyes were directed to Fort Santiago, watching for the appearance of the American flag.—The musquito fleet of the two steamers and five schooners, could be seen to glide gracefully in between the city and castle.—Suddenly the flag looked for arose to the top of the staff, and unrolled its stars and stripes to the breeze, and, at the same instant, the guns below it, which had been belching their thunders against it, spoke out as clear for its honour, and announced that the city was ours.

Simultaneously with its discharges, came a full salute from the field-pieces on the plain, another from the batteries, still another from the musquito in the harbour, and one also from every vessel of war at Sacrificios. The first glimpse of the flag as it rolled out, was the signal for all to fire together; and their mingled roar appeared to shake the hills. The whole fleet was completely enveloped in smoke.—When this grand discharge had ceased its thunders, the bands of music commenced, and the strains of "Hail Columbia," rose in power on the air, and the enthusiasm of the American army was aroused to its highest pitch. General Worth's division was put in motion: dragoons, artillery and infantry, swept by, to the quick and inspiring national air of "Yankee Doodle;" and thus they entered the city.

The impressive scene closed with the entrance into the gates of the heavy column.—The other troops were marched back to their encampments and dismissed, and the general exclamations of all were of the events of the day, and the wonder expressed was, whether they should ever see the like again.

The Mexicans had all gone, and the surrounding country was full of them, as they pursued their various courses,—some north, some south,—carrying in every direction the news of their defeat.—At the gates of the city were immediately placed sentinels, to prevent the entrance of any more soldiers,—General Scott being fearful of disturbance or disorder. Many of the soldiers, however, anxious to see the city, entered, through the breaches battered in the walls.

On approaching these, we were struck by the preparations that had been made for defence against an assault:—deep holes were dug along in three parallel lines, with lance heads set in the bottom;—a thick growth of prickly pear was within these. At every distance of two hundred yards, the solid stone forts stood out from the walls.

We entered into the "railroad fort."—Six heavy cannon were there;—piles of .shot lay near each; the rammers, sponges, &c., were laid across them, as the artillerists had left them in the morning.—Blood had stained the whole place, where the Mexican soldiers had fallen at their posts;—bags of sand had been placed upon the breaches of the walls.

We passed out of this, inside of the battered city wall, along the wide avenue between that and the buildings, to the next fort,—or the "red fort," as we called it,—which had done so much injury to our batteries, and received so much in return. Six heavy cannon of brass, cast in Spain a hundred or more years ago,—in 1707, 1750, 1694, &c., were here;—the cannon shot, rammers, &c., lay as in the other, and with them several large boxes of Congreve rockets, and piles of grape and canister shot. Some of these guns had been injured by our fire, and the battlements of the fort were torn down, but had been rebuilt, during the intervening time, with bags of sand. Large stains of blood were on the whole area.

Turning from this, we passed down to the fort of Santiago. This was much larger than the others; was battered, but not so much as the city wall or other forts.

We turned into the streets, and a scene of destruction and desolation was before us.—Bombs had fallen thickly, making, in their descent, large holes in the pavements; and the explosions that had followed, had thrown the ragged pieces of iron, and the round paving stones, through the sides of the buildings, doors, and windows, tearing and crashing all before them. Very many had fallen, too, upon the stone and tiled flat roofs, which had failed to protect the interior: for the ponderous shells had torn and descended, through the rooms and the floors, to the basement. The effect of their explosions was terrible.—The floors, and in many instances the stone walls, were lifted, crashed, and all fell in—a mass of timbers, plank, plaster, stone and brick—upon the mangled inmates.

The streets were covered with heaps of broken walls, plaster, and brick; heavy pieces of exploded shells were scattered in and about their deep, torn out beds. In all the southern part of the city the heavy cannon shot had ranged in straight lines, doing terrible execution;—whole sides of stone blocks had fallen before them. The interiors of some of the churches were ripped and torn in a scene of confusion and destruction difficult to imagine. The chequered marble floors were thrown up, the images were broken and scattered, the plastering tumbled in; and in one, a shell had taken off the head of an image of Christ upon the cross.

We were looking within the walls of a fine, two story, lofty building, and observing the complete havoc made by a bomb, when a Mexican woman came by, (the first that we had seen within the walls: for the streets were nearly deserted). Throwing up her hand from under her *reboso*, and fixing her eyes upon us, with a wild and terrified look, she exclaimed, *"Muchas bombas Americanos! mui malo, mui terrible!"* (multitude of American bomb-shells! very bad, most terrible!)—and, after gazing upon us for a moment, with grief and terror depicted in her countenance, she passed on.

The owner of a large store invited some of us to follow him into the second story of his buildings. In a room, on the shelves, a great quantity of China and Liverpool ware had been stowed. Many large and splendid looking-glasses had been hung up around. On one side of the apartment had been a range of costly furniture,—tables of the richest mahogany and rosewood, secretaries and sideboards, with black and white marble slabs on their tops; Grecian chairs, &c., &c.

Into this costly collection a heavy bomb, breaking in an instant through the thick roof, which the owner had fondly believed to be proof against them, had descended and exploded; and the complete destruction of everything, with the fallen quantities of plaster and stone, could not be justly described. We were struck with amazement. The owner contemplated the scene for a moment, and pointing upwards to the large hole, through which we could see the blue sky, exclaimed, "*bomba*" and throwing his hand around towards the heaps of property, so shattered in an instant, repeated, "*mucho malo! mucho malo!*" and shook his head despondently.

The city had been well prepared to resist an assault.—The parapet walls of the houses, around the roofs, had been piled higher with sand bags. Ditches had been dug in every street, and embankments placed before them, with cannon pointed over them. The streets, near the city walls, were barricaded with posts ten feet high, set in the ground. Quantities of hand grenades, or small bombs, to light with a match, and throw down upon troops in the streets below, had been carried up to the tops of the houses. And we found that, in addition to the force within, every citizen had been fully armed from the public arsenal, thus nearly doubling the force for defence.

But their calculations were destroyed by our shower of bombs, against the effect of which there had been no protection. They were miserably disappointed in the manner of attack; and now, some of the English and French, who had remained within the city to witness the slaughter of our troops, in the expected assault, and who had suffered most grievously in their families and property, by the shells and shot, had the impudence to complain most bitterly of it, saying that General Scott, when directing them to leave the city, did not inform them that he was going to bombard it; as if they expected our general to tell them and the Mexicans the plan of his future operations. They refused to leave the city when they might have done so; and, undoubtedly, many of them had anticipated the pleasure of popping at us from behind the parapet walls of their high stone buildings, or dropping hand grenades, to burst among our troops in the streets below;—they remained at their own peril.

General Worth was immediately appointed governor of the city and castle, and entered upon the discharge of his duties.—Ten thousand rations of bread, rice, beans, and meat, were ordered to be distributed among the poor of the city, who crowded to receive this unexpected bounty, given by those, who but a day or two before, were destroying them by hundreds.

The vessels were removed from the anchorage at Sacrificios, to the harbour of the city.—The custom-house was opened, and business commenced.—A Mexican printing-office was hired, and a newspaper, styled the *Vera Cruz Eagle*, soon made its appearance. The *rancheros* came into market, with provisions and vegetables to sell; the *burreros* with their jackasses, to resume their business, of bringing in wood, coal, &c.—The stores were reopened; and many American establishments were added, the goods of which had, until then, been on board the vessels in the harbour.

Immense quantities of stores were landed in the city, and placed in security.—The castle and city were thoroughly cleaned up, the rubbish taken away, and the citizens, finding themselves secure in person and property, began rapidly to rebuild and repair their immense damages. The *fondas*, or eating-houses, were opened; the religious services, in their great variety, were carried on; one of the first of which was a *funcion*, or religious thanksgiving, to show their gratitude to the saints, that their city had been surrendered to *"los Americanos,"* before it had been entirely destroyed, and its inhabitants cut off by the terrible *bombas*.

The inhabitants who had fled, began to return; and in less than a week Vera Cruz was in a more brisk and thriving state, as it regarded business, than it had been for years. The American soldiers, who garrisoned the forts and castle, were found to be less oppressive than those of their own nation.—Money was plenty, labour wanted; a market for everything, their lives and property safe, their religion respected, and in its ceremonies General Scott, himself, took a part, much to their surprise and gratification; and no one would have judged the Americans and Mexicans, that were now mingled, buying and selling from each other, to have been, but a few days before, deadly enemies; but so it was.—Such stores of goods and merchandise had been sent by the vessels, that anything needed, could be bought almost as cheap as in New Orleans.

The camps of the troops of Worth's and Patterson's divisions, were brought up near the city. General Quitman's brigade, of the Georgia, Alabama, and South Carolina troops, with Lieutenant Steptoe's artillery, were sent off to take Alvarado,—about thirty miles to the south-east; while a powerful naval force, under Commander Perry, of the frigate *Potomac*, the steam frigate Mississippi, the sloop-of-war *St. Marys*, the steamers *Spitfire*, *Vixen*, *Water Witch*, the brig *Porpoise*, one bomb-ketch, and the five schooners of the musquito fleet, sailed to make, in conjunction with General Quitman, this third attack on Alvarado. But Commander Perry having sent the little steamer *Scourge*, Lieutenant Hunter, to lie off the port, that officer receiving from the authorities propositions for a surrender, accepted them, and hoisted the American flag over the place, and also over another small town above, to the utter astonishment of the commodore and his officers, when the fleet arrived, and no less so to the army of General Quitman, when they came before the place.[3]

Colonel Harney, with his dragoons, made a descent upon the town of Antigua, eighteen miles north of Vera Cruz, and took the place, capturing a number of lancers, and much ammunition and arms.—The navy, to atone for the loss of the anticipated active operations against Alvarado, projected, and carried into execution, shortly after this, an expedition against the town of Tuspan, about one hundred and thirty miles to the north-west of Vera Cruz, defended by General Cos. After some brisk fighting, they took this town, and, with its fall, the whole of the eastern coast of Mexico, bordering on the Gulf, came under the

---

3. For this act Lieutenant Hunter was arrested by Commodore Perry, tried by a court-martial, and sentenced to be reprimanded and sent home; which was done. But the President of the United States, not agreeing with the proceedings of the commodore, complimented Lieutenant Hunter for his conduct. The expression of public opinion was also in his favour and a splendid sword was presented to him for the act

power of the United States.—But we are getting ahead of our subject. A little to be said of Vera Cruz and the Castle of San Juan de Ulloa, now in our possession, and we leave this city for the next scene of action, in the interior, now approaching to the vital part of Mexico.

Vera Cruz, or "the true cross," is a closely-built city, entirely surrounded by a wall; without which is a barren sand plain, save on the south, where is a dilapidated part of its former extent, and a stone walk for pleasure, called the *Paseo*. The streets are regular and well paved, with side-walks of smooth cement. The houses, mostly of two lofty stories, square, with court-yards within, as has been described at Tampico. There is not a garden, or a tree, or a single green leaf of shrub or plant, or vacant spot of ground from the city wall on one side, to the same on the other.

It is a heavy mass of stone, brick, and mortar, throughout; and is like a vast citadel surrounded by its heavy fortifications. It has a splendid aqueduct, built in 1725, for supplying it with water from the interior. It is most liberally furnished with churches; not all of which, however, are used. The oldest one, built in 1630, can partly be seen in the view opposite, taken by the author, of the Gate of Mercy, or principal gate on the southern side of the city, and the same out of which the Mexican army marched to the surrender.

The reader can see there, the railroad, which runs but a few miles into the interior, made thus far by English capitalists; the car, with the cannon-ball hole through it; the road, torn up by the explosion of shells,—shot, and pieces of shell around; a *burrero*, driving in his two jacks with coal; a Vera Cruz cart, with three mules abreast;—beyond is seen the double gate, one of our wagons going in, and the sentinels there; on the left of it some tables, at which the Mexicans sell *pulque*, pineapples, oranges, &c.

The walls and the buildings are battered with shot, though, directly at this spot, they did not suffer very much. The shell that entered the dome of the old church above the window, did much damage in the interior, and killed several women that were praying within to the Virgin Mary. The building, seen only by its interior corner, on the extreme left, was the barracks for the troops; but it was so riddled through in hundreds of places, by our shot, as to be untenable by the Mexicans during the bombardment. On the right, are seen two guns of the "white fort." In the cart are a couple of women, with their *rebozos* drawn over their heads.—On entering this gate, you come directly into a crowded street.—The materials of which the walls, the buildings, the aqueduct, and the whole castle are constructed, is a porous, hard, coral rock, which is obtained from the reefs in the harbour, before mentioned. Their lime, for mortar, is burnt from the same rock.—Vera Cruz has always enjoyed most of the foreign trade of the city of Mexico, and would, from its position, be a much larger city, but for its poor harbour, exposed to the northers, (being only protected from their force by the reefs and castle), and its fatal yearly visits of yellow fever or *vomito*.

The castle of San Juan de Ulloa[4] is built on a small island opposite the city. The waves beat against its massive walls on every side but the north-east, where is a small beach.—It is divided within into three separate fortresses, with canals between, which are crossed by draw-bridges; (for view of one, see frontispiece). It is of immense strength;—the walls are from fifteen to eighteen feet thick, of solid stone;—the flat roof, supported on arches, is nearly as thick.—The area on the top of this is so extensive that thousands of infantry and squadrons of cavalry might parade upon it.

There is a large *plaza* in the interior or main fortress.—On the top, and in the water batteries, or lower forts, the cannon are arranged along in formidable rows;—there are many sixty-eight and eighty-four-pounders among them, and several mortars. Magazines are placed in various parts of the large extent. The whole fort covers between seven and eight acres.—Its full complement of cannon is three hundred and seventy; complete garrison, two thousand five hundred men. In the *plaza* below, or paved square, and the courts and streets, it resembles a city,

---

4. A disputed word sometimes spelled "Ulloa," and at others, "*Ulua* ."

with its lofty houses around.—On the top, one is struck with its extent, magnitude and strength.

Its water tanks are filled by the rain which descends on the extensive stone area above. These tanks hold a sufficient quantity to serve the whole garrison for two years.—Its immense arches below; its subterranean apartments; its large square; its extensive canals, fine bridges, thick walls, solid roofs, and its excellent adaptation for defence, and its durability, (for one cannot see why it should not remain a thousand years), excite wonder and astonishment in the mind of the beholder. The magazines were filled with powder: its *plaza* piled with shells and shot.

Many of its guns are of old Spanish and French manufacture, and are beautifully carved, and most have upon them the name of Philip V, of Spain. This castle was commenced in building near two hundred and eighty years since; has been improved and built upon continually since, or until the Spaniards lost it;—has cost upwards of fifty millions of dollars, according to the accounts of the different expenditures; and now, with an American garrison in it, it would bid successful defiance to the navies of the world. To describe it, so as, part by part, to bring it fully before the reader's mind, would take a volume of hundreds of pages. A correct view of its outside appearance from a distance, to the south, is shown in the picture of the bombardment.

The Spaniards held possession of it eighteen months after they had lost the city opposite, and, in fact, every foot of land in Mexico, save that; and even then were starved out. The Mexicans might have set at nought all our efforts to take it, had they been supplied with provisions, and been willing to abandon the city to its fate; for General Scott refused, at last, to accept the surrender of the city without the castle; and, while the garrison of the latter had laid in sufficient powder, shot and shells, for a siege of years, they had not provisions in it for more than a few weeks. And so had fallen the city of Vera Cruz before American arms; one castle, the strongest in America; nine other forts, well mounted with artillery; over four hundred good pieces of cannon and mortars, of every calibre, and an abundance of ammunition for them; near six thousand stands of muskets, and many other arms; and five thousand prisoners, besides inhabitants.

Gate of Mercy at Vera Cruz

CHAPTER 5

Return March

We were not allowed much rest in Vera Cruz, for General Scott had determined on an immediate advance towards the city of Mexico; but he was delayed in his operations for a few days, by the want of transportation.—Mules enough could not be procured, and those sent from the United States were slow in arriving.

While these events of the investment, bombardment and capture of Vera Cruz and the castle of San Juan de Ulloa had been carried on, General Santa Anna, upon whom all the hopes of the Mexicans depended, had not been idle; but, after reaching San Luis Potosi, about the 5th of March, on his return from his bloody battle with General Taylor, at Buena Vista, remained there only a few days.

Spurred on by the difficulties that surrounded him,—the actual existence of a revolution in the city of Mexico, raised by General Peña y Barragan, against the power of Gomez Farias, the vice president, who held the reins of government,—by the descent of General Scott upon Vera Cruz, of which he was previously aware, from the captured dispatches, he left San Luis on the 14th of March, and attended by two brigades of infantry and one of cavalry, commenced his movement for the city of Mexico, leaving a force at San Luis, and another, under General Miñon, on the road between that place and Buena Vista, to oppose any onward movement that General Taylor might project. He had previously sent four thousand of his veterans, under

General Vasquez, to the seat of government.

His reception at the towns on his route was that of a triumphant conqueror;—deputations from Congress met him to congratulate him on his glorious achievements:—the municipal authorities of the towns vied with one another in endeavouring to do him honour, so completely had the whole people been deceived with regard to his action at Buena Vista. New recruits, in crowds, joined his standard, eager to march against the Americans, to accomplish other glorious actions.

He arrived near Mexico on the 20th March, having, a week previous, written letters to Gomez Farias, and to General Barragan, the chiefs of the opposing factions in the capital, to suspend all hostilities until his arrival; and which direction by each had been obeyed. He took the oath of office, as President of the Republic of Mexico, on the 23rd, and, reconciling both the contending armies, united their forces to his own. He impressed many wagons and *atajos* of mules into his service, and at the head of his army quickly marched by the national road towards Vera Cruz, adding to his force the troops at Puebla, Perote, and Jalapa. At the latter place he borrowed from the *alcaldes* twenty thousand dollars, to pay to his force. He made a stand with his army, then swelled to thirteen thousand men, with forty-two pieces of artillery, at the pass of Cerro Gordo—a strong position, about sixty miles from Vera Cruz, and twenty-seven from Jalapa.

This pass, which had before been the scene of contest, in their civil wars, as well as in that between Mexico and Spain, had always been regarded as impregnable to an attack made by an enemy advancing from the coast, and as impossible to be turned.[1] The heights, here overhanging the road, already strongly fortified, he farther strengthened, and placed in position his pieces of artillery. His right was protected by a ravine of several hundred feet perpendicular depth, and his left by the height of Cerro Gordo; his front was covered with hills, among which the road lay for miles, and came up through his centre, between

---

1. Santa Anna's vindication, published at the city of Mexico soon after the battle of Cerro Gordo.

the heights, and was thus rendered utterly impassable. Here he waited, to prevent the advance of Scott, confident of victory, from his position, situation of artillery, and amount of force. No stronger place could have been found.—He was not obliged to wait long, as the sequel will show.—In the interval, let us speak of this section of country.

The land upon which Santa Anna had now posted himself, belonged, as private property, to him. His vast estate comprehends the whole slope of the mountains, from Jalapa to Vera Cruz, near ninety miles, including, in one sense, the land of the torrid and of the temperate zones; for, as land rises, the air becomes cooler, and at Jalapa is almost like that of a perpetual spring. On the lower part of Santa Anna's estate, towards Vera Cruz, in the *tierras calientes*, or hot lands, can every rich fruit of the torrid zone be produced: oranges, lemons, limes, figs, pineapples, *zapotes*, tunas, *anonas*, bananas, plantains, cocoa-nuts, and sugarcane; while upon the *tierras templadas*, or temperate lands, flourish corn, cotton, small grains, and the fruits and flowers of the temperate zones. The oak, the sycamore, and the other forest trees to which he is accustomed, meet the eye of the northern soldier in every direction; the air is cool and balmy; the dreaded *vomito*, or yellow fever, that so rages in the *tierras calientes*, never reaches here.

On this large estate, the Mexican chieftain has three principal *haciendas*; one in the hot regions, eighteen miles from Vera Cruz; a stone building splendidly furnished, roomy and capacious, with marble floors, &c. This is called Manga de Clavo.—Another is near the Puente Nacional, or National Bridge, about half way to Jalapa.—The scenery around this is of the most wild and romantic character; the bridge and fort overlooking it, has been the scene of many a combat and bloody fight, between the Spaniards and Mexicans, the different factions of the Mexicans themselves, and lately between the guerrilla forces and small bodies of American troops.[2]

The bluff from which this picture was taken is of perpen-

---
2. The National Bridge

dicular rock, about two hundred feet in height. The mountain torrent, or the Rio Antigua, as it is called, rushes against the base of this rock, and turns off to the left around it. The bridge is of solid stone, of magnificent proportions and structure; and will remain, unless forcibly destroyed, for ages. Near the foreground of the picture, not shown therein, is another fort, the guns of which, when in position, bear down upon the bridge, and upon the road, as it descends the opposite hill.

On that slope perceived, the Mexicans afterward defeated the detachment of Captain Wells, by means of cannon on the high fort seen on the hill, and also others on this bluff; their cross-fires were terrible. After that event, it was found necessary what at first should have been done to place an American garrison in the works. Since this, the guerrillas do not come near it. This national road has been by some travellers described as one most miserable; but this representation resulted from the fact of their starting from Vera Cruz in the night, in the *diligencia*, or stage, and going at a rapid rate; the road, in places, being out of repair, they were jolted exceedingly.

The truth is, that the road was, originally, and would be now, with small repairs in paving, the best on the continent of America. One who marches slowly along it, is astonished at the magnitude of the whole work; hills are dug down, and the valleys filled up; every water-course, and even little brook, is spanned by a magnificent bridge, which, even the most common ones, exceed, in stability and beauty, anything of the kind to be found in the United States. Let the traveller, instead of rolling in the close coach, take his horse, and ride over the road at his leisure; descend the ravines, and pass under the magnificent arches below, and he will be astonished at the work.

The travelling public of the West are familiar with the stone arch over the canal at Louisville, Ky; but that does not compare with any one of the arches of the splendid national bridge, seen in the view. Though from the height which you are supposed to look down upon that, these appear much lower than they really are. Every object of nature around is upon such a vast scale, that one does not perceive the immense strength and size of the bridge, until he is on or under it This road, when first it leaves the city of Vera Cruz, passes over the level, loose sands that surround that city; after three miles it enters the *chaparral*-covered sand hills; eight miles distance through these, brings one upon it to the little town of Santa Fe, in the midst of a beautiful, undulating country: eighteen miles, to Manga de Clavo, a section more hilly, wooded, green, and fertile, with many ranchos scattered about.

It now begins to ascend, and, at the national bridge, winds among wild hills, more barren and sterile; beyond this, it rises continually, ranging around the bases of the mountainous hills, until, by a rapid and circuitous rise, near Cerro Gordo it leaves the hot lands, and enters the temperate regions, but among scenery so rugged and mountainous, that there are but few ranchos or inhabitants. It, continues rapidly to rise, until, at Encerro, it passes through a fine grazing country, where sheep and cattle are innumerable, in the undulating pastures, which are enclosed by stone walls, of miles in extent.

Still rising, and passing through the town of Jalapa, it brings one to a most lovely country; and then pursues its course towards the city of Mexico. For its whole extent it is paved, or covered with *tunastate* rock, which, when pulverized, makes a macadamized road of the finest kind. If the pavements were repaired in some places, it would, as said before, be the best road in America. The cost of it to the Spanish government was immense. The Mexicans have done nothing to it of benefit

A view of the bridge from the rocky bluffs on the lower-side, is given in the sketch; and the *hacienda* of Santa Anna, spoken of, is seen on the right, though the large village near it, is concealed by the rocks, that the artist who sketched it from the Author's drawing, has piled up too freely there.

Santa Anna's third *hacienda* is at Encerro, a few miles east of Jalapa, and in the temperate regions. By varying his residence from Manga de Clavo or Encerro to the other, only about sixty miles apart, on the same road, he enjoys as much variety of cli-

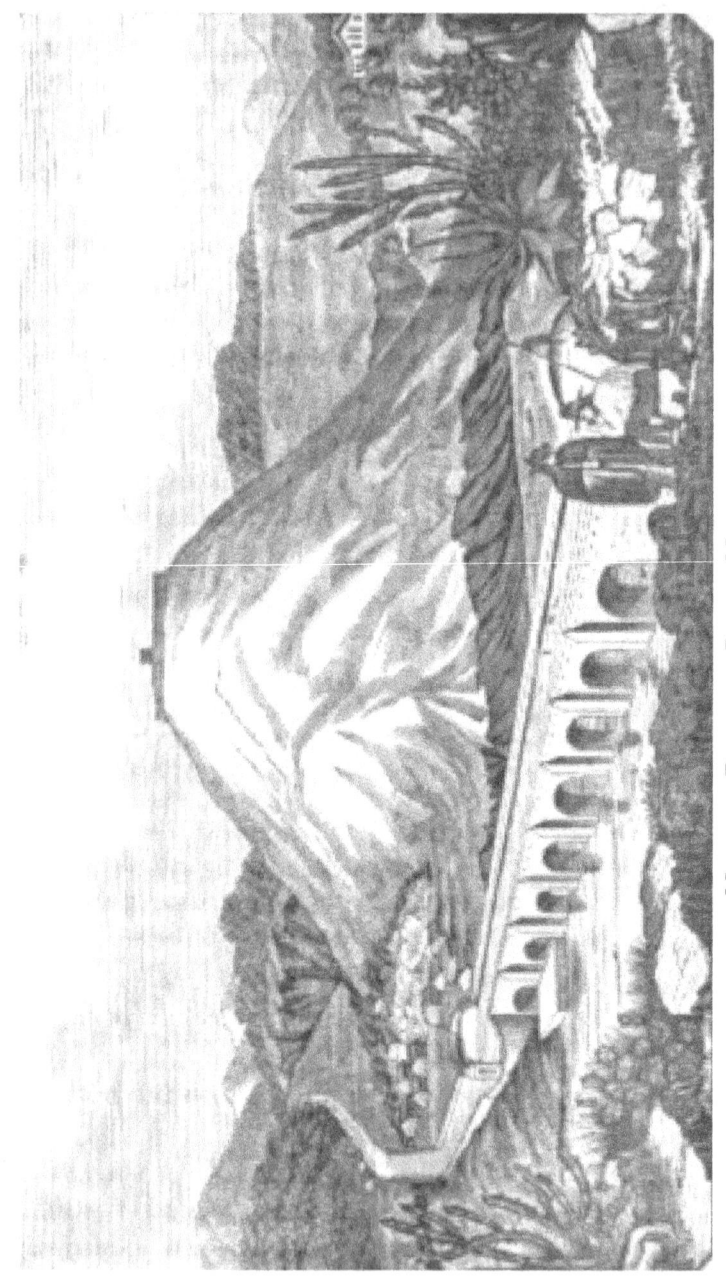

National Bridge or Puente Nacional

mate, change of scene and air, and view of the different productions of the earth, as one would find in travelling from Maine to Florida. He can suit himself. If at Manga de Clavo he is weary of the rich fruits and hot sun of the torrid zone, one day's ride takes him to the medium clime at the national bridge; or another to the healthful, temperate, grazing region about Encerro.— His *haciendas* are all beautiful. That at Encerro appears to be the more richly furnished; while the stock of fine wines, &c., into which our men dipped, at Manga de Clavo, showed that he had laid up much for use there. Between Encerro and the national bridge, at the supposed impregnable hills of Cerro Gordo, as before said, he awaited with his hosts, to give battle to General Scott.

Four days after Vera Cruz was taken, on April 3rd, the latter general issued orders to his army to prepare for the march to the interior, stripping themselves of all extra baggage, and leaving all tents behind, save three for each company for sick, wounded, and protection of arms, in case of rain. On the 8th of April, the second division of regulars, under General Twiggs, commenced the march towards Jalapa, all anxious to leave this sickly climate, before which, already, many were falling;—the hospitals were filled with sick, and the dreaded scourge, the *vomito*, began to make its appearance.[3]

On Saturday, April 10th, two days after the departure of General Twiggs, the large division of volunteers under General Patterson, followed.—These were the first and second Tennessee infantry, under Colonels Campbell and Haskell, and one company of our regiment of cavalry, Captain Caswell; the first and second Pennsylvania regiments, Colonels Roberts and Wyncoop; and Captain Williams' independent company of Kentuckians:— forming the brigade of General Pillow, (the remainder of our regiment being left behind, on account of our horses not yet

---

3. There was less spirituous liquor drank at Vera Cruz than at any other town we took; the soldiers being afraid of its effects in the sickly climate, and moreover being particularly cautioned to abstain from its use by the officers, both general and inferior. Even the old soakers took but little stronger than wine; claret was freely used.

having arrived); and the third and fourth regiments Illinois, under Colonels Foreman and Baker; and the New York regiment, Colonel Burnett, composing the brigade of General Shields.

On Monday evening, the 12th, (two days after this), General Scott and his staff left, with an escort of dragoons.—On the next day, (Tuesday, the 13th), the whole division of General Worth, with field artillery, followed with part of the siege train of heavy artillery. On the same day that General Scott departed, the large fleet of frigates, sloops of war, armed steamers and schooners,—in all sixteen vessels,—sailed, as before mentioned, to attack Tuspan.

On Sunday, April 18th, the remainder of the forces, General Quitman's brigade, marched for the interior, bringing up the rear of the army, and leaving as a guard in the city and castle the First regiment Regular Infantry and two companies Louisiana Volunteers. General Quitman's brigade was composed of the Alabama regiment, Colonel Coffee, the Georgia regiment, Colonel Jackson, and the South Carolina regiment, Colonel Butler, with four companies of our regiment of cavalry, Colonel Thomas, the horses of the remaining companies not yet having fully arrived.—The horses of our companies, which now started, were in fine condition, having been well attended to at Tampico, and having had a short passage from thence.

The brigade marched rapidly, for we had heard of the position of the enemy ahead, and wished to be in the battle; but we were too late, for the battle was fought on this day, and our bri-

---

4. These guerrillas lay concealed at every bridge, and fired upon any small parties of our men that passed. Sergeant Tucker and four men, of the regular dragoons, came dashing into camp late in the night, carrying an express of the news of the battle of Cerro Gordo to Vera Cruz. Hundreds of shots had been fired at them; they were closely pursued to near our sentinels, and three of the men were bleeding freely from wounds received. We were amused at one of our men, A. G. McCandllas, who was so anxious to have a hand-to-hand conflict with these guerrillas, that he went to General Quitman and begged to be allowed to go back to Vera Cruz with their little escort, thinking that they would be fired upon again. On account of the wounded men, the general permitted him to go. Although disappointed previous to reaching Vera Cruz, yet, in returning, near Jalapa, he was gratified by having a fight, and killing a guerrilla captain.

gade had none of the work, save a little skirmishing with [4]guerrillas along, who had killed the stragglers of the other divisions. The mutilated bodies we found here, and there on the road. In these skirmishes three of our men—Roach, King and Luker, of Captain Haynes' company—were slightly wounded. We did not arrive at Plan del Rio, near Cerro Gordo, until the second day after the battle.

We had marched from the national bridge.—The day was hot and the road dusty.—As the column neared Plan del Rio, and wound over the hills, we came to a burnt rancho. Here the dragoons had had the first skirmish with the advance parties of Mexicans before the battle. Another mile brought us to a bridge crossing a creek in which were many beautiful cascades, and shortly after to another bridge, and beyond it a small plain, embosomed, as it were, in among crags and mountains.—This was Plan del Rio, and here we found encamped the second Tennessee infantry. As we approached, they came to meet us, crowding in among our horses; and the advance was almost stopped, so eager were all of us to learn particulars from them.—There was inquiry among us for this one, for that one, &c.

The answers were various:—some were safe; others had lost arms or legs, or had been otherwise wounded, while the inquiry for others was answered by their pointing to the long rows of fresh graves by the side of the road. The enemy had been completely defeated, but many brave men had fallen in our ranks.

We visited the wounded after encampment, and then rode to the battle-ground, on which we found detachments of men piling up muskets, bringing off the wounded, burying the dead, &c., over the extended hills. We examined the ground thoroughly, and many unpleasant scenes were presented before us, of which we will speak after giving an account of the battle.

The battle-ground of Cerro Gordo is difficult to be described, on account of its being but a vast collection of massive hills, divided by deep and precipitous ravines.—No view of the whole ground can be obtained from any one place, save the height of Cerro Gordo itself, that rises nine hundred and fifty feet above the river, which runs in a deep ravine on its southern side.—The only way in which the Author can possibly present to the mind of the reader a correct idea of the extraordinary strength of this place, and the difficulties that our gallant troops had to surmount in the attacks upon the enemy's strong works, is to draw his attention to the plan and views combined. (See plan and frontispiece).

In the first place, imagine yourself standing at General Pillow's position, marked on the plan. You are on a high hill, facing to the north-west,—and you have before you the view seen in the picture. Behind you is a dense growth of *chaparral*. In front of you are the batteries of the enemy's left,—Nos. 1, 2, 3,— running on the tops of the hills, and separated by ravines. These works are of stone.

The space between you and the batteries is very rough, of irregular stones, overgrown with briers;—the thorny musquit has been cut down, and so left: for, as the enemy expected the main attack here, every precaution was taken to ensure success in defence.—To the left of the whole picture, a little beyond the view, is the edge or perpendicular side of the principal ravine— an awful chasm, between four and five hundred feet in depth, and two-thirds of a mile in width.—Far down in this meanders the river.—Behind you are rugged, stony hills, covered with thick *chaparral*, and with tremendous ravines between, rendering them impassable. If you turn and look in that direction, you can see far down over their rugged tops to Plan del Rio, and the American camp quietly reposing in the narrow valley.

The national road, as you also perceive by the plan, leaves Plan del Rio; runs eastwardly, up the side of the mountain base; then north, rising rapidly; then west; then north again, until, down in the valley, where General Worth's position is marked, it comes within long range of the guns on the right of the fort before you. There it winds around the next hill, and takes a northwestern course, directly through the "pass," where you see it is exposed in its approach to the guns of battery No. 3, which are high up above it; and, after it enters the pass, to those of No. 4, which bear directly down upon it; also to those of the height of Cerro Gordo,—opposite which, you observe that battery No. 5 entirely closes the road, and its guns point directly down the pass. From No. 4 to No. 5 is a continued breast-work on the side of the rising hill, within pistol range of the pass below.—Turn again to this picture of the batteries and you observe part of No. 3, on the right; and, over the top of the hill upon which that is placed, under the letter X, there placed, and looking down on the road in the pass, is the position of No. 4. The hill of Cerro Gordo you observe rising above, in the distance. Observing the position of the battery No. 4, on the plan, and from this picture described, in imagination proceed there in a direct line,—crossing the ravine,—leaving battery No. 3 to your right.

On arriving at No. 4, you have the picture, shown in the frontispiece before you, which was also taken after the battle:—the pass below you; the hills of Cerro Gordo and Telegrafo, in front; Cerro Gordo being to the left. Telegrafo is the hill on which the fighting of the 17th took place; and Cerro Gordo rises high, the key of the whole position. A body of our troops are placed going through the pass, toward the head, or the farther extremity, at which is battery No. 5, shown on the plan;—the guns of this bear directly along the pass, as above mentioned.

Now, reader, from your last position (battery No. 4) imagine yourself across the pass, and on the summit of Cerro Gordo, and then you look down on, and have a direct view of the whole ground, and, with the aid of the plan first mentioned, can gain a clear idea of the field of operations.—In the first place, facing to the south-east, below you is the pass, and the hill beyond it, rising from battery No. 5, and continually ascending, until it ends at batteries No. 1, 2 and 3. Still farther on, in the same direction, you look far over the mountainous hills, which are between you and Plan del Rio. To the south, you see over this hill of batteries, and observe that on its southern side it is abruptly terminated by the terrible chasm or ravine before mentioned.—Over the ravine, you observe but distant mountains, thrown together in nature's wildest style.

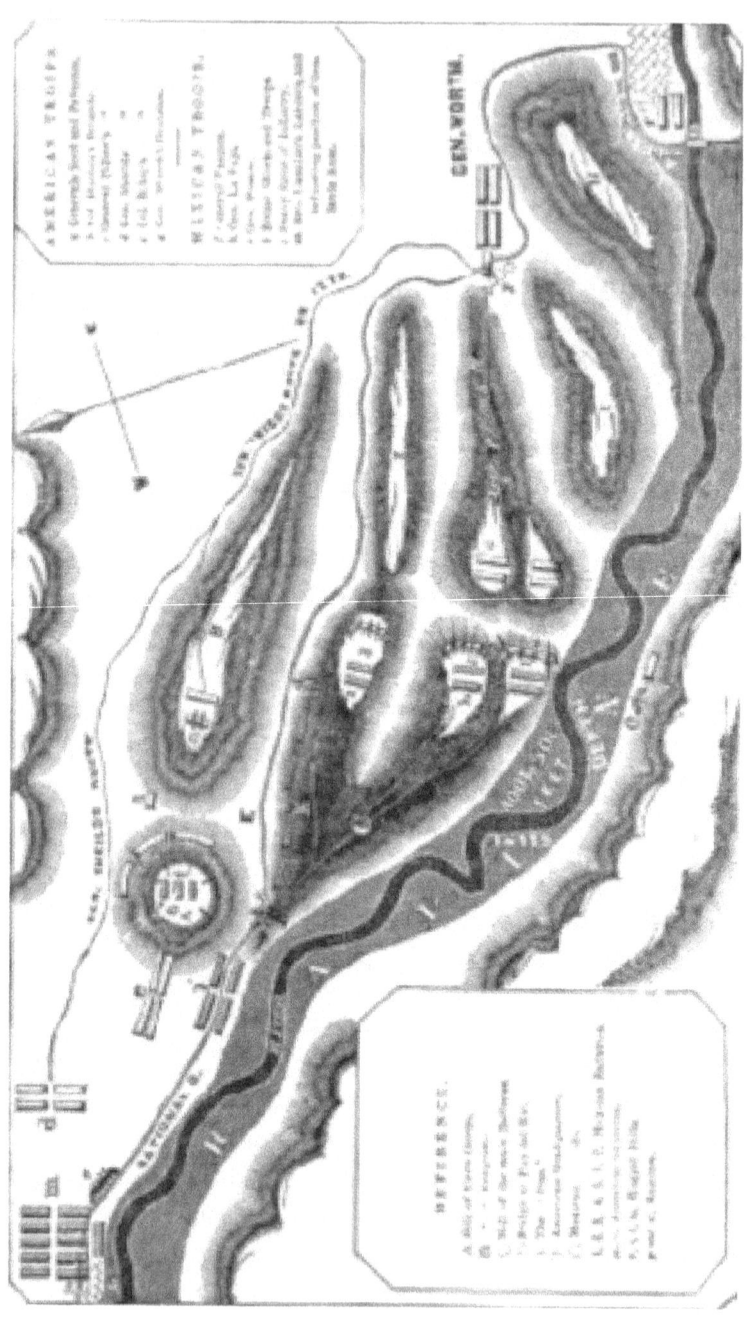

Plan of Battleground of Cerro Gordo

View of Battery No.2, at Cerro Gordo

Looking down from your high elevation to the west, you observe the plain, bounded by the same ravine, which, at battery No. 5, comes nearly to the road at the base of the mountain, and this road follows up the bank of the ravine to where is marked Santa Anna's headquarters;—there the road branches off, and loses itself in other hills.

Now look to the north.—At the base of the mountain is another ravine, apparently impassable;—beyond that, the rugged mountains are piled upon one another far as the eye can reach.

Now look to the east, still consulting the plan. Below you is the hill of Telegrafo;—it stretches long and high. Between it and the hill of batteries Nos. 1, 2, 3 and 4, the road runs up. Over this hill of Telegrafo, surrounded as it is by tremendous chasms, your vision extends far off to the eastward;—rugged hills succeed to others still lower, until, thirty miles in the distance, you observe the more level and faint outlines of the lower lands of the sea coast.

The view all around you is of the wildest of nature's work, and you wonder at the exceeding strength of this place. You see that no force can approach by the south, for the terrible ravine forbids.—You think it utterly hopeless to endeavour to come around to the north, for the ravines appear impassable.—You perceive no way to come, save directly up the road from the south-east along the pass; but if that was attempted, you perceive, from the plan, that they would be exposed to a flank fire from fort No. 2, as they crossed the valley below, and then would be annihilated as they came up the pass, by the lofty batteries. Nos. 3 and 4, and the direct fire of No. 5, added to that of No. 6, on the summit of the hill of Cerro Gordo. You can perceive no opportunity for a force ever to be able to come so near as to attack any of the works, save the batteries on the extreme south,—Nos. 1 and 2,—which may be approached by a difficult path through the *chaparral* on the rocky hills, marked as General Pillow's route.

Well, reader, so it appears, and so Santa Anna and his officers thought; and into that part of the line, consequently, he had placed the best troops and strongest collection of artillery; their opinion was made certain by a German,—one of our regular dragoons,—who, confident, from their position, that they must gain the victory, deserted from our troops on the night of the 17th, and passed over to them, informing them that they were to be attacked on the next morning, and that the principal effort was to be made against those batteries,—Nos. 1 and 2. On this information, General La Vega, who commanded on the height of Cerro Gordo, changed places with General Vasquez in command of the batteries on the hill; and every preparation was made to receive the attack.

But this deserter was wrong in his idea: the main assault was not to be made there, but at the eminence of Cerro Gordo itself, in the face of all the natural difficulties that surrounded it; and his tale, therefore, and its effect in change of the Mexican movements, in strengthening these batteries, and waiting there for the main attack, was in the highest degree subservient to the glory of the American arms: for General Scott, although commanding an assault to be made against these batteries, yet had from the first intended to direct his main movements to the right; and so confident was he of his plans securing the victory, notwithstanding the immense advantage of position and numerical force of the enemy added to their overpowering number of artillery, that his orders were only directed to that end, and nothing is said in them of the possibility of defeat; but the troops are directed as to the manner of pursuit of the routed foe.

GENERAL SCOTT'S ORDERS PREVIOUS TO THE BATTLE
OF CERRO GORDO.

Headquarters of the Army of the United States of America,
Plan del Rio, April 17, 1847.
General Orders, No. 111.

The enemy's whole line of entrenchments and batteries will be attacked in front and at the same time turned, early in the day tomorrow, probably before ten o'clock, a. m.

The second (Twiggs') division of regulars is already advanced within easy turning distance towards the enemy's left. That division has instructions to move forward before daylight tomorrow, and take up position across the National Road in the enemy's rear, so as to cut off a retreat towards Jalapa. It may be reinforced today, if unexpectedly attacked in force, by regiments one or two taken from Shields' brigade of volunteers. If not, the two volunteer regiments will march for that purpose at daylight tomorrow morning, under Brigadier General Shields, who will report to Brigadier General Twiggs on getting up with him, or the general-in-chief, if he be in advance.

The remaining regiment of that volunteer brigade will receive instructions in the course of this day.

The first division of regulars (Worth's) will follow the movement against the enemy's left at sunrise tomorrow morning.

As already arranged, Brigadier General Pillow's brigade will march at six o'clock tomorrow morning along the route he has carefully reconnoitred, and stand ready as soon as he hears the report of arms on our right, or sooner, if circumstances should favour him, to pierce the enemy's line of batteries at such point the nearer the river the better as he may select. Once in the rear of that line, he will turn to the right or left, or both, and attack the batteries in reverse, or if abandoned, he will pursue the enemy with vigour until further orders.

Wall's field battery and the cavalry will be left in reserve on the National Road, a little out of view and range of the enemy's batteries. They will take up that position at nine o'clock in the morning.

The enemy's batteries being carried or abandoned, all our divisions and corps will pursue with vigour.

This pursuit may be continued many miles, until stopped by darkness or fortified positions, towards Jalapa. Consequently, the body of the army will not return to this encampment, but be followed tomorrow afternoon, or early the next morning, by the baggage trains of the several corps. For this purpose, the feebler officers and men of each corps will be left to guard its camp and effects, and to load up the latter in the wagons of the corps. A commander of the present encampment will be designated in the course of this day.

As soon as it shall be known that the enemy's works have been carried, or that the general pursuit has been commenced, one wagon for each regiment, and one for the cavalry, will follow the movement, to receive, under the directions of medical officers, the wounded and disabled, who will be brought back to this place for treatment in general hospital.

The surgeon general will organise this important service, and designate that hospital, as well as the medical officers to be left at it.

Every man who marches out to attack or pursue the enemy, will take the usual allowance of ammunition, and subsistence for at least two days.

By command of Major General Scott:

H. L. Scott, A. A. A. General.

General Twiggs had already opened a road around, with infinite labour, and, after a hard fight on the 17th, taken possession of the hill of Telegrafo, driving off the enemy with great loss; and, on this evening, he was reinforced by General Shields' brigade of volunteers, consisting of the Third Illinois infantry, Colonel Foreman, the fourth do., Colonel Baker, and the New York regiment, Colonel Burnett.

General Twiggs' division slept on their arms, on the ground they had so gallantly won.(See report). In the night, three pieces of artillery, twenty- four pounders, two of them howitzers, under the command of Captain Steptoe, and the other under that of Lieutenant Seymour, were dragged up the new road opened by General Twiggs (marked on the plan), with incredible labour, by the regulars, the Illinoisans, and the New York regiment, and on the summit of Telegrafo placed in position. This battery commenced the action of the 18th, at seven o'clock a. m., by a heavy upward fire upon the enemy's battery, on the adjacent height of Cerro Gordo.

Twigg's Action on the 17th:

The forces of General Twiggs engaged in the battle of the 17th, the object of which was to gain possession of Telegrafo, were under the immediate command of Colonel Harney; were composed of the regular rifle regiment, Major Loring, first artillery, Colonel Childs, and one company of the seventh regular infantry, under Lieutenant Gardner, with the mountain howitzer and rocket company, under Captain Talcott, and was a spirited battle, in which Colonel Harney and his command conducted themselves with great gallantry and success; driving the numerous bodies of the enemy from the hill of Telegrafo, and repulsing three heavy charges that they made with a heavy force from Cerro Gordo, to regain possession. While this action was going on, General Santa Anna was on the height of Cerro Gordo above, and the action was thus fought beneath, his eye, and directed, on the part of the Mexicans, by his orders. By referring to the frontispiece, the reader has a full view of Telegrafo, and the hollow between that and Cerro Gordo, which, as well as the hill, was the scene of the severe fighting of this day.

We will now speak of the disposition of the Mexican troops at this moment, and the arrangements made for receiving the attack.—In the fort, at the top of the hill of Cerro Gordo, were six pieces of artillery, and near three thousand men, under General Vasquez; General Santa Anna and General Ampudia were there, also, during the commencement of the fight, but cleared themselves quickly afterward.—At the foot of Cerro Gordo, and near the battery No. 5, were about two thousand men and five cannon. On the hill of the batteries Nos. 1, 2, 3, and 4, were about four thousand men, and twenty-four pieces of artillery—five in No. 1, eight in No. 2, eight in No. 3, and three in No. 4. These were under the commands of General La Vega and General Pinson.

The fact of there being artillery in Nos. 1 and 2 was unknown to our attacking force, the pieces being masked by brush, like that which lay cut down and dry before them, and there having been no opportunity of making a correct reconnaissance of the position.

At Santa Anna's headquarters, were a body of infantry and artillery, with six cannon, and four thousand lancers, under General Canalizo; making in all about thirteen thousand men, with forty-two pieces of cannon.

The battle now commenced with the utmost spirit. General Twiggs' three brigades—Colonel Riley's, Colonel Harney's (General P. F. Smith, the commander, being sick), and General Shields' volunteers were already on the ground;—General Pillow's brigade—composed of the 1st and 2nd Tennessee regiments, under colonels Campbell and Ilaskell, 1st and 2nd Pennsylvania do., under colonels Roberts and Wyncoop, the Independent company of Kentuckians, Captain Williams, and one company of the Tennessee Cavalry, Captain Gaswell—was on the route from camp, at Plan del Rio, but having three miles to march round, before it could reach the enemy's left batteries, was not able to arrive at these until after the general commencement of the fight at Cerro Gordo, on the other extremity, although the gallant brigade was making every exertion to get there. The firing commenced sooner than had been anticipated.

Colonel Harney's brigade of the 1st Artillery, Colonel Childs, 3rd Infantry, Captain Alexander, 7th Infantry, Lieutenant Colonel Plympton, and the rifle regiment, Major Loring, descended from Telegrafo, into the valley (seen in the frontispiece) between that and Cerro Gordo, and then rapidly charged up the sides of the steep mountain, upon the fort, exposed to the fire from above, and partly to that of the three pieces, seen in the foreground, which fired with fatal effect across to the mountain.

While these were attacking the hill, the 2nd brigade, under Colonel Riley, passed to the right, around the base of Cerro Gordo, and engaged the enemy at and near its base. At the same time, the volunteer brigade, under General Shields, also passing under the base of Cerro Gordo. and crossing a ravine, moved up on its right bank, and, to the perfect astonishment of Santa Anna, vigorously attacked his headquarters, which were protected by the battery of six cannon, and supported by General Canalizo's body of lancers

While these three brigades were thus moving, the enemy, perceiving the movements, apparently became alarmed, lest the main attack should be in that direction, instead of on the other extremity; and a heavy body of near two thousand infantry were put in motion, to proceed across and strengthen the post of Cerro Gordo. But at that moment the heavy firing upon their left announced the attack of General Pillow, and this body were immediately recalled to the resistance of what they supposed to be the main attack of the American army.[5]

Harney's brigade, after sharp fighting and heavy loss, entered the breast-works on top of Cerro Gordo, from opposite points, and, finishing the work with the bayonet, drove the enemy down the hill, where Colonel Riley's brigade was already routing the force there stationed.—General Shields' Illinoisans,[6] with the New York regiment, charged upon the battery at Santa Anna's headquarters, and upon the lancers beyond, in a most gallant manner, that drew upon them the admiration of the whole army, and the highest compliments from the generals. Their brave and accomplished leader, General Shields, fell, shot through the breast; and Colonel Baker, of the 4th Illinois, as-

---

5. Never, in any battle, have been a superior and excellently fortified force more completely out-generalled, and more decisively and promptly defeated in consequence, than were the Mexicans in their almost impregnable position at Cerro Gordo. Strong as was the main hill, they relied too much upon it. The very opinion of the Mexicans, that their left was the only place that could be assailed, and the formidable preparations there made for the reception of the Americans, and their confidence of being able to repulse them, proved their ruin; for although they were thus enabled to repulse General Pillow, yet the attention and force to do this, thus withdrawn from Cerro Gordo and their right, lost them those positions, before the sweeping, resistless charges of Colonel Harney, Colonel Riley, and General Shields; and their batteries on the left were then untenable, being completely commanded by Cerro Gordo.

6. As the 1st and 2nd Illinoisans distinguished themselves at Buena Vista, under General Taylor, so did the 3rd and 4th, of the same State, gain equal honours at that action, under General Scott.

sumed the command.

The battery was taken, and the lancers routed; Santa Anna barely escaping, by a rapid flight; and the rout of all the forces of the enemy became complete, save that upon the hill of the batteries Nos. 1, 2, 3 and 4. These surrendered prisoners of war. The remainder, that fled towards Jalapa, were pursued by General Twiggs, with two sections of artillery, the regular dragoons, captains Hardee and Blake, under Major Beal, and the Illinoisans and New Yorkers. A scene of slaughter and capture extended for miles; the routed forces escaping in the *chaparral*, wherever they could, throwing away their arms in their flight.

But we are getting ahead of our account. We left General Pillow's brigade arriving before the enemy's left batteries. Not ready—but the firing having already become heavy at Cerro Gordo, that general, too hasty in the movement, instantly ordered the 2nd Tennessee, accompanied by Captain Williams' Kentucky company, to charge upon battery No. 2, to be supported by the 1st Pennsylvania; and the enemy opened with artillery into the *chaparral* in which the arriving troops were forming, killing and wounding some, and, of the latter, the general himself, as he was riding over to the other column, the 2nd Pennsylvania, supported by the 1st Tennessee, which was to attack battery No. 1.

The 2nd Tennessee had dashed ahead, towards its object. A short distance brought them out into the open space, of which the covering *chaparral* had been cut down, and now, for the first time, all saw the position of the works here; (for, as said before, it had not been possible to closely observe them previously, on account of the strong Mexican pickets, in the *chaparral*, which completely prevented the approach, sufficiently near, of a reconnoitring party).

Before them, for two hundred yards, the *chaparral* trees lay over the ground in every direction. The large rocks beneath lay piled on each other, covered with a coarse grass, which grew up between, and concealed their ragged, irregular crevices. In front, at battery No. 2, eight pieces of artillery were loaded to the muzzles with canister, and eighteen hundred infantry were ranged behind them. To the right, in battery No. 3, five pieces of artillery, within musket shot, loaded with canister, and supported by infantry, were ready to fire crosswise; on the left, in battery No. 4, were three pieces, in the same manner, to cross-fire in the other direction, supported in the same manner.

Thus had they here prepared to receive the main attack of the American army.—As the column emerged from the *chaparral*, the glance around them upon the obstructions of the ground, and the terrible preparations to receive them, did not daunt, in the least degree, the courage or the enthusiasm of this noble regiment of Tennesseans, and the equally gallant company of Kentuckians;—delivering their fire at the serried, protected ranks before them, they answered the clear strains of the Mexican bugles with a wild shout of defiance, and over the rocks, brush and fallen trees, as rapidly as they could get, they dashed firmly forward with the bayonet.

The Mexican artillery in front opened upon them; the battery on the right swept them with grape, and that on the left crossed its showers of canister through their ranks, while the deadly fire of two thousand muskets poured upon them. The air was filled with the storm of iron, copper, and lead; the trees and brash flew in splinters, the rocks were shattered on every surface; and the gallant command, pressing nearly to the forts, fell like leaves before the whirlwind. Their heroic colonel, Haskell, maddened in seeing his men thus falling around him, and that the consummation of the assault with his force was absolutely impossible, his lieutenant-colonel, major, adjutant, and most of his company officers having fallen, with his cap torn from his head by a grape-shot, his hair streaming wildly in the wind, loudly ordered his men to fall back until supported.

This was done; and then the whole brigade put in columns, to attack Nos. 1 and 2 simultaneously. But now it was unneces-

---

7. The reader has only to look at the view of these batteries, (see picture) and in imagination to fill up the fortifications with the crowded ranks of the enemy, to be able fully to appreciate the daring valour and unflinching bravery of this 2nd Tennessee regiment, with its accompanying band of Kentuckians.

sary—the object had been gained.[7] For the heavy Mexican column, that had been proceeding to the assistance of the force on the height of Cerro Gordo, was stopped in its course, and turned back with all speed, by the firing at the left; and before they could return, Cerro Gordo, the key to the whole position, had been taken; the forces there entirely routed, and, immediately after, those in the batteries displayed a white flag for surrender, and the battle was over.

The rout was complete.—Not a thing was saved by the flying enemy; all order was lost, and every one escaped in the best way he could.—There fell into the hands of our victorious army forty-two pieces of cannon, (most of them brass), many wagons and pack mules, four thousand prisoners,[8] six or eight thousand stand of arms (not numbered), five generals,—Pinson, Jarero, La Vega, Noriega, and Obando; (another, General Vasquez, was killed on Cerro Gordo, fighting to the last); many colonels, lieutenant-colonels, and other officers (two hundred and fifteen in all); most abundant supplies of excellent powder; cannon and musket cartridges; cannon-balls, grape-shot and canister, of copper, iron, and lead; Santa Anna's travelling carriage, and his effects, including sixteen thousand dollars, in silver—a good part of which fell into the hands of the victorious Illinoisans and others; and, in fact, everything that the enemy possessed.

Santa Anna escaped to the town of Orizaba, on the foot of the mountain of the same name. The Mexican army dispersed in every direction, and the largest body was pursued sixteen miles, to Santa Anna's *hacienda* at Encerro, and many were cut down.

At Encerro, a few miles from Jalapa, the pursuing column of Illinoisans, of both regiments, of the New York regiment, and of regular dragoons, directed by General Twiggs in person, was halted by Major General Patterson, on account of the extreme fatigue of the men and horses, many of the latter dropping dead,

---

8. About one thousand of these escaped, for the want of a full escort in the *chaparral*-lined road, between the battle-field and Plan del Rio, whither they were conducted. The remainder were released on parole, given by their officers, that they should not again bear arms against the United States during the present war.

from over-exertion; the miserable fugitives left of the Mexican army were unnoticed farther. On this route, General Ampudia and his staff were nearly caught: for, hemmed in by a wall, they could not escape, and they took the bold movement of advancing directly towards General Patterson and his staff, who supposed that they were coming up to surrender themselves; but the wily Mexicans had no such idea: by this movement they came to a lower part of the wall, and Ampudia leaped his splendid gray horse, which he calls "General Taylor," over it, followed by the rest, like a flock of sheep, and away they went. The dragoon horses were too much fatigued to pursue them, and General Patterson was disappointed in capturing his supposed prize.

This gallant general had been, during the day, and for several days before, quite sick, enough so to be confined to his bed; but, on the approach of the battle, could not be kept in by the surgeons, but joined General Scott at the base of Cerro Gordo during the battle; and was in the whole of the subsequent pursuit. General Smith was sick, so that he could not get out, and therefore Colonel Harney had command of his brigade.

The hopes of the Mexicans were, for the time, wholly destroyed; and, as the fruits of victory, the fine city of Jalapa yielded, on the next day, to the conquerors; and, in two days more, the strong castle of Perote, second only to San Juan de Ulloa, followed,—having within it fifty-six cannon and seven mortars, and an abundance of small arms; and in a few days the splendid city of Puebla surrendered, upon the advance of General Worth, and was taken possession of by that officer, and the road to the city of Mexico was open.[9]

Such was the battle of Cerro Gordo, which, although admired, has not received its merited degree of praise; for the position of the enemy; his greatly superior force; his vast supplies; the excellent generalship displayed in the attack: the complete

---

9. In less than two months after General Scott had landed at Vera Cruz, he had taken nine thousand prisoners, and among them ten generals; three large cities; two famous fortresses; five hundred pieces of cannon, over ten thousand stand of arms, and an immense quantity of materiel of war; had routed and dispersed the Mexican armies, and driven their great general, a fugitive, into the mountains for safety.

and sudden overthrow and defeat; the dispersion of his army; the vast materiel captured, and the consequences of the victory, render it one of the most brilliant actions of the Mexican war. The least estimate made by the Mexican officers, of their loss in killed and wounded, was about one thousand; but from the number of dead, and the wounded which fell into our hands, it was afterwards universally conceded that it could not have been less than one thousand five hundred. The loss of the Americans, as listed below, was four hundred and twenty-five.

Killed and Wounded, First Brigade of Volunteers.

For the list of Tennesseans and Kentuckians, the Author is indebted to the politeness of the acting adjutant of the second Tennessee regiment.

First Brigade of Volunteers.—wounded.

Brigadier General G. J. Pillow, slightly.

Second Tennessee Regiment, Colonel Wm. Haskell.

Wounded—Lieutenant Colonel David Cummings, Major Farquarharson, Adjutant Wiler P. Hale, (since dead).

Company A, Captain W. G. McCowan.—Killed—Private Samuel Floyd. Wounded Sergeant And. Carson, Privates H. Mowry, Peter Wheeler, Aaron Dockery, Aaron Capps, S. G. Williams

Company B, Captain Henry F. Murray.—Wounded —Captain H. F. Murray; Privates J Kent, (since dead), Moreau Brewer, Benj. F. Bibb.

Company C, Lieutenant W. G. McAdoo Killed—Private Wm. England, Geo. W. Keeny. Wounded Sergeants T. R. Bradley and E. H. McAdoo; Privates Wm. Bennet, Isaac N. Graham, Lewis L. Jones, Samuel Davis.

Company D, Lieutenant F. B. Nelson.—Killed—1st Lieutenant F. B. Nelson; Private Chas. Sampson. Wounded—Josiah Prescott, Benj. O'Haver, Chas. Ross.

Company E, 1st Lieutenant W. B. Davis—Killed—2nd Lieutenant C. G. Gill, Sergeant H. L. Bynum, Privates R. L. Bohannon, John J. Gunter. Wounded —Privates John Gregory, A. Gregory, F. G. Robinson, B. Plunkett. John P. Isler.

Company F, 2nd Lieutenant A. P. Greene.—Killed—Sergeant F. Willis; Privates W. O. Striblin, Eph. Price, Thos. Griffin, Robert Keirnan. Wounded—Sergeant George A. Smith.(mortally); Privates L. W. Fusseil, Alonzo White, John Burrus, Christopher Johnson, James Whittington, Thos. H. Boyd.

Company G, Captain W. J. Standifer. —Wounded —Sergeant John Cowan; Private James Allison.

Company H, Captain John D. Lowry.—Killed—Sergeant W. F. Brown. Wounded —1st Lieutenant Wm. Yearwood, (since dead), 2nd Lieutenant Jas Forest; Privates James Woods, John D. Armon, George Sherman, (since dead), a free coloured boy, who persisted in going into the action.

Independent company Kentuckians, from Clark county, Captain John S. Williams, attached to 2nd Tenn.—Killed—Corporal W. F. Elkin; Privates W. Durham, Alfred Hatton. Wounded —2nd Lieutenant George S. Southerland, Sergeant A. T. Mocabee; Privates W. W. Keith, Henry Williams, Minor T. Smith, Ira Storm, Henry Brewner, Joseph J. Langston, Wm. Bruce, Willis F. Martin, James Muir, William Chism

First Tennessee, Colonel Campbell.

Killed—Private S. W. Lauderdale. Wounded —Captain Maulding, Adjutant Heiman, Adjutant Corporal Johnson; Privates S. G. Steamers. M. Burns, W. F. McCrory. S. W. Garnette.

First Pennsylvania, Colonel Roberts.

Wounded—Privates J. Lindhurt, David Lindsay, Albert Cudney, J. R. Davis, C. F. Keyset, John Sheleen, G. Sutton. A. Lovier, D. W. C. Kitchen, D. K. Morrison.

Second Pennsylvania, Colonel Wynkoop.

Wounded—Corporal John Smith: Privates A. Holand, J. Shultz. John Chambers, Jacob Simons, Ed. Cruse, Jacob Miller, D. M. Davidson, Wm. Wilhelm, P. Somers, James Shaw, Thos. Hann, Josiah Horn.

Second Brigade Volunteers.

Wounded —Brigadier General Shields, severely.

Third Illinois, Colonel Forman.

Killed —Private Benjamin Merrill. Wounded —Sergeant Allen, Corporal J. F. Thompson; Privates Andrew Browning, T. W. Haley, John Roe, Levi Card, H. Dimond, S. White, A. McCollum, S. C. B. Ellis, G. Hammond, T. Harlow. S. Bullock, J. Mellburn, John Maulding.

Fourth Illinois, Colonel Baker.

Killed —1st Lieutenant George M. Cowardin. Corporal H. H. Miller, Private Joseph Newman. Wounded—Lieutenants Richard Murphy, Charles Maltby, And. Forman; Sergeants J D. Sanders, J. M. Handsby, James B. Anderson, Uriah Davenport: Corporals Thomas Hissey. G. W. Nelson; Privates James A. Banel, James Depen, John Walker, Wm. E. Lee. James Mahon. John Arahood, Laban Chambers, George Carver, E. Rice, James Shephard, David Hoffman, Robert Jackson, Leroy Thornley, Thomas Tennery, John Price, Joseph Tharp, Irwin Becker. J. J. D. Todd, Charles Lanning, Frederick Brancher, S. Browne, Wm. Morris

The first and second lieutenants of company F, Scott and Johnson, and eleven others in that company are also known to have been killed or wounded; but the names the author has not been able to procure.

First New York. Colonel Burnett.

Wounded —Captain Pearson; Privates E. Cook, R. Hedrick, John Silver, Henry Heveras Christopher Newman.

First Brigade Regulars, Colonel Marnet.

Mounted Riflemen, Major Semper.

Killed—Sergeant James Harlison, Corporal Danley Ware; Privates Thomas J. Pointer, Benp McGee, Conrad Kuntz, Charles Wills, Wm. Cooper, George Collins, Wm. McDonald.

Wounded—Major E. V. Summer, commanding regiment, Captain Stephen T. Mason, First Lieutenant Thomas Ewell, (since dead), Second Lieutenant Thomas Davis, Second Lieutenant G. McLean, Brevet Second Lieutenant Dabney H. Maury. Brevet Second Lieutenant Alfred Gibbs; Sergeants Jeremiah Beck. Thomas Sloan, Carter L. Vigus, H. Louis Brown, Charles H. W. Boln: Corporals Thomas Williams, Ferdinand Littlebrand, Wm. R. Leachman, Thos. Goslin, Lewis P. Arnold; Privates John McCormick, W. W. Miller, John McCauley, T. J. Hester, D. Hesling,

R. Ross. S. N. Ritner, W. F. Ford, E. N. Brown, John Sampson, W. W. Breedon, E. Allen, A. Evans, W. Butterfield, J. Meyers, D. Carpenter, G. W. Gillespie, John Raney, J. Windle. H. Zimmerman, James McGowan, W. A. Miller, C. Jones, W. J. Scrivener, Jas. A. Adams, George Stempson, David Bear, W. Hammersly, Samuel Gilman, John W. Robinson, Justus Freemaux. Adam Ryan, J. Hooker, L. Hooker. John Walker, H. Hill, W. Higgins, W. Forbes, Ira White, George Tucker, C. A. Alburn, H. Bell, W. H. Preston, W. Scheder, J. Lipp, J. Vorle, J. Spencer, T. Conway, A. L. Ogg, C. Bruner, F. Workman, Hiram Melviar, M. Lang, D. Ferguson, C. Foster, G. Bacurine, G. Brydong, S. Ranison, J Schraman, T. Moll, N. J. Campbell.

First Artillery, Colonel Childs.

Killed—Sergeant Caldwell Armstrong; Privates Patrick Casey. Daniel Doty, Amant Harsman, Charles Skinner, Joseph Wood. Francis Perrod, Michael Dailey, Griffin Budd, Samuel M. Roberts, Hugh Croley. 11.

Wounded —Sergeants J. M. Holden, (mortally), John Haymes, John Teahan; Privates John, Bandorf, Adam Kock, R. M. Huntington, Michael Griffin, James Welsh, Thomas Sullivan, Sergeant S. F. Simpson, Privates John Gornaley, Thomas Matheron, Wm. B. Williams; Corporal Ferdinand Littleward; Artificer Hiram Melvin; Privates Marinus Lang, David Ferguson, Charles Forster, Gollert Barnrule, George Bridung, Konradt Fisher, Stephen Rineson, Julius Schramm, Frederick Molte, Nathaniel J. Campbell; Corporal Thomas Williams; Privates Patrick Anthony, Samuel Downey, Anthony Bracklin, Mathew Faganberg, George Harnblin, Michael Harley, James Keegan, Orrin Lawton, John Rooney. John A. Sloane, Wm. H. Webber, John Wooley, James Burnett, Thomas Lynes, Andrew Wright, Patrick Kane, Sergeant Thomas Geff. 43.

Seventh Infantry, Lieutenant Colonel Plympton.

Killed—Sergeant Robert Wright; Corporal Edmund Toley; Privates Wm. Myers, Lewis Bodie, J. M. Derby, John M. Seaton, John Lynch, Francis O'Neill, Isaac Dolen.

Wounded—1st Lieutenant N. T. J. Dann; Sergeants John

Heynes, John Teahan, James M. Holden, H. J. Manson, Samuel Cline, R S. Cross, Jonathan Marsh, James Ecles, John Brayman; Corporals Nicholas Bradley, John Carter, Patrick Duneghar, James Garrard, John Jones; Privates Anthony Bracklin, Samuel Downey, Matthew Fagan, George Hamlin, Michael Harly, James Keigan, Orrin Lawton, John Rooney, J. A. Sloane, W. H. Webber, John Wooley, James Burnet, Thomas Myres, Andrew Wright, John Bandorf, Adam Kock, Patrick Kane, R. R. Huntington, N. Griffin, James Welsh, Thomas Sullivan, Jacob Halpin, D. McCrystal, E. Lyons, E. Peters, C. Elliott, James Godfrey, C. S. Hassner, William Longwell, I. Gilleze, C. Johnson, James Joice, J. Lee, John McMahon, T. O'Callaghan, W. Robinson, John Smith, George Wakeford, C. Bierwith, John Keelan, John Burnes, Niell Donelly, P. Henley, D. Downs, John Trunks, S. Ratcliff, P. Mahoney. John Davidson, Michael Dwyer, James Flinn, M. Ryan, Walter Roob, D. Reed, Peter M. Calee,— Thompson, A. Hansford, Jame Harmer, Wm. Sprague, D. Whipple, Daniel McCrae, Joseph Brewer. K. Fisher.

Second Brigade, Colonel Riley. Second Infantry.

Killed—Sergeant Michael Christal; Privates James Olsen, John Schenck. Andrew Devine, Wm. Turner.

Wounded—Captain George W. Patten; Lieutenant C. E. Jarvis; Sergeants Francis Doud, Alpheus Russell; Privates Wm. Pollock, D. Hogan, Patrick Sheridan, Jacob Carr, George W. Derry, James Harper, Morris Welsh, Henry Yuill, Lyman Hodgden, Timothy Byrne, Jas. McCulhough, Richard Crangle.

Third Infantry, Captain Alexander.

Wounded —Lieutenants J. N. Ward, B. E. Bee; Sergeant George Reed; Corporal David Kerr; privates Henry Carleton, George Dunn, R. Toulden, R. Vickers, Nicholas Tyans, J. D. Lore, J. B. Richardson, Wm. Keaner. C. Smith, J. Matten, Silas Chappel, A. Marsh, Joseph Gallion, A. E. Marsh, John McConville, Stephen Garble. P. Levy, S. Corey.

Appearance of the Ground after the Battle.

Now, reader, having given an account of the glorious action

of Cerro Gordo, as it may be interesting to many, we will speak, in this note, of the appearance of the battle-ground afterward, as it appeared to us of the four companies of cavalry, who had come up with General Quitman's brigade. We remained there for a few days, to assist the 2nd Tennessee regiment, who had been left, with one company of regulars, to guard the hospitals of wounded, and to spike the cannon, burn the muskets, blow up the magazines, and, as much as possible, to destroy all the immense materiel of war, which, with so much labour and expense, had been collected at this stronghold by Santa Anna, in the vain hope of entirely defeating us, and which materiel was now not wanted by our army.

Quitman's brigade passed on. and joined the main army at Jalapa, and we commenced our laborious task. Having, in our work, for three days, to traverse, again and again, all parts of the ground, we became more familiar with every position, than any other portion of the army had the opportunity to be; and the more we walked over its strong positions, the more we were struck with admiration of the glorious results of the battle. A battle-ground, after the fight, especially when such a rout as this has taken place, presents a melancholy appearance.

We will give a short sketch of the scenes around, commencing at Plan del Rio. The hospital here presented a painful spectacle; all the little cane buildings on the side of the road were filled with wounded, who ware ranged along on blankets, stretched upon the bare, hard earth. Their situation was uncomfortable; the pain they were suffering was dreadful.

They lay in their ordinary clothing, which, in many instances, was stiff with blood. Some had been shot through the body, and lay groaning in pain; others, being struck by cannon balls, had lost their arms or legs; some were shot in the head, neck, or sides; in every possible manner were they wounded. Some apparently suffered but little, and lay quietly, without a word; others, unable to move, were in good spirits, and freely conversed upon the battle, and their part in it.

Walking around, were many who had been slightly wounded;

several with the stump of an arm tied up in a bandage; some were shot in two or three places. One young man was shot by a canister ball, through the thigh, and another ball had wounded him, at the same instant, m the left side, while another had taken the cap from his head. The groans of many were heart-rending.

One, who had been hit near the ear, by a canister ball, which had ranged down into his neck, and lay deep against the back bone, so deep that it could not be extricated, every few moments was delirious with pain; he groaned and rolled in intense agony, and in no position could he be relieved; he turned upon his side, his back, or, rising on his hands and knees, would press his fevered forehead against the earth; most earnestly and piteously did he continually beg of the attendants to be killed it was his only prayer; death, that night, came to his relief.

Near him, another young man, clotted with gore, from a terrible wound on his head, by grape shot, was sinking under its effects; he lay quietly, and murmured sometimes incoherently, and sometimes plainly, of scenes at home; called upon his mother and his sisters, in terms of endearing affection, and was, in imagination, at the place of his childhood again; but never would he be there in reality, for, before he had been brought from the battlefield, the flies had clustered upon his wound, and the worms were already working within, beyond the reach of the surgeon to remove. His was a horrible death.

Another lay near, whose jaw was shattered, tongue torn out, part of his neck gone, and his power of speech departed; but still he lived; and the quick, restless movements of his eyes, showed that he was fully aware of his terrible situation. The scene in all the houses was the same; men, wounded in every way, all suffering, all bloody; some improving, some shrieking with pain, some dying, and some dead; while the new burial ground, near, was receiving continually, the victims.

Here, too, were some Mexican soldiers, severely wounded. After gazing at these painful scenes, the Author with a companion, saddled their horses, and proceeded up the road, to the nearest batteries on the hills, those that had been attacked by

Pillow's brigade, and entered No. 2. The dead and wounded had from here been taken down; the blood, where so many had yielded up their lives, was caked upon the ground, and the rocks were smeared with it. Inside the batteries, the cannon, which had been employed in the work of death, still looked grim and threateningly; piles of shot were by them; tin canisters, containing about two hundred and fifty balls each, were ready to be forced down their muzzles; the spongers and rammers lay as they were left; great quantities of ammunition were in the magazines, nearby.

We crossed to No. 3. The same scenes of abandoned cannon, piles of shot, and cases of powder, were here; but with them, too, were great numbers of muskets. From No. 4, to the road at 5, the way was strewed with muskets, bayonets, cartridge-boxes, belts, and scabbards, an, in many places, the ground was literally covered with loose cartridges.

Here, at this battery, No. 5, were four old Spanish cannon, richly carved and with them one new one, that had recently been cast at the city of Mexico, with its name in large letters upon it, "*El Terror di los Norte Americanos,*" ("the terror of the North Americans"); but not much terror had it inspired in our troops. A great quantity of arms and ammunition lay around here, trampled underfoot.

We passed up the steep height of Cerro Gordo. Soldiers, with litters, were still bringing down the wounded; and their groans, as we passed, were distressing. On the summit, were the blackened cannon, the marks of the deadly conflict, and blood in abundance; around the hill, and all up its side towards Telegrafo, and on the north, the corpses lay thickly, as they fell, their guns in their hands, or by them. In one place were fifteen, almost in a pile; some stabbed with bayonets, some shot in the head, some through the heart; one had fallen by a ball through his brain, as he was holding his gun in his left hand, and biting off the end of a cartridge held in his right; although dead his face had a stern expression of defiance, and his left hand yet grasped his gun, and the cartridge was still in the fingers of the right.

Another had fallen on his face so violently, that his cartridge-box was thrown over his shoulder; his gun was still in his hand, the hammer of the lock was drawn back, and, on opening the pan, we found it loaded. We turned him over, to see where he had been hit, to be killed so suddenly; a large hole between his eyes, showed the passage of the fatal ball. On opening the cartridge boxes of the dead that lay on their faces, we saw that they had yet plenty of powder and ball.

Here five lay almost over each other, as they had fallen, in defending the same spot; the life-blood of the upper ones, had saturated the clothing of the lower. Some had died apparently in much agony; for their countenances were awfully distorted, and their bodies were drawn up and stiffened in convulsive movements. Some, lower down the hill, had evidently crawled some distance, as shown by the trail of clotted blood behind them, before they died.

Many had their heads blown open; while the entrails of others were out; and one presented a horrible appearance, having crawled twenty yards or more, in that terrible situation; several had died with their hands covering their faces. One, in this way, was leaning back against a rock, and appeared as if alive, among the corpses stretched out around him. Some, down in the valley, appeared to have been shouting as they were killed, or else uttering their cries of mortal agony; for their mouths were opened to their utmost. In almost every instance where balls had passed through the vitals, the hands were pressed upon the wounds.

One muscular body lay with the arms and legs stretched widely out, but without a head; the bloody stump was terribly lacerated. One had his stomach entirely torn away, by a cannon shot. So, horribly mangled, they lay thickly to one another, as they fell. The dead bodies of the Americans had been selected out, and buried. Hundreds of buzzards and vultures sailed around, but appeared not to touch these Mexican dead; at least, we did not see in the multitude any that appeared to have been torn by them.

Descending the hill, towards the scene of Colonel Riley's

and General Shields' attack, the same sights were before our eyes, until we were sick of the spectacle. Hearing a groan in the bushes, close by a number of dead, we looked in, and saw a lancer, lying stretched out bloody, and unable to move; his *escopeta* lay by him; he held up his hands and cried piteously for *agua* (pron. ah-wah), water. We had none to give him; but determined to see that the poor fellow should be attended to. At the scene of Shields' and Baker's attack, the dead had been buried, and the wounded taken in.

The dead horses of Canalizo's lancers, shot in the furious attack of the Illinoisans, covered a large space of ground; some of the mules of the ammunition wagons were dead in their harness; a universal scene of destruction was all around. There was a *rancho* of several cane houses here, and they were now occupied as hospitals. Entering those on the left side of the road, we looked at the numbers of Mexican wounded, thickly covering the floors of the houses; attended by fine-looking Mexican surgeons; many Mexican soldiers in attendance. On the other side, the buildings were used for the American wounded. The scenes in these large and crowded hospitals were equally painful as those at Plan del Rio.

We entered the Mexican hospital first, and informed the officer in charge, of the wounded lancer, and were promised that he should be attended to. After looking at the scenes of pain and distress crowded around, till our hearts were sick with the sight of so much misery and suffering, we retraced our steps; turned out again from the road, to hunt up the lancer among the dead. On coming to the place, we found with him a Mexican soldier, who had been sent to his assistance carrying to him a large bottle of water and a double handful of raw corn! which the poor fellow was munching with great eagerness. He was soon after conveyed to the hospital; and we returned to Plan del Rio.

The labour of blowing up the magazines and destroying the muskets was hard, and we were all rejoiced, when, after three days, we were ordered to leave for Jalapa; for the dead men and horses now had become most offensive, and a sickening air seemed to rest over the hills and field of carnage. We had lost, while here, Adjutant Reese Porter, an officer who had gained the good will of the whole regiment. He died at Plan del Rio, directly after our arrival.

One of Captain Newman's men, while out on a foraging party, had accidentally shot himself, and was brought in dead.—One of Captain Caswell's men, J. L. Robertson, on a foraging party, had been killed, in a fight with some lancers, a few days before. There were so many deaths now, every day, from violence and sickness, that the Author found himself unable to keep an account of those even in his own regiment.

It was a bright morning when, to the cheering sound of our bugles, we saddled up, formed our lines, and leaving the scenes at Plan del Rio, commenced ascending the long slopes, winding round and up the rugged hills. The road was excellent, and we travelled fast; stopping at battery No. 5 a short time, again we looked down into the terrible ravine below, on the south. It was a grand sight to gaze below, as the winding river ran through the vale; but so awful the depth, that few, from giddiness, could bear to look a moment down.

We marched over the burnt and blackened ruins of Santa Anna's headquarters; then by the hospitals, where Americans and Mexicans—friends and foes—were together suffering, and still dying; then passed through the scene of the slaughter of Canalizo's lancers; then on up the long paved road, that ascended the mountain's elevation. Mile after mile, we continued so to ascend, while the air began perceptibly to change. Sixteen miles brought us to the lovely valley of Encerro, with its sparkling river, dashing over the rocks; crossed by the road on a stone bridge, of construction equal to those before mentioned. Here the sight of dead horses and fresh graves, by the side of the road, which had met our eyes all along, from Cerro Gordo, ceased; for at this place that terrible slaughter ended.

Encerro was a beautiful section; green pastures took the place of sterile hills, and clear water was abundant.—Just before arriving at the bridge, we crossed a little ditch which had been made by the Mexican army for the whole distance to Cerro Gordo, in order to convey a stream of water into camp; and this ditch, winding around, encircling the hills, carried the waters rapidly. At this spot in its course it completely deceived the eye; and there was not one man in a hundred, of the troops that passed over it, to whom it did not have the appearance of water running up hill. Some declared that it did so, the illusion was so complete. Neither could that be corrected by a renewed look; for, judging by the eye alone, the more we gazed at the ground, the more perfect was the deception, caused by the ditch winding around the brow of the green eminence.

During the halt of an hour, near the bridge, in this delightful, sunny valley of Encerro, some of us went up to Santa Anna's *hacienda*, which was about half a mile off, on a long, verdant hill, to the left of the road; commanding, in its position, a view of the valley, the river, and the rugged mountains beyond, overlooked by the snowy peak of Orizaba—as beautiful a scene as could be desired.—Entering the lofty gateways, we followed a curved, paved way up to the house; where, though at first coolly received by the domestics in charge, yet were soon most cordially welcomed, as they found by our actions that we wished not to disturb, but to view the place.

They showed us, freely, through the house; opened to our observation the arched *piazzas*, and splendid rooms above; the private office of Santa Anna below, with its furniture as he had left it a few days before; and pointed out to us the fine framed pictures that adorned the apartments. These were, a series of Napoleon's battles; another, of Hannibal's history; a set of hunting scenes, as acted in various parts of the world; and the plan of a splendid monument to be erected in honour of the Mexican chief.—The glasses were large, the carpets fine, the furniture excellent, the pictures splendid.

In the long gallery, we smiled as we observed one of the general's artificial legs lying there, booted finely, and excellently manufactured. We were shown his services of China and table ware, of the best kind; and every plate and every cup had his name upon it, in ornamental scrolls. We were conducted through his pleasure grounds; observed the cascades of falling water, in the small river which had been dammed up, and now fell about fifteen feet, in a sheet on the rocks below, and then wound off in several clear channels, which lost themselves among the little islands of thick shrubbery, among which it hurried along towards the valley below.

The stone stables, at some distance down the slope of the hill, were capacious enough to hold the horses of a cavalry regiment. We could have spent several hours in strolling about the beautiful place, but the mellow sound of the bugles arose from the valley; and, on looking down, we saw the column forming for the advance. Mounting our horses, we rode over the paved way to the gates, then down a long slope to another brook, then up to the road, where we remained a few moments, until the column came, took our places in ranks, and continued our course.—Yet upwards we rose;—the air became more invigorating, the scene fresher, the green of the foliage deeper.

Oaks appeared, the first we had seen for a long time;—black jack, sycamore, alder bushes, of enormous size, and many of the plants of the temperate zone, to which we were Accustomed at home, met our eyes. Maguey plants, of the largest size, were closely growing among them. *Ranchos* became thickly scattered along the road; good houses, fine stone walls around the green fields, more cultivation of the toil, and, in fact, the best appearance met our eyes, both in country and people, that we had viewed in Mexico. All were exhilarated and delighted by the balmy, bracing air and delightful garb of nature. Still we were rising, and occasionally, from a height, could look down on the vast regions of the torrid zone beneath us.

A little before sunset, we came over a verdant hill, and before and below us was the beautiful city of Jalapa, universally acknowledged by travellers to be one of the most delightful places in the world. The tall mountains rose above it, green even to the edge of the dazzling snow that eternally covered the summit of the loftiest, Orizaba. The city stood in the valley, upon several little hills, with its ancient spires, its white stone buildings in its large extent, relieved by the groves of every sort of tree of freshest green, fragrant flowers, and richest fruit.—A fine clear stream coursed by it.

We closed up our ranks, and descending, crossed the bridge, and entered the clean paved streets, with wide side-walks and spacious houses of stone on either side. The *tiendas* or stores were all open, the people engaged at their various occupations, the streets crowded with Americans and Mexicans, and business was briskly going on, and all were apparently friendly. At their iron barred windows were many of the ladies, who gazed upon us without fear,[10] and, to our surprise, we noticed them as extremely beautiful.

The busy view of life, activity and enjoyment, immediately banished from our minds, as it had from those of the rest of the army who were participating in it, all thought of the scenes of death, destruction, and suffering, that we had left behind.

We marched through the crowded streets and market-places up the long slope of the city beyond, and passing on by the farther boundary, continued our course over the hills, looking down into valleys of beauty unknown to us before, and in one of these, on the right of the road, encamped with the volunteer division.

Saturday, May 1st, 1847. We have now been at Jalapa near a week, and the time has flown so quickly that it seems but a day; for every attraction had been presented to the senses and mind. It is the most beautiful spot that any of us ever saw—the finest air that ever we inhaled.—The sun shines with unusual splendour, and there is not that sickly sensation to its heat, although great at noon-day, that is so strongly felt in the regions on the

---

10. After Vera Cruz had been taken, General Morales, who there gallantly commanded the Mexican forces, passed through Jalapa, and informed the people that the American army would soon advance upon the interior, and that, if General Santa Anna, should be defeated by General Scott, their city would fall into the hands of the Americans; and advised them, in that case, not to be alarmed for fear of ill treatment, but to go on with their regular business; assured the females that in such a case they need apprehend no danger from the American soldiers.

coast. It has rained a little every night, and the beauty of the morning, as we see it from camp, is difficult to conceive—much more so to describe.

All nature is fresh and green, dressed in smiles; the lofty mountains are tinted then with rosy hues;—clouds of rolling majesty, in brilliant whiteness, lay in massive, strongly defined volumes, around in the valleys, at their bases.

Orizaba, lifting high its dazzling top of snow, appears to be but a few miles off, in fact close at hand; but forty miles will hardly reach its base. Its head is elevated seventeen thousand feet above the level of the sea;—our Alleghanies and Blue Ridge at home would appear like small eminences, when compared with this majestic mountain. On that lofty summit no human foot has disturbed the eternal snows, which have looked down, from age to age, upon the changing races in the lovely and extensive valleys below.

One can have no idea of the vastness of the scale in which mountains, hills and valleys are here thrown together. You gaze on a beautiful valley beneath you, on the height near the city. It appears close under you; for the opposite mountain, in its grandeur, covered with a robe of verdure, is near to you, apparently; but half a dozen miles will hardly carry you across to it. The extraordinary clearness of the air assists in the deception. There is no light blue haziness, caused by vapour in that distance, as is seen elsewhere, but every object, far and near, is plain and distinct.

Not only is nature so attractive in her appearance of landscapes in this favoured section, but she also seems to have poured out here, profusely, her richest gifts of grains, of fruits, and flowers, and every store that can conduce to the comfort of man. And to that, she has added health robust, and driven away those lurking causes of disease that infest other sections, as intruders who have no right to enter this, her chosen paradise.—We had heard before of the beauty and richness of this section, but it excelled all our previous ideas;—not a person in the army but was agreeably disappointed in finding it more beautiful than he anticipated.—Attempts to describe its attractions are idle;—to see it, to enjoy it, to breathe the air, is only to know it.

The city, too, taking everything into consideration, was the finest that we had seen in Mexico. We were now where we could observe the true Mexican character and customs more perfectly than before.—We saw, in comparison to what we witnessed in the valley of the Rio Grande, just what a foreign traveller would see in the United States, in New York, Pennsylvania, or any of the older states, compared with the frontiers of the west. The same language was spoken, and many of the same customs were observed; yet one could learn more of Mexicans and Mexico here in a week, than there in months. But few pretty women had we seen on the frontier, and many soldiers, whom the fortune of war kept during the campaign in northern Mexico, now firmly believe there are but few in the whole country; yet it is saying nothing more than the truth to observe, that the ladies of Jalapa are, with few exceptions, beautiful—strikingly so; and their manners are most agreeable and pleasing.

The male population are, as a body, superior to those that we had before met with; more industrious and enterprising. Several cotton and woollen factories are on the streams about the city, and all the business within it was brisk and flourishing.

We have before spoken of the principle of "protection and remuneration to the Mexicans." This was exemplified at Jalapa, by forcing the volunteer divisions, who were mostly without tents, to camp out. and take the cold rains, at night, (which were the first that had fallen upon them for months), as they could, while there was plenty of room in the city for their shelter. This principle was carried to its utmost extent, and never produced the slightest beneficial results; but. on the contrary, excited ridicule and contempt among them.

For instance: at Jalapa, a Mexican proprietor, in less than three days after the battle of Cerro Gordo, presented a bill to the quartermaster for the use of fifty of his mules, furnished to Santa Anna to haul a twelve pound brass cannon up the height of Cerro Gordo, which piece had opened upon our troops a perfect shower of grape and canister, killing many and wounding more! Another, who had supported a large body of the Mexican lancers for some time previous to the battle, called also, to inquire about getting his pay for it!

Monday, May 3rd. Reader, will you, on this lovely morning, again accompany the Author into town, to observe something more of Mexican manners and customs, than yet you are acquainted with. We will have but little to say of the scenery to be viewed on both sides of the wide, paved road thither, of mountain and valley, and most luxuriant vegetation, for we have glanced at that already; but will hurry on to the upper part of town nearest to us, passing the crowds of soldiers going in and returning to the camp, the numerous *burreros*, with their loaded jacks, bearing fodder, wood, charcoal, fruits, &c., going in; and, besides these, you see another class, that you have not noticed before: the lowest order, or pure descendants of the Indians, which are yet distinct in this section.

You observe that these are ragged and dirty; the men have large *panniers*, or square baskets of oranges, pine-apples, &c., on their heads, and as they stoop forward, in moving with their load, the basket is held to its place by a broad band, which passes around their foreheads. They carry enormous burdens. The squalid women have each a child lashed to their backs. There are many of these miserable looking creatures passing.

We enter the city, and are in a crowd, up and down the hilly streets. We will glance at the meat-market, in the "*Plaza de la Constitucion,*" and you will notice the neatness of the stalls, and of the whole establishment, and the way in which they cut their meat, into long strips, for the purchasers. But although a very busy crowd are around, there is nothing more of interest, and we will pass on down, peeping into the iron-barred windows of house after house, to gaze at the pretty *señoritas*, who sit, with their fans in hand, and rich *rebosos* over their glossy hair, and observe all that passes. It is no impoliteness here thus to notice them; in fact, you will be greeted with a smile, from as lovely lips as ever you looked upon, for the compliment you thus pay them.

They are beautiful, indeed.—See them, as they come out of their houses in numbers, to proceed to the *yglesia,* or church, to hear mass. They walk finely, look neat, and their bright black eyes sparkle with intensity of feeling.—Amid these, and among the crowd of officers, soldiers, citizens, *rancheros, burreros,* Indians, pack mules, and *burros,* with here and there wagons of our own, we force our way down to the vegetable market, near the principal church. This market-place is rather small, and, as you enter it, you are astonished at the throng within, and the immense quantities of vegetables and fruits arranged around on stands, or spread on mats, to sell; the piles are near one another, as close as they can be placed in rows; and the buyers and vendors are mingled together.

Look around, a few minutes, and think if ever you have heard of a vegetable, or of many fruits, that are not here for sale. Here is an anomaly among markets. This *ranchero* has brought in a fine quantity of pineapples, tunas, *anonas, sapotes,* coconuts, &c.; and another, bananas, plantains, oranges, and lemons, all the products of the torrid zone; while another has brought black-berries, currants, apples, peaches, nectarines, apricots, &c., growing only in the temperate zone; and another has fine cherries, plums, and other fruits, which grow only, in perfection, still farther north; and yet these different persons live not a half day's ride from the city.

The *ranchero,* from the torrid zone, meets with his brother, who lives in the temperate, every week; and this last performs regular trips, oftener than that, into the frigid; and makes a business of bringing the snow and ice therefrom, and selling it in the market. You can buy drinks, cooled with the snows and ice of Orizaba, at the same stand where you purchase the juicy fruits of the torrid zone; and both have been brought to market that morning.—Many other articles are here, besides fruits and vegetables. Here are stands of sweet-meats and confectionery, of kinds, of the making of which our people know nothing; thousands of trinkets, of every kind, are for sale; calicoes, silks, *som-*

breros; and, in fact, every article that a Mexican needs, can here be procured.

On one side of the square, is the *parochia*, or parish church, a large, old building, most elaborately ornamented within; its images and wealth had not been disturbed on the approach of our army. Many worshippers are kneeling there, on the marble floor, before the Virgin Mary. From this church proceeds the "host," or the sacramental bread, when going to the death-bed of a citizen. And as this ceremony is always most imposing, and is the same in all Catholic countries, a full description of it is given in the note; which, as it is minute and correct, will be found interesting.

The Procession of the "Host."

Whenever a person is about to die, it is indispensable, according to their faith, to the repose of his soul, that he confess his sins to the priest, receive absolution, and partake of the holy sacrament; which is commonly carried to him in the twilight of evening, so that its display to the population will be greater. The ceremony universally followed is this: One of the boys attached to the vestry *sacristia*, or establishment of the church, steps out in front of the *parochia*, and violently rings a large hand-bell; thus announcing to all the faithful, that the body of Christ (sacramental bread), or holy unction of the sacrament, is about to proceed upon its mission to the bed of the dying believer.

At the sound of the bell, there soon collects, within and at the door of the church, a large body of persons, mostly women, each of whom is supplied with a lighted wax candle. The *parochial* coach drives up before the doorway. The officiating priest, with holy reverence, takes the vase containing the consecrated wafer, from within its resting place, in the altar at the extremity of the church, and bears it towards the doorway, preceded by two boys, dressed in their church habiliments red and white robes.

One carries a wooden cross, about five feet high; the other swings a censer, in which incense is smoking, diffusing a pleasant odour around. At the instant the "host" is thus lifted from the altar, and borne towards the door, the bells in the tower of the church commence a rapid ringing, which is kept up, without intermission, as long as the procession, about to start, continues in sight of the *parochia*. The vase of bread, or "host," at the door, is reverently placed, by the priest, in the centre of the coach, with a lighted taper by it; the priest enters, seats himself on the back seat, and remains with his head uncovered in its holy presence. The boy with the censer of incense enters before him, and seats himself on the front seat.

The procession is then formed. First, the boy with the bell, still ringing, advances about forty yards in front; following him, after an interval, the white and red robed youth, with the sacred cross; then a band of music, clarinets, fifes, bugles, and drums, then an escort of soldiers, if there are any in the town, with muskets shouldered; then the *parochial* coach, with its sacred contents; around the coach, and in its rear, follow the crowd of the faithful, with their lighted candles, every one repeating prayers; in this order they proceed towards the dwelling of the dying.

The din of the bells of the *parochia* ceases, as the procession is lost to view in the distant street; but if it comes in sight of another church, the bells of that commence, and keep up the same noise, while it is within the view of the ringers. Amid the din of these bells, the wild strains of the music, the deep sounds of the drums, and the confused chant of prayers, from the devout, candle-bearing crowd, whose numbers are increased at every step, by others with their tapers, the solemn procession moves slowly on.

The sharp, well-known sound of the hand-bell gives notice to all of its close approach; the inhabitants of the buildings on either side, grasp and light their candles, advance to their doorways, windows, and even upon the side-walks, and instantly kneel in reverential awe, and so remain while the holy train is within their sight. By so doing, they are taught that they gain much favour from the blessed Virgin Mary, and secure the forgiveness of many of their smaller transgressions , and not only so, but the law forces them so to do; and, therefore, every foreigner, who resides in a Mexican city, whenever he hears the bell, absents himself from view.

The lighted throng continues to increase, as the procession advances, until, at its arrival at the house of the sick, it not unfrequently numbers five hundred or more candle-bearers, of both sexes and all ages. Arrived, the priest with the vase of holy bread, accompanied by the boy with the censer, from the coach, proceeds into the house, leaving the crowd and the escort, who continue to chant their prayers, without.

A table within has been prepared for the reception of the host, being covered and adorned with pictures of the Virgin, *Nuestro Señora de Gaudaloupe*, the peculiar name of the blessed Virgin in Mexico. The sacrament is administered, and the procession returns by different streets from those by which it came, followed by the still increasing crowd; and as now it is commonly dark, it makes, with the kneeling worshippers at the houses, and the innumerable lights, a most imposing appearance. When in sight of the *parochia*, the bells of that again commence their rapid ringing, and cease not, until the vase of sacred bread is deposited within the altar. The crowd then disperses.

Such is the procession of the host; precisely the same in every city and town of Mexico, and at all times, with only this difference: that when, on account of the rapid approach of death, it must be carried to the sufferer in the day time, the coach is not used; the priest walks, bearing the vase, and four men hold over him a splendid satin canopy. Respect is always shown to this consecrated bread in the church, by raising the hat when passing the door. Every Mexican does this at every church, whether he is riding or walking.

On emerging from the church into the large square again, we notice, opposite, a large building, with several of our regular soldiers crowded around the arched doorway. This is their barracks. The building belongs to the government of Mexico, and has been used continually for military barracks. Observe the inscription painted around the arches: "*Cuarto de la Guarda Nacional*" (quarters of the National Guard). You must not suppose, however, though this belongs to, it was built by the government: for the government of Mexico never has done the slightest thing towards improvement of old national edifices, or building new ones.

It has been occupied with revolutions, and has not kept in repair the splendid works that the Spanish power erected. It owns much property, though, in every large town;—some of the most magnificent buildings in the republic belong to it.—The reason is this:—When the order of Jesuit priests, which had become wealthy in Mexico, was abolished, and the priests themselves banished by the old Spanish power, all their property—churches and private buildings was taken by the government then existing; and, after the revolution, the whole fell into the hands of the Mexican government, save the cathedrals and *parochias*, which had been given to the new establishment of the church.

These numerous buildings are rented out, used as barracks, devoted to city purposes, &c., &c.—Some have been given to every town, in charge of the president of the *ayuntamiento*, for the purpose of the rents thereof being applied to keeping up a public school for children, where these might be instructed in reading, writing, a little arithmetic, and in all the numerous ceremonies and doctrines of the church; which, in fact, is their principal object of education.

Mexican children are always more precocious and brighter than those of our country at the same age. One is astonished at the genius and talent exhibited by the boys at from eight to fourteen years of age;—but at that age they become dull and stupid, and so afterward continue.

Let us look into the school near here, and you will acknowledge the truth of the remark, from the very intelligent appearance of the countenances of the children.—It is a perfect Babel in sound, for everyone is studying his creed, the history of some saint, or his spelling book, at the top of his voice; and such screaming, yelling and chattering is going on, that you will be glad to get out of it instantly. The old *pedagogue*, who looks so uneasily, is rejoiced to see you about to go, though he makes many bows and polite salutations before you leave.

You will observe that most of his persuasive arguments addressed to the boys are with a sort of rattan, which he lays upon them in a manner that shows him equal, in that method of education, to those of our country,—a method which should have been long since abolished in our own land, but may yet answer in Mexico.

These young ones can tell you all about every saint in the calendar, and recount miracles that they have wrought; can rattle over the creed and *Ave Marias, Padre Nuestros,* &c., &c., and can inform you all about the church ceremonies;—can tell you minutely how even the longest one is done, (*Corpus Christi,* which takes a week in performance);—can write beautifully; read, and cipher a little, but cannot tell you whether St. Petersburgh is in Europe, Asia, or New Holland;—is taught that Mexico is the most powerful nation on the earth, and that Spain is the next.

Most of the schools are of the Lancasterian order, and are of but little advantage. Before we leave the crowded, noisy room of bright looking urchins, we will examine their written copies and these from the universally beautiful execution, will astonish you; and it is surprising, when compared with the performances of our youth.—Every Mexican, that writes at all, writes finely; some excelling even our best writing-masters. The immense amount of their army papers and reports, that we have captured from time to time, are executed in a style nearly equal to that of copper-plate printing.

CORPUS CHRISTI—*FUNCION GRANDE DI LA TOLENSA.*

Of all the church ceremonies in Mexico in which the people blend religion, recreation, pomp, fun and folly, this festival of *Corpus Christi,* of the holy week, is the longest, most format and most imposing, and is strictly attended to in every town of the republic, when it yearly comes round. At Vera Cruz, this year, it was neglected: for, at the time it should have commenced, the surrender to our troops had prevented it. At Jalapa, though, it had been celebrated with unusual pomp; for there were Mexican soldiers to take part in it. It comes on immediately after

Lent, in the latter part of March. The ceremony, as related to the Author by those who had just acted it, and who acted it every year, is as follows:

Sometime in the week previous, the curate of the *parochia*, with much ceremony, goes to the president of the *ayuntamiento*, and delivers to him the keys of the church; thus acknowledging the inferiority of the ecclesiastical to the civil power. The president immediately issues a proclamation to the people of the city, ordering all shops to be closed, all business to be suspended, and every animal and vehicle to be kept out of the streets from Wednesday morning until Saturday noon of the following week, under penalty of fine and imprisonment; and enjoining upon all the inhabitants the necessity of having the streets, through which the various processions will pass, cleanly swept and continually sprinkled; and also of having curtains hung before their windows and doors, &.c.

All the population now commence preparing in earnest for the approaching festival; the showy dresses of the wealthy, and every article of finery of the lower class, is hunted up and put in order; in fact, these preparations commenced two or three weeks before for the grand celebration in which they are to hunt up Jesus Christ, who will escape their hands, to be again apprehended by the aid of Judas, who will betray him. They will try. and condemn him; will crucify him; raise him from the dead; then exalt and worship him; and finally will wreak their vengeance on Judas Iscariot.

On Monday morning the priests go, in a body, to the president of the ayuntamiento, and humbly beg of that officer the keys of the *parochia*, that they may dispense the consolations of the gospel to the inhabitants of the city for the ensuing year. That functionary grants their prayer, delivers to them the keys, and with these they return, and the closed *parochia* is again opened. In the afternoon of this day, at four, p. m.. the first procession of the festival makes its appearance from the church, coming out in a most imposing manner.

First advances a band of music, followed by various banners

and crosses of the *parochia*, borne by the church boys, dressed as has been mentioned in the procession of the host. These banners are commonly surrounded by a crowd of idlers. Next, under a splendid silken canopy, supported by four men at the corners, come the body of the priests, in their robes; these, in a loud voice, chant prayers as they march, and are answered in the responses to these by the multitude behind. Next comes a full length figure of St Peter, borne on a frame supported upon the shoulders of four men. The saint has in his hand a bunch of large keys (in allusion *Matthew 16: 19*.) Following this are many persons with long lighted wax candles, and all with their heads uncovered,

Then, upon another such a frame, comes the Virgin Mary, but borne by four richly dressed ladies. Her right arm is extended, and from her hand is suspended a golden cup. A beautiful radiating crown encircles her head. Following her are many women, each with their lighted tapers, and many of the other sex in the same manner. Next, borne on a like frame, is the large image of Christ, with a long flowing beard, bearing a heavy cross, of perhaps ten feet in height, and the timbers apparently a foot in diameter; then numerous files of persons again, with their tapers.

Following along at intervals in the dense procession, come, in the same manner, the figures of St. Paul, St. John, St. Matthew, and a host of others. This long procession, which is often from a mile to a mile and a half in extent, with all persons uncovered, and with so many hundreds, often thousands, of candles, makes a most brilliant display. From the moment that the head of the procession moves off from the *parochia*, and while it winds its length through the streets of the city, all the bells keep up a ceaseless clatter until it returns again. So ends the first day.

On Tuesday, early in the morning, in every street may be seen one or more men, dressed peculiarly with clothing of all colours : most have white roundabouts, striped with red across their backs; with strange shaped caps, something like the old style of dragoon helmets, with red sashes, depending from their topmost ridges, hanging over their backs. These carry in their hands slender poles of cane from twelve to sixteen feet in length, haying a bunch of red, white and blue ribbons streaming from the upper ends.

These are the Roman soldiers, and they are now hunting for Jesus Christ. With an anxious, hurried and wild appearance, these soldiers run up to every passer-by, with great eagerness inquiring, "*As visto V Jesu Christo?*" (have you seen Jesus Christ). Each one thus addressed, with perfect seriousness answers "No," and then away rushes the soldier, to ask another.

This search is continued the whole day but they do not find their object. In the afternoon the procession starts out again, the same in its parts as on the day before, save that the figure of Christ is missing, and the advance is a body of fifty or sixty of these Roman soldiers, with their long staffs, who are still continuing their search for Jesus Christ; many are blowing clearly on little wind instruments, something like our fifes.

On Wednesday, the next day, the bells all cease their sounds. Not a horse or vehicle it seen in the streets. Christ has been apprehended during the night, by the treachery of Judas, and the Roman soldiers are seen, in high glee, to collect around the doors of the *parochia*, rejoicing in the successful termination of their search In the afternoon the procession again moves out, but is materially changed in its order.

As before, first comes the music, crosses and banners; then the Roman soldiers, with the ends of their long poles trailing behind them, the ribbons flying in the air before and above them, vibrating with tremulous motion. In the midst again, as a prisoner, appears the image of Christ, with the cross. After him follow the priests, chanting prayers and responses in a loud and wild manner.

Next is the Virgin Mary, in deep mourning; then Joseph, and Mary Magdalene, Peter and others. This night the soldiers keep watch over Christ; but he escapes: is hunted and overtaken the next morning. On this day, Thursday, comes the full acting of the scene of crucifixion, in the manner described by the evangelists. His clothes are divided by lot, &c.; and the one who kills

Christ (called by the crowd the Christ-killer) is borne around the streets in triumph.

When Jesus is thus crucified, the bells stop their former clanging, and are not heard again for two days The body is asked for and obtained by persons representing Joseph, of Arimathea, and Nicodemus; (see *St. John 19 : 38*). In the afternoon it is carried about in the procession within a frame coffin, with glass sides, for all to see and all to worship.

The remainder of the procession is like that of the day before, the Virgin Mary in deep mourning. The only other difference is in the missing sound of the bells; but that is compensated by thousands of rattles (like those of our watchmen), which, in the hands of boys and men, keep up a ceaseless clatter, assisted by a large clacking wheel, in the belfry of the church.

To the church the body is brought, and placed near the altar, and a guard of two persons at a time keep watch over it the remainder of the day and following night, on Friday, and Friday night, until Saturday. These guards are regularly detailed from the best of the population, and, with lighted candles in their hands, stand their time of thirty minutes, when they are relieved by others. And thus ends Thursday.

On Friday, is an entirely changed scene. The churches are lit up with the utmost splendour from five to eight hundred candles diffuse their light around in each; while every decoration that can, by the ingenuity of the inhabitants, be placed within, is added; nothing is omitted that can increase the splendour. The people, dressed in their richest attire, go in groups, companies, or families, from church to church, repeating prayers all the while, as they pass with heads uncovered. This they call their pilgrimage; and every church in the city must be on foot thus visited, in the course of the day, by every person, rich or poor. This brilliant scene is kept up until twelve o'clock at night.

The next day, Saturday, is called *Sabado de Gloria*, Sabbath of Glory: and at about eleven o'clock the bells, which so long have been silent, burst out from every church, in one peal thus announcing that Jesus Christ has risen from the dead ! And now comes a scene. A moment before, the horses were standing saddled in the yards; the coaches were harnessed; the boys were collected at the corners of the streets; the Roman soldiers, in their odd dress, were walking in consequence about, having crucified Jesus; and everything was unusually still. But at the first clap of the bells, rises through the city a wild hurra and uproar. Christ has risen.

The Roman soldiers run as if for life, with the rabble in pursuit of them. In every direction the court-yard gates open, and hundreds of horsemen issue into the street, and wildly gallop to and fro. The streets are crowded; the curtains, that hung at the windows and doors, disappear in a twinkling; all is noise, confusion, fun, frolic, and mirth for the Redeemer lives !

The next day, Sunday, gives the end to this *funcion grande de la Yglesia* (grand ceremony of the church), which is, the vengeance to be taken by the mob upon Judas Iscariot. who betrayed his master. The first part of the day is spent in adoration of the risen Saviour; and about twelve o'clock the indignation of the people appears to be aroused against the traitor. "*Van a quemara Judas*" (they are about to burn Judas) is clamoured in one street, echoed in another, and vociferated by the boys and rabble, everywhere.

Immediately after this a crowd, with music, advances into the principal square, bearing aloft, on a pole, the full length figure of the traitor, with his right hand holding to his hat on his head. He has been ingeniously constructed by the Sacristan, or sexton; and is composed entirely of a mass of rockets, crackers, and other fireworks, and is commonly made a facsimile of some foreign merchant, who may reside in the place, and who is a Protestant or heretic.

The pole is planted in the earth; the tumultuous crowd sway to and fro, in their excitement; highly elevated on the pole is Judas, awaiting his doom; the combustible string, that leads up to him is ignited; the little flame runs up, and the traitor immediately experiences the most awful torments; his hands, his body, and head burst out in numberless small explosions and flames; he whirls round and round on the pole; his hat flies off, and with it his arm extends itself with a jerk, and he turns faster as the flames are more severe: they reach within, and a loud explosion, amid the shouts of the delighted populace, blows Judas to the four winds of heaven. And so ends the grand ceremony of the church, in Mexico.

We will leave them, and come again into the street; and, passing on, we will observe that many of the spacious courts within the houses are provided with fountains and jets of water, producing a fine effect.—We observe a public washing place, of long, stone reservoirs, with roofs above them; washing benches—one built on either side, of the same material; and scores of women are there washing.—We notice that everything around us is entirely Mexican in appearance. But our observations must close, for here rides up an officer, ordering all of us to camp, preparatory to another march, to be immediately made to Puebla, on the road to the city of Mexico.

Tuesday, May 4th. This day General Scott countermanded the orders given yesterday, for a farther march; and, as the time of the twelve months' volunteers was nearly expired, he had suddenly concluded to discharge them, and thus enable them to leave Vera Cruz before the *vomito* should reach its height.

Accordingly, on the next day,—Wednesday, May 5th,—Major General Patterson issued the order in the note below,—being the last general order addressed to us.

> Headquarters, Volunteer Division,
> Jalapa. Mexico, May 5th, 1847.

Orders, No. 17.

In accordance with the orders from the Headquarters of the army, the Tennessee cavalry the 1st and 2nd Tennessee, the 3rd and 4th Illinois, the Georgia and the Alabama regiments of infantry, and Captain Williams' company of Kentucky volunteers, will be held in readiness to march to Vera Cruz, thence to embark for New Orleans, where they will be severally and honourably mustered out of the service of the United States, and paid off by the proper officers on duty there.

To facilitate the march. Colonel Campbell, with the regiment of Tennessee Horse, the 1st and 2nd Tennessee Infantry, and the company of Kentucky Volunteers, will march to-morrow morning, the 6th instant.

The 3rd and 4th Illinois regiments, under Colonel Forman, will march tomorrow, at two, p. m.

The Georgia and Alabama regiments, under Colonel Jackson, will march on the morning of the 7th instant.

The troops will march with their arms, ten rounds of ammunition, and their personal effects, and will turn in at this place all tents, and such other articles of camp equipage as may not be indispensable on the return march.

Each man will take in his haversack hard bread for four days, and bacon for two days. The brigade commissaries will obtain from the chief commissary money to purchase fresh beef, on the road, for two days.

The quartermasters of the command will make the proper requisitions on the acting quartermaster general for the necessary transportation.

In promulgating this order for these gallant regiments to return to the United States, the major general, while he regrets that the term of their service will not afford another opportunity for these troops to gather additional fame in the future events of this already brilliant campaign, cannot forget that the recollections of a glorious past will be carried to their homes The services of the twelve months' volunteers will ever be perpetuated in their country's history with the remembrances of Monterey, Buena Vista, Vera Cruz and Cerro Gordo.

The major general avails himself of this occasion to take leave of the 1st and 2nd Pennsylvania, the South Carolina and the New York volunteers, and to tender his thanks to Brigadier General (now Major General) Quitman, and them, for their obedience to orders, attention to duty, and their faithful, ready and cheerful support, under all emergencies, since they have been under his command; and he assures these fine corps, and their gallant and accomplished commander, that he will always be happy to meet,

and to serve with them.
By order of Major General Patterson:
(Signed) Wm. H. French,
Acting Asst. Adjutant General.

We commenced the return march, from the city of Jalapa on the morning of the 6th of May. It was a lovely day; the air was clear, and Orizaba showed its height of snow more plainly than usual. For a sketch of this mountain, taken this morning, see picture.

In the foreground of this view the artist was directed to place part of the column of cavalry and infantry of the twelve months' volunteers, as they commenced the return march, and which, from want of time, had not been placed on it by the author. When again he saw the picture, on being finished, he perceived that only part of one company of cavalry had there been placed, and those were represented as going at full speed, as if on a charge, apparently delighted at the idea of return. But, however gratifying this might have been to them, the march was made in regular columns of twos, with the same steady motion as at all other times, save in the charge, or in pursuit of the enemy. A long plume and beaver had also been placed on the head of one of the officers. The author has no recollection of ever seeing one of these in the American army in Mexico, save upon one occasion that worn by General Worth, at the scene of the surrender of Vera Cruz. Being amused, however, at the idea of the hurry to return, expressed by the position of these soldiers, and thinking that it would perhaps strike the minds of his former comrades in the same manner, he allowed the picture to remain unaltered. It gives a correct view of Orizaba and the neighbouring mountains.

We arrived at Vera Cruz, on the 8th, without any circumstances worthy of note, save some skirmishing with guerrillas. We sold our horses there, to the quartermaster's department, and immediately embarked on board the ships ready in the harbour, and a few days' sail brought us to New Orleans; where, on the last of May, we were mustered out of the service of the United States, with the other twelve months' volunteers, who were arriving from General Taylor's division. We were paid off and discharged, and, for the first, time in near twelve months, felt ourselves at liberty.—Every man commenced thinking, planning, and acting for his future interests; and each experienced a feeling of pride, upon reflecting that he had nobly served his country for one year of his life. But with our joy a feeling of sadness was mingled, when we thought of the many brave spirits that a year before had gone out with us, who now returned not,—fallen in the ranks before the enemy, or sunk beneath the baneful effects of a sickly climate.—Of the eighteen thousand twelve months' volunteers that then had been marshalled for the conflict, not twelve thousand could now be mustered.

And now, reader, the long account is brought to a close; and if to the minds of his former fellow-soldiers the Author has succeeded in bringing past scenes freshly in review,—and if to the general reader he has given a clear idea of those transactions and events,—his object is fully accomplished.

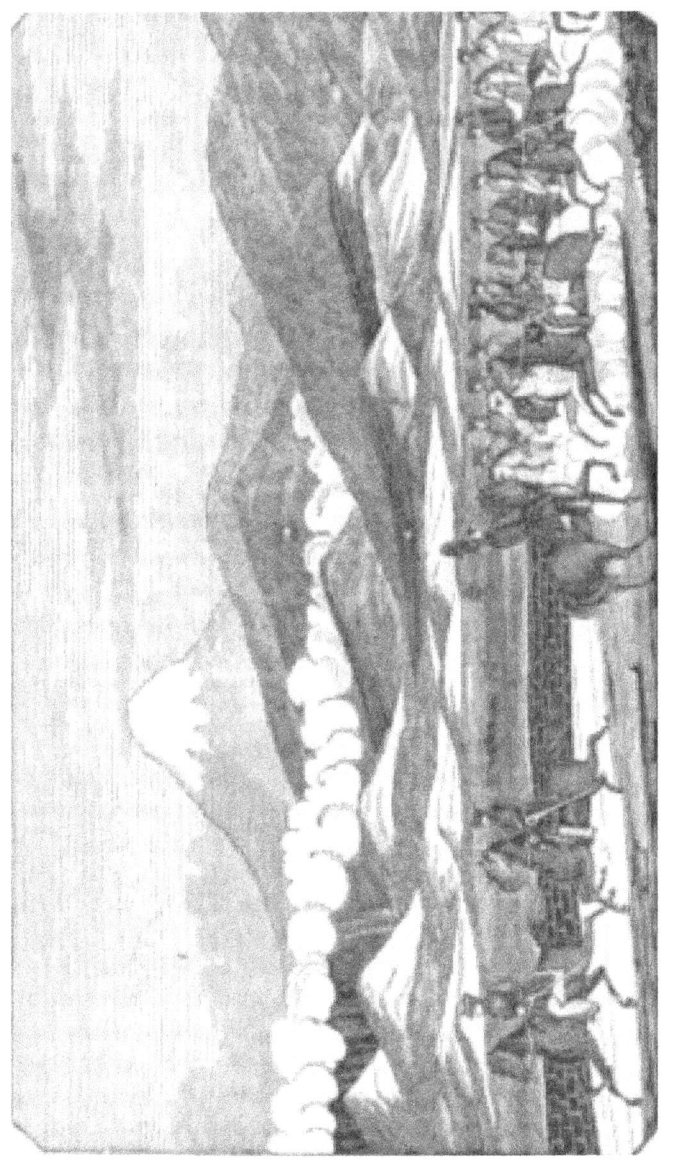

Mountain of Orizaba

Appendix

SUBSEQUENT OPERATIONS.

After the twelve months' volunteers had left the army, General Scott remained at Puebla, which had been previously taken, until he was reinforced by the arrival of other troops, from the United States, all of which were mustered in for the war. As these reinforcements moved up from Vera Cruz, along the national road, they were violently opposed in their progress by- bodies of guerrillas, now become formidable, and whose method of fighting was without quarter, or in their own words, "without pity unto death."

These had severe conflicts with the forces of General Pillow, General Cadwalader, General Pierce, General Lane, Major Lally, and others; but they were worsted in every conflict, save one, at the National Bridge, in which they defeated the small detachment of Captain Wells, and forced him to retreat, with the entire loss of his train, and many men killed and wounded. Major Lally's command fought nearly every foot of the way from Vera Cruz to Jalapa; the report having spread among the guerrillas, that in the train he had with him was contained, in specie, over a million of dollars.

On the 6th of August, the army commenced the march from Puebla. towards the city of Mexico. Now, the Mexican army, in great numbers, posted in strong fortifications, awaited them; having entirely recovered from the effects of the rout at Cerro Gordo.—For an account of the succeeding glorious battles, and the final capture of the city of Mexico, the reader is referred to the dispatches of General Scott :

Headquarters of the army,
Tacubata, at the Gates of Mexico, August 28, 1847.

Sir; My report, No. 31, commenced in the night of the 19th instant, closed the operations of the army with that day.

The morning of the 20th. opened with one of a series of unsurpassed achievements, all in view of the capital, and to which I shall give the general name the battle of Mexico.

In the night of the 19th, brigadier generals Shields, P. F. Smith, and Cadwalader, and Colonel Riley, with their brigades, and the 15th regiment, under Colonel Morgan, detached from Brigadier General Pierce, found themselves in, and about, the important position, the village, hamlet, or *hacienda*, called indifferently. Contreras. Ansalda, San Gerenano—half a mile nearer to the city, than the enemy's entrenched camp, on the same road, towards the factory Magdalena.

That camp had been, unexpectedly, our formidable point of attack, the afternoon before; and we had now to take it, without the aid of cavalry or artillery, or to throw back our advanced corps upon the road from San Augustin to the city, and thence force a passage through San Antonio.

Accordingly, to meet contingencies, Major General Worth was ordered to leave, early in the morning of the 20th; one of his brigades to mask San Antonio, and to march with the other, six miles, *via* San Augustin, upon Contreras. A like destination was given to Major General Quitman, and his remaining brigade, in San Augustin replacing,—for the moment, the garrison of that important depot, with Harney's brigade of cavalry, as horse could not pass over the intervening rocks, &c., to reach the field of battle.

At three o'clock. a, m. the great movement commenced on the rear of the enemy's camp, Riley leading, followed successively, by Cadwalader's and Smith's brigades: the latter temporarily under the orders of Major Dimmick, of the 1st Artillery—the whole force being commanded by Smith, the senior in the general attack, and whose arrangements, skill, and gallantry, always challenge the highest admiration.

The march was rendered tedious, by the darkness, rain, and mud; but about sunrise, Riley, conducted by Lieutenant Tower, engineer, had reached an elevation behind the enemy, whence be precipitated his columns, stormed the entrenchments, planted his several colours upon them, and carried the work —all in seventeen minutes.

I doubt whether a more brilliant or decisive victory, taking into view, ground, artificial defences, batteries, and the extreme disparity of numbers, without cavalry or artillery, on our side, is to be found on record. Including all our corps directed against the entrenched camp, with Shields' brigade at the hamlet, we positively did not number over four thousand five hundred, rank and file; and we knew, by sight, and since, more certainly, by many captured documents and letters, that the enemy had actually engaged on the spot seven thousand men, with at least twelve thousand more hovering within sight, and striking distance—both on the 19th and 20th. All, not killed or captured, now fled with precipitation.

Thus was the great victory of Contreras achieved: one road to the capital opened: seven hundred of the enemy killed : eight hundred and thirteen prisoners, including among them, eighty-eight officers, four generals, besides many colours and standards: eighty-two pieces of brass ordnance half of large calibre thousands of small arms and accoutrements, and immense quantities of shot, shells, powder, and cartridges, seven hundred pack mules, many horses. &c., &c.—all in our hands.

One of the most pleasing incidents of the victory, is the recapture, in the works, by Captain Drum, 4th Artillery, under Major Gardner, of the two brass six pounders, taken from another company of the same regiment, though without the loss of honour, at the glorious battle of Buena Vista—about which guns the whole regiment had mourned for so many long months. Coming up a little later, I had the happiness to join in the protracted cheers of the gallant 4th, on the joyous event; and indeed, the whole army sympathises in its just pride and exultation.

The battle being won before the advancing brigades of Worth's and Quitman's divisions were in sight, both were ordered back to their late positions. Worth, to attack San Antonio in front, with his whole force, as soon as approached in the rear, by Pillow's and Twiggs' divisions—moving from Contreras, through San Angel and Coyoacan. By carrying San Antonio, we knew that we should open another—a shorter and better—road to the capital, for our siege and other trains.

Arriving at Coyoacan, two miles by a cross road, from the rear of San Antonio, I first detached Captain Lee, engineer, with Captain Kearney's troops, 1st Dragoons, supported by the rifle regiment, Major Loring, to reconnoitre that strong point; and next dispatched Major General Pillow, with one of his brigades (Cadwalader's), to make the attack upon it, in concert with Major General Worth, on the opposite side.

At the same time, by another road to the left, Lieutenant Stevens, of the engineers, supported by Lieutenant G. W. Smith's company of sappers and miners, of the same corps, was sent to reconnoitre the strongly fortified church, or convent, of San Sablo, in the hamlet of Churubusco, one mile off. Twiggs, with one of his brigades (Smith's less the rifles), and Captain Taylor's field battery, were ordered to follow, and to attack the convent. Major Smith, senior engineer, was dispatched to concert with Twiggs, the mode and means of attack, and Twiggs' other brigade (Riley's), I soon ordered up to support him.

Next (but all in ten minutes) I sent Pierce (just able to keep the saddle), with his brigade (Pillow's division), conducted by Captain Lee, engineer, by a third road, a little farther to our left, to attack the enemy's right and rear, in order to favour the movement upon the convent, and cut off the retreat towards the capital. And, finally, Shields, senior brigadier to Pierce, with the New York and South Carolina Volunteers (Quitman's battalion), was ordered to follow Pierce, closely, and to take the command of our left wing. All these movements were made with the utmost alacrity by our gallant troops and commanders.

Finding myself at Coyoacan, from which so many roads conveniently branched, without escort or reserve, I had to advance, for safety, close upon Twiggs' rear. The battle now raged from the right to the left of our whole line.

Learning, on the return of Captain Lee, that Shields, in the rear of Churubusco, was hard pressed, and in danger of being out-flanked, if not overwhelmed, by greatly superior numbers, I immediately sent under Major Sumner, 2nd Dragoons, the rifles (Twiggs' reserve), and Captain Sibley's troop, 2nd Dragoons, then at hand, to support our left, guided by the same engineer.

About an hour earlier, Worth had, by skilful and daring movements upon the front and light, turned, and forced San Antonio—its garrison, no doubt much shaken by our decisive victory at Contreras.

The forcing of San Antonio was the second brilliant event of the day. Worth's division, being reunited in hot pursuit, he was joined by Major General Pillow, who, marching from Coyoacan, and discovering that San Antonio had been carried, immediately turned to the left, according to my instructions, and, though much impeded by ditches and swamps, hastened to the attack of Churubusco.

The hamlet, or scattered houses, bearing this name, presented, besides the fortified convent, a strong field-work (*tete de pont*), with regular bastions and curtains, at the head of a bridge, over which the road passes from San Antonio to the capital.

The whole remaining forces of Mexico—some twenty-seven thousand men, cavalry, artillery, and infantry, collected from every quarter—were now in, on the flanks, or within supporting distance of those works, and seemed resolved to make a last and desperate stand; for if beaten here, the feebler defences at the gates of the city—four miles off could not, as was well known to both parties, delay the victors an hour. The capital of an ancient empire, now of a great republic, or an early peace, the assailants were resolved to win. Not an American, and we were less than a third of the enemy's numbers, had a doubt as to the result.

The fortified church, or convent, hotly pressed by Twiggs, had already held out about an hour, when Worth and Pillow—

the latter having with him only Cadwalader's brigade began to manoeuvre closely upon the *tete de pont*, with the convent at half gun-shot, to their left.—Garland's brigade (Worth's division), to which had been added the light batalion under Lieutenant Colonel Smith, continued to advance in front, and under the fire of a long line of infantry, off on the left of the bridge; and Clarke, of the same division, directed his brigade along the road or close by its side. Two of Pillow's and Cadwalader's regiments, the 11th and 14th, supported and participated in this direct movement; the others (the *voltigeurs*), were left in reserve. Most of these corps particularly Clark's brigade—advancing perpendicularly, were made to suffer much by the fire of the *tete de pont;* and they would have suffered greatly more by flank attacks from the convent, but for the pressure of Twiggs, on the other side of that work.

This well-combined, and daring movement, at length reached the principal point of attack, and the formidable *tete de pont* was, at once, assaulted and carried by the bayonet. Its deep wet ditch was first gallantly crossed by the 8th and 5th infantry, commanded, respectively, by Major Waite and Lieutenant Colonel Scott, followed closely, by the 6th Infantry (same brigade), which had been so much exposed in the road, the 11th regiment, under Lieutenant Colonel Graham, and the 14th, commanded by Colonel Trousdale, both of Cadwalader's brigade, Pillow's division, About the same time, the enemy, in front of Garland, after a hot conflict of an hour and a half, gave way, in a retreat towards the capital.

The immediate results of this third signal triumph on the day were: three field pieces, one hundred and ninety-two prisoners, much ammunition, and two colours, taken in the *tete de pont*.

Finally, twenty minutes after the *tete de pont* had been carried by Worth and Pillow, and at the end of a desperate conflict of two hours and a half, the church or convent the citadel of this strong line of defence along the rivulet of Churubusco— yielded to Twiggs' division, and threw out on all sides signals of surrender. The white flags, however, were not exhibited until the moment when the 3rd infantry, under Captain Alexander, had cleared the way by fire and bayonet, and had entered the work. Captain J. M. Smith and Lieutenant O. L. Shepheard, both of that regiment, with their companies, had the glory of leading the assault. The former received the surrender, and Captain Alexander instantly hung out, from a balcony, the colours of the gallant 3rd. Major Dimick, with a part of the 1st Artillery, serving as infantry, entered nearly abreast with the leading troops.

Captain Taylor's field battery, attached to Twiggs' division, opened its effective fire, at an early moment, upon the outworks of the convent and the tower of its church. Exposed to the severest fire of the enemy, the captain, his officers and men, won universal admiration; but at length, much disabled, in men and horses, the battery was, by superior orders, withdrawn from the action thirty minutes before the surrender of the convent.

The immediate results of this victory were: the capture of seven field-pieces, some ammunition, one colour, three generals, and 1,261 prisoners, including other officers.

Captain E. A. Capron and M. J. Burke, and Lieutenant S. Hoffman, all of the 1st Artillery, and Captain J. W. Anderson and Lieutenant Thomas Easley, both of the 2nd Infantry, five officers of rare merit—fell gallantly before the work.

The capture of the enemy's citadel was the fourth great achievement of our arms in the same day.

In a winding march of a mile around to the right, this temporary division found itself on the edge of an open wet meadow, near the road from San Antonio to the capital, and in the presence of some four thousand of the enemy's infantry, a little in rear of Churubusco, on that road.—Establishing the right at a strong building, Shields extended his left parallel to the road, to outflank the enemy towards the capital. But the enemy extending his right, supported by 3,000 cavalry, more rapidly, (being favoured by better ground), in the same direction, Shields concentrated the division about a hamlet, and determined to attack in from. The battle was long, hot and varied; but ultimately, success crowned the zeal and gallantry of our troops, ably directed by their distinguished commander. Brigadier General Shields. The 9th, 12th and 15th regiments, under Colonel Ransom, Captain Wood, and Colonel Morgan, respectively, of Pierce's brigade, (Pillow's division), and the New York and South Carolina volunteers, under Colonels Burnett and Butler, respectively of Shields' own brigade, (Quitman's division), together with the mountain howitzer battery, now under Lieutenant Reno, of the ordnance corps, all shared in the glory of this action—our fifth victory in the same day.

Brigadier General Pierce, from the hurt of the evening before—under pain and exhaustion fainted in the action. Several other changes in command occurred on this field.

Shields took 380 prisoners, including officers; and it cannot be doubted that the fate of the conflict between him and the enemy, just in the rear of the *tete de pont* and the convent, had some influence on the surrender of those formidable defences.

As soon as the *tete de pont* was carried, the greater part of Worth's and Pillow's forces passed that bridge in rapid pursuit of the flying enemy. These distinguished generals, coming up with Brigadier General Shields, now also victorious, the three continued to press upon the fugitives to within a mile and a half of the capital. Here, Colonel Harney, with a small part of his brigade of cavalry, rapidly passed to the front, and charged the enemy up to the nearest gate. The cavalry charge was headed by Captain Kearney, of the 1st Dragoons, having in squadron, with his own troop, that of Captain McReynolds, of the 3rd —making the usual escort to general headquarters; but being early in the day detached for general service, was now under Colonel Harney's orders. The gallant captain, not hearing the recoil, dashed up to the San Antonio gate, sabring, in his way. all who resisted.

So terminated the series of events, which I have but feebly presented. My thanks were freely poured out on the different fields—to the abilities and science of generals and other officers to the gallantry and prowess of all the rank and file included. But a reward infinitely higher the applause of a grateful country and government will, I cannot doubt, be accorded, in due time, to so much merit, of every sort, displayed by this glorious army, which has now overcome all difficulties—distance, climate, ground, fortifications, and numbers.

It has in a single day. in many battles, as often defeated 32,000 men; made about 3,000 prisoners, including eight generals, (two of them ex-presidents), and 205 other officers; killed or wounded 4.000 of all ranks besides entire corps dispersed and dissolved: captured thirty-seven pieces of ordnance—more than trebling our siege train and field batteries—with a large number of small arms, a full supply of ammunition of every kind, &c.. &c. These great results have overwhelmed the enemy.

Our loss amounts to 1.053 killed. 469, including sixteen officers; wounded, 876, with sixty officers. The greater number of the dead and disabled were of the highest worth. Those under treatment, thanks to our very able medical officers, are generally doing well.

I regret having been obliged, on the 20th, to leave Major General Quitman, an able commander, with a part of his division the fine 2nd Pennsylvania volunteers, and the veteran detachment of United States' marines at our important depot, San Augustin. It was there that I had placed our sick and wounded; the siege, supply and baggage trains. If these had been lost, the army would have been driven almost to despair, and considering the enemy's very great excess of numbers, and the many approaches to the depot, it might well have become, emphatically, the post of honour.

After so many victories, we might, with but little additional loss, have occupied the capital the same evening. But Mr. Trist, commissioner. &c. as well as myself, had been admonished by the best friends of peace intelligent neutrals, and some American residents against precipitation; lost, by wantonly driving away the government and others dishonoured we might scatter the elements of peace, excite a spirit of national desperation, and thus indefinitely postpone the hope of an accommodation. Deeply impressed with this danger, and remembering our mission to conquer a peace the army very cheerfully sacrificed to patriotism to the great wish and want of our country the éclat that would have followed an entrance sword in hand into a great capital. Willing to leave something to this republic of no immediate value to us on which to rest her pride, and to recover temper I halted our victorious corps at the gates of the city, (at least for a time), and have them now cantoned in the neighbouring villages, where they are well sheltered, and supplied with all necessaries.

On the morning of the 21st, being about to take up battering or assaulting positions, to authorize me to summon the city to surrender, or to sign an armistice, with a pledge to enter at once into negotiations for a peace—a mission came out to propose a truce. Rejecting its terms, I dispatched my contemplated note to General Santa Anna—omitting the summons. The 22nd, commissioners were appointed by the commanders of the two armies; the armistice was signed the 23rd, and ratifications exchanged the 24th.

All matters in dispute between the two governments have been thus happily turned over to their plenipotentiaries, who have had several conferences, and with, I think, some hops of signing a treaty of peace.

There will be transmitted to the adjutant general reports from divisions, brigades, etc., on the foregoing operations, to which I must refer with my hearty concurrence in the just applause bestowed on corps and individuals by their respective commanders. I have been able—this report being necessarily summary—to bring out. comparatively but little of individual merit not lying directly in the way of the narrative. Thus, I doubt whether I have, in express terms, given my approbation and applause to the commanders of divisions and independent brigades; but left their fame upon higher grounds the simple record of their deeds and the brilliant results. To the staff, both general and personal, attached to general headquarters, I was again under high obligations for services in the field, as always in the bureaux.

I had the valuable services, as volunteer aids, of Majors Kirby and Van Buren, of the pay department, always eager for activity and distinction; and of a third, the gallant Major J. P. Gaines, of the Kentucky Volunteers.

I have the honour to be, sir, with high respect,
Your most obedient servant,
Winfield Scott.
Hon. Wm. L. Marcy, Secretary of War.

The foregoing dispatch of Major General Scott, with regard to the operations of the army from the time of its arrival near the city of Mexico, to that of the armistice being concluded between the opposing forces, can be better understood by a perusal of the following clearly written review of the same, by a correspondent of the N. O. Picayune. Taking this in connection with the map of the vicinity of the city of Mexico, the reader can be at no loss in forming a clear and definite view of the plan of those gallantly fought engagements.

"We do not think that either the dispatches of General Scott, or the reports of his subordinates, have been remarkably clear as historical narration. As military papers, they are, no doubt, all that they ought to be; but in reading them one becomes absolutely puzzled with the mincing up of facts with the names of divisions, brigades and regiments, officers and soldiers, and a mass of details, which it requires almost an adjutant general to disentangle and understand. The task of forming a clear idea of the plan of operations, as a whole, is to a civilian a difficult one; and, perhaps, his satisfaction in accomplishing it is one reason why he may be permitted to spread the result of his labours on paper, for the benefit of those who, like himself, have known little more than that Mexico is ours, and that it cost a certain number of killed, wounded and missing, to make it so.

"About the middle of August last, General Scott, with the army that marched from Puebla, was at Buena Vista not the Buena Vista, but a place of the same name about twenty miles from the city of Mexico Let us imagine ourselves at his side, looking straight towards the city, and able to see it, and the intervening country, as we do on the map before us as we write.

Directly in front is the great high road to Mexico. Immediately to the left is a large lake, along whose northern shore the road runs; and some miles further on, still to the left as we look, and to the south of the road, but at a distance from it and reaching to within a few miles of the city, is another lake.

"The first of these, is the lake of Chalco; the second, or farthest off, is the lake of Xochilmilco. So much for what we see on the left of the highway as we look towards Mexico. On the right, and opposite to the lake of Chalco, the country is open, but farther on and directly opposite the lake of Xochilmilco is the lake of Tezcuco the lake in whose waters was throned the Tenochtillan of Montezuma—but now dwindled to a comparatively small sheet of water, which does not approach much nearer to the modern city than the lake of Xochilmilco, on the opposite side of the high road. travelling, therefore, from Buena Vista to Mexico, you have first the lake of Chalco on your left hand, with open country on your right, and afterwards the lake of Tezcuco close on the right, and the lake of Xochilmilco opposite to it, but much farther off on the left; and so you continue on between the two lakes until, passing their western extremities, you travel through an open country on either hand up to the *garita* of Penon, one of the entrances into the city.

"Now, this was the best road for the diligence, but not for General Scott; for close to that part of the road which, as we have seen, lies between the lakes of Tezcuco and Xochilmilco. was the fortress or fortified hill of the Penon—the old Penon—for there is another Penon nearer the city.

"The ground on either side of the road was marshy and impassable; and an approach to Mexico, by this route, would have been a most murderous business—something like marching a body of men from the Bridge up Baltimore street to the Eutaw House, supposing the latter turned round across the street, with cannon loaded with round and grape shot at every window. Tempting, therefore, as was the smooth highway between the lakes, it was not to be thought of; and, instead, therefore, of pursuing it. General Scott turned off to the left at Buena Vista, nearly at right angles to the road he had travelled from Puebla, and, keeping close to the lake of Chalco, which was. of course, then on his right hand, came to Ayocingo at its southern extremity.

"Here, he turned again short round to the right, and keeping close to the southern shores, first of the lake Chalco, and afterwards of Xochilmilco, upon a road which he cut for the occasion, marched north-westwardly on a line nearly parallel with the highway he had left, and separated from it by the last named lakes. In this manner, and soon after leaving the lake of Xochilmilco, at La Novia, he came to San Augustin—about as far from the city as he could have been had he taken the main road and stopped at the Penon, but without the loss of a man; whereas thousands might have been sacrificed in an attempt on the latter fortress. This was the first out-generalling of the Mexicans, who never dreamed that anyone would prefer cutting around the lakes of Chalco and Xochilmilco to going between them and the lake Tezcuco upon the smooth highway.

"Now. if the Mexicans had stayed at the Penon, there would have been little to prevent the Americans from marching at once into the city; but, as soon as the latter turned round the eastern end of the lake of Chalco to reach San Augustin, the former, leaving the Penon, went round the western end of the lake of Xochilmilco to head the invaders, and established themselves at Churubusco, San Antonia, Contreras—a very necessary change of position, well conceived and promptly executed, and which again placed the whole Mexican army between General Scott and the capital.

"Let us now imagine ourselves with General Scott, looking towards the city of Mexico, which is due north, and much nearer than it was at Buena Vista. Immediately in front is a road nearly straight leading to the city; passing first through the village of San Antonio, about—miles off; then about—miles farther, crossing the Churubusco river, at the village of that name, where there is a large convent and a bridge, the entrance to which is defended by a fortification, called among soldiers, a *tete du pont* or bridge head. Beyond Churubusco, is the village

VICINITY OF MEXICO

of Los Portales, and beyond that the road is a fair and smooth one to the *garita* of San Antonio Abad, one of the entrances into Mexico. At first sight, it would seem that nothing was to be done but to march upon the Mexicans at San Antonio drive them to the Churubusco river, defeat them there, and hurry on to the "Halls of the Montezumas." But, then, to the left of General Scott—whom we imagine to be looking towards Mexico from San Augustin and almost at right angles to the road into the city, is a body of men, the flower of the Mexican army, under General Valencia—veterans from San Luis Potosi men who had been in the fight of the Buena Vista.

"To have marched directly on Churubusco would have placed Valencia in Scott's rear, which would have been at the mercy of the Mexican general; and this would never have done. Therefore, although Contreras was a good deal out of the way, and, although going to Mexico, via Contreras, was like going to Philadelphia via York, Pa., or to Richmond *via* Norfolk, there was no help for it; and to Contreras a force was accordingly sent to put Valencia *hors du combat*. Santa Anna, who saw that Valencia could do no good under such circumstances, ordered him to retire on Churubusco which was what he ought to have done to aid in the stand which it was intended to make there against the Americans.

"But Valencia was a fool, and preferred staying to be routed in a battle, commencing on the evening of the 19th of August, by a feigned attack in front, and followed up on the morning of the 20th. by an attack in the rear that did the business thoroughly. This was a fine move on Scott's part, though it would have been counteracted had Valencia obeyed orders and joined Santa Anna either at San Antonio or Churubusco. The roads from Contreras and San Augustin to Mexico, came together at Churubusco, forming a V, the point of which was at the latter place. San Antonio, as we have seen, was between San Augustin and Churubusco. Scott, marching on the Contreras road towards Mexico, would, therefore, have got into the rear of Santa Anna at San Antonio; and Santa Anna, seeing this, ordered the troops at the latter place, to Tall back on Churubusco. And here a word of collateral explanation is necessary.

"When Scott reached San Augustin, he was nearer San Antonio than to Contreras, and, therefore, had he sent his whose force to Contreras, Santa Anna, by advancing from San Antonio, could have attacked his rear before Valencia was beaten. In other words, Scott would then have been between Santa Anna and Valencia. To prevent this, but a part of the American army was seal to Contreras, and with the remainder San Augustin was held, and a movement was made towards San Antonio, keeping Santa Anna in check, as it is termed. Thus, when the force which had beaten Valencia advanced towards Churubusco, there was another force advancing on the Mexicans from San Augustin; so that, although Santa Anna's order to fall back from San Antonio on Churubusco was obeyed, it was not obeyed in time to prevent collision with the Americans.

"Had Valencia obeyed Santa Anna had the force at San Antonio fallen back in lime, the lines at Churubusco would have been held by fresh forces, in good spirits, behind excellent defences, and fighting in sight of their homes and firesides. As it was, the defeat at Contreras. the conflict at San Antonio, disheartened the Mexicans, and they fought the battle of Churubusco at a great disadvantage. But they fought well, notwithstanding. Up to this time, the game of war had been a succession of most skilful and able moves, for, to deny that Santa Anna has all the attributes of a great general, is idle.

"The next move was the Battle of Churubusco. The Mexicans were routed and demoralized; and no one can doubt; that if General Scott had marched forward, instead of stopping at Los Portales, he would have taken the city of Mexico without further loss. We say no one can doubt, because we have read the intercepted mail taken at Tacubaya. and translated and published in Mexico, showing the state of feeling in the capital on the day of the battle of Churubusco. Our purpose, however, is not to criticise the armistice.

"After the battle of Churubusco, there was a pause. The

Americans advanced to Tacubaya, and the Mexicans remained in the city, strengthening their defences, and making those preparations for a renewal of the contest, which the armistice gave them an opportunity of doing.

"The movement to Tacubaya was an able one. It is true, that from Churubusco to the capital, there was an open and undefended causeway leading up to the gate of San Antonio Abad, and to get to the city by way of Tacubaya. was as round about as to get to Churubusco from San Augustin byway of Contreras, for Churubusco is nearly due south of Mexico, and Tacubaya almost south-east. But Tacubaya is close lo Chapultepec. and it was necessary to take Chapultepec before attacking Mexico. We have heard this doubted, but the necessity was plain. If Mexico had been taken first, the army, instead of retreating towards Guadalupe, would have retired to Chapultepec; and to have left Mexico then, to take the fortress, would, with Scott's small army, have been to abandon the city and the wounded Americans to the *leperos*. The whole Mexican army would then have been the garrison of Chapultepec. As it was, the army was divided between the fortress and the city; and, as it was, it was no child's play to take Chapultepec.

"Thus far. with the exception of the armistice, about which there is room for difference of opinion, Scott had made not one mistake in the valley of Mexico. With a most able man opposed to him. he had met the emergency. He was now in sight of the city, and the next thing was to take it. There was little room for scientific combinations. Hard knocks were to settle the day."

But this armistice was only used by Santa Anna for the purpose of reuniting his scattered troops, and of throwing all their power together, for a desperate defence of the city. Santa Anna openly avows this, in a letter to one of his subordinates, found afterwards in the palace when the city was captured. With the accustomed duplicity and faithlessness of their nation, the Mexican commissioners met Mr. Trist. with every appearance of fairness, to negotiate a treaty of peace, but prolonged the discussion for every moment possible. In the meantime, an assault was committed by the Mexican populace upon an American train proceeding under the authority of the armistice, into the city, for provisions.

This and other outrages following, brought a letter from General Scott to General Santa Anna, lo which the latter, having completed his arrangements, returned an answer of almost defiance and absolute insult, accusing falsely, the American forces of robbing the churches, and of every other outrage, of which in fact, the Mexican forces were alone guilty. Negotiations were broken off on the 6th of September, and on the 8th. General Worth attacked the strong position of *Molino del Rey*, or King's Mill, and took it, but with severe loss on both sides. The following is the official report of the engagement

BATTLE OF MOLINO DEL REY

Report of General Worth.

Headquarters, 1st Division,
Tacubaya, September 10, 1847.

Sir: Under the inconvenient circumstances incident to recent battle, and derangement from loss of commanders—staff, commissioned and non-commissioned and amid the active scenes resulting therefrom, I proceed to make a report, in obedience to the orders of the general-in-chief, of the battle of *El Molino del Rey*, fought and won on the eighth of September, 1847, by the first division, reinforced as follows:

1st. Three squadrons of dragoons, and one company of mounted riflemen 270 men, under Major Sumner, 2nd dragoons.

2nd. Three pieces of field artillery, under Captain Drum.

3rd. Two battering guns, (twenty-four pounders,) under Captain Huger.

4th. Cadwalader's brigade, 784 strong, consisting of the Voltigeur regiment, the 11th and 14th regiments of infantry.

Having, in the course of the 7th, accompanied the general-in-chief on a reconnaissance of the formidable dispositions of the enemy near and around the castle of Chapultepec, they were found to exhibit an extended line of cavalry and infantry, sustained by a field battery of four guns occupying directly, or sustaining, a system of defences collateral to the castle and summit. This examination gave fair observation of the configuration of the grounds, and the extent of the enemy's force; but, as appeared in the sequel, an inadequate idea of the nature of his defences they being skillfully masked.

The general-in-chief ordered that my division, reinforced as before mentioned, should attack and carry those lines and defences, capture the enemy's artillery, destroy the machinery and material supposed to be in the foundry, (*El Molino del Rey*;) but limiting the operations to that extent. After which, my command was to be immediately withdrawn to its position, in the village of Tacubaya.

A close and daring reconnaissance, by Captain Mason of the engineers, made on the morning of the 7th, represented the enemy's lines collateral to Chapultepec to be as follows: His left rested upon and occupied a group of strong stone buildings, called *El Molino del Rey*, adjoining the. grove at the foot of the hill of Chapultepec, and directly under the guns of the castle which crowns its summit. The right of his line rested upon another stone building, called *Casa Mala* situated at the foot of the ridge that slopes gradually from the heights above the village of Tacubaya to the plain below. Midway between these buildings was the enemy's field battery, and his infantry forces were disposed on either side to support it. This reconnaissance was verified by Captain Mason and Colonel Duncan, on the afternoon of the same day. The result indicated that the centre was the weak point of the enemy's position; and that his flanks were the strong points, his left flank being the stronger.

As the enemy's system of defence was connected with the hill and castle of Chapultepec, and as my operations were limited to a specific object, it became necessary to isolate the work to be accomplished from the castle of Chapultepec and its immediate defences. To effect this object, the following dispositions were ordered: Colonel Garland's brigade to take possession on the right, strengthened by two pieces of Captain Drum's battery, to look to *El Molino del Rey* as well as any support of this position from Chapultepec; and also within sustaining distance of the assaulting party and the battering guns, which, under Captain Huger, were placed on the ridge, five or six hundred yards from El Molino del Rey, to batter and loosen this position from Chapultepec.

An assaulting party of five hundred picked men and officers, under command of Brevet Major George Wright, 8th Infantry, was also posted on the ridge to the left of the battering guns, to force the enemy's centre. The 2nd (Clarke's) brigade, the command of which devolved on Colonel McIntosh, (Colonel Clarke being sick,) with Duncan's battery,—was to take post further up the ridge, opposite the enemy's right, to look to our left flank, to sustain the assaulting column if necessary, or to discomfit the enemy, (the ground being favourable,) as circumstances might require. Cadwalader's brigade was held in reserve, in a position on the ridge, between the battering guns and McIntosh's brigade, and in easy support of either. The cavalry, under Major Sumner, to envelop our extreme left, and be governed by circumstances to repel or attack, as the commander's judgement might suggest.

The troops to be put in position under cover of the night; and the work to begin as soon as the heavy metal could be properly directed. Colonel Duncan was charged with the general disposition of the artillery. Accordingly, at 3 o'clock in the morning of the 8th, the several columns were put in motion, on as many different routes; and when the gray of the morning enabled them to be seen, they were as accurately in position as if posted in midday for review. The early dawn was the moment appointed for the attack, which was announced to our troops by the opening of Huger's guns on *El Molino del Rey,* upon which they continued to play actively until this point of the enemy's line became sensibly shaken; when the assaulting party, commanded by Wright, and guided by that accomplished officer, Captain Mason of the engineers, assisted by Lieutenant Foster, dashed gallantly forward to the assault.

Unshaken by the galling of the musketry and canister that

was showered upon them, on they rushed, driving infantry and artillery-men at the point of the bayonet. The enemy's field battery was taken, and his own guns were trailed upon his retreating masses; before, however, they could be discharged, perceiving that he had been dispossessed of his strong position by comparatively a handful of men, he made a desperate effort to regain it. Accordingly, his retreating forces rallied and formed, with this object. Aided by the infantry, which covered the housetops (within reach of which the battery had been moved during the night), the enemy's whole line opened upon the assaulting party a terrific fire of musketry, which struck down eleven out of the fourteen officers that composed the command, and non-commissioned officers and men in proportion; including, amongst the officers, Brevet Major Wright, the commander; Captain Mason and Lieutenant Foster, engineers: all severely wounded.

This severe shock staggered, for a moment, that gallant band. The light battalion, held to cover Captain Huger's infantry, under Captain E. Kirby Smith. (Lieutenant Colonel Smith being sick,) and the right wing of Cadwalader's brigade, were promptly ordered forward to support, which order was executed in the most gallant style; the enemy was again routed, and this point of his line carried, and fully possessed by our troops.

In the meantime, Garland's (1st) brigade, ably sustained by Captain Drum's artillery, assaulted the enemy's left, and after an obstinate and very severe contest, drove him from his apparently impregnable position, immediately under the guns of the castle of Chapultepec. Drum's section, and the battering guns under Captain Huger, advanced to the enemy's position, and the captured guns of the. enemy were now opened on his retreating forces, on which they continued to fire until beyond their reach.

While this work was in progress of accomplishment by our centre and right, our troops on the left were not idle. Duncan's battery opened on the right of the enemy's line, up to this time engaged; and the 2nd brigade, under Colonel McIntosh, was now ordered to assault the extreme right of the enemy's line.

The direction of this brigade soon caused it to mask Duncan's battery the fire of which, for the moment, was discontinued, and the brigade moved steadily on to the assault of *Casa Mala*, which, instead of an ordinary field entrenchment, as was supposed, proved to be a strong stone citadel, surrounded with bastioned entrenchments and impassable ditches an old Spanish work, recently repaired and enlarged. When within easy musket range, the enemy opened a most deadly fire upon our advancing troops, which was kept up, without intermission, until our gallant men reached the very slope of the parapet of the work that surrounds the citadel.

By this time a large proportion of the command were either killed or wounded, amongst whom, were the three senior officers present Brevet Colonel McIntosh, Brevet Lieutenant Colonel Scott, of the 5th Infantry, and Major Waite, 8th Infantry; the second killed, and the first and last desperately wounded. Still, the fire from the citadel was unabated. In this crisis of the attack, the command was. momentarily, thrown it into disorder, and fell back on the left of Duncan's battery, where they rallied. As the 2nd brigade moved to the assault, a very large cavalry and infantry force was discovered approaching rapidly upon our left flank, to reinforce the enemy's right.

As soon as Duncan's battery was masked, as before mentioned, supported by Andrews' *voltigeurs* of Cadwalader's brigade, it moved promptly to the extreme left of our line, to check the threatened assault on this point. The enemy's cavalry came, rapidly, within canister range, when the whole battery opened a most effective fire, which soon broke the squadrons, and drove them back in disorder.

During this fire upon the enemy's cavalry, Major Sumner's command moved to the front, and changed direction in admirable order, under a most appalling fire from *Casa Mala*. This movement enabled his command to cross the ravine immediately on the left of Duncan's battery, where it remained, doing noble service, until the close of the action.

At the very moment the cavalry were driven beyond reach,

our own troops drew back from before the *Casa Mala*, and enabled the guns of Duncan's battery to reopen upon this position; which, after a short and well-directed fire, the enemy abandoned. The guns of the battery were now turned upon his retreating columns, and continued to play upon them until beyond reach.

He was now driven from every point in the field, and his strong lines, which had certainly been defended well, were in our possession. In fulfilment of the instructions of the general-in-chief, the *Casa Mala* was blown up, and such of the captured ammunition as was useless to us, as well as the cannon moulds found in *El Molino del Rey,* were destroyed.

After which, my command, under the reiterated orders of the general-in-chief, returned to quarters at Tacubaya, with three of the enemy's four guns, (the fourth having been spiked, was rendered unserviceable,) as also a large quantity of small arras, with gun and musket ammunition, and exceeding eight hundred prisoners, including fifty-two commissioned officers.

By the concurrent testimony of a prisoner, the enemy's force exceeded fourteen thousand men, commanded by General Santa Anna in person. His total loss, killed, (including the 2nd and 3rd in command, Generals Valdarez and Leon,) wounded and prisoners, amounts to three thousand, exclusive of some two thousand who deserted after the rout.

My command, reinforced as before stated, only reached three thousand one hundred men of all arms. The contest continued two hours, and its severity is painfully attested by our heavy loss of officers, non-commissioned officers and privates, including in the first two classes some of the brightest ornaments of the service.

Accompanying is a tabular statement of casualties, with lists, by name, of rank and file killed, *viz.*; nine officers killed, and forty-nine wounded; seven hundred and twenty-nine rank and file killed and wounded.

I have the honour to be, very respectfully, your obedient servant,   W. J. Worth,   Brevet Major General Commanding.

To Captain Scott, A. A, Adjutant General, headquarters.

THE BATTLE OF CHAPULTEPEC, AND THE ASSAULT UPON AND CAPTURE OF THE CITY OF MEXICO.

Report of Major General Scott

(No. 34.) Headquarters or the Army.
National Palace of Mexico,
September 18, 1847.

Sir At the end of another series of arduous and brilliant operations, of more than forty-eight hours' continuance, this glorious army hoisted on the morning of the 14th, the colours of the United States on the walls of this palace.

The victory of the 8th at the *Molino del Rey*, was followed by daring reconnaissances, on the part of our distinguished engineers—Captain Lee, Lieutenants Beauregard, Stevens, and Tower Major Smith, senior, being sick, and Captain Mason, third in rank, being wounded. Their operations were directed principally to the south—towards the gates of Piedad, San Angel (Nino Perdido) San Antonio, and the Paseo de la Viga.

This city stands on a slight swell of ground, near the centre of an irregular basin, and is girdled with a ditch in its greater extent a navigable canal of great breadth and depth—very difficult to bridge, in the presence of an enemy, and serving at once for drainage, custom-house purposes, and military defence—leaving eight entrances of gates, over arches; each of which we found defended by a system of strong works, that seemed to require nothing but some men and guns, to be impregnable.

Outside and within the crossfires of those gates we found to the south, other obstacles, but little less formidable. All the approaches near the city, are over elevated causeways, cut in many places (to oppose us), and flanked on both sides by ditches, also of unusual dimensions. The numerous crossroads are flanked in like manner, having bridges at the intersections, recently broken. The meadows thus chequered, are moreover, in many spots under water, or marshy: for it will be remembered, we were in the midst of the wet season, though with less rain than usual, and we could not wait for the fall of the neighbouring lakes, and the consequent drainage of the wet grounds at the edge of the city the lowest in the whole basin.

After a close personal survey of the southern gates, covered by Pillow's division and Riley's brigade of Twiggs', with four times our numbers concentrated in front, I determined on the 11th, to avoid that network of obstacles, and to seek, by a sudden inversion to the south-west and west, less unfavourable approaches. To economise the lives of our gallant officers and men, as well as to insure success, it became indispensable that this resolution should be long masked from the enemy; and again, that the new movement, when discovered, should be mistaken for a feint, and the old as indicating our true and ultimate point of attack.

Accordingly, on the spot, the 11th, I ordered Quitman's division from Coyoacan, to join Pillow, by daylight, before the southern gates, and then, that the two major generals, with their divisions, should, by night, proceed (two miles) to join me at Tacubaya, where I was quartered with Worth's division. Twiggs, with Riley's brigade, and captains Taylor's and Steptoe's field batteries—the latter of twelve-pounders was left in front of those gates, to manoeuvre, to threaten, or to make false attacks, in order to occupy and deceive the enemy. Twiggs' other brigade (Smith's), was left at supporting distance, in the rear, at San Angel, till the morning of the 13th, and also to support our general depot at Miscoac.

The stratagem against the south was admirably executed throughout the 12th, and down to the afternoon of the 13th, when it was too late for the enemy to recover from the effect of his delusion.

The first step in the new movement was to carry Chapultepec, a natural and isolated mound, of great elevation, strongly fortified at its base, on its acclivities, and heights. Besides a numerous garrison, here was the military college of the republic, with a large number of sub-lieutenants, and other students. Those works were within direct gun-shot of the village of Tacubaya, and, until carried, we could not approach the city on the west, without making a circuit too wide and too hazardous.

In the course of the same night (that of the 11th), heavy batteries, within easy ranges were established. No. 1, on our right, under the command of Captain Drum, 4th Artillery (relieved late next day, for some hours, by Lieutenant Andrews, of the 3rd), and No. 2, commanded by Lieutenant Hagner, ordnance both supported by Quitman's division Nos. 3 and 4, on the opposite, supported by Pillow's division, were commanded, the former by Captain Brooks and Lieutenant S. S. Anderson, 2nd Artillery, alternately, and the latter by Lieutenant Stone, ordnance. The batteries were traced by Captain Huger, and Captain Lee engineer, and constructed by them, with the able assistance of the young officers of those corps and the artillery.

To prepare for an assault, it was foreseen, that the play of the batteries might run into the second day; but recent captures had not only trebled our siege pieces, but also our ammunition, and we knew that we should greatly augment both, by carrying the place. I was, therefore, in no haste in ordering an assault before the works were well crippled by our missiles.

The bombardment and cannonade, under the direction of Captain Huger, were commenced early in the morning of the 12th. Before nightfall, which necessarily stopped our batteries, we perceived that a good impression had been made on the castle and its outworks, and that a large body of the enemy had remained outside, towards the city, from an early hour, to avoid our fire, and to be at hand on its cessation, in order to reinforce the garrison against an assault. The same outside force was discovered the next morning, after our batteries had reopened upon the city, by which we again reduced its garrison to the minimum needed for the guns.

Pillow and Quitman had been in position since early in the night of the 11th. Major General Worth was now ordered to hold his division in reserve, near the foundry, to support Pillow; and Brig. General Smith, of Twiggs' division, had just arrived, with his brigade, from Piedad (two miles), to support Quitman. Twiggs' guns, before the southern gates, again reminded us, as they did before, that he, with Riley's brigade, and Taylor's, and Steptoe's batteries, was in activity, threatening the southern gates, and there holding a great part of the Mexican army on the defensive. Worth's division furnished Pillow's attack with an assaulting party of two hundred and fifty volunteer officers and men, under Captain McKenzie, of the 3rd Artillery; and Twiggs' division supplied a similar one commanded by Captain Casey, 2nd Infantry, to Quitman.

Each of those little columns was furnished with scaling ladders. The signal I had appointed for the attack, was the momentary cessation of the fire of our heavy batteries. About eight o'clock in the morning of the 13th, judging that the time had arrived, by the effect of the missiles we had thrown, I sent an *aid-de-camp* to Pillow, and another to Quitman, with notice that the concerted signal was about to be given. Both columns now advanced with an alacrity that gave assurance of prompt success.

The batteries, seizing opportunities, threw shot and shells upon the enemy, over the heads of our men, with good effect, particularly at every attempt to reinforce the works from without, to meet our assault. Major General Pillow's approach, on the west side, lay through an open grove, filled with sharpshooters, who were speedily dislodged; when, being up with the front of the attack, and emerging into an open space, at the foot of a rocky acclivity, that gallant leader was struck down by an agonizing wound. The immediate command devolved on Brigadier General Cadwalader, in the absence of the senior brigadier (Pierce) of same division, an invalid since the events of August 19th

On a previous call of Pillow, Worth had just sent him a reinforcement Colonel Clark's brigade. The broken acclivity was still to be ascended, and a strong redoubt, midway, to be carried, before reaching the castle on the heights. The advance of our brave men, led by brave officers, though necessarily slow, was unwavering, over rocks, chasms, and mines, and under the hottest fire of cannon and musketry. The redoubt now yielded to their resistless valour, and the shouts that followed, announced to the castle the fate that impended. The enemy were steadily driven from shelter to shelter. The retreat allowed not time to fire a single mine, without the certainty of blowing up friend and foe.

Those, who, at a distance, attempted to apply matches to the long trains, were shot down by our men. There was death below, as well as above ground. At length the ditch and wall of the main work were reached; the scaling-ladders were brought up and planted by the storming parties; some of the daring spirits, first in the assault, were cast down, killed, or wounded; but a lodgement was soon made; streams of heroes followed; all opposition was overcome, and several of our regimental colours flung out from the upper walls, amid long-continued shouts and cheers, which sent dismay into the capital. No scene could have been more animating or glorious.

Major General Quitman, nobly supported by Brigadier Generals Shields and Smith (P. F.), his other officers and men, was up with the part assigned him. Simultaneously with the movement on the west, he had gallantly approached the south-east of the same works over a causeway, with cuts and batteries, and defended by an army strongly posted outside, to the cast of the works. These formidable obstacles Quitman had to face, with but little shelter for his troops, or space for manoeuvring. Deep ditches, flanking the causeway made it difficult to cross, on either side, into the adjoining meadows, and these again were intersected by other ditches.

Smith and his brigade had been early thrown out to make a sweep to the right, in order to present a front against the enemy's line (outside), and to turn the two intervening batteries, near the foot of Chapultepec. This movement was also intended to support Quitman's storming parties, both on the causeway. The first of these, furnished by Twiggs' division, was commanded in succession, by Captain Casey, 2nd Infantry, and Captain Paul, 7th Infantry, after Casey had been severely wounded; and the second, originally under the gallant Major Twiggs, marine corps, killed, and then Captain Miller, 2nd Pennsylvania Volunteers.

The storming party, now commanded by Captain Paul, seconded by Captain Roberts, of the rifles, Lieutenant Stewart, and others of the same regiment, Smith's brigade, carried the two batteries in the road, took some guns, with many prisoners, and drove the enemy posted behind in support. The New York and South Carolina volunteers (Shields' brigade), and the 2nd Pennsylvania Volunteers, all on the left of Quitman's line, together with portions of his storming parties, crossed the meadows in front, under a heavy fire, and entered the outer enclosure of Chapultepec, just in time to join in the final assault from the west.

Besides Major Generals Pillow and Quitman, Brigadier Generals Shields, Smith and Cadwalader, the following are the officers and corps most distinguished in those brilliant operations:—The Voltigeur regiment, in two detachments, commanded, respectively, by Colonel Andrews and Lieutenant Colonel Johnstone—the latter mostly in the lead, accompanied by Major Caldwell; Captains Barnard and Biddle, of the same regiment—the former the first to plant a regimental colour, and the latter among the first in the assault; the storming party of Worth's division, under Captain McKenzie, 2nd Artillery, with Lieutenant Seldon, 8th Infantry, early on the ladder and badly wounded; Lieutenant Armistead, 6th infantry, the first to leap into the ditch to plant a ladder; Lieutenants Rogers of the 4th, and J. P. Smith of the 5th Infantry, both mortally wounded;—the 9th Infantry, under Colonel Ransom, who was killed while gallantly leading that gallant regiment; the 15th Infantry, under Lieutenant Colonel Howard and Major Woods, with Captain Chase, whose company gallantly carried the redoubt, midway up the acclivity; Colonel Clarke's brigade, (Worth's division), consisting of the 5th, 8th, and part of the 6th Regiments of Infantry, commanded, respectively, by Captain Chapman, Major Montgomery and Lieutenant Edward Johnson, the latter specially noticed, with Lieutenants Longstreet, (badly wounded advancing colours in hand), Pickett and Merchant, the last three of the 8th Infantry: portions of the U. S. Marines, New York. South Carolina, and 2nd Pennsylvania Volunteers, which delayed with their division (Quitman's) by the hot engagement below, arrived just in time to participate in the assault of the heights—particularly a detachment, under Lieutenant Ried, New York Volunteers consisting of a company of the same, with one of marines; and another detachment, a portion of the storming party. (Twiggs' division, serving with Quitman), under Lieutenant Steele, 2nd Infantry—after the fall of Lieutenant Grant, 7th Infantry.

In this connexion, it is but just to recall the decisive effect of the heavy batteries, Nos. 1, 2, 3 and 4, commanded by those excellent officers, Captain Drum, 4th Artillery, assisted by Lieutenants Benjamin and Porter of his own company; Captain Brooks and Lieutenant Anderson, 2nd Artillery, assisted by Lieutenant Russell, 4th Infantry, a volunteer; Lieutenants Hagner and Stone, of the ordnance, and Lieutenant Andrews,—3rd Artillery the whole superintended by Captain Huger, chief of ordnance an officer distinguished by every kind of merit. The mountain howitzer battery, under Lieutenant Reno, of the ordnance,—deserves, also, to be particularly mentioned. Attached to the *voltigeurs*, it followed the movements of that regiment, and again won applause.

In adding to the list of individuals of conspicuous merit, I must limit myself to a few of the many names which might be enumerated:—Captain Hooker, assistant adjutant general, who won special applause successively in the staff of Pillow and Cadwalader; Lieutenant Lovell, 4th Artillery, (wounded), chief of Quitman's staff; Captain Page, assistant adjutant general, (wounded), and Lieutenant Hammond. 3rd Artillery, both of Shields' staff; and Lieutenant Van Dora, 7th Infantry, *aid-de-camp* to Brigadier General Smith.

These operations all occurred on the west, south-east, and heights of Chapultepec. To the north, and at the base of the mound, inaccessible on that side, the 11th Infantry, under Lieutenant Colonel Herbert, the 4th, under Colonel Trousdale, and Captain Magruder's field battery, 1st Artillery—one section advanced under Lieutenant Jackson—all of Pillow's division had, at the same time, some spirited affairs against superior numbers, driving the enemy from a battery in the road, and capturing a gun. In these the officers and corps named gained merited praise. Colonel Trousdale, the commander, though twice wounded, continued on duty till the heights were carried.

Early in the morning of the 13th. I repeated the orders of the night before to Major General Worth, to be with his division at hand, to support the movement of Major General Pillow from our left. The latter seems soon to have called for that entire division, standing momentarily in reserve, and Worth sent him Colonel Clarke's brigade. The call, if not unnecessary, was, at least, under the circumstances, unknown to me at the time; for. soon observing the very large body of the enemy in the road in front of Major General Quitman's right, was reinforcements from the city less than a mile and a half to the east —I sent instructions to Worth, on our opposite flank, to turn Chapultepec with his division, and to proceed, cautiously, by the road at its northern base, in order, if not met by very superior numbers, to threaten or to attack in rear, that body of the enemy. The movement, it was also believed, could not fail to distract and to intimidate the enemy generally.

Worth promptly advanced with his remaining brigade—Colonel Garland's Lieutenant Colonel C. F. Smith's light battalion, Lieutenant Colonel Duncan's field battery—all of his division and three squadrons of dragoons, under Major Sumner, which I had just ordered up to join in the movement.

Having turned the fortress on the west, and arriving opposite to the north centre of Chapultepec, Worth came up with the troops in the road under Colonel Trousdale, and aided by a flank movement of a part of Garland's brigade in taking the one-gun breastwork, then under the fire of Lieutenant Jackson's section of Captain Magruder's field battery. Continuing to advance, this division passed Chapultepec, attacking the right of the enemy's line, resting on that road, about the moment of the general retreat consequent upon the capture of the formidable castle and its outworks. Arriving some minutes later, and mounting to the top of the castle, the whole field, to the east, lay plainly under my view.

There are two routes from Chapultepec to the capital—the one on the right entering the same gale, Belen, with the road from the south, *via* Piedad; and the other obliquing to the left, to intersect the great western, or San Cosme road, in a suburb outside of the gate of San Cosme. Each of these routes (an elevated causeway) presents a double roadway on the sides of an aqueduct of strong masonry, and great height, resting on open arches and massive pillars, which, together, afford fine points both for attack and defence. The sideways of both aqueducts, are, moreover, defended by many strong breastworks at the gates, and before reaching them. As we had expected, we found the four tracks unusually dry and solid for the season.

Worth and Quitman were prompt in pursuing the retreating enemy—the former by the San Cosme aqueduct, and the latter along that of Belen. Each had now advanced some hundred yards. Deeming it all important to profit by our successes, and the consequent dismay of the enemy, which could not be otherwise than general, I hastened to dispatch from Chapultepec, first Clarke's brigade, and then Cadwalader's, to the support of Worth, and gave orders that the necessary heavy guns should follow. Pierce's brigade was, at the same time, sent to Quitman, and, in the course of the afternoon, I caused some additional siege pieces to be added to his tram.

Then, after designating the 15th Infantry, under Lieutenant Colonel Howard—Morgan, the colonel, had been disabled by a wound at Churubusco—as the garrison of Chapultepec. and giving directions for the care of the prisoners of war, the captured ordnance and ordnance stores, I proceeded to join the advance of Worth, within the suburb, and beyond the turn at the junction of the aqueduct with the great highway from the west to the gates of San Cosme.

At this junction of roads, we first passed one of those formidable systems of city defences, spoken of above, and it had not a gun;—a strong proof.—1. That the enemy had expected us to fail in the attack upon Chapultepec, even if we meant anything more than a feint; 2. That in either case, we designed, in his belief, to return and double our forces against the southern gates—a delusion kept up by the active demonstrations of Twiggs and the forces posted on that side; and, 3. That advancing rapidly from the reduction of Chapultepec, the enemy had not time to shift guns—our previous captures had left him, comparatively, but few—from the southern gales.

Within those disgarnished works, I found our troops engaged in a street fight against the enemy posted in gardens, at windows, and on housetops—all flat—with parapets. Worth ordered forward the mountain howitzers of Cadwalader's brigade, preceded by skirmishers and pioneers, with pick-axes and crow bars, to force windows and doors, or to burrow through walls. The assailants were soon in an equality of position fatal to the enemy. By eight o'clock in the evening, Worth had carried two batteries in this suburb. According to my instructions, he here posted guards and sentinels, and placed his troops under shelter for night.—There was but one more obstacle; the San Cosme gale (custom-house) between him and the great square in front of the cathedral and palace—the heart of the city; and that barrier, it was known, could not by daylight, resist our siege guns thirty minutes.

I had gone back to the foot of Chapultepec, the point from which the two aqueducts begin to diverge, some hours earlier, in order to be near that new depot, and in easy communication with Quitman and Twiggs, as well as with Worth. From this point, I ordered all detachments and stragglers to their respective corps, then in advance; sent to Quitman additional siege guns, ammunition, entrenching tools; directed Twiggs' remaining brigade (Riley's) from Piedad, to support Worth, and Captain Steptoe's field battery, also at Piedad, to rejoin Quitman's division.

I had been, from the first, well aware that the western, or San Cosme, was the less difficult route to the centre and conquest of the capital; and, therefore, intended that Quitman should manoeuvre and threaten the Belen or south-western gate, in order to favour the main attack by Worth knowing that the strong defences at the Belen were directly under the guns of the much stronger fortress called the citadel, just within. Both of these defences of the enemy were also within easy supporting distance from the San Angel (or Nino Perdido) and San Antonio gates. Hence the greater support, in numbers, given to Worth's movement at the main attack.

Those views I repeatedly, in the course of the day, communicated to Major General Quitman; but, being in hot pursuit—gallant himself, and ably supported by Brigadier Generals Shields and Smith—Shields badly wounded before Chapultepec, and refusing to retire—as well as by all the officers and men of the column—Quitman continued to press forward, under flank and direct fires carried an immediate battery of two guns, and then the gate, before two o'clock in the afternoon, but not without proportionate loss, increased by his steady maintenance of that position.

Here, of the heavy battery, 4th Artillery, Captain Drum and Lieutenant Benjamin were mortally wounded, and Lieutenant Porter, its third in rank, slightly. The loss of those two most distinguished officers the army will long mourn. Lieutenants J. B Moragne and Wm. Canty, of the South Carolina volunteers, also officers of high merit, fell on the occasion—besides many of our bravest non-commissioned officers and men—particularly in Captain Drum's veteran company. I cannot, in this place, give names or numbers; but full returns of the killed and wounded of all corps, in their recent operations, will accompany this report.

Quitman, within the city—adding several new defences to the position he had won, and sheltering his cores as well as practicable—now awaited the return of daylight, under the guns of the formidable citadel, yet to be subdued.

At about four o'clock next morning (Sept. 14th), a deputation of the *ayuntamiento* (city council), waited upon me to report that the federal government and the army of Mexico had fled from the capital some three hours before, and to demand terms of capitulation in favour of the church, the citizens, and the municipal authorities.

I promptly replied that I would sign no capitulation; that the city had been virtually in our possession since the lodgements effected, by Worth and Quitman, the day before; that I regretted the silent escape of the. Mexican army; that I should levy on the city a moderate contribution for special purposes; and that the Mexican army should come under no terms, not self-imposed such only, as its own honour, the dignity of the United States, and the spirit of the age, should, in my opinion imperiously demand and impose.

At the termination of the interview with the city deputation, I communicated, about daylight, orders to Worth and Quitman, to advance slowly and cautiously (to guard against treachery), towards the heart of the city, and to occupy its stronger and more commanding points. Quitman proceeded to the great plaza, or square, planted guards, and hoisted the colours of the United States on the national palace—containing the halls of Congress, and the executive apartments of federal Mexico.

In this grateful service, Quitman might have been anticipated by Worth, but for my express orders, halting the latter at the head of the *Alamate* (a green park), within three squares of that goal of general ambition. The capital, however, was not taken by any one or two corps, but by the talent, the science, the gallantry, the prowess of this entire army. In the glorious conquest, all had contributed early and powerfully the killed, the wounded, and the fit for duty at—Vera Cruz, Cerro Gordo, Contreras, San Antonio, Churubusco (three battles), the *Molino del Rey*, and Chapultepec as much as those who fought at the gates of Helen and San Cosme.

Soon after we had entered, and were in the act of occupying the city, a fire was opened upon us, from the flat roofs of the houses, from windows, and corners of streets, by some two thousand convicts, liberated the night before by the flying government—joined by, perhaps, as many Mexican soldiers, who had disbanded themselves, and thrown off their uniforms.— This unlawful war lasted more than twenty-four hours, in spite of the exertions of the municipal authorities, and was not put down till we had lost many men, including several officers, killed or wounded, and had punished the miscreants.

Leaving, as we all feared, inadequate garrisons at Vera Cruz, Perote, and Puebla—with much larger hospitals; and being obliged, most reluctantly, from the same cause (general paucity of numbers), to abandon Jalapa, we marched (Aug. 7-10), from Puebla, with only 10,738 rank and file. This number includes the garrison of Jalapa, and the 2.420 brought up by Brigadier General Pierce, August 6th.

At Contreras, Churubusco, &c., August 20th, we had but 8,497 men engaged—after deducting the garrison of San Augustin (our general depot), the intermediate sick, and the dead; at the *Molino del Rey*, Sept. 8th, beat three brigades, with some cavalry and artillery making in all 3,251 men—were in the battle; in the two days—Sept. 12th and 13th—our whole operating force, after deducting again, the recent killed, wounded, and sick, together with the garrison at Miscoac—the then general depot—and that of Tacubaya, was but 7,180; and, finally, after deducting the new garrison of Chapultepec. with the killed and -wounded of the two days, we took possession, Sept. 14th, of this great capital, with less than 6,000 men! And I reassert, upon accumulated and unquestionable evidence, that, in not one of these conflicts, was this army opposed by fewer than three and a half times its numbers in several of them, by a yet greater excess.—I recapitulate our losses, since we arrived in the basin of Mexico:

August 19th, 20th —Killed, 137, including fourteen officers. Wounded, 877, including sixty-two officers.—Missing (probably killed), thirty-eight rank and file. Total. 1.052.

September 8th—Killed, 116, including nine officers. Wounded. 655, including forty-nine officers. Missing. eighteen rank and file. Total, 789.

September 12th, 13th, 14th—Killed. 130, including ten officers. Wounded. 703, including sixty-nine officers. Missing, twenty-nine rank and file. Total, 862. Grand total of losses, 2,703, including 383 officers.

On the other hand, this small force has beaten, on the same occasion, in view of their capital, the whole Mexican army, of (at the beginning) thirty odd thousand men. Killed or wounded, of that number more than 7,000, officers and men, taken 3,730 prisoners, one-seventh officers, including thirteen generals, of whom three had been presidents of this republic, captured twenty colours and standards, seventy-five pieces of ordnance, besides fifty-seven wall pieces, 20.000 small arms, and an immense quantity of shot, shells, powder, &c., &c.

I have the honour to be, sir, with high respect, your most obedient servant,

Winfield Scott.
Hon. Wm. L. Marcy, Secretary of War.

Santa Anna fled with part of his shattered army, and proceeding back to Puebla, joined in the attack then making by General Rea, upon the small but heroic garrison left under the gallant Colonel Childs. for the occupation of that city.

The American army were now in possession of the valley of Mexico, as well as of the cities on the route to the coast, and an American governor, General Quitman, the first of his race, swayed the rule over that city, for the possession of which, three hundred and thirty years before, the Spanish army under Cortez, had fought with such desperation, and at last, with such triumphant success; and which the descendants of that nation had since held untouched and unapproached by foreign foe.

The scene of battle for each, was the same;—the object the same;—the city approached by the same causeways, the work of the ancient Aztec race, who fell before their conquerors, then also the conquerors of the richest parts of the new world, which in its vast extent, and its incalculable riches, had but a few years before been revealed to the knowledge of the older continent.— But in the lapse of these three centuries, the glory of the Spanish race has departed. Corrupted by riches and enervated by luxury, it has fallen, and the rich colonies planted by them in the new world, are now but the shadows of nations, possessing the names and territories, without the power.

While the hardy and intelligent Anglo Saxon race, springing from a then inferior nation, and planted a hundred years after the former upon the shores of America, in its less favoured, and more cold and sterile sections, has increased into a mighty nation, long the superior of its south-western neighbour, and now its conqueror.—The same tall, majestic and ancient cypresses, standing on the hill of Chapultepec, the former royal residence of the emperors of the Aztec race, have seen that empire in all its glory, when its capital city, in its magnificence, sat before them in the midst of the waters, and tributary nations around acknowledged the sway of its semi-barbaric, but mighty sovereign.

They saw too, the small but gallant array of Spanish cavaliers, with their train of Indian allies, as they descended from the mountains on the coast, into the lovely and populous valley. They witnessed the terrible struggles, and finally the downfall of the ancient dynasty. Three hundred years after, they have seen another army, of another race, approaching over the same mountains, to gain possession of the same city, from the descendants of its former conquerors.

They have witnessed the same deadly strife fought on the same grounds as before, and with the same result.—The city was dyed in the blood of its defenders. Another flag unrolled its folds from the lofty turrets, and the North American descendants of the English, banished the enervated descendants of the Spanish race, and trod in triumph the "Halls of the Montezumas."

The city of Mexico, into which the American army under General Scott had now entered, is the oldest of the American continent. Originally it was situated on some islands in Lake Tezcuco and was transversed in various directions by canals. It was but little elevated above the surface of the water, and at this period, although the waters of the lake have retired nearly a league from the city walls, they are but four feet below the level of the streets.

The city was connected with the main land, on the north, the south, and the west, by long and solid causeways of stone and mortar, the shortest of which, that on the west, was about two miles in length. Besides these, was a narrower causeway running through the lake to Chapultepec, the principal use of which was to convey a large pipe of water from the reservoir on that hill, throughout the city, for the use of the inhabitants, the construction of fountains, &c. Although as said before, the waters of Lake Tezcuco have far retired and the city is no longer, like a second Venice, situated in the midst of the waters, yet these causeways stilt remain an imperishable monument of the skill of their builders, and are yet the main thoroughfares to the city.—

After Mexico was taken by Cortez, in 1521, most of the buildings were torn down to make way for the more lofty residences of the conquerors; the pagan temples gave place to the Catholic churches; the streets were widened, but retained their same courses, over the same ground—The Spaniards endeavoured to rebuild the capital in a style that should eclipse in splendour the cities of the old world; and to such an extent did they soon succeed in doing this, that a traveller who visited it about twenty years after the conquest, gives it as his opinion, that no city of Europe could, at that time, equal it in magnificence.

A portion of the wealth that fell into the possession of the Spaniards was devoted to add to the splendour of the churches, and this was increased also by munificent gifts of Charles V, and the succeeding monarchs of Spain.—In all the internal convulsions of Mexico, this vast wealth of the churches has remained undisturbed, and now, in its magnificent display, excites the wonder and astonishment of the beholder.

But Mexico of modern time, has but little, save this splendour of in ancient buildings, and the wealth of its churches, to excite admiration;—and from all other cities of the Mexican republic, it is distinguished for the great number of inhabitants, who are in a state of the utmost indigence, and indeed of beggary; having no habitation save the shelters of the public edifices, and no method of obtaining a livelihood. These *leperos.* as they are called, clothed in rags, crowd the streets, begging, as their only reliance for food.—The ecclesiastical portion of the population or the various grades of the priests, in their number, would exceed the belief of a citizen of the United States. These also are drones, living only by the exercise of the half religious, half superstitious feelings of the mass of the people.—But little, that would interest the reader, can be said of this miserably governed city, the head of a worse governed nation.

We will pass on to a glance at the succeeding operations of the war and first take up

The Siege of Puebla.

This siege, on account of the disparity of the forces engaged, and the almost unparalleled gallantry of the little body of United States' volunteers and regulars, together with the size of the city, which they held in defiance of their assailants, and the length of time they withstood the assault, and the hardships undergone, is one of the most brilliant affairs, not only recorded of this war, but of all the annals of warfare throughout the civilized world.—A garrison of not quite four hundred men, infantry, artillery and cavalry, in the heart of a city of 70,000 inhabitants, assailed by all the available population, and by the additional force of 8,000 men under Generals Santa Anna and Rea, holding that city in a continued fight of thirty days and nights, against these united efforts, supported by artillery, appears more like romance, or an act of the days of chivalry, than like the reality of modern warfare.

When the American army passed on from Puebla towards Mexico, Colonel Childs was left as the military commander. His force consisted of six companies 1st Pennsylvania regiment, under Lieutenant-Colonel Black two companies of artillery, Captains Kendrick and Miller; one company of cavalry, Captain Ford. He was encumbered with 1,800 sick American soldiers in hospital.—Not until after the first battles near the city of Mexico, was he interrupted. On the night of the 13th September, a fire was commenced upon his force in the *Plaza* of the city; renewed on the 14th, and then kept up by night and day until the 12th of October, when as General Lane was rapidly approaching the city from the east, the Mexican force retreated to Atlixco.— General Santa Anna, when he abandoned the city of Mexico, on the night of Sept. 13th, to its gallant and almost desperate invaders, moved with a large force of his withdrawn troops, directly back upon Puebla; joined forces with General Rea, in the attack upon Colonel Childs and his little band, expecting to crush him and thus revive the spirits of the Mexicans, by cutting off the passage of the Americans.

Part of Colonel Childs' force was in the fortified convent of Loreta, on the heights overlooking the city. When the Mexican reinforcements under their commander-in-chief appeared in sight, on Sept 22nd, the numerous bells of the city rang out in triumph: but their noise was soon silenced by a destructive discharge of shot and shell from the Americans above them.—Santa Anna on the 25th, with an imposing display of his forces, sent a demand to Colonel Childs for surrender; but he received an answer no more favourable to his purpose, than the memorable one sent to him by "Old Zack," on a previous occasion. Here was a little band of the "same sort" for him to contend with.

The battle then raged furiously and without intermission. Barricades of cotton bales and stone were raised in the streets, and a fire of artillery opened upon the American forces in the *Plaza*. The houses around gave shelter to the assailants, who from every window, and every parapetted roof poured a continual shower of lead, copper and iron, upon the little American band therein. All force was concentrated upon it—the heights not being attacked, but a fire from them continually sent death and destruction through the city.

The besieged threw up defences in the *Plaza*, dug through the walls of the buildings, even to the rear of the enemy's barricades, and issuing therefrom, sword in hand, and with the bayonet, routed them, and burned their works. They took and blew up the buildings from which the enemy annoyed them the most.—The utmost enthusiasm prevailed among the American troops. Having been fortunate enough to collect thirty cattle and four hundred sheep at the commencement of the attack, in addition to their other provisions, they determined to resist to the last.

This attack was continued by all the Mexican forces until the evening of the 30th of Sept. when General Santa Anna, with about 4,000 men, withdrew to meet General Lane, then rapidly advancing from Perote on the east: while General Rea with about the same number, continued the assault with unremitted ardour, until the 12th of October; when General Lane, having met and defeated Santa Anna at Huamantla, advancing upon Puebla, Rea and his forces retreated to Atlixco, leaving Colonel Childs and his little band in possession of the fair city. Let us now turn our attention to Santa Anna, as he left Puebla to meet General Lane, whom he had met before at Buena Vista, and note his success at the ensuing

Battle of Huamantla.

General Lane, who by his rapid movements and indefatigable energy, in pursuing and breaking up the band of guerrillas, after this time acquired the name of the Marion of Mexico, was now advancing from Vera Cruz toward Puebla, with a force of one regiment of Indiana Infantry, Colonel Gorman; one do. Ohio, Colonel Brough; four companies Georgia mounted men, Major Lally; nine additional companies infantry, two batteries of artillery, and a large wagon train. Santa Anna—moving from Puebla. took a position at some distance from the national road, at Huamantla, with the intention of allowing the force of General Lane with the train to pass him on its route, and then with his whole strength, suddenly to fall on the rear of the Americans, at a time when as he says, "they would least expect it."

General Lane encamped in the neighbourhood on the night of the 6th of October;—on the following morning, the 7th, the Mexican forces silently commenced the march for the appointed place of surprise. But Lane at the same time having heard of the position of Santa Anna, determined at once to attack him, and on the same morning, having placed the train compactly together on the road, leaving with it Colonel Brough's Ohio regiment, with three other companies of infantry and a battery of artillery, he rapidly marched with Gorman's Indianans. Walker's Georgia Mounted men, Wyncoop's Pennsylvanians. and a battery of five pieces of artillery, for Huamantla.

The mounted men of the advance under Walker, charged rapidly on, entered the town and immediately were engaged hand to hand with the force left there. In this bloody conflict the gallant Walker lost his life. This fight was maintained by the cavalry for three quarters of an hour, when they succeeded in putting the enemy to flight; capturing two pieces of cannon. During this time, the infantry and artillery were hurried to their utmost speed towards the city to support the cavalry, and at the same time the whole Mexican army were endeavouring by another road, in full view of the Americans, to get back into the town;—Santa Anna from a lofty watchtower, having seen the movement of the Americans from the road, had counter-marched his forces from their original destination.

In this exciting race between the two opposing armies, the Mexicans, from the nature of their road, succeeded in arriving first at the town, and succouring their broken battalions, which were now flying before the chivalrous cavalry. Instantly the lancers charged upon and drove the American Cavalry back into the town, and, rapidly pursuing them, were met in their turn by the column of American Infantry, with the artillery, and a sharp engagement ensued, in which, the Mexicans were totally routed, and dispersed with a loss of about one hundred and fifty men;—American lost thirteen killed, eleven wounded.

This was Santa Anna's last attempt, in person, against the Americans.—Abandoning the town after destroying the great amount of military stores found there, General Lane with his force rejoined his train, and proceeded on towards Puebla; which he entered on the 13th, clearing the way before him by volleys of musketry, and relieving the gallant detachment under Colonel Childs, who so long had defended the place against overwhelming numbers. The Mexican general, Rea, on Lane's approach, retired to Atlixco, but the indefatigable American, on the morning of the 19th, left Puebla in pursuit of him. This movement led to the next action,

THE BATTLE OF ATLIXCO.

General Lane, taking as his force, Colonel Brough's 4th Ohio, and Colonel Gorman's 4th Indiana regiments; Colonel Wyncoop's battalion of 1st Pennsylvanians; Captain Heintzleman's battalion, all infantry; Major Lally's Georgia cavalry; a squadron of regular cavalry under Captain Ford, with two batteries of artillery, under Captain Taylor and Lieutenant Pratt, left Puebla on October 19th to seek the forces of General Rea, at Atlixco. They came up with the advance of the enemy at one p. m.—A fight ensued.—The Mexicans retreated a mile and a half, and made another stand; were gallantly charged by the American cavalry; They again retreated, falling back four miles upon their main body, drawn up on a hill of *chaparral*.—Upon this body the cavalry—charged; dismounted,—fought hand to hand;—drove them towards Atlixco, one and a half miles distant.

The artillery and infantry came up;—marched on, took possession of a height above the city, and cannonaded it by moonlight three quarters of an hour, when it was surrendered, but the Mexican force had retreated.—The Mexican loss, from the battle and cannonading, was heavy;—being 219 killed, 300 wounded.—American loss was very light,—only one killed, one wounded. General Lane with his force marched on to the city of Mexico, and for a few days took up his quarters in the "Hails of the Montezumas."

Troops from the United States were now pouring into Vera Cruz.— About a month after General Lane had passed up, General Patterson with a large force and heavy train moved up from the coast.—Following General Patterson, with four more regiments, Major General Butler, already distinguished in the northern army under General Taylor, commenced his march towards the city.—The guerrillas now were becoming scarce. On the arrival of these troops.

General Scott had under his command, at Mexico, Puella, Jalapa and Vera Cruz, a little over 20,000 available men, increased afterwards by the arrival of the force of General Marshal.—The whole country now was becoming more tranquil.

All hopes of successfully resisting the American power, were leaving the minds of the Mexican people, and an anxiety for peace was becoming prevalent among all the better classes—Santa Anna endeavoured to regain the presidency; but in this was foiled.—Of war the Mexicans had had enough. The northern army under General Taylor, after the battle of Buena Vista, had done but little times there, at Matamoras, Camargo, Monterey, Saltillo, and in all the camps, had become extremely dull, enlivened only by the continued reports of the fighting at the south. Many of the officers returned on leave of absence, and among others, Old Zack himself, left the camp at Monterey on the 8th of November, and hastened to his home, greeted in his coming, most heartily, by all parties and classes in the United States.

The northern army in New Mexico under General Price, had suffered much from hardships; Chihuahua having again been taken possession of by the hostile forces of the enemy, that general prepared to move against it.—In California, all being quietly in possession of the forces of the United States, the two leading officers of the land forces, General Kearney and Colonel Fremont, returned by land to Washington city.

An unhappy difference having occurred between them, it was referred to a court martial, the testimony before which, tended principally to show that the minds of the most meritorious officers are not free from a narrow jealousy of one another; a love of power and praise, and envy of others possessing the same, superior or yet inferior. A difficulty of the same kind, but more extended in its character, arose in the southern army, between General Scott, General Worth, General Pillow, and other officers.—The most ridiculous vanity and jealousy were shown by those who had been fellow actors in the same glorious scenes; the details of this will not repay the perusal; they will never be remembered in history, while their glorious actions will shine forth never to be forgotten.

The remaining events until the termination of hostilities, are of lighter moment When the court of inquiry was ordered to proceed to Mexico, to examine the grounds of complaint, between the above named generals, the command of the army devolved on Major General Butler.—General Lane now was actively engaged in scouring the country, and hunting down the various guerrilla bands, and in several minor actions in pursuit of Santa Anna, Paredes, and Jarauta. a renegade priest; in these he proved himself emphatically, by active promptness and gallantry, a second Marion.

In these arduous expeditions he was most ably seconded by his officers Colonel Hays, and Major Polk of the dragoons.—Paredes returned to Mexico in disguise, and endeavoured unsuccessfully to regain his power.—Santa Anna sought and obtained leave to depart from the country, which he did.—The Mexican government was directed first by President Pena y Pena, and then Anaya, both favourable to peace; and under their efforts commissioners were appointed, who met Mr. Trist near the city of Mexico, and after much consultation, a treaty of peace was signed, as given below, and on the 29th of February, an armistice was agreed upon to carry into effect its provisions.

All fighting now ceased, save with scattering guerrillas, and the gallant action of San Resales, fought by General Price, in Chihuahua, to regain possession of the capital of that state,—he being ignorant of the armistice. This action of San Resales, like all others, ended in the complete rout of the Mexican forces, under the command of General Angel Trias, and the re-occupation of the city of Chihuahua, before so gallantly taken by the troops of Colonel Doniphan.

The following synopsis of the treaty of peace will be found interesting and important.

TREATY OF PEACE, FRIENDSHIP, LIMITS AND SETTLEMENT.

Between the United States of America. and the Mexican Republic concluded at Guadalope Hidalgo, on the second day of February. and ratified with amendments, by the American Senate, March 10, 1848.

In the name of Almighty God:

The United States of America and United Mexican States,

animated by a sincere desire to put an end to the calamities of the war which unhappily exists between the two republics, and to establish on a solid basis relations of peace and friendship, which shall confer reciprocal benefits on the citizens of both, and assure the concord, harmony and mutual confidence wherein the two people should live as good neighbours, have for that purpose appointed their respective plenipotentiaries; that is to say, the President of the United States has appointed N. P. Trist, a citizen of the United States, and the President of the Mexican Republic has appointed Don Louis Gonzaga Cuevas, Bernardo Conto, Don Miguel Atristain, citizens of the said republic, who, after a reciprocal communication of their respective powers have, under the protection of Almighty God, the Author of peace, arranged, agreed upon and signed the treaty of peace, friendship, limits and settlement, between the United States of America and the Mexican republic.

Article 1.

There shall be firm and universal peace between the United States of America and the Mexican Republic, and between their respective countries, territories, cities, towns and people, without exception of places or persons.

Article 2.

Immediately on the signature of this treaty, a convention shall be entered into between a commissioner or commissioners, appointed by the general-in-chief of the forces of the United States, and such as may be appointed by the Mexican Government, to the end that a provisional suspension of hostilities shall take place, and that in the places occupied by the said forces, constitutional order may be re-established, as regards the political, administrative, and judicial branches, so far as this shall be permitted by the circumstances of military occupation.

Article 3.

Immediately upon the ratification of the present treaty, by the government of the United States, orders shall be transmitted to the commanders of their land and naval forces, requiring the latter, (provided this treaty shall then have been ratified by the Government of the Mexican Republic) immediately to desist from blockading any Mexican ports; and requiring the former, (under the same condition) to commence, at the earliest moment practicable, withdrawing all troops of the United States then in the interior of the Mexican Republic, to points that shall be selected by common agreement, at a distance from the sea-ports not exceeding thirty leagues; and such evacuation of the interior of the republic shall be completed with the least possible delay; the Mexican Government hereby binding itself to afford every facility in its power for rendering the same convenience to the troops on their march, and in their new positions, and for promoting a good understanding between them and the inhabitants.

In like manner, orders shall be dispatched to the person in charge of the custom houses at all points occupied by the forces of the United States, requiring them (under the same condition) immediately to deliver possession of the same to the persons authorized by the Mexican Government to receive it, together with all bonds and evidences of debt for duties on importations and exportations, not yet fallen due.

Moreover, a faithful and exact account shall be made out, showing the entire amount of all duties on imports and on exports, collected at such custom houses, or elsewhere in Mexico, by authority of the United States, from and after the day of the ratification of this treaty by the government of the Mexican Republic; and also an account of the cost of collection, and such entire amount, deducting only the cost of collection, shall be delivered to the Mexican Government, at the city of Mexico, within three months after the exchange of ratifications.

The evacuation of the capital of the Mexican republic by the troops of the United States, in virtue of the above stipulation, shall be completed in one month after the orders there stipulated for shall have been received by the commander of said troops, or sooner, if possible.

Article 4.

Immediately after the exchange of ratifications of the present treaty, all castles, forts, territories, places and possessions, which have been taken and occupied by the forces of the United States during the present war, within the limits of the Mexican republic, as about to be established by the following Article, shall be definitely restored to the said republic, together with all the artillery, arms, apparatus of war, munitions, and other public property, which were in the said castles and forts when captured, and which shall remain there at the time when this treaty shall be duly ratified by the government of the Mexican republic.

To this end, immediately upon the signature of this treaty, orders shall be dispatched to the American officer commanding such castles and forts, securing against the removal or destruction of any such artillery, arms, apparatus of war, munitions or other public property. The City of Mexico, within the inner line of entrenchments surrounding the said city, is comprehended in the above stipulations, as regards the restoration of artillery, apparatus of war, &c..

The final evacuation of the territory of the Mexican republic by the forces of the United States, shall be completed within three months from the said exchange of ratifications, or sooner, if possible; the Mexican republic hereby engaging as in the foregoing Article, to use all means in its power for facilitating such evacuation, and rendering it convenient for the troops, and for promoting a good understanding between them and the inhabitants.

If, however, the ratification of this treaty by both powers should not take place in time to allow the embarkation of the troops of the United States to be completed before the commencement of the sickly season, at the ports of the Gulf of Mexico, in such case a friendly arrangement shall be entered into between the general in-chief of the said troops and the Mexican Government, whereby healthy and otherwise suitable places, at a distance from the ports not exceeding thirty leagues, shall be designated for the residence of such troops as may not yet have embarked, until the return of the healthy season. And the space of time here referred to as comprehending the sickly season,—shall be understood to extend from the first day of May to the first of November.

All prisoners of war taken on either side, on land or on sea. shall be restored as soon as practicable after the exchange of the ratifications of this treaty. It is also agreed, that if any Mexicans should now be held as captives by any savage tribe within the limits of the United States, as about to be established by the following Article, the government of the United States will exact the release of such captives, and cause them to be restored to their country.

Article 5.

The boundary line between the two republics shall commence in the Gulf of Mexico, three leagues from land, opposite the mouth of the Rio Grande, otherwise called Rio Bravo del Norte, or opposite the mouth of its deepest branch, if it should have more than one branch emptying directly into the sea; from thence up the middle of that river, following the deepest channel, where it has more than one, to the point where it strikes the southern boundary of New Mexico; thence, westwardly, along the whole southern boundary of New Mexico (which runs north of the town called Paso,) to its western termination; thence northward along the western line of New Mexico, until it intersects the first branch of the river Gila; or if it should not intersect any branch of that river, then to the point on the said line nearest to such branch, and thence in a direct line to the same:) thence down the middle of the said branch and of the said river, until it empties into the Rio Colorado; thence across the Rio Colorado, following the division line between Upper and Lower California, to the Pacific Ocean.

[The second clause of this Article provides that the boundary line between Upper California thus ceded to the United States, and Lower California retained by Mexico, shall consist of a straight line drawn from the mouth of the Gila River directly to the Pacific Ocean, striking the same, one marine league south of the port of San Diego, and provides also, that each government shall appoint a commissioner and surveyor, who shall meet at San Diego within one year from the date of ratification of the treaty, and shall run this line through to the mouth of the Gila.

The clause also provides that the southern and western boundaries of New Mexico thus ceded to the United States, shall be the same as those laid down on Disturnell's map of the United States, and that hereafter these boundary lines shall not be changed, except by free consent of both governments.] (*Author.*)

Article 6.

The vessels and citizens of the United States, shall, in all time, have a free and uninterrupted passage by the Gulf of California, and by the river Colorado, below its confluence with the Gila, to and from their possessions situated north of the boundary line defined in the preceding Article; it Being understood that this passage is to be by navigating the Gulf of California and the river Colorado; and not by land, without the express consent of the Mexican Government.

[The second clause of this 6th Article, stipulates that, if hereafter it may be found advantageous to construct a road, railroad, or canal along the bank of the river Gila, that both governments will form an agreement for its construction.] (*Author.*)

Article 7.

[This Article stipulates, that the river Gila, and that part of the Rio Grande which lies below the southern boundary of New Mexico, as ceded to the United States, shall be free for the navigation thereof by the vessels of both nations. That neither shall interrupt or impede this, by works on the river, or by any taxes on vessels navigating the same. That if it is necessary, in order to improve the navigation of wide rivers, to lay any tax on such navigation, that both governments shall consent to the same.] (*Author.*)

Article 8.

[This Article provides, that the Mexican inhabitants of the

territory thus ceded to the United States, are at liberty to move back into Mexico, with their effects, without tax or charge; or they may remain, and become citizens of the United States, or continue citizens of Mexico, at their option: but they must make this selection within one year after the ratification of the treaty. It also provides, that the property of Mexicans in the ceded territory, shall be guaranteed to them as fully as though they were citizens of the United States.] (*Author.*)

Article 9.

[This Article was rejected by the United States' Senate; it provided, 1st, that those Mexicans who might become citizens of the United States, in the ceded territory, should be admitted to the full rights of said citizenship; that, until that is done, they shall be protected in person and property according to the Mexican laws. 2nd. That the priests and ecclesiastics in the said territory, be guaranteed the exercise of all their religious privileges, and in the possession of all property dedicated to Roman Catholic worship, churches, houses, schools, hospitals, etc.. And 3rd. that the Catholic Mexicans thus becoming citizens of the United States, should be under the same ecclesiastical government as before, even should such ecclesiastical authority be within the limits of the Mexican republic, until new districts should be laid off conformable to the laws of the Roman Catholic church.

The effect of this would have been, to have placed the Mexicans in the ceded territory, in the character of political citizens of the United States, but religiously subject (to them the strongest bond) to the ecclesiastical authority of Mexico. Rejecting, therefore, this Article, the Senate of the United States adopted and inserted substantially the third Article of the treaty with France, of 1803, for the cession of Louisiana, to the effect that inhabitants of the ceded territory shall be incorporated in the Union of the United States, and admitted as soon as Congress shall determine, according to the principles of the federal Constitution, to the enjoyments of all the rights, advantages and immunities of citizens of the United States: and in the meantime they shall be maintained and protected in the full enjoyment of their liberty, property, and the religion which they profess.] (*Author.*)

Article 10.

[This Article related to the grants of land by the state of Texas. It was rejected by the United States' Senate. It provided, that those persons who had received grants of land in Texas from the Mexican government, prior to March 2nd, 1836. and who on account of the war between Texas and Mexico, had not performed the conditions of said grants, should now perform the same, in the given period of time, as before, but dating from the ratification of this treaty; and such grants not thus complied with by the grantees, should not be obligatory upon the state of Texas; the same provisions were also extended over the other ceded territory on grants issued prior to May 13th, 1846.

As this Article, if agreed to. would have proved a prolific source of disagreement and litigation in Texas and the ceded territory, and as the Mexican government was justly regarded as having now no right to interfere with the lands forever ceded from it, this Article was wisely rejected by the Senate of the United States.] (*Author.*)

[The next Article, 11th, will, if complied with by the United States, as they are most solemnly pledged to do, inevitably lead to a war with the powerful Indian tribes of Comanches, Apaches. Navajos, and other minor ones, who, for a long course of years, have been continually in the practice of making predatory excursions into the Mexican territories. The whole power of the northern states of Mexico has so far, been unavailing in preventing these, and the Mexican republic has now shrewdly thrown the burden thereof on the United States, looking to that power for security; a security of more value to Mexico than all the territory that by this treaty she has ceded; for her northern and best provinces will be secure; multitudes of *haciendas*, now deserted, will be re-peopled, and her richest mining district of Sonora. before unavailable on account of the dreaded Indians, will be opened to her; while the United States will be saddled with a long continued and troublesome war with these formidable savages. This Article is one of the most carefully written of the whole treaty, and in its result, will be of far more benefit to Mexico, than the 15,000,000 of dollars which by the succeeding Article, are to be paid to her.] (*Author.*)

Article 11.

Considering that a great part of the territories which, by the present treaty, are to be comprehended, for the future, within the limits of the United States, is now occupied by savage tribes who will hereafter be under the control of the government of the United States, and whose incursions within the territory of Mexico would be prejudicial in the extreme, it is solemnly agreed, that all such incursions shall be forcibly restrained by the government of the United States, whensoever this may be necessary: and that when they cannot be prevented, they shall be punished by the said government, and satisfaction for the same shall be exacted all in the same way, and with equal diligence and energy, as if the same incursions were committed within its own territory, against its own citizens.

It shall not be lawful, under any pretext whatever, for any inhabitant of the United States to purchase or acquire any Mexican, or any foreigner residing in Mexico who may have been captured by Indians inhabiting the territory of either of the two republics, nor to purchase or acquire horses, mules, cattle, or property of any kind, stolen within Mexican, territory by such Indians, with firearms, or ammunition, by sale or otherwise.

And in the event of such person or persons captured within Mexican territory by Indians, being carried into the territory of the United States, the government of the latter, engages and binds itself in the most solemn manner, so soon as it shall know of such captives being within its territory, and shall be able so to do, through the faithful exercise of its influence and power, to rescue them and return them to their country, or deliver them to the agent or representative of the Mexican government.

The Mexican authorities will, as far as practicable, give to the government of the United States notice of such captures, and its agent shall pay the expenses incurred in the maintenance and transmission of the rescued captives, who, in the meantime, shall be treated with the utmost hospitality by the American authorities at the place where they may be. But if the government of the United States, before receiving such notice from Mexico, should obtain intelligence through any other channel of the existence of Mexican captives within its territory, it will proceed forthwith to effect their release, and deliver them to the Mexican agent as above stipulated.

For the purpose of giving to these stipulations the fullest possible efficacy, thereby affording the security and redress demanded by their true spirit and intent, the government of the United States will now and hereafter pass, without unnecessary delay, and always vigilantly enforce, such laws as the nature of the subject may require. And finally, the sacredness of this obligation shall never be lost sight of by the said government when providing for the removal of Indians from any portion of said territories, or for its being settled by the citizens of the United States; but, on the contrary, special care shall then be taken not to place its Indian occupants under the necessity of seeking new homes, by committing those invasions which the United States have solemnly obliged themselves to restrain.

Article 12.

[Provides for the payment of 15,000.000 of dollars to Mexico by the United States, for the extension of territory of the latter power. It also indicates two methods of payment of this, sum. The first method, by the creation of stock by the United States, was rejected by the United States' Senate, and the second adopted; that is, the payment of 3,000.000 immediately upon the ratification of the treaty, and 3,000,000 yearly for four years; to be paid at the city of Mexico, together with interest on each instalment, at the rate of six *per cent, per annum.*] (*Author.*)

Article 13.

[By this Article the United States also agree to pay the amounts due by the Mexican Government to American citizens, as determined by the conventions of April 11th, 1831, and Jan. 30th, 1843, and to release the Mexican Government from all liability therefore.] (*Author.*)

Article 14.

[By this Article the United States furthermore agree to release the Mexican Government from any additional claims on the part of citizens of the United States, that may have arisen after said conventions, up to the time of the date of this treaty, assuming the consideration, allowance and payment of the same on the part of the United States.] (*Author.*)

Article 15.

[The United States by this Article, after repeating the entire exoneration of the Republic of Mexico, from the demand of those claims mentioned in the 14th Article, agree to pay and satisfy the same to the amount not exceeding 3,260,000 dollars. And it also provides for the establishment of a Lord of commissioners for deciding upon the validity of said claims, and makes provision, that the Mexican government shall furnish the said board with such documents as shall be in its possession, and which may be deemed necessary by said board, for its decision upon said claims.] (*Author.*)

Article 16.

Each of the contracting parties reserves to itself the entire right to fortify whatever point in its territory it may judge proper so to fortify, for its security.

Article 17.

[Provides for the renewal of the treaty of amity, commerce and navigation of April 5th 1831, for the next eight years afterwards; said treaty to be abrogated by either party, by giving one year's notice to the other.] (*Author.*)

Article 18.

[Provides, that when the custom-houses of the ports shall have been restored to Mexico, that no duties shall be laid upon such articles as shall be sent by the government of the United States, for the use of her troops not then embarked, and that this shall continue while any of the United States' troops shall remain in Mexico.] (*Author.*)

Articles 19 and 20.

[These articles refer to the security of goods and merchandise imported into Mexico through those ports of which the forces of the United States have possession, during that period. They are of no other interest to the general reader.] (*Author.*)

Article 21.

[This Article provides, that in case of misunderstanding between the two republics with regard to the interpretation of this treaty, or any other subject, that both parties shall use their utmost endeavours to preserve the state of peace between the two nations, and settle, if possible, such difference, by negotiation or arbitration; not to resort to hostilities, reprisals, &c., unless the party that considers itself aggrieved shall, after mature consideration, deem that milder measures would be "altogether incompatible with the nature of the difference or the circumstances of the case."] (*Author.*)

Article 22.

[As this refers to the manner of carrying on a future war, it is inserted in full.] If (which is not to be expected, and which God forbid!) war shall unhappily break out between the two republics, they do now, with a view to such calamity, solemnly pledge themselves to each other, and to the world, to observe the following rules, absolutely, where the nature of the subject permits, and as closely as possible in all cases where such absolute observance shall be impossible.

1. The merchants of either republic then residing in the other, shall be allowed to remain twelve months (for those dwelling in the interior), and six months (for those dwelling at the seaports), to collect their debts and settle their affairs; during which periods, they shall enjoy the same protection, and be on the same footing, in all respects, as the citizens of subjects of the most friendly nations; and, at the expiration thereof, or at any time before, they shall have full liberty to depart, carrying off all their effects without molestation or hindrance; conforming therein to the same laws which the citizens or subjects of the most friendly

nations are required to conform to.

Upon the entrance of the armies of either nation into the territories of the other, women, children, ecclesiastics, scholars of every faculty, cultivators of the earth, merchants, artisans, manufacturers and fishermen, unarmed, and inhabiting unfortified towns, villages, or places, and in general, all persons whose occupations are for the common subsistence and benefit of mankind, shall be allowed to continue their respective employments unmolested in their persons. Nor shall their houses or goods be burnt or otherwise destroyed, nor their cattle taken, nor their fields wasted by the armed force into whose power, by the events of war, they may happen to fall; but if under necessity to take anything from them for the use of such armed force, the same shall be paid for at an equitable price. All churches, hospitals, schools, colleges, libraries, and other establishments for charitable and beneficent purposes, shall be respected, and all persons connected with the same, protected in the discharge of their duties, and the pursuit of their vocations.

2. In order that the fate of prisoners of war may be alleviated, all such practices as those of sending them into distant, inclement, or unwholesome districts, or crowding them into close and noxious places, shall be studiously avoided. They shall not be confined in dungeons, prison-ships, or prisons; nor be put in irons, or bound, or otherwise restrained in the use of their limbs. The officers shall enjoy liberty on their paroles, within convenient districts, and have comfortable quarters, and the common soldiers shall be disposed of in cantonments, open and extensive enough for air and exercise, and lodged in barracks as roomy and good as are provided, by the party in whose power they are, for its own troops.

But if any officer shall break his parole, by leaving the district so assigned him, or any other prisoner shall escape from the limits of his cantonment, after they shall have been designated to him, such individual, officer, or other prisoner, shall forfeit so much of the benefit of this Article, as provides for his liberty on parole or in cantonment. And if an officer so breaking his parole, or any common soldier so escaping from the limits assigned him, shall afterwards be found in arms, previously to his being regularly exchanged, the person so offending, shall be dealt with according to the established laws of war.

The officers shall be duly furnished, by the party in whose power they are, with as many rations, and of the same articles, as are allowed, either in kind or by commutation, to officers of equal rank in their own army; and all others shall be daily furnished with such rations as is allowed the common soldier in his own service; the value of all which supplies shall, at the close of the war, or at periods to be agreed upon between the respective commanders, be paid by the other party, on a mutual adjustment of accounts for the subsistence of prisoners; and such accounts shall not be mingled with or set off against any others, nor the balance due on them be withheld, as a compensation. Each party shall be allowed to keep a commissary of prisoners, appointed by itself, with every cantonment of prisoners in possession of the other; which commissary shall see the prisoners as often as he pleases; shall be allowed to receive, exempt from all duties or taxes, and to distribute whatever comforts may be sent to them by their friends, and shall be free to transmit his reports in open letters to the party by whom he is employed.

And it is declared that neither the pretence, that war dissolves all treaties, nor any other whatever, shall be considered as annulling or suspending the solemn covenant contained in this Article. On the contrary, the state of war is precisely that for which it is provided; and during which, its stipulations are to be as sacredly observed as the most acknowledged obligations under the law of nature or nations.

Article 23.

This treaty shall be ratified by the President of the United States of America, by and with the advice and consent of the Senate thereof; and by the President of the Mexican republic, with the previous approbation of its General Congress; and the ratifications shall be exchanged in the city of Washington, in four months from the date of the signature hereof, or sooner if practicable.

In faith whereof, we, the respective plenipotentiaries, have signed this treaty of peace, friendship, limits, and settlement; and have hereunto affixed our seals respectively. Done in quintuplicate, at the city of Guadalope Hidalgo, on the second day of February, in the year of our Lord one thousand eight hundred and forty-eight.

N. P. Trist, [l. s.]
Luis G. Gervis, [l. s.]
Bernardo Conto, [l. s.]
Nio. Atristain, [l. s.]

[In addition to this, was a secret Article, providing that the term of eight months should be given for the ratification of the treaty. This Article was rejected by the Senate of the United States.] (Author.)

This treaty of peace between the United States and the Republic of Mexico, thus amended, was ratified by the Senate of the United States on the evening of the 10th of March, 1848, by the following vote, Ayes thirty-seven, Nays fifteen.

Messrs. Sevier and Clifford were appointed commissioners to Mexico, and the treaty thus amended, transmitted to the Mexican Congress, to be assembled at Queretaro. This done, it was laid before that body, and on the evening of the 19th of May, 1648, was ratified by the Mexican Lower House or Chamber of Deputies, by the following vote, Ayes fifty-one, Nays thirty-five. Then passed to the Mexican Senate, and by that body was ratified on the 25th of May, 1848, by the following vote, Ayes thirty-three, Nays four.

And thus ended the war with the Mexican republic, after a duration of a little more than two years, and the army of the United States immediately commenced its preparations for evacuating the soil of Mexico.

ALSO FROM LEONAUR
AVAILABLE IN SOFTCOVER OR HARDCOVER WITH DUST JACKET

CAPTAIN OF THE 95th (Rifles) by *Jonathan Leach*—An officer of Wellington's Sharpshooters during the Peninsular, South of France and Waterloo Campaigns of the Napoleonic Wars.

BUGLER AND OFFICER OF THE RIFLES by *William Green & Harry Smith* With the 95th (Rifles) during the Peninsular & Waterloo Campaigns of the Napoleonic Wars

BAYONETS, BUGLES AND BONNETS by *James 'Thomas' Todd*—Experiences of hard soldiering with the 71st Foot - the Highland Light Infantry - through many battles of the Napoleonic wars including the Peninsular & Waterloo Campaigns

THE ADVENTURES OF A LIGHT DRAGOON by *George Farmer & G.R. Gleig*—A cavalryman during the Peninsular & Waterloo Campaigns, in captivity & at the siege of Bhurtpore, India

THE COMPLEAT RIFLEMAN HARRIS by *Benjamin Harris as told to & transcribed by Captain Henry Curling*—The adventures of a soldier of the 95th (Rifles) during the Peninsular Campaign of the Napoleonic Wars

WITH WELLINGTON'S LIGHT CAVALRY by *William Tomkinson*—The Experiences of an officer of the 16th Light Dragoons in the Peninsular and Waterloo campaigns of the Napoleonic Wars.

SURTEES OF THE RIFLES by *William Surtees*—A Soldier of the 95th (Rifles) in the Peninsular campaign of the Napoleonic Wars.

ENSIGN BELL IN THE PENINSULAR WAR by *George Bell*—The Experiences of a young British Soldier of the 34th Regiment 'The Cumberland Gentlemen' in the Napoleonic wars.

WITH THE LIGHT DIVISION by *John H. Cooke*—The Experiences of an Officer of the 43rd Light Infantry in the Peninsula and South of France During the Napoleonic Wars

NAPOLEON'S IMPERIAL GUARD: FROM MARENGO TO WATERLOO by *J. T. Headley*—This is the story of Napoleon's Imperial Guard from the bearskin caps of the grenadiers to the flamboyance of their mounted chasseurs, their principal characters and the men who commanded them.

BATTLES & SIEGES OF THE PENINSULAR WAR by *W. H. Fitchett*—Corunna, Busaco, Albuera, Ciudad Rodrigo, Badajos, Salamanca, San Sebastian & Others

AVAILABLE ONLINE AT **www.leonaur.com**
AND OTHER GOOD BOOK STORES

www.ingramcontent.com/pod-product-compliance
Lightning Source LLC
Chambersburg PA
CBHW020730160426